Jay E. Harris, MD

How the Brain Talks to Itself
A Clinical Primer
of Psychotherapeutic Neuroscience

Pre-publication
REVIEWS,
COMMENTARIES,
EVALUATIONS . . .

"**T**his book is a treasure for the practitioner who wants to think about why and how people change in therapy. Jay Harris offers an integrated understanding of the complex new language of brain function with ways to understand and alter behavior.

Remarkable progress has been made in recent years in understanding how the brain functions and how we think and feel. Relatively little of this information has as yet been brought to bear on the process of psychotherapy. Harris's book is a scholarly summary of the expanding knowledge from available neuroscience and how that information can guide the process of change in psychotherapy."

Sandra Lee Harris, PhD
Professor and Dean,
Graduate School of Applied
and Professional Psychology,
Rutgers University

More pre-publication
REVIEWS, COMMENTARIES, EVALUATIONS . . .

"**D**r. Jay Harris skillfully interweaves neuroscience with cognitive therapy and psychoanalysis into a richly textured tapestry of human identity. It is rare to have someone so knowledgeably at home in such disparate fields. He is able to humanize neuroscience for the nonspecialist in his discourses on identity. This book is as relevant to the practicing mental health clinician as it is to the scientist and theoretician."

Alan Roland, PhD
psychoanalyst in private practice,
New York City;
Faculty, National Psychological
Association for Psychoanalysis

"**T**his intriguing book treats the reader to new ways of understanding how social and psychological phenomena are closely interwoven with underlying neural substrates. Jay Harris, MD, is a psychiatrist who is equally at home in the disciplines of psychoanalysis, cognitive science, and neurobiology. He deftly draws on the literature of each to lay out a sophisticated theory of human behavior that highlights the centrality of human identity formation and its associated neural structures. Harris, as a practicing clinician, demonstrates how his theoretical propositions can be applied to the understanding and treatment of the major psychiatric disorders. This volume is a conceptual tour de force that leads the way to an exciting dialogue between the fields of psychotherapy and neuroscience."

Stanley B. Messer, PhD
Professor and Chairman,
Department of Clinical Psychology,
Graduate School of Applied
and Professional Psychology,
Rutgers University

"**I**nterweaving the constructs of psychoanalysis, cognitive and anatomic neuroscience, psychopathology, mythology, and poetry with well-described case material and the guidelines of DSM-IV, Dr. Harris provides the basis for an integrated psychiatry. This *chef d'oeuvre* is of interest to advanced students in psychiatry, the allied mental health disciplines, and philosophy."

Max Fink, MD
School of Medicine,
Department of Psychiatry
and Behavioral Science,
Health Sciences Center,
State University of New York
at Stony Brook

How the Brain Talks to Itself

Talks to Itself

A Clinical Primer of Psychotherapeutic Neuroscience

THE HAWORTH PRESS
Advances in Psychology and Mental Health
Frank De Piano, PhD
Senior Editor

Beyond the Therapeutic Relationship: Behavioral, Biological, and Cognitive Foundations of Psychotherapy by Frederic J. Leger

How the Brain Talks to Itself: A Clinical Primer of Psychotherapeutic Neuroscience by Jay E. Harris

Cross-Cultural Counseling: The Arab-Palestinian Case by Marwan Dwairy

The Vulnerable Therapist: Practicing Psychotherapy in an Age of Anxiety by Helen W. Coale

How the Brain Talks to Itself

A Clinical Primer of Psychotherapeutic Neuroscience

Jay E. Harris, MD

The Haworth Press
New York • London

The Haworth Press, Inc., 10 Alice Street, Binghamton, NY 13904-1580

Cover design by Monica L. Seifert.
Cover illustration by Keelin Murphy.

Library of Congress Cataloging-in-Publication Data

Harris, Jay, 1936-
    How the brain talks to itself : a clinical primer of psychotherapeutic neuroscience / Jay E. Harris.
        p. cm.
    Includes bibliographical references and index.
    ISBN 0-7890-0408-9 (alk. paper).
    1. Cognitive neuroscience. 2. Psychoanalysis. 3. Identity (Psychology) 4. Neuropsychiatry.
I. Title.
    [DNLM: 1. Mental Disorders—diagnosis. 2. Mental Disorders—therapy. 3. Mental Processes—physiology. 4. Psychoanalytic Theory. 5. Neuropsychology. WM 140 H314h 1997]
    RC454.4.H365 1997
    612.8'2—dc21
    DNLM/DLC
for Library of Congress
                                          97-20703
                                            CIP

I dedicate this book to Nandor Balazs, who helped me maintain my belief in the efficacy of this decade-long endeavor, when common sense led me to think of giving up the fight. The ideas advanced in this text build upon earlier ones that I set forth in my book, *Clinical Neuroscience: From Neuroanatomy to Psychodynamics* (1986). I am eternally grateful to my wife, Jean Harris, who edited this manuscript in each of its developmental phases, as she did the previous one. Without her help, many essential ideas would have remained in their juvenile phase.

ABOUT THE AUTHOR

Jay E. Harris, MD, is a Consulting Psychiatrist at the Stony Brook University Student Health Counseling Center on Long Island. He was also Director of Residency Training in Psychiatry at Stony Brook University Hospital Medical Center, Director of Psychiatric Education for Medical Students, and Chairman of Grand Rounds. He has held appointments at several other prominent medical schools, including Albert Einstein Medical School, New York University Medical School, Cornell University Medical Center, and New York Medical College, where he is presently Adjunct Clinical Associate Professor of Psychiatry. Dr. Harris was the Director of Residency Training in Psychiatry at Cabrini Medical Center for nearly five years, where he developed a four-year teaching program, coordinated residency accreditation site visits, and developed an affiliate program for expansion of the residency. The author of *Clinical Neuroscience: From Neuroanatomy to Psychodynamics* (1986), he has published articles in *Psychotherapy and Psychosomatics,* the *Journal of Psychohistory,* and *Integrative Psychiatry.* He is also the co-author of three books: *Murals of the Mind: Image of a Psychiatric Community* (1973), *The Roots of Artifice: The Origins of Literary Creativity* (1982), and *The One-Eyed Doctor: Sigmund Freud, Psychological Origins of His Works* (1984).

CONTENTS

Introduction

How the Brain Talks to Itself may sound like the title of a Steve Martin movie or a *Star Trek* episode, but the amazing truth is: the human brain uses language—the same language I am communicating with at this very moment—to arrange its inner life as an organ. Figuring out how to talk about a process that is so natural and overt yet so technical and covert is a little like entering a hall of mirrors . . . or a world containing an infinite regress of smaller beings. In modern scientific jargon, we might say the brain contains multiple domains of nested templates. Such a statement is as potentially beautiful and true as it is ridiculous. The problem of this work is how to scientifically embrace both the brain's identity as observer and its identity as the observed in the same context.

The purpose of this work, then, is to create a coordinated picture that illuminates the brain's functions along with its structures. Its method is to derive functional and structural principles from all of the disciplines relevant to the brain's *development, information processing, problem solving, and syndrome formation.* Reconciling these principles, I have tried not to violate the fundamental truths of one discipline at the expense of another. The relevant disciplines include, but are not limited to the following:

- psychoanalytic psychology (including ego psychology, object relations psychology, and self-psychology)
- cognitive neuroscience (including cognitive and behavioral psychology, neuropsychology, and clinical neuroscience)
- clinical psychiatry (including DSM-IV diagnostic syndromes and neuropsychiatry)
- neurology (limited to developmental neuroanatomy, the formation of distributed neural systems, and computerized EEG, including event-related potential and functional brain imaging)
- linguistics (including neurobiological, social, cultural, and mytho-poetic influences)

The major thesis of this book is that intrapsychic identity, which presides executively at the apex of the brain's hierarchy of structural organizations, stabilizes the brain's functional coherence. Its corollary is that bilateral prefrontal assessment cortex integrates functionally distinct identity zones and synthesizes them in an intrapsychic identity system.

The minor thesis of this book is that in its temporal domains, the brain creates neural organizations that range from microsecond molecular effects, to macrosecond neurohormonal effects, to decades of life maturational transformations, to social effects that evolve over millions of years. The corollary to this is that each structural organization maintains functional equilibria in its own temporal domain, while engaging and altering contiguous temporal domains during periods of rapid structural change in the brain.

In organizing my hypotheses, I have used the following test of validity: the structural and functional principles derived from relevant disciplines must fit congruently. In other words, if conclusions reached in one discipline explain the brain's structural and functional relationships, they will match similar conclusions reached in other disciplines. I realize that no one person can encompass the relevant informations derived from so many fields of inquiry. Therefore, I have tried to encompass only the gist of the findings in each discipline. Interpolating integrations among disciplines, I am sure that I have made various factual errors, which I hope will serve as stimulus for further research or refinement. For instance, the mechanisms I have cited for long-term potentiation and the organization of distributed neural systems may become outdated. Nevertheless, I hope the framework and terms I have set out will enhance interdisciplinary communication.

A member of any particular discipline may find various contents of this book either naive or esoteric. I acknowledge these criticisms in advance. I believe, however, that fresh integrations can stimulate interdisciplinary research and lead to more comprehensive forms of therapy and diagnosis.

HOW DOES THE BRAIN TALK TO ITSELF?

I recently heard Michael Gazzaniga, PhD, speak about "Cognitive Neuroscience and the Future of Psychiatry," a subject close to my heart. At the time, Gazzaniga was keynote speaker at the January 1996 meeting of the American Association of Directors of Residency Training in Psychiatry in San Francisco. It seems that fifteen years ago, Gazzaniga had worked with Roger Sperry. Together, they studied the effect of cutting the corpus callosa in patients who had intractible epilepsy. Today, years after severing the interhemispheric links, some of the patients' right brains have begun to speak—in a way that their left brains cannot understand. Ordinarily, the left brain controls articulation. When the right brain begins to talk, the left brain experiences cognitive dissonance. It is as if the passenger, whose job it is to read the map, were suddenly driving the car.

Gazzaniga described a patient whose right brain was shown a picture of a wagon. Trying to verbally identify the picture, the patient's right brain said, "w . . . w . . . something that goes around." The left brain heard the consonant whoosh straining in the utterance. Gazzaniga asked the patient what "w" word he had meant to say and the patient's left brain came up with "windmill," a quixotic rationalization. Gazzaniga followed up with "Why windmill?" The patient began a long-winded explanation about saving energy and cleaning the farm environment. Everyone at the conference laughed. The left brain seemed fatuous in its willingness to come to conclusions on flimsy phonic evidence.

Clearly, the left hemisphere's reason was detached from the right's reality. In Gazzaniga's view, the right hemisphere's consciousness of the social world and of its affective response to it is hostage to the left's semantic narration. For this reason, Gazzaniga asserted that cognitive therapy works by reinforcing the left hemisphere's capacity to produce well-reasoned narration of experience.

As the conference unfolded, many psychiatrists seemed willing to concur. For instance, Daniel J. Siegal, MD, said that the aftereffects of trauma are due to the left hemisphere's stunned inability to perform its narrative function, which is to record source memory—memory of the actual event or episode—during a traumatic experience. Failure to perform the narrative function exposes the patient to the right hemisphere's naked affect.

Gazzaniga and the psychiatrists missed two essential points. First, neither hemisphere functions autonomously. Second, the right hemisphere normally contributes a great deal to both hemispheres' consciousness. The right hemisphere does more than perceive the world and regulate affect. It observes and records experience in its emotional and social context. More than this, the right hemisphere experiences a situation in the present as a variant of a past affective episode. In other words, the right hemisphere reallocates episodes of source memory. I would even say that the right hemisphere transfers episodic memory to the present. In this way it creates psychodynamic *transference*.

Like Siegal, other psychiatrists at the conference wanted to enhance their therapy with neuroscience. A popular and overly simple idea emerged: cognitive therapy is a left hemisphere endeavor. In this view, the cognitive therapist trains the patient's left hemisphere to listen more positively to reason. But cognitive therapy is not entirely a left hemisphere project. Look at it this way: If the therapist's position were "Don't do as I do, do as I say," there would be no cognitive therapy. Why?—because the patient has to have a positive identification with and transference to his cognitive therapist. The right hemisphere's transference incites the left hemisphere to reason.

Therapy without recognition of transference is like making love without stroking or kissing, a purely mechanical performance. Like love, therapy is not a machine's job, as the following example shows. I recently saw a depressed cognitive therapist as a patient. This man could not understand what a relationship is. He had been trained in childhood to keep his feelings to himself and to abide by his father's controlling, nonemotional way of doing things. His mother often said, "Father knows best," and that maxim ruled the house. Imagine the patient's surprise on learning that two people who have the will to relate and the ability to acknowledge their feelings can enter a *process* of relating. Imagine a world where no one learns to relate. What would it be like if no one valued individual identity? How might therapy occur in such a world?

When we cut the corpus callosum, we do not cut all avenues of communication between the hemispheres, only the ones that transact *conscious* communication. As I see it, cutting prefrontal communications (i.e., the bulk of anterior cortex) disrupts *identity* (our conscious sense of human coherence), which divides it into two portions: one subjective, one objective. *This text explores how the prefrontal cortex unifies identity that is both hemispherically divided and parceled into cognitive, social, and emotional integrative zones.*

For now, let us say we can still coordinate our cognitive, social, and emotional lives in rudimentary ways. As this text's study of the brain will show, after severing the corpus callosum:

- rhinal cortex (limbic system cortex that distributes sensory information) still compares left verbal and right pictoral data,
- supplementary motor cortex (an anterior cortex that facilitates behavioral release) still bilaterally augments our behaviors, and
- the amygdalae (limbic nuclei) still compare left and right emotional signals, and still regulate our social bonding patterns, as they have done since infancy.

That is why Gazzaniga addressed his remarks to the patient—one patient—not two patients, each lodged in a separate hemisphere.

It seemed to me that in responding to Gazzaniga's image of the wagon, both of his patient's hemispheres struggled valiantly to make sense of a farm vehicle that contributes to a farmer's survival. Both hemispheres also struggled to bond with Gazzaniga while answering his question about their own operations. His tacit question to each was, "What do you do with data?" Complying, the patient's two hemispheres spoke about how they used data to guide behavior, which is what Gazzaniga asked them to demonstrate.

The right hemisphere *prepares* for behavior by defining the context in which it will take place. To do this, it whisks data back and forth between its prefrontal cortex and its parietal cortex until it contextualizes the data in holistic gestalts. That is why Gazzaniga's patient's right prefrontal cortex enacted its way of integrating perceptual data, which is to make it complete a circuit such as a wagon wheel.

Because the left hemisphere *formulates* behavior as goals, its prefrontal cortex relates to objects as extensions of gestures—as tools. Luria (1980) taught us that tools extend left hemisphere gestures. Indeed, the left hemisphere's sequential analysis of phonemes and articulemes makes speech a tool for prefrontal organization. Following this line of reasoning, it was natural that Gazzaniga's patient's left hemisphere talked about its tool function—achieving motor goals. Why not? Wagons, and sometimes windmills, are farm tools.

WHAT DOES THIS TEXT DO?

This text synthesizes a world of recent discoveries in cognitive neuroscience with a psychoanalytic understanding of human dynamics and a working model for clinical diagnosis. It includes a guide to late twentieth century clinical neuroscience and a broad revision of human sciences. For neuroscience to contribute to our therapeutics, we need to:

- create a model that explains how functioning together, the hemispheres provide a sense of identity that fits us into our social world,
- look at identity as a set of prefrontal metafunctions that organizes the brain's problem-solving cognitive activity, and
- see how psychodynamics and transference convey the present and past emotional life into the realm of identity.

This text makes human identity the focus of neuroscience, diagnosis, and treatment.

With such a wide interdisciplinary scope, this book has to cultivate its audience. Data will be introduced bit by bit, as it is needed to make neuroscience a human science. This is another way of saying that this text sees the brain through the lens of human identity. It has to: my brain sees this text through the lens of my human identity. To put the case more strongly, it is time for neuroscience to take human identity seriously, because that is what our brains do. Assessing data prefrontally, we create identity. Our executive metafunction wields identity, like a personal, indwelling Zeus, as it reconciles each brain's unique organic universe with the social and physical universe.

Learning the terms that describe the brain's communication with itself will carry the reader to a fascinating new province, and yet it is one we have always known was there. Looking at the brain as it talks to itself is like studying the view of Central Park from the sculpture garden on the roof of the Metropolitan Museum—a place you thought you knew from intimate acquaintance with its pleasures and dangers discovers itself in fresh new patterns of paths and arborizations. I believe that the reader will acclimate quickly, and to assist that process, I have done my best to include a wealth of case histories, clinical vignettes, and diagnostic examples of mental status dialogues with patients.

As regards to method, I begin with *problem solving*. The core topic for both *cognitive* and *ego psychology*, problem solving is, I think, the key to understanding how we create, unify, and use identity. Our identity begins in the ego, "I" and "me," subject and object synthesized in a single entity. Ego psychology, the Gulf Stream of human science, holds that the ego's main work is to solve problems. Cognitive therapists presume we solve problems by framing them in an identity-based belief and value system. Essentially, we have to solve problems to survive.

From this text's perspective, innate crises arise in our brain's neurodevelopmental *neoteny* (cyclic neural maturation during our life span). These crises inevitably precipitate big problems. We solve them by creating newly functional human coherence. Solving small problems every moment or two, we affirm our identity more than ten million times in our lives.

Because our prefrontal cortex has a modular infrastructure that is both malleable and mutable, each solution reinstates and slightly sculpts who we are. I have tried to dissect identity by following natural divisions in the brain's way of assessing and encoding data. I have then resynthesized the brain's working structure as an illustrated model of six prefrontal identity zones. I have depicted this resynthesis in *The Acropolis of the Mind*, illustrated in Chapter 1. Its iconography personifies prefrontal functions to help the reader intuit how the brain communicates with itself. When I personified the executive function as Zeus, I foreshadowed.

Prefrontal dissection is possible because the prefrontal system uses parallel lateral, intermediate, and medial networks to integrate the types of data we assess in each identity zone. I locate six parallel processing prefrontal networks, which I call *experiential loops* because of their feedback operations. Each loop links: (1) adjacent cortex, (2) transcallosal cortex, (3) posterior (sensory) cortex, (4) rhinal cortex, and (5) amygdala.

I attribute a mythical persona to each loop to indicate what type of experience each loop integrates. Personification is a common, if unacknowledged, practice in neuroscience. Thus, when neuroscientists talk about executive or supervisory functions, they personify prefrontal metafunctions. The truth is: human qualities pervade important conceptualizations of brain function.

We all know, I think, that our sense of identity expands throughout neoteny. As the prefrontal networks develop a functional hierarchy, our executive reflection on identity matures through several neurodevelopmental cycles. In this way, the monumental human capacity to record and unify decades of experience arises from the flexible interaction of a hierarchial prefrontal system with subordinate distributed neural systems.

To merge the cognitive and psychoanalytic sciences with neuroscience, we need guiding principles. I have derived principles for mind/brain integration from Jean Piaget, Sigmund Freud, Alexander Luria, Dan Stern, Margaret Mahler, Noam Chomsky, Gerald Edelman, Joaquin Fuster, and many others. I respect each author's core concepts, both while building interdisciplinary models, and while applying them clinically.

How do we organize behavior? Freud called this organization *practical thinking*. Using *articulatory rehearsal* (thought as trial action), the prefrontal cortex joins perceptual and motor networks twice over. Four principles account for how the prefrontal system integrates its structure with its function:

1. *Each hemisphere thinks and behaves differently.* The right hemisphere organizes procedures based on its experience of mimicking objects' perceived qualities. Based on its motor experience of how an object's tool qualities extend our gestures, the left hemisphere initiates planned actions.

2. *Solving problems, the brain talks to itself.* A person who is solving a problem pays attention to the flow of speech through the prefrontal system. This flow operates as a hierarchical, functional mind/brain signal system for the prefrontal system's activated distributed networks. The process is like a person's using a computer to solve a problem. First, she uses a hierarchy of function keys or icons. Then, the computer, like the brain, operates its own built in modes of data transmission. The results translate back into human solutions.

Solving problems, the brain talks to itself in functional codes as we move down the prefrontal system's hierarchy from: *metafunctions* (executive, supervisory, self-observing), to *identity functions* (agent, social subject, subject and procedural self, social self and self), to *higher cortical functions*, known as ego functions (memory, perception, synthesis, integration, defense, etc.) to *neuropsychological functions* (phonemes, morphemes, articulemes, cadence, prosody, salience, significance, etc.). The particular combination of functions that the brain uses as it solves problems determines which modules and networks are activated, and in what order.

3. *Each module has a life of its own.* Each unit of mental structure responds to diverse neural influences. Each prefrontal module is like a citizen of the mind who uses the Internet. She is well connected to her district, to her province, and indeed to her brain's whole organic universe. She receives e-mail from scouting messengers in the posterior field, emotional messages from her amygdalar social relations, financial messages from her biogenic amine system (which uses dopamine, norepinephrine, serotonin, and acetylcholine), and almost irresistible messages from close neighbors as well as from her relatives in the other hemisphere. She sends out messages herself, often to urge that operations begin.

4. *Consciousness develops cyclically.* During neoteny, the brain develops in three cyclical spirals, from left hemisphere to right and from lateral to medial zones in each. These maturational spirals induce characteristic paths of integration in the two hemispheres. In each cycle, the left hemisphere expands its capacity to analyze data, while the right expands its capacity to make holistic integrations.

WHAT IS IN THIS PRIMER?

An individual's neural and psychic development is a microcosm of its own evolution. Taking a *neurally Darwinian* approach to human development, Chapter 1 presents a model in which amygdalar and hippocampal *excitotoxicity* determine which excitatory neurons survive as functional experiential links. Many neuroscientists believe these links are built by long-term potentiation (LTP) of excitatory synapses. Extreme LTP manifests a genetically predetermined, programmed neuronal self-destruction, *apoptosis*, which destroys a postsynaptic neuron. Excitotoxicity determines which neurons will survive as functional links in neural systems, and which, in a redundant primary repertoire, will not.

We start life with a vast overabundance of budding neurons. By destroying neurons we do not need, our personal neoteny sculpts our memory and experience out of the primary repertoire. A human being's unique experience has the same effect on his brain that Michelangelo had on a piece of stone. Michelangelo got rid of the part he did not need to make a statue of Moses. Each brain gets rid of what it does not need to form our adult identity.

Chapter 1 picks up where excitotoxicity leaves off. It creates an operational definition of the many forms of memory that bring data into consciousness when they are needed for problem solving. In other words, it follows the process through which data enters memory and memory enters experience. This text sees Freud's *system-consciousness* as the prefrontal system. It looks at prefrontal zones in terms of their cognitive, social, and emotional contributions to experience.

But what happens when data seem to be absent? Chapter 1 examines how the right brain forms *constructs* (allusion to what is not there). What is in the world is always partly unknown. Because the right hemisphere eschews chaos, we have to feel that our identity is coherent. The right hemisphere makes mental constructs, representations and symbols that compromise among what we know, what we cannot know, and what we do not want to know.

Chapter 2 sees the hippocampal neurons that survive potentiation as the ones that initiate long-term memory. This is another way of saying that initial excitotoxic events determine an individual's capacity to build source memories. At the cellular level, intracellular glucocorticoid stress receptors conclusively fix the functional synaptic linkages of surviving neurons within CA 1 and CA 3 hippocampal populations. This happens because the neurophysiological sequelae of stress induce excitotoxic destruction in some hippocampal neurons and potentiate others. Thus, stress selects which neurons survive. What happens when infant stress reaches traumatic levels? A combination of functional neural selection and long-term potentiation highly condition the limbic cortex that comprises the prefrontal intermediate zones in infantile patterns. At the same time, the same combination forms excess hippocampal source memory in infantile patterns. From infancy on, each person's capacity to record experience is multiply determined by genetic factors, neurophysiological factors, types of stress, and external response to the person's problem-solving dilemmas. Each human brain consequently initiates, responds, and records as an instrument of its singular neoteny.

Nevertheless, we all share instinctual tendencies that form templates for experience. Phylogenetically determined neural linkages make human beings social animals. As we come to know our own instinctual tendencies, we narrate them to ourselves and sense their presence in our identities. Collectively, our narrated instinctual tendencies produce recognizable types of people, whom we recognize in a variety of critical problem-solving situations. For this reason, narrated instinctual development leaves traces in collective mythologies that record humanity's social becoming.

Chapter 3 establishes the neurobiological foundations for human development. To survive phylogenetically, a complex organism needs:

- a *consummatory instinct* that reaches to the environment for resources to maintain its internal milieu and for mating,
- a *vigilant instinct* that deals with threats to survival, and
- a *vital instinct* that balances the other two.

In order for a human being to survive, these instincts need to be tamed—conditioned—as they contribute to the development of an individual's identity.

In infancy, the amygdala conditions the three basic instincts by linking them to three prefrontally regulated drives. These are a *left hemisphere, dopaminergic libidinal drive*, a *right hemisphere, noradrenergic aggressive drive*, and a *bilateral serotonergic-acetylcholinergic neutralizing drive*. Observers report that infants cycle among these three drive states.

Each biogenic amine (or aminergic) system's synaptic effects last for a second or two while data processing and behavioral preparation occur. Thus, in a state of consummation pressure, dopamine rapidly energizes the prefrontal system's search for salience (satisfying stimuli). Similarly, in a state of vigilance pressure, norepinephrine quickly energizes the prefrontal system's search for significance (relevant stimuli). When consummatory or vigilant states must be maintained longer, the central serotonergic and acetylcholinergic drive reenforces them.

States of acute and chronic stress alter drive regulation. In recent decades, researchers and psychiatrists have believed that *upregulation* or *downregulation* of each aminergic system accounts for the formation of various syndromes. I will argue that to regulate an aminergic system is to regulate a drive system. I will maintain consequently that the findings of psychoanalysis are supported by neuroscientific research and that psychoanalytic discoveries explain neurobiological findings. On the basis of their clinical findings, classical psychoanalysts believe that libidinal, aggressive, and neutral drives pressure the ego to solve problems. If an amine system is a drive system, it follows that unrequited consummation pressure, or continuing external threats, can exhaust the problem-solving capacity lent by the drives and produce a state of neurophysiological urgency.

Chapter 3 provides several lines of evidence that the left hemisphere evolved to coordinate the consummatory, libidinal drive, and that the right hemisphere evolved to coordinate the vigilant, aggressive drive. The nature of that evolution includes the organization of two signal systems, which yield two different forms of speech. The left hemisphere's innately derived *inner speech* is oriented toward consummating action, while the right hemisphere's imitative *social speech* uses social phrases in an aggression-binding idiom. Prefrontal synthesis of the two forms of language provides the balance we need for pragmatic problem solving.

Chapter 4 uses a neural system's perspective to unify cognitive and psychoanalytic views of development. Human development advances in cyclic stages. As new data sources emerge during critical periods in each stage, excitotoxicity fashions structural changes in the neural systems. Because a maturing prefrontal cortex is structurally flexible, its identity organization can accommodate newly conditioned associations and new source memories. Conditioned associations form the compost from which socialized identity flowers.

Chapter 4 advances the thesis that cyclic stage changes are *endogenously traumatic.* As his neural system unfolds along genetically predetermined lines, an individual encounters survival problems that require him to radically transform his neural systems and his identity. This explains such critical psychoanalytic concepts as the *universal primal scene* experience and the *shattering of the Oedipus complex.* It seems to me that these identity-shattering experiences necessarily accompany and triggers massive excitotoxic processes that usher in new developmental stages.

Chapter 5 follows the maturation of identity from hemisphere to hemisphere. In the course of my study I have discovered (and illustrate here) a *spiral synthesis* model for development that depicts sequential periods of emotional, social, and cognitive maturation in each hemisphere. *Developing alternately, each hemisphere provides the foreground for new higher cortical functions. The spiral process culminates three times in the synthesis of new stages of intrapsychic identity.* Prefrontal identity systems undergo three hierarchical transformations.

Quantitative electroencephalogram (EEG) findings strongly support this developmental thesis. While quantitative (Q)EEG findings show new nodes of integration emerge in the massively reconditioned hemisphere, developmental findings show that the other hemisphere concurrently provides a reliable foreground for its prefrontal functions. Thus, while endogenous primal-scene trauma at eighteen months triggers left hemisphere synaptogenesis and excitotoxicity, the right hemisphere stabilizes new observing metafunctions, identity functions, ego functions, and neuropsychological functions. Chapter 5 weaves the developmental findings of neoteny, ego psychology, and cognitive psychology into a unified portrait of human identity.

Chapter 6 looks at how the adult brain uses its experience, memory, and functional hierarchy to solve adult problems. Using the *Acropolis of the Mind* figure to form an iconography of the prefrontal system's identity functions, Chapter 6 looks at the interaction between the social world and the adult, working brain. I propose that:

- human prefrontal cortex has evolved in equilibrium with the social and physical world,
- the social and institutional world has evolved as an extension of humanity's collective prefrontal cortex,
- the disparate institutions that govern us have evolved socially as extended operations of particular identity zones, and
- the interplay between the extant social world and the more personally imagined social world that we each externalize is mediated by linguistic organization.

Put another way, externalized, socialized structures such as language, iconography, and mythology mediate our social interactions. After humanity externalizes prefrontal functions as social structures, the structures evolve socially. And yet, the social impacts the personal. Externalized prefrontal structures become templates for the brain's inner communication, and they regulate the prefrontal system's identity.

Extending the theme of social organization as externalizing prefrontal functions, the text narrowly defines two terms. *Coping* is the left hemisphere's response to social challenges to one's narcissistic integrity. *Adaptation* is the right hemisphere's response to challenges to one's objective social standing. The text also classifies left hemisphere coping personalities as *Type 1*, and right hemisphere adaptive personalities as *Type 2*. I posit that individuals are genetically predetermined to use one hemisphere more than the other and to use particular identity zones more than others.

Continuing to look at how the adult brain uses data, Chapter 6 scrutinizes the brain's data evaluation in millisecond epochs. A review of event-related potential (ERP) studies (quantitative EEG reports on the brain's cumulative synaptic response to stimuli) suggests that data evaluation proceeds in serial epochs. Within a second or two, data are serially (1) registered, (2) processed, (3) discriminated, (4) assessed, and (5) enter executive reflection.

Finally, Chapter 6 retraces the origins and development of (1) neuropsychological functions (zero to forty-two months), (2) ego functions (three and one-half to eleven years), and (3) metafunctions (age twelve to twenty-one). Each of these functional brain domains emerges from a new cycle of neoteny, and supports a higher level of consciousness. Figure 1, Identity

FIGURE 1. Identify Synthesis and Cognitive Foundations

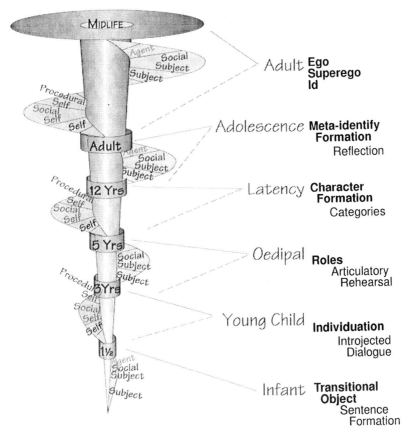

Synthesis and Cognitive Foundations, depicts the brain's cognitive development in each cycle.

Chapter 7 provides the reader with a novel biopsychosocial context for understanding syndromes and treating patients. Health professionals use the DSM-IV (*Diagnostic and Statistical Manual of Mental Disorders, Fourth Edition*) to classify syndromes. I reclassify DSM-IV syndromes according to the hemispheric zones that trigger them. Triggering may result from endogenous or exogenous causes.

By *endogenous causes*, I mean genetic, organic, metabolic, neurophysiological, endocrine, or medical processes that trigger excitotoxicity.

Neurophysiological defenses against excitotoxicity (known as "damping" or "forced normalization") play a role in the clinical presentation of excitotoxic syndromes such as bipolar disorder or temporal lobe epilepsy. By *exogenous causes*, I refer to social, interpersonal, and conflictual processes that contribute to the ultimate shape of a syndrome. Exogenous causes may or may not trigger excitotoxicity.

Post-traumatic stress disorder (PTSD), the defining syndrome of our era, is the prime example of an exogenous syndrome's provoking excitotoxicity or forced normalization. PTSD occurs most frequently in genetically vulnerable individuals who experience a loss of reliable social and family authority. This loss is tantamount to restraint stress. Without escape, individuals chronically damp their cognition.

As I see it, when individuals with PTSD lose their social templates for their belief and value systems, severe trauma triggers excitotoxicity of experiential neural loops. This permanently alters stress responses, cognitive capacity, intrapsychic identity, and social adaptation. I infer that PTSD replicates neurodevelopmental change as exogenous trauma triggers endogenous process. Trauma induces massive reconditioning and source memory formation. This brings a new load of identity structures into an already loaded identity system, which triggers pathology. The traumatized person is no longer the same person.

Chapter 8 presents a model for exogenous causes of syndrome formation. How do interpersonal conflicts and dynamics produce changes in the brain's organization? Looking at each identity zone and considering its hierarchy of functions gives rise to a multitude of clinical hypotheses about the integration of mind and brain. The illustrated *Where Syndromes Come From* presents these hypotheses in graphic form within this chapter. What all these clinical hypotheses have in common is each identity zone has predictable

- drive and neurotransmitter resources,
- symptoms emerging from under- or overuse of that zone, and
- interpersonal psychopathology.

Narcissism, for example, distorts left prefrontal regulation. Looking at the illustrations in Chapter 8 tells us that narcissists manifest faulty ideals, empathy, intersubjective identifications, and shame regulation. In left hemisphere syndromes, dopamine and serotonin regulation are abnormal. Borderline disorder distorts right prefrontal regulation. The illustrations in Chapter 8 tells us that borderlines show faulty morality, interpersonal relating, and self-esteem. They identify with the aggressor, use denial, and are anxious about novelty. In right hemisphere syndromes, norepinephrine and serotonin regulation are abnormal.

Focusing on the syndromes classified in DSM-IV, Chapter 9 provides a unified theory of syndromes. The basic premise is that each syndrome has a core

- neural mechanism,
- symptom-triggering flash point,
- distortion in intrapsychic identity,
- dynamic conflict,
- cognitive bias, and
- social cause.

Diagnosis and treatment involves analyzing relations among core elements, as the included case presentations show.

Arising from core causes in this way, patterns of syndrome development emerge mechanistically in stages. To give an example: Genetically vulnerable people undergo abnormal excitotoxicity and develop psychosis. Psychosis produces endogenous trauma. Psychoses' excitotoxicity literally scars neural networks. Altered networks produce enduring changes in emotionally organized source memory. Psychotically transformed source memory modifies personality.

Answering the question, "Where does the mind go when we lose it?", Chapter 10 follows the schizophrenic's journey to oblivion. Tracing schizophrenia's regression from prodrome through chronicity, this chapter develops closely reasoned neural and intrapsychic explanations for schizophrenia's dramatic symptoms.

To put the case in a nutshell, endogenous psychosis is a traumatic experience that self-perpetuates in mechanistic steps. The intense and unrelenting panic, terror, stress, and intrapsychic dissolution that accompany *acute schizophrenia* induces excitotoxicity. Consequently, in a restitutional, *subacute stage*, the schizophrenic person's brain reorganizes all of its networks. As acute and subacute stages repeat their vicious circle, the mutable prefrontal cortex undergoes a pathological change that marks the start of *chronicity*.

This steadily building endogenous trauma affects the patient's intrapsychic identity. In the acute stage, the schizophrenic's prefrontal system attempts to experience its own identity in a coherent way, even as it loses its sense of regulating its parallel processing networks. When the schizophrenic's synthesis of intrapsychic identity fails, she lose the capacity to ascribe reflections, thoughts, and causes to her own sense of identity. This experience is the essence of primary delusions. Auditory hallucinations and a formal thought disorder occur when the left dorsolateral zone loses its capacity for semantic integration. It seems to me that when the left hemisphere's working memory fails to integrate auditory data that has been registered, raw data enters into left dorsolateral processing and hallucinations result.

Chapters 11 and 12 provide a new perspective on the *mental status examination*. Every element of the mental status is reexamined under the lens of structural analysis. The neural systems model structurally redefines the functions that give rise to symptoms and syndromatic phenomenology. To give a simple example, *effort*, a left hemisphere function, is separable from *concentration*, a right hemisphere function. They should not both be included under the rubric of concentration.

When our right eye locks in gaze fixation with the patient's right eye, we can read the patient's left hemisphere's allocation of libidinal drive. Thus, right eye to right eye reads libidinal warmth. In this way, the practiced examiner can tell if the patient's narcissism is available for investment, whether the patient is capable of reflection, and whether the patient is impulsive. When we gaze lock with the patient's left eye, we can read the disposition of his aggressive energy. Seeing a look of deadness there is a sign of depression.

Chapter 12 realigns our understanding of cognitive disorders such as delirium and dementia. Memory, for example, is reclassified in terms of disruptions in metamemory, source memory, short-term memory, working memory, and immediate memory. These memory types and their disturbances are defined in a context of their structural triggering zones. This approach replaces simple functional concepts of retention and recall.

If the examiner dissects his own reciprocating responses to the patient and deliberately observes his own data analysis, he can figure how fast the patient is processing data. How long do we have to wait for answers that require the patient to use his sourced cognitive data? Is the patient consistent in producing images and even symbols of painful episodic source memory?

Placing phenomenology within a neuroscience model of clinical syndromes, Chapters 11 and 12 offer researchers and clinicians a testable paradigm for predicting where functional brain images and quantitative EEG will show the brain's hot and cold spots.

Chapter 13 presents a new form of integrative treatment, *structural therapy*. To recover from a syndrome that compromises his identity, a person needs to cognitively reconstruct the endogenous and exogenous forces that altered his identity. Adequate cognitive explanations can restore, to some extent, disequilibrium in metafunctions that regulate identity. Using the neural systems model, therapist and patient together form a more viable account of the life of the person's mind. That account becomes a prosthesis which the patient can absorb in his symbiotic transference with the therapist. This technique helps highly motivated patients. I illustrate the use of this technique in several of the text's cases.

Individual dynamics and identity conflicts arise from family disequilibria as well as from familial myths that pathologically account for these disequilbria. The second aspect of structural therapy is therefore to provide an account of this process. In therapy, the patient learns to see that the need to dwell on the past is more than a need to live out fantasies or repeat traumata in belated attempts at mastery. The patient revisits the past in an attempt to repair the lies and myths that have distorted her cognitive world.

One cannot successfully treat a traumatized or a psychotic person without taking into account the change in her sense of identity. For instance, a psychotic person always suffers a profound change in identity. Good, supportive therapy explains the identity changes to the patient. A therapeutic focus on identity altering experience reconciles cognitive therapists with object relations therapists and self psychologists.

Chapter 13 presents a rationale for psychopharmacological interventions that follows from seeing syndromes both in their zonal context and in the context of excitotoxicity or forced normalization. Treating such left hemisphere syndromes as atypical or narcissistic depression, we have to pay attention to stabilizing dopamine and serotonin systems. Right hemisphere syndromes require us to attend to norepinephrine and serotonin stabilization. It seems to me that mania and acute exogenous and acute endogenous trauma (which occurs in acute psychosis), can benefit from drugs that interrupt excitotoxic processes.

* * *

Because we are the sum of our neural possibilities and life experiences, we cannot solve the simplest problem of living without deriving every element of our solution from who we are and what we have gone through. In studying how the brain talks to itself to solve survival problems, this text looks at two sets of situations. In the first, neural possibilities mesh adaptively. In the second, dysfunction clouds the picture. Something has gone wrong in the brain, in the life, or in a combination that ends in the cascading distortions of clinical syndromes. Our goal is to view the brain's distortions of experience through the lens of a phenomenology informed by dynamics and neuroscience.

Introspection is a fundamental tool of the psychoanalyst, the behaviorist, and the neuroscientist, as each tries to plumb the genesis of such basic ego functions as memory, thought, speech, or perception. By describing the development of the consciousness of identity as it occurs in well-defined stages, this text strives to extend the reader's introspection further into his interior structures and processes of consciousness. In the end, the text helps each of us know how our brain answers the question, "Who am I?"

Chapter 1

The Functional Anatomy
of Consciousness

Man is a structure-making, problem-solving animal.

This is a chapter about the relationship between the brain's structure and its problem-solving function. Human survival skills reside in the prefrontal system's evolved capacity to create structures that solve problems. This capacity has two dimensions. The brain talks to itself, and it talks to others. The brain's structure determines how it talks to itself, and its function determines how it talks to others. Because the brain is an interactive structure that eschews chaos, the question we have to ask ourselves is, how does the brain coordinate its inner speech with its outer speech to resolve problems? [1]

A NEURAL SYSTEMS APPROACH
TO THE BRAIN'S INNER LANGUAGE

When we start thinking about this question, we face a problem right away. The infant brain does not work exactly as the child's brain does, and the child's brain does not process data as an adult's does. Mature brains and old brains also have their own neurobiological systems. A cognitive neuroscience model will have to create a developmental portrait of the brain as it elaborates human and individual identities. Thus, our model will have to employ a *neural systems* top down approach that focuses on relevant identity changes that demarcate the stages of life.

But there is more to the brain's internal communication than infant brain talking to infant brain, adult brain talking to adult brain, and so forth. The infant brain talks to the adult brain, and as it is *de rigueur* to say, the adult talks to the child within. The brain's capacity to access our life's experience is more than impressive. The way we solve problems recapitulates the development of our intrapsychic identities.

To understand and use this neural systems approach, we will follow the principles elaborated in the introduction:

Solving Problems, the Brain Talks to Itself

Using language as a coding system, the problem solver keeps track of activated prefrontal modules. These activated associations are the products of *parallel-processing,* prefrontal networks.

Each Hemisphere Thinks and Behaves Differently

Cognition organizes language to formulate behavior. Each hemisphere employs its own form of cognition. Left prefrontal dorsolateral cortex (the agent's inner speech zone) organizes *planned* behavior. Right prefrontal dorsolateral cortex (the procedural self's social speech zone) organizes *responsive* behavior. The executive unifies the two forms of cognition as a simple sentence before we act or speak (*articulatory rehearsal*).

Each Module Has a Life of Its Own

A module is the basic structural unit of cortex. Modules are links in associational networks. Each prefrontal hemisphere has three kinds of data inflow networks: *cognitive* (lateral cortex), *social* (intermediate cortex), and *emotional* (medial cortex). In addition to its participation in one of these six possible data inflow networks, each prefrontal module also participates in the prefrontal system's *behavioral* outflow.

Consciousness Develops Cyclically

Functional distributed systems develop in three cyclical spirals. The spiraling begins in the left hemisphere and moves to the right. Within each hemisphere, the movement is from lateral to medial cortex. These spirals induce characteristic paths of integration in the two hemispheres. Each cycle triggers new paths of integration, and these paths are hierarchically superior to the earlier ones. Prefrontal networks consequently develop hierarchically organized modular fields. The closer a module is to the top of a pyramid, the more abstract the data it codes.

We have to deduce these principles, because we experience *system consciousness* (reflection on experience organized by identity) in a unified way. Having deduced them, we can see that to solve problems, we filter data through parallely distributed networks of prefrontal structures *(agent, social subject, subject, procedural self, social self, and self)*. These structures are intrinsic to our personal identities. When we have a problem, we use them to assess whether processed data can trigger behavior compatible with our identities.

Let us summarize the types of assessments that the prefrontal cortex makes. The lateral zones code cognitive formulations of ongoing significant and salient experience. When present experience evokes them, the intermediate zones code signals derived from previously conditioned social experience. The medial zones code feedback from our emotional responses. Since every sentence solves a problem, every sentence includes contributions from our cognitive, social, and emotional life.

Here is an example of how our prefrontal identity system works to coordinate its component zones. In order to use anxiety as a signal system, we have to first sample the feedback from a minor anxiety discharge. Then we code the signal anxiety in language. Only then can we modify our behavior. If warranted by intermediate and medial signals, the executive can also evoke long-term, emotionally organized source memory. These are masses of explicit associations available to cognition.

HOW DOES THE BRAIN MANAGE CONSCIOUSNESS?

In his *Project for a Scientific Psychology*, Freud saw *system consciousness* as an indwelling sense organ that perceives the activity of those neural systems that make the most direct and simultaneous contact with the sensory world and our biochemical milieu (1895). System consciousness is the sixth sense. This executive, observing sense uses language to code how the brain is working. Thus, as a prefrontal assessment system, system consciousness makes data suitable for entering the *executive* structures of our personal identity.

Freud's system consciousness also manifests a motor quality—*attention*. Together, the thalamus and cerebellum create quick motor shifts in attention that focus perception. The thalamus evokes consciousness of sensory stimuli by passing signals from the ascending reticular activating system to the frontal and prefrontal areas. If, like general lighting on a theater's stage, the thalamus sets the stage for consciousness, then the cerebellum spotlights the data we attend. The cerebellum is a

> computational system for providing the optimal context for the smooth interdigitated, coordinated neural action of whatever systems are needed from moment to moment to achieve a specified goal within the context of continuously fluctuating internal and external contexts. (Courchesne et al., 1994, p. 861)

Once aroused and attending, executive *metafunctions* regulate a hierarchy of activated perceptual and motor networks required to solve problems. First, an executive sense of unified identity brings our *higher cortical functions* into selected and simultaneous use. Higher cortical functions *are* the *ego functions*; they are not the *ego*, which will be defined later. Each higher cortical function—thought, initiation, apperception, synthesis, defense, adaptation, etc.—derives from a different reference point in identity.

HOW DO METAFUNCTIONS REGULATE INTRAPSYCHIC IDENTITY?

The brain's two hemispheres are not identical twins. The dominant left hemisphere organizes our initiatives, while the nondominant right hemisphere organizes our responses. The division of labor shows up at the highest level of prefrontal organization. Hereafter I will use the following anthropomorphisms:

— *executive* to refer to the executive metafunction that transcallosally synthesizes speech and identity
— *supervisor* to refer to the left prefrontal, supervisory metafunction that integrates what we mean to do or say
— *observer* to refer to the right prefrontal metafunction that represents the reality of the self in the world

In later chapters, I will show that these anthropomorphisms are justified, for metafunctions embody intrapsychic identity.

Using our functional model, we can say that while solving problems prefrontally:

- the left hemisphere *supervises inner speech,*
- the right hemisphere *observes social speech,* and
- the executive function *synthesizes* inner with social speech as *articulatory rehearsal.*

Without the mediation of language, the brain cannot embody its left hemisphere's volition, its right hemisphere's observation of reality, or its reflection on its intrapsychic identity states. The advantage that language confers on us as problem solvers is that it codes both sensory representations and motor schema.

WHAT IS ARTICULATORY REHEARSAL?

When the brain uses articulatory rehearsal to talk to itself, it fuses subjective and objective identity into *das ich,* the ego, by which Freud meant "I"/"me." At the twin centers of behavioral preparation, the simple use of the subject, *I*, summons supervisory volition, while the object, *me*, prepares observational reaction. Equipped with dual consciousness, the executive enables us to act upon the world and react to it.

Protosentences, of which "Ah wa da—I want that—" is an example, occur at eighteen months, when the infant brain synthesizes a transcallosal identity. A legacy of early hemispheric linkage, protosentences underlie later intrapsychic communications. A simple example of the brain's talking to itself occurs in the protosentence "I need me to open the window." Of course, one never hears such sentences because a Chomskian transformation translates them into "I need to open the window." The full purposes of the ego are nevertheless served by the untransformed base sentence, in which the subject initiates and the object reacts.

WHAT IS INNER SPEECH?

Inner speech is mainly a sequence of action verbs that the left brain encodes for *volitional* discharge. We are all familiar with what the left brain has to say. For example, while watching the 1994 Winter Olympics, I heard one of the miked figure skaters vocalizing as she went through her routine. The inner speech with which she instructed her actions was, "back, back, back, through." This is familiar enough, and to be sure, anyone who has watched professional golf on television will recognize the players' inner speech. Almost all men or women golfers "follow through" verbally with instructions to the ball such as: "left, left, roll, sit!" Inner speech joins action, and extends volition into the arena of effects as "body English."

WHAT IS SOCIAL SPEECH?

As we fall asleep and lose the point of intention, we relapse into the social speech of young childhood. Perhaps this is why, for some of us, the dissolution of identity that accompanies the entrance to sleep feels dangerous and leads to insomnia. As we fall asleep, we need to feel that our identity is simple and coherent and that we will awaken revitalized.

At sleep's portal, however, we begin to fuse with language and sensory images. As we fall asleep, we notice phrases floating and joining without meaning. Meaning dissolves without intention, and our only intention is to fall asleep. In other words, jetsam from the sea of words—ideas, idioms, phrases, and images—fuses with our entrance into sleep, as our sense of unified identity melts.

This sea is the stuff of social speech, detached from thought. On several occasions, I was treated to displays of social speech by each of my daughters when each was two and falling asleep. Whole phrases I had used during the day must have gone streaming into their mental seas, and now, they articulated whole phrases that had to have been beyond their complete comprehension.

In waking life, the executive actively selects ideas, idioms, and phrases that we absorb from social speech and combines them with the inner speech that derives from our voluntary expression. This articulatory rehearsal, the legacy of the brain's later childhood, is the thought that constitutes trial action. In problem solving, the executive's articulatory rehearsal organizes metafunctions by linking our behavioral repertoire of inner speech with the verbally encoded data of observation.

Legacies of the brain's development of inner speech, social speech, and articulatory rehearsal are vulnerable to organic damage as well as to dynamic conflicts. Particular areas of *damaged* prefrontal cortex produce characteristic disruptions in speech functions. In the prefrontal cortex, damage to:

- the left dorsolateral zone results in the utterance of simple sentences, much like inner speech;
- the left orbital frontal zone causes unfocussed, impulsive utterance;
- the right orbital frontal zone globally disorganizes syntax (Kaczmarek, 1984); and
- either medial cortex gives rise to a tendency to *initiate* vocalization in monkeys and humans (Kling and Brothers, 1992). Thus, the prefrontal cortex is a system of branched networks that freely unifies left semantic classes of meaning with right linguistic forms. Each zone contributes to the regulation and organization of articulatory rehearsal.

FUNCTIONAL/STRUCTURAL LINKS
IN SYSTEM CONSCIOUSNESS

A. R. Luria called prefrontal cortex "social cortex," because it mediates the shared problem solving that gives humans a survival advantage (1980). Prefrontal cortex uses a social medium, language, to unify intrapsychic identity in terms that flexibly link the inner life of needs and emotions to outer, social reality. We call this social synthesis *reflection*, because it provides a sense of indwelling social observation. Reflecting in preparation for behavior, the executive unifies its prefrontal system's lateral cognitive data, intermediate socially conditioned data, and medial emotional feedback data. The executive scrutinizes diverse data structures that are all relevant to solving the problem at hand.

Perhaps our brain's evolutionary advance can be ascribed to its separation of these three dichotomous streams of emotional, social, and cognitive associations. After their separation, which allows careful scrutiny of data, the streams are reunified by articulatory rehearsal. Our uniquely human identity is formed, then, from a stream of thought that includes finely honed elements of emotion, social conditioning, and cognition.

The executive's identity can undergo an infinite series of transformations. Piaget called the generalizing capacity for assessment of assessment—thinking about thinking about feeling, etc.—*formal thought*. This hierarchical, detaching quality of reflective identity confers a uniquely human survival advantage.

How did we evolve this capacity to reflect and generalize our experience? The answer resides, I think, in the development of cortex that can assess assessment cortex. The redundant availability of prefrontal assessment cortex is an evolutionary advance that enables our capacity for symbolism, abstraction, generalization, and metaphor. I conjecture that supraordinate cortex evolved from genetically induced, redundant assessment ensembles, which conferred a survival advantage. We get further away from the concrete experience of reality as we engage our higher order sense of organized intrapsychic identity. There is no end to the levels of reflective intrapsychic identity; instead, they seem to merge into the ineffable sense of God.

HOW DO WE EXPLAIN
THE DUALITY OF CONSCIOUSNESS?

Having explored the first principle: *solving problems, the brain talks to itself,* let us elaborate the second principle: *how each hemisphere thinks and behaves differently.* Frontal cortex provides dual behavioral formats for action and response (Miller, Galanter, and Pribram, 1960). The left brain's *action program* contingency is: first do this, then do that. The right's *response program* procedural contingency is: if this is so, then do that. Regardless of which hemisphere initiates behavior, supplementary motor association cortex bilaterally activates behavioral discharge that inner speech mediates (Eccles, 1982; Pfurtscheller and Berghold, 1989). The brain talks to itself as it acts, whether behavior is voluntary or the result of it following procedural rules. Reflection is dichotomous; discharge is not.

Each behavioral step is contingent upon detecting salient and significant data in posterior perceptual networks. We build apperception by fixating on objects' *salient* (need relevant) and *significant* (reality relevant) features. Salience and significance are verified by the supplementary visual cortex, which uses the eye muscles to motorically palpate objects. These *saccades,* also known as *fixation-stops,* palpate percepts; which is to say that our eye muscles make sure that salient and significant objects have the requisite features.

Among the distributed posterior areas that provide salient and significant data to the prefrontal system's lateral, cognitive associational network:

- inferior temporal cortex provides visual features,
- posterior parietal cortex provides somesthetic (muscle and pressure sense) and tactile features, and
- superior temporal cortex provides auditory phonemes.

By integrating posterior perceptual networks (representations) into anterior motor networks (schema), the left hemisphere's *agent* acts spontaneously. By integrating its anterior schema into posterior networks of representations, the right hemisphere's *procedural self* reacts procedurally.

> Perception and motor action are functionally interrelated, and both are part of many representational networks. The functional relationship between perceptual and motor memory and the interplay of their networks, constitute the basis of the *perception-action* cycle. This is the circular course of information processing, serial and parallel, through posterior cortex, through anterior cortex, and through the environment, that shapes and characterizes any sequential structure of novel behavior. (Fuster, 1995, p. 3, emphasis in original)

The right dorsolateral prefrontal cortex constructs *procedures* (perceptual copies of the world) from multimodal feedbacks during motor responses to objects. It mimes the composition of objects by *simultaneously* associating vestibular, somesthetic, tactile, and visual data feedbacks. Motor responses to objects give rise to serial, holographic snapshots—perceptual *representations* of the objects. The procedural self uses motor schema to guide action by replicating objects (making them appear again) or by imitating perceptions of how others act.

As we prepare to act, then, we balance two perspectives about the world: we mime an object procedurally, and as Luria said, our initiatory actions reciprocate those tool qualities of an object (such as a bat or ball) that extend our gestures (1980). Our right hemisphere's self-observant representational function tells us what is in the world and where we stand, and our left hemisphere's semantic analysis predicts how we will affect the world. Integrating two sets of motor and perceptual data about the world provides us with an overlapping capacity to know *what* is in the world and *how* we can effect that world.

For this reason, behavior is either spontaneous (led by action) or procedural (led by perception). When agency determines behavior, we are spontaneous. Spontaneous behavior arises from clear and salient perception. When procedure determines behavior, we premeditate. Procedural behavior tries to create its own perceptions.

Let us think about what happens in baseball. When the batter is on his game, the ball looks as big as a watermelon coming over the plate. The batter's agent follows the ball's path so accurately that when the batter unleashes his swing, he hits the ball with the fat part of the bat. When the batter is off his game though, his procedural self swings where it thinks the ball will be and the ball itself looks as small as a pill. Now, consider the pitcher. On his game, he pitches spontaneously and follows through. Off his game, he takes aim. What happens when he thinks procedurally about how to get the ball to go where he wants it to go? Any fan will tell you, taking aim makes the ball go awry. Aiming is all procedure. It is not about action; it is about what is in the world.

Most of our behavior, though, is communication via speech. For communication to occur, we need both to receive and express language. To understand how the prefrontal cortex uses language to arrange our business, we will need to distinguish *operants* from *procedures*. The agent's left dorsolateral cortex generates *sequential* verbal associations called *operants*. Operants lead action. *Phonemes* and *morphemes* code sequential kinaesthetic feedbacks from the muscles of articulation (*articulemes*) as *operant speech*. In effect, the left dorsolateral cortex uses perceptual coding to form semantic (and gestural) schema of the world. The agent uses these operant schemata as templates to initiate spontaneous behavior through its anterior networks.

As for verbal communication behavior, the prefrontal system's double coding combines an infinite array of percepts and schema. During seconds of preparation, the brain reflectively articulates its behavioral rehearsal. Then we act—spontaneously.

DISTRIBUTED SYSTEMS

Let us now amplify the third principle: *each module has a life of its own.* To do this, we will need to see where modules stand in the brain's structural and functional organization. We will want to understand how a module becomes specially facilitated to participate in a functional neural system.

Let us say that you, the reader, are a rock climber who has to find significant features in the facade of a rock wall, which may be a good metaphor for how you see this book before you master it. You are particularly interested in the chinks that will give you the toeholds you need to keep climbing. Each chink is a necessary feature. You need each one to get to the top where vistas clarify. When you have surmounted many difficulties in the course of arduous problem solving, you will feel an enhanced sense of identity. Defining yourself against the mountain—that is, the *Acropolis of the Mind* (see Figure 1.1)—you will know yourself better than you did before. Our question here is, how do distributed systems turn novel chinks and toeholds, significant features, into welcome signs for the ego? The short answer is that on its way to reflection, a datum runs the gamut of the brain's coding systems. Distributed systems determine its course.

Distributed systems are composed of excitatory neurons that transmit excitation to other excitatory neurons in a regulated way. In other words, distributed systems are *flexible cortical-subcortical links* that structure an interactive equilibrium among modular data processing units (Bechtereva, 1978). The flexible cortical and subcortical links determine which fields of a network participate in higher cortical functions at a particular moment. Posterior cortical tails of prefrontal networks are so vast and multiply distributed that most sensory modules are within one or two synapses of the prefrontal cortex. The amygdalar and rhinal cortical neurons that provide the heart and soul of experience are one synapse away from the prefrontal cortex.

Some data are always critical to the resolution of particular problems. As a rock climber, you will want to find as many such toeholds as you can. The brain needs a mechanism for permanently facilitating critical features. When the climber knows he has used a particular toehold before, his way is eased. Similarly, facilitated modules are welcome signs in distributed systems.

The brain's mechanism for facilitating synapses adapts to its neurophysiology and its experience. We call this mechanism *long-term potentiation* (LTP). LTP induces quasipermanent synaptic facilitation among excitatory neurons, which are linked by glutamate (the main excitatory neurotransmitter). Experience potentiates synapses. It makes neural systems' linkages potentially conscious. Familiar data follows old ruts. Novel data makes new ruts by engaging the LTP mechanism.

Distributed neocortical systems constantly change their fields of receptive integration. To give an example, tape a monkey's fingers together for a long time. During that time, let the monkey perform repeated intricate

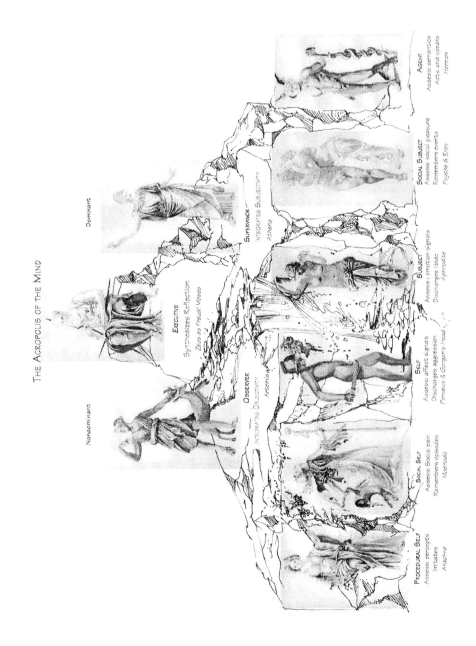

The Acropolis of the Mind

hand maneuvers. Pretty soon, the cortical field for hand representation will have massively remodeled (Merzenic, 1994). Merzenic concludes that the whole neocortex is "self-organizing." If you as a rock climber damage one finger, but you want to keep being a climber, your somatosensory cortex will reorganize itself to keep intact your identity as an explorer of vistas.

Inducing an overly rapid plasticizing of the prefrontal networks to which they contribute, overstimulated hippocampal and amygdaloid ensembles can *transfer* their LTP to other modules. When these overstimulated modules contribute to identity, they can induce a cascading plasticity in the prefrontal zones that may give rise to pathological syndromes. It is better not to be deluged by too much emotionally intense, novel information over a short period of time.

MEMORY

Memory is a disparate set of functions that mediate between neural systems and mental process (see Figure 1.2). Let us tease these functions apart. *Metamemory* is the memory we know in consciousness. It arises from our reflectively synthesizing the linguistically coded assessments derived from each of the six prefrontal zones: the right cognitive, social, and emotional zones, and the left cognitive, social, and emotional zones. When we talk about metamemory, we are not talking about how we use our prefrontal identity structures. We are talking about how we know we are using them. we will begin our study of memory by looking into the life of modules in different brain systems.[2]

What are modules to memory? One module equals one association. Each association is either knowable (explicit) or unknowable (implicit). The life of a *prefrontal module* varies. In its network, it can engage (1) experience, (2) short-term memory, and (3) long-term memory. How can this be? Experience is a knowable product of the totality of activated modules. Some of the links that a prefrontal module activates have to be verbal ones in order for a person to own an experience.

The distinction between short- and long-term memory depends on the difference between variant and invariant associations. Associational links are like ruts: the more they are used, the deeper they get. Often used verbal associations get quite deep. Long-term memory usually has well graven links, and these invariably lead to familiar verbal conclusions. To further understand the distinction between short and long-term memory, we will have to see it in a context of prefrontal modules' malleability.

Each module has tens of thousands of potential inputs. A module participates in multiple regulations, functions, and networks. It can have its

FIGURE 1.2. The Brain

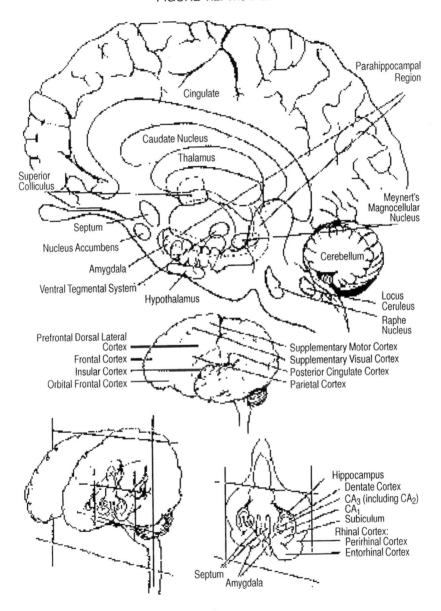

own associations, which is to say its own range of potentiated links that are part of a long-term memory network, and it can form new corticocortical associations to expand its long-term memory. Looked at this way, long-term memory is a particular web of the same associations so tightly linked, that conscious access to one association automatically invokes the others.

A prefrontal, pyramidal neuron's output excites reciprocating modules in linked neocortex (Morrison and Hof, 1992). Such excitatory linkages form distributed neocortical systems. Multiplying each module's links by factors of millions provides us a model of the *prefrontal system*. This system is plastic insofar as its modular links can rapidly potentiate. One could say that each prefrontal module is a "web site."

Data converges on six-layered prefrontal modules. Each module contains a vertically aligned pyramidal output neuron and hundreds of inhibitory gabaminergic (GABA) neurons, which regulate the pyramidal neuron's synaptic contacts in different layers of the module. Thousands of input neurons synapse with the pyramidal neuron in all six layers. The upper layers contain dendritic synapses, the lower layers, axonal synapses.

In layers two and three, a prefrontal module's pyramidal neuron synapses dendritically with inputs from other cortical cells. In layers three and four, it synapses with facilitatory inputs from thalamic, rhinal cortical, and often amygdalar neurons. In the lower three layers, the pyramidal neuron sends axons to other cortical neurons, the thalamus, the rhinal cortex, and sometimes the amygdala. In layers five and six, it sends axons down the motor hierarchy to effect behavior. All of the synapses, especially those in layers two and three where excitatory N-methyl-D-aspartate (NMDA) synapses concentrate, undergo regulations by central dopaminergic, norepinephrine, serotonergic, and acetylcholinergic fibers (Morrison and Hof, 1992). In sum, each cortical module is the potential center of a web of networks.

Activated by its links, a prefrontal module participates in experiential assessment. In its short-term memory function, it responds to selected sensory features that have already been activated by the rhinal cortex. The module potentiates when the amygdala recurrently amplifies the module's excitation. The amygdala can directly enhance a module's excitation, and indirectly enhance it through the amygdala's concurrent effect on the module's biogenic amine regulation. When some of a prefrontal module's cortico-cortical links potentiate, those links participate in a *long-term memory* network.

TERMS FOR TYPES OF MEMORY

If metamemory is the prefrontal reflective functional memory that the executive uses for problem solving, we have to define other types of func-

tional memory. Neuroscientists talk about local anatomical synaptic charac-
teristics of *associative* (explicit) or *nonassociative* (implicit) memory. When
Daniel Schacter introduced this distinction into cognitive neuroscience, he
meant that only explicit memory is available to verbal recollection (1985).
Tulving introduced *semantic memory* into the neuroscience vocabulary.
This form of memory contains verbal abstractions and concepts so often
used that they no longer have specifiable long-term memory sources (1992).
Indeed, even the verbal categories that are frequently used lose their specifiable cognitive sources. Thus, in adult problem solving, the individual finds
the activated associations he needs because they are included in a semantic
hierarchy. All roads lead to the Rome of well-known meaning.

A module of a dorsolateral prefrontal neural net catches a butterfly of
semantic meaning or perceptual representation. Associative (explicit) memory enters the prefrontal verbal system, whereas nonassociative (implicit)
memory cannot. As we process data, we entrain them in distributed systems
that radiate like wheel spokes from their hub in the rhinal cortex to assessment zones in the prefrontal cortex. From there, data mobilizes structures that
engage the prefrontal system's steering mechanism. we will distinguish prefrontal memory *functions* from: (1) the location of memory fields, (2) synaptic types of memory formation, and (3) neural systems that convey data.

Eichenbaum and Buckingham (1995) understand *implicit* data to include
the following:

- *primed*—precognitively facilitated sensory cues
- *procedural*—prebehaviorally facilitated motor skills and habits
- *conditioned*—preemotionally facilitated sensory (*classically conditioned*) or motor (*operantly conditioned*) data

With regard to location, the rhinal cortex surrounding the hippocampus,
like thick bark on a tree, registers data. Some rhinal cortex populations
register implicit data, others configure and store the hippocampus' explicit
outflow. The rhinal cortex's *entorrhinal* cortex primes verbal cues for extended, day-long use, while its *perirrhinal* cortex primes pictoral images
for potential visual feature detection. In cases of hippocampal destruction,
when the rhinal cortex remains intact, the capacity for verbal and pictoral
priming remains intact (Eichenbaum and Otto, 1992).

Buffering and Priming

Depending on the constellations of higher cortical functions, data vary
in importance at any moment of processing. The brain, therefore, employs
mechanisms to extend the availability of data for critical examination. We

call this extended availability *sensory priming* when the rhinal cortex of the limbic system maintains it, *motor priming* when the neocerebellum maintains it, and *buffering* when the prefrontal system keeps it available.

Sensory priming provides a day-long recognition context. Once a datum registers in the rhinal cortex, it is facilitated in case it is needed. Motor priming provides an extended cerebellar context that enhances our readiness for appropriate behavior. Buffering is a short-term memory mechanism. It keeps data available to the prefrontal system's scrutiny during searches for *salience*—need gratification—and *significance*—relevance to reality. Buffering contributes to the prefrontal system's assessment of data's relevance to problem solving by keeping the prefrontal system in contact with widespread modules.

Maintaining activation within the distributed links of a higher cortical function, buffering supports delayed response. When Goldman-Rakic explored buffering with positron emission tomography (PET) functional brain scans during monkeys' delayed responses, she found that the prefrontal system's modules remain activated—buffered—during several seconds of delayed response: "Prefrontal cortex is divided into multiple memory domains, each specialized . . . such as the location of objects, the features of objects—semantic and mathematical knowledge" (1992, p. 115).

On its way to explicit, prefrontal use, data can:

1. remain nonassociated—*primed* in the rhinal cortex,
2. pass immediately through the hippocampus—a passage that we call *processing,* or
3. later pass through the hippocampus and develop associative significance or meaning through *delayed processing.*

Brenda Milner discovered explicit memory's link to the hippocampus' CA 3, CA 1, and subicular populations in 1953, when she found that the now famous H.M. lost his capacity to consciously recall new experience after bilateral hippocampal ablation (Milner and Teuber, 1968). Since then, other cases verify that we cannot store verbal and pictoral memory when damage curtails our subicular outflow paths to the rhinal cortex. After bilateral hippocampal damage, people cannot retain present experience. Left damage impairs the capacity to record verbal experience, right impairs the capacity to record pictoral experience.

What causes data streams to segregate so that verbal data are processed in the left hemisphere and pictoral data in the right? As I understand it, the hippocampus *processes* data only after they have already been hemispherically segregated. The rhinal cortex receives sensory inputs that have been *preprocessed* by the primary sensory cortexes, the prefrontal system, thalamus, basal ganglia, and the cerebellum. Sensory data is facilitated or inhibited before the hippocampus explicitly redistributes it.

During problem solving, we have to seek out data that will flesh out a behavioral program. To do this, we need to use functional forms of memory. Thus, during *recognition,* the prefrontal system can cause primed data poised in the rhinal cortex to undergo delayed processing. During *recall,* the prefrontal system activates its own relevant networks, and signals the rhinal cortex to confirm their sources. During *retrieval,* the hippocampus reactivates sourced memory associations from their warehouse in the rhinal cortex.

A TOP-DOWN INFORMATION-PROCESSING MODEL

I now propose the following information processing model: the prefrontal system synthesizes a parallel set of distributed systems, some linked to associative memory, some to conditioned memory, and some to nonassociative, preattentive, primed memory. The executive serially coordinates various metamemory functions that each bring different types of data on line. Each problem requires a unique memory constellation for its solution. Organized as distributed network links, facilitated memory modules modify the ongoing experience that the executive uses to make behavioral decisions. Thus, the executive's metamemory links memory structures from multiple brain locations.

How do we use implicit, conditioned, and nonverbal data to solve problems? Missing data, ambiguous data, denied data, and implicit data are sometimes the key to problem solving. I propose that the *right hemisphere* provides social speech to code:

- *ideas* from perceptual representations,
- *constructs* from classically conditioned data, and
- *procedures* from nonconscious habits, imitations, and operantly conditioned data.

Ideas, constructs, and procedures are often imbedded in *idioms.* Idioms are social speech forms that organize underrepresented data. Platonically, an idea is a transcendent linguistic entity that is a real pattern for imperfect representations.

Visual percept representations fall into a different category of data analysis than semantic classification. While they are potentially explicit, visual percepts can effect our problem solving without becoming completely explicit. Visual percepts can penetrate the observing function without our knowing it. Advertising icons, for instance, can influence our behavior without our semantically encoding their perceptual significance. In addition to the implicit-explicit distinction, data can be *potentially explicit* and still affect our behavior. Thus, we will also reckon with *preconscious* percepts.

Neuroscientists who look at memory exclusively through a synaptic lens from the vantage of particular anatomical locales do not account for how the right hemisphere processes constructs, procedures, and percepts through a hierarchy of structures. Nevertheless, it seems to me that it is only at the executive level of that hierarchy that social speech codes all the types of data integration and behavioral preparation that are organized in the right hemisphere.

Oliver Sacks says that right hemisphere memory is confounding: "It is impossible for patients with certain (right) syndromes to know their own problems—they may demand a new . . . neurology, a personalistic, or a romantic science . . . for the physical foundations of the *persona*" (1987, p. 5). As I see it, right hemisphere *constructs* fill gaps in data processing, which, empty, would block the observer's capacity to assess her own social self in the world. The executive semantically encodes the observer's constructs. Because the right hemisphere interpolates experience, our sense of reality is incomplete.

"Filling in represents a basic interpolation process . . . at many levels in the neocortex. It is . . . what is meant by a constructive process" (Crick and Koch, 1992, p. 156).

INFORMATION-PROCESSING SYSTEMS

To better understand how the brain encodes its problem solving data, we will study the interaction of four memory systems.

1. *Immediate memory* registers and regulates data.
2. *Working memory* forms cognitive items from raw data.
3. *Short-term memory* enters items into thought.
4. *Metamemory* reflects on thought.

Let us consider each memory system in turn.

Immediate memory registers sensory input, including after-images in all the modalities. Then, after thalamic, cerebellar, and neocortical primary and secondary registration, data stream through the rhinal cortex for preliminary implicit or explicit processing at about 100 milliseconds (msecs). Novel data also engages various amygdaloid nuclei that promote orientation, somatic discharge, classical conditioning, operative conditioning, and prefrontal arousal (Everitt and Robbins, 1992).

Working memory processes precognitive associations that have been configured by their hippocampal passage at around 300 msecs. It integrates items of potential consciousness, both left hemisphere *semantic strings* and right *hemisphere visual percepts.*

Short-term memory grammatically and syntactically synthesizes prefrontal memory networks between 300 and 600 msecs, but sometimes these intervals extend for several seconds. Short-term memory synthesizes eight to fourteen items of inner and social speech as the trial thought that precedes action. Probably, for this reason, a thesis sentence should always boil down to a simple sentence of fourteen words or less. The thesis sentence is the trial thought. The essay is the action. Although some investigators condense short-term with working memory, I would like to preserve a distinction. In my view, working memory forms associative *items* (integers of consciousness). Sometimes, working memory extends its epoch to create an item.

Metamemory uses executive reflection on articulatory rehearsal to judge whether to go ahead with an action or response program at the one-second epoch. Proceeding with discharge depends on the presence of salient and significant items in short-term memory. If these items are not present, the executive extends or repeats the whole processing cycle in order to introduce fresh items. Lacking new items, anxiety and emotional signals determine the course of behavior.

HOW THE BRAIN IS SOCIALIZED

We have paid scant attention to the socially conditioned intermediate prefrontal zones and the emotionally assessing medial prefrontal zones. Obviously, these zones effect problem solving as much as cognition does. The functional beauty of the prefrontal system is that it joins limbic assessments of socially conditioned emotional data with neocortical cognitive feedback.

The medial and intermediate identity zones, both extensions of the limbic system, have evolved to provide emotional signals, social signals, and to initiate social behavior. The *medial, anterior cingulate cortex* assesses amygdaloid-determined hypothalamic discharges of emotions (Rolls, 1992). The *insular cortex*, a temporal lobe limbic cortex that is highly interactive with the *intermediate, orbital frontal cortex*, mediates the amygdala's influence on the retention of aversive experiences (McGaugh et al., 1992). Orbital frontal cortex assesses amygdaloid outputs from emotional facial processing, a vital source of social representation (Rolls, 1992). Thus, both the medial and intermediate prefrontal cortex respond to amygdaloid output with socialized behavioral tendencies.

Implicitly conditioned somatic associations exert a bulk signal effect on the intermediate prefrontal cortex. Thus, they determine the course of problem solving at least as much as cognition does. Explicit associations *do* accompany intense emotional experience. They remain available to link current experience with emotionally organized source memories, unless they have been repressed. During intense emotional experience, the amygdala conditions many associations implicitly, while the hippocampus provides explicit records of that same experience.

For their solution, many problems require that we compare present emotional experience with past emotional experience. When this happens, we need to plumb the source of emotionally organized experience. Conditioned social signals summon clusters of explicit emotional memories to produce what Tulving called *episodic memory* (1992). Unlike Tulving, I distinguish hemispheric forms of *emotionally organized source memory*:

- *Episodic memory* refers to right hemisphere clusters of explicit source memory *simultaneously* centered by an affect.
- *Event memory* refers to left hemisphere *temporally sequenced,* explicit source memories attached to motives.

HOW IDENTIFICATIONS MEDIATE THE BRAIN'S SOCIALIZATION

Language Is an Instrument for Regulating Behavior

Identifications are founded in body states and translated into social regulations as a linguistic signal system. Socially conditioned relationships are reexperienced as emotional signals. These somatic signals indicate how to proceed with relationships. This assessment of social *regulations* occurs in the prefrontal system's intermediate zones. Each prefrontal zone contains populations that respond to the amygdala's instinct-triggered output with a tendency to form social communications. Chapter 2 will examine the amygdala's role in first producing, then reenforcing these socially conditioned associations, which form the bedrock of our emotional organization as well as the roots of social identifications. We will be devoting a lot of attention to understanding how identifications mediate the brain's commerce with the social world. Since speech is an innate signal system, and language is a social structure that is learned from others, the brain must have a mechanism for internalizing language, for turning what is objective into what is subjectively and voluntarily produced as an instrument for regulating behavior.

By introjecting conditioned social speech at three years of age we form identifications with the aggressor. By internalizing conditioned dialogues at six years, we make social speech available to assimilation by inner speech. By associating inner speech with social speech, internalized dialogue produces the cognitive, social foundations of *latency identifications*.

At all levels, social identity sinks roots into the compost of identifications. Both the left hemisphere's social subject and the right hemisphere's social self depend on identifications for their substance. In order to contribute integrity to the intermediate identity zones, the social subject, and the social self have to make masses of implicit social conditioning available to executive encoding.

Left hemisphere identification with others, which integrates the social subject, extends our subjective needs as *narcissistic identification*. When our social subject bonds with another's social subject, we feel reciprocated or rejected, which conditions our empathy. Right hemisphere identification with others, which integrates the social self, extends our affective, objectified identity as *anaclitic identification*. When our social self relates to another person's social self, we feel affect: pain or relief of pain, and this conditions our *object relations*. In Piaget's terms, left hemisphere identifications *assimilate*, while right hemisphere identifications *accommodate* what is outside.

We *overlay* our conditioned associations when we encode their somatic signals. We *integrate* our sense of social identity whenever we remember the explicit source of our past social experience. Intense experience is both emotionally conditioned and cognitively structured. Analysts use the term *emotionally organizing memories* when they refer to the past's impact on our present social identity. Emotionally organized long-term memories are dichotomous. The left hemisphere produces sequenced narrations of *events* that give us a sense of subjective continuity. The right yields *apercus*, moments in which affect-centered past social *episodes* become metaphors for our present affective experience of the social world.

When we need to, we evoke event and episode memory to reenforce our sense of who we are. Each of us collects true and false stories from our past and our family's history, as well as social and historical myths and stories which inspire us. These event memories stock our left hemisphere. We renarrate them selectively when we need to enhance our motivation to carry through our ambitions. On the other hand, past moments of high affect are available to explore in needed detail when reality presents us with a tough choice of responses. These episode memories, some traumatic, stock our right hemisphere. We use them to make adaptively guiding metaphors and analogies.

THE ANATOMY OF THOUGHT

What follows is an annotated, illustrated, technical manual. How does the prefrontal machine work during problem solving? (See Figure 1.3.) The manual looks at medial emotional, intermediate social, and lateral cognitive functions. This machine has feedback loops. In this system, emotional signals give feedback about how the problem-solving program is running, social signals reenforce or switch programs, and cognitive signals reenforce programs.[3]

What Are the Medial Functions?

Event-related potential (ERP) studies show that the medial zones regulate nonspecific processes of short- and long-term activation. These take place with the aid of the speech system (Luria, 1980). Need and affect pressure the lateral prefrontal system to solve problems (Luria, 1980, pp. 265-266). *Left anterior cingulate cortex* assesses need pressure (unsatisfied/satisfied), *right anterior cingulate cortex* assesses affect pressure (frustration/relief) (Rehak et al., 1992). This emotional signal system determines when behavioral programs may conclude.

What Are the Intermediate Functions?

Together, intermediate *orbital frontal* and *insular* cortex signal the executive how to arrange the constellation of working zones to solve present problems as they associate somatic signals of past emotional response with present social contexts (Damasio, Tramel, and Damasio, 1990; Goldenberg et al., 1991). Damage to the orbital cortex dysregulates behavior, which produces a disinhibition syndrome (Crowe, 1992).

When this social signaling system of our emotionally conditioned past interrupts problem solving, the executive searches the rhinal warehouse of emotionally organized source memory, assesses its impact in our insular cortex, and verbally analyzes the past's impact on the present. In this way, intermediate cortex determines when behavioral programs must be modified.

What Are the Lateral Functions?

The left hemisphere's lateral frontal area maintains a repertory of action programs. The right's maintains a repertory of response programs (Miller, Pribram, and Galanter, 1960). As a program unfolds, the prefrontal system feeds back and forward with frontal, supplementary motor, supplementary visual, premotor, sensory-motor, cerebellar, thalamic, caudate, and striatal systems to regulate behavioral sequences.

FIGURE 1.3. Prefrontal System Consciousness Loops

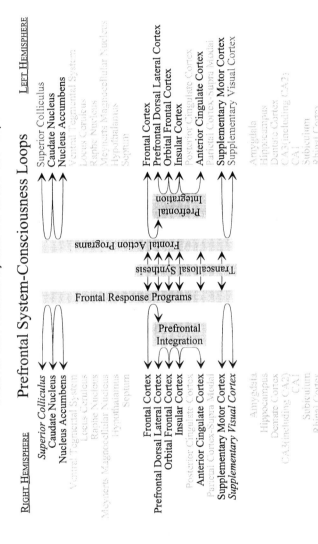

Bold structures show functional activations, *italicized* show differential increased hemispheric activation.

*Arrows point to and/or from that anatomy in the corresponding horizontal row which participates in the given neural system.

All the loop figures are most useful for suggestive examination after the material in the first three chapters has been studied.

First, prefrontal cortex derives intrapsychic identity through (1) dorsolateral, *cognitive* (2) orbital and insular, *social* and (3) anterior cingulate, *emotional* data analysis. The *executive* transcallosally synthesizes each hemisphere's working networks. The *observer* integrates (1) procedures, (2) social roles, and (3) affects into objectified, self-observant identity. The *supervisor* integrates (1) plans, (2) interpersonal empathy, and (3) motives and goals into volitional, subjective identity. Then, frontal response and action programs prompt problem-solving behaviors, using supplementary visual and motor analysis.

Our adult problem-solving repertory contains *action programs orga-nized by the left hemisphere* and *response programs organized by the right hemisphere* so that behavior can be directed over prolonged time periods. During long periods, we parcel our goals and responses into behavioral segments which we accomplish during brief intervals. If behavior needs to be prolonged over considerable periods, we plan action programs for the follow-ing day. Then, before falling asleep, we relinquish volition and response. This can be painful. Last night, for example, I anxiously dreamed that I had revised this chapter for the umpteenth time, only to find that my computer had gone dead and that I had lost the whole revision.

When we plan our day, there are many projects we want to set up. Each has many details to account. We attend to them before undertaking any particular program. Because we cannot get to all our intentions however, we prioritize them according to how vital they are to our sense of coherent intrapsychic identity.

The executive uses articulatory rehearsal to track the progress of action and response programs. Then, as each program runs, *left dorsolateral asso-ciation cortex* assesses inner speech (Damasio and Damasio, 1992) and *right dorsolateral association cortex* assesses social speech. Social speech encodes perception as apperception, which can be instilled in thought.

NEOTENY: CONSCIOUSNESS DEVELOPS CYCLICALLY

Finally, we will explicate the fourth principle, *neoteny.* Homo sapiens' brain size mandates considerable postnatal development. The result is that after birth, brain functions mature slowly, in characteristic stages. This long, slow development socializes us in stages. We are presently concerned with the mechanisms that integrate these periodic, developmental changes.

Neoteny consolidates in slow periods, which are punctuated by stages of rapid development. Psychoanalysts, psychologists, family therapists, social scientists, and cognitive scientists characterize stages and periods in terms of psychosexual development, ego development, cognitive develop-ment, and social development. We have already looked at evidence that neoteny unfolds cyclically. What needs to be said now is that while each stage emphasizes one hemisphere over the other, it is also true that as one hemisphere develops *neurally* from lateral to medial, the other hemisphere matures *functionally* in corresponding zones.

In Edelman's vision of *neural Darwinism,* optimally and functionally stimulated neurons survive (1987). All neurons are embryologically simi-lar. Those that undergo functional stimulation give rise to differentiated populations. Each population's genome expresses characteristic protein and peptide molecules that determine its functional properties.

Edelman compares neural Darwinism with the clonal antibody theory: the immune system begins with a stochastic array of globulins, and only functional ones survive. Particular globulins survive and clone when indigenous proteins stimulate functionally active molecules. Thus, cortical modules may also "represent a structural record of the rules that govern synaptic growth and development, rather than any imperative related to higher brain function" (Purvis, Riddle, and Lamantia, 1992, p. 362).

I believe that beginning with a *primary repertoire of redundant neurons*, the prefrontal system easily develops assessment layers that link it in stages to distributed systems. This is why, maturing in functional stages, prefrontal cortex develops successive hierarchical assessment layers. As the limbic system transfers massive long-term potentiation during the stage changes of neoteny, new prefrontal layers develop.[4]

If neural Darwinism explains stage changes, then the presence of more selective changes within distributed systems explains the effect of experience on forming memory within stages. The limbic system is phylogenetically programmed to form networks conditioned by pain and pleasure. These connect to higher centers during human learning:

> Neuronal groups tied in classification couples within global mappings, linked in reentrant fashion to hedonic centers . . . provide a basis for the assignment of values. . . . The connection to groups in global mappings subserving motor output allow revisions by search until the input fulfills expectancies based on the preceding categorization ("memory") and reduces the reentrant drive from the limbic system. (Edelman, 1987, p. 304)

This is another way of saying with Freud that we develop the reality principle in order to learn to solve problems, reduce drive pressure, and avoid mental pain.

In stage changes, neural centers rededicate to new functions (Edelman, 1987). How, during stage changes, can neural systems change their linkage patterns to form new higher cortical functions? How does limbic stimulation determine new identity? We approached these questions earlier in the chapter when we discussed how transfer LTP produces compatibility in separate networks. Now we can add that *experience that is necessary and sufficient to create stage appropriate endogenous trauma triggers neural selection. Consequently, new functional ensembles form.* Thus,

1. if experience stimulates the survival of functional neurons,
2. and if experience determines the structure of brain systems,
3. then, experience determines memory's structural organization.

LONG-TERM POTENTIATION (LTP)

What are the brain's mechanisms for harnessing and linking neural excitation? Excitation is a concept that spans levels, from the effect of nitric oxide and ionic calcium on organic molecules to the effect of stress or trauma on intrapsychic experience. Let us now define kinds of neural excitation and the mechanisms the brain uses to harness excitation for the purpose of forming memory and communicating experience:

- *Potentiation* is an excitatory synapse's semipermanent or permanent tendency to be engaged by its neurotransmitters.
- *LTP* is a permanent or semipermanent synaptic potentiation that enhances functional transmission.
- *Epilepsy* is pathologically increased neural transmission.
- *Kindling* lowers the seizure threshold.

By locally lowering the threshold for forming LTP, kindling induces new excitatory links in a neural system (Lynch and Baudry, 1984). Irregular stimulation of the hippocampal formation for thirty to forty minutes permanently reduces (kindles) the local threshold for LTP (Goddard, McIntyre, and Leech, 1969). Many neuroscientists have proposed that LTP selects and links neurones to form distributed systems. Crick and Koch, for instance, see the N-methyl D-aspartate (NMDA) receptor's readiness to receive excitatory, ionic calcium (CA^{++}) during LTP as the hallmark of memory formation (1992). The NMDA receptor is well suited to play a critical role in establishing new transmission patterns because it is heavily regulated by a variety of biochemical lock and key mechanisms. The formation of structures that register and transmit information is critical to our survival.

Accounting for 50 percent of all brain synapses, glutamate populations form distributed systems. When higher cortical functions form their array of processors, these distributed systems contain facilitatory and inhibitory links. Glutamate systems form distributed systems when their NMDA synapses:

- are potentiated through intense stimulation and
- are colocalized with ordinary ionic—AMPA—receptors.

Glutamate neurons use their ionic sodium (Na^+) AMPA receptors for ordinary data transmission. During intense excitation, glutamate neurons use their colocalized NMDA receptors. As in many other neurotransmitter regulated cellular systems, it is the Ca^{++} reception that induces system changes, and the Na$^+$ reception that serves ordinary transmission. Glutamate neurons also have *metabotropic* receptors. Metabotropic receptors release molecular *second messengers* that produce a cascade of energizing effects that promote intracellular maintenance and stability.

THE REGULATION OF LONG-TERM POTENTIATION

The hippocampus engages in prolific synaptic potentiation that triggers long-term memory storage. Its LTP is regulated by the following:

- all the biogenic amine systems.
- local gabaminergic (GABA) systems present in about 25 percent of all brain synapses (McDonald and Johnston, 1990).
- various peptides coexisting in synaptic secretory vesicles with biogenic amines and GABA (Hokfelt, 1991).
- genome regulating neurohormones (McEwen et al., 1992).
- mRNA's expression of synapsin—the protein building block of excitatory synapses (Greengard, 1995).

Thus, LTP is determined by (1) aminergic regulation, (2) selective inhibition, (3) hormonal modulation, (4) genome activation, and (5) mRNA expression. Multiple determinants provide the brain with a flexible LTP mechanism that adapts to experience while it mediates neoteny's reorganization.

Consider each determinant. Long-range biogenic amine systems branch out from neural centers deep within the midbrain. Each biogenic amine neuron (e.g., dopamine, norepinephrine, serotonin, and acetylcholine) is a system unto itself as it communicates with and regulates multiple modules in many brain areas. Biogenic amine systems' neural centers develop early in the brain's embryogenesis. These neurons shepherd the formation and location of excitatory systems, for they actively determine new axonal/dendritic connections as they facilitate the moving tip of developing axons with the help of growth regulating proteins. The life and death of biogenic amine neurons regulates the operation of neural systems from embryo to old age.

Beginning in middle age, many biogenic amine neurons die. This causes the remaining ones to carry a greater regulatory load. As we will see in later chapters, biogenic amine systems *are* drive systems. Which is to say, they collectively determine behavioral states—the amount and type of problem solving pressure on the prefrontal system.

If excitation is the key to neural transmission and linkage, then selective *inhibition* must be just as important to the regulation of synapses and functional neural systems. Local GABA neurons selectively inhibit excitatory synapses. GABA receptors inhibit by regulating the postsynaptic neuron's polarizing chloride channel. Just as excitation spans the gap from the ionic and molecular to the experiential, so also does inhibition span the same gap. Thus, benzodiazepine drugs dampen experience. The antiepileptic action of GABA-enhancing drugs such as the benzodiazepines (e.g., diazepam—valium) demonstrates the inhibitory *and* sedative force of GABA neurons. GABA neurons' inherent periodicity regulates the pace of excitatory transmission. In the hippocampus as well as the prefrontal cortex, for instance, GABA neurons surround glutamate output neurons with inhibition.

Often coexisting with other neurotransmitters, sometimes in the same secretory vesicle, *neuropeptides* are local modulators that regulate the temporal domain of biogenic amines, GABA inhibition, and glutamate excitation. GABA neurons contain neuropeptides that modulate the periodicity of their inhibition. Vasoactive intestinal polypeptide (VIP) extends norepinephrine's metabotropic effect on the postsynaptic neuron. Endogenous opioids are another kind of local neuromodulatory peptides. Thus, neuropeptides are local biological clocks.

McEwen and colleagues discovered that hippocampal glutamate neurons have genome-regulating, cytoplasmic hormone receptors (1992). This puts the regulation of memory formation right into the main stream of the hypothalamic pituitary axis (HPA). Cortisone, cortisone releasing factor (CRF), and thyroid have a profound, long-lasting effect on LTP. Accessing the genome of excitatory neurons, circulating hormones and locally produced hormones change the rate of metabolism and protein production. Prolonged neurohormonal stimulation of glutamate neurons increases the likelihood that they will undergo LTP under threshold condition. Prolonged stress or changes in the levels of sexual neurohormones can change the likelihood of LTPs occurring.

LONG-TERM POTENTIATION OF DISTRIBUTED SYSTEMS

How does LTP promote distributed systems?

- Modules that develop LTP undergo postsynaptic loss of their gabaminergic inhibition (Kamphius and Lopes da Silva, 1991).
- After LTP, contiguous modules develop *long-term-depression* (LTD), that inhibits the spread of LTP (Kuba and Kumamoto, 1990).
- Inhibitory and facilitatory modules interdigitate (Purvis, Riddle, and Lamantia, 1992).

Thus, LTP/LTD *segments* new excitatory transmission.
Glutamate neurons participate in distinct processes:

- *synaptic transmission,*
- *presynaptic sensitization* or *postsynaptic potentiation,*
- *pre- and postsynaptic facilitation* (*full LTP*), and
- *excitotoxic apoptosis*—genetically programmed destruction.

Pre- and postsynaptic potentiation may either precede LTP or temporarily facilitate neurotransmission. Apoptosis destroys postsynaptic neurons. In this way, it segregates presynaptic neurons from further participation in data processing. [5]

Marriages in the Hippocampus

The marriage of CA 1 pyramidal cells with their Schaffer collaterals is the most highly studied form of LTP. Each Schaffer collateral to CA 1 relationship actually consists of multiple synapses between the same two cells (Lisman and Harris, 1993). The size and number of these synapses increases after LTP has occurred. A potentiated relationship between two cells is like a close marriage that requires increasing faithfulness and energy exchange between the involved cells.

In Chapter 2, we will explore the repercussions of hippocampal LTP marriages. we will see how they convey their covenant to other neural populations, how they sometimes part company, and how they act during exigencies in the life of the brain.

Chapter 2

Foundations of Clinical Neuroscience

Named Kindberg . . . child mountain . . . a town which they reach at night . . . the place, at last, where one can change, tasting good shelter; and soup in a large silver tureen, breaking the bread and giving the first piece to Lina . . . then she blows on it . . . in that way seeing Lina's bangs rise up a little and tremble as if the blowing on the hand and bread were about to raise the curtain in a tiny theater, almost as if from that moment on Marcelo could see Lina's thoughts come onstage, Lina's images and memories as she sips savory soup still smiling. (1984, pp.185-186)

—Julio Cortazer

"A Place Named Kindberg" is a tale of suicide. An older man, a younger woman, both travelers—displaced Latin Americans in Central Europe: traveling salesman and hitchhiker—Marcello and Lina are the faces of a coin. They stop at an inn where experience becomes Gothic. Bringing Lina onto the stage of his present identity, Marcello merges his experience of her youth with everything in his own gut memories. Who is Lina? For Marcello, she is a child of his own mind, a person who grows silently stronger as Marcello prepares to end his own life as if to relinquish his identity to Lina's. But the suicide takes place at the end of the story. Like Proust's induction by tea and madeleine, this passage is about the way gut memories play themselves out on the stage of the present. Gut memories—taste, smell, emotion—come center stage when the amygdala evokes them.

These visceral memories radiate associations like arrows on a compass that point to the sources of past emotional experience. Freud recognized this as the process of overdetermination, which underlies the multifarious origin of imagery in symptoms and dreams. Freud pointed out that we can never completely analyze any image or get to the navel of any dream because an overabundance of associations and causes combine to emotionally organize each source memory (1900). The multiplicity makes each emotionally organized source memory into a large neural net that can be retrieved later by cognitive associations.

The brain's anatomy is our potential destiny. The amygdala, the hippocampus, and the surrounding rhinal (entorrhinal, perirhinal, and parahippocampal) cortex contain many of the brain's most easily potentiated circuits. Here, the impetus to form emotional source memory and to surround it with explicit associations transfigures experience. But . . . given early trauma, explicit associations will not form. Conditioned associations will.

Each emotional source memory forms a center around which identity crystallizes. Just as dust forms the center of a crystal, too much emotional dust—too much experience too early in life—forms a plethora of crystallized identity. The overabundant experience causes these crystals to precipitate before their time. When this happens, an individual's adult identity will be overly laced with an infant's conditioning. A person plagued by too many conditioned associations may never experience the social and personal unity that gives mature life dignity.

When they are prematurely dedicated, amygdaloid emotional circuits and hippocampal precognitive circuits both play an overly important role in the formation of identity. Metaphorically speaking, high infant stress creates a wartime economy that the adult cannot govern in peacetime. The battle wages inside.

If too many amygaloid and hippocampal neurons and rhinal modules dedicate during infancy, they will not be available to transfer potentiation to a flexible intrapsychic identity, which the prefrontal system later forms. The neural resources that formed conditioned associations and primitive memories will be unavailable to later purposes. Each developmental stage has its own vulnerability to fixation (i.e., excessive amygdalarly induced pleasure conditioning) and trauma (excessive amygdalarly induced pain conditioning), with predictable effects on the formation of a stable sense of identity. Each new stage has to be flexible enough to override some fixations and traumata.

Our metaphor becomes a social and political reality when we speak of millions of infants' and children's traumata. High developmental stress triggers syndromes in individual brains, and the syndromes cascade transgenerationally. A traumatized generation raises its children stressfully. Together, both generations form pathological, social, and political structures, and the traumatically conditioned populace is likely to engage in violent activities. If history cycles, the biopsychosocial mechanism of individual and collective trauma and the resulting selection of brains that survive, make it cycle.

In some historical epochs, individual survival depends on the left hemisphere's capacity for libidinal initiative and coping; in others, it depends on the right's capacity for aggressive exploration and adaptation. As we continue, we will explore the idea that human beings have evolved genetically, so that some people tend toward left hemisphere initiative, others toward right hemisphere responsiveness. The concept of our brains' extending their conflicts and structures into the social world's conflicts and structures presents a biological as well as a social proposition: (1) the brain's two hemispheres may be at odds and (2) like Athens and Sparta, pacifistic and warlike sociopolitical systems may be at odds.

The biopsychosocial equilibrium of causes circles in both directions. If a country is abandoned to its own fate after a war, if the gratification seeking left hemisphere's way of processing experience adjusts to wartime experience, then primitive fixations to gratification emerge socially and economically, and criminal free enterprise becomes the *modus vivendi*. If the population cannot acknowledge the presence of its underground economy, then like the left hemisphere's identity, the identity of that country fragments narcissistically. However, if a country is occupied by a foreign power after a war, then that country will identify itself with the foreign invaders. In that case, if the right hemisphere's way of processing its experience denies its trauma, unstable, rigid, "borderline" bureaucratic identifications with the aggressor will split the person's and the country's sense of its legitimate identity from itself.

Returning to neuroscience, this chapter poses several questions:

- Does experience effect amygdalar and hippocampal anatomy?
- What is the hippocampus' role in cognitive development?
- What is the amygdala's role in emotional development?
- Do limbic structures potentiate prefrontal structures?
- How does prefrontal cortex unify intrapsychic identity?

When we have answered these questions, we will see that the amygdala gives our experience heart, the hippocampus gives it soul, the rhinal cortex joins heart and soul, and the prefrontal cortex brings heart and soul to human identity.

Evolution has segregated our emotional and our cognitive lives and then reintegrated them at the prefrontal level, where human identity resides. Understanding how data streams segregate and then reintegrate prefrontally will illustrate why we need both a psychoanalytic and a cognitive neuroscience and why the two must be synthesized. Personal experience intersects with neoteny—the human evolutionary legacy of slowed, staged development. An individual's progress from *instinctual*, to *condi-*

tioned animal, to *socialized human identity* makes the prefrontal system's social and linguistic organization preeminent in our adult being.

WHAT IS AN EXPERIENCE?

According to Gloor, an experience "is the unique pattern woven within a distributed neuronal network . . . the entire matrix once created can be reproduced by activating only a part of it" (1992, p. 522). Gloor adds that networks are "part of the emerging distributed neuronal matrix representing the experience as a whole, with other neurons . . . located in the amygdala and in the hippocampal system" (p. 524). Gloor's amygdala provides experience with emotional depth as it:

- primes the autonomic and endocrine system,
- reenforces the hippocampal input of explicit data, and
- potentiates hippocampal output to the prefrontal cortex.

In what follows, we will use the term *experiential loops* to refer to distributed, prefrontal networks that process three types of experience: *cognitive, social, and emotional.* Each loop links anterior and posterior cortex, thalamus, cerebellum, and basal ganglia, as well as the rhinal cortex and the amygdala. Each hemisphere's prefrontal system coordinates:

- a cognitive lateral (dorsolateral cortex),
- a social intermediate (orbital frontal and insular cortex—which are highly interactive), and
- an emotional medial (cingulate cortex) experiential loop.

The prefrontal system serially unifies all six loops, providing us with a coherent sense of intrapsychic identity before we act (see Figures 2.1, 2.2, and 2.3).

SOURCES OF LATERALITY

The prefrontal system regulates laterality. Within this system, the cognitive function is lateralized, and the left temporal semantic reception area may be larger than the right in humans. Percept formation is lateralized to the right. The left hippocampus forms verbal memory; the right forms pictoral memory. The left amygdala is larger than the right in humans (Reynolds, 1992), which may mean that humans are predisposed to taking pleasure in their semantic functions. However, amygdaloid populations innervate all levels of visual processing, but only some levels of auditory,

FIGURE 2.1. Cognitive Experiential Loops

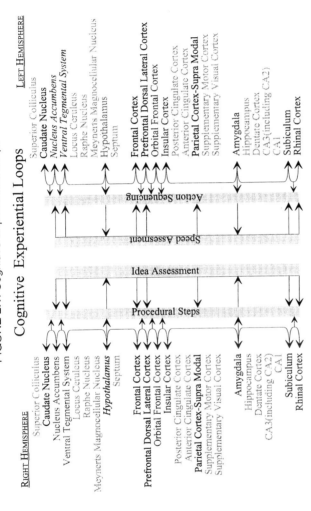

Bold structures show functional activations, *italicized* show differential increased hemispheric activation.

*Arrows point to and/or from that anatomy in the corresponding horizontal row which participates in the given neural system.

All the loop figures are most useful for suggestive examination after the material in the first three chapters has been studied.

Cognitive loops use the right hemisphere's *social speech*—preformed ideas—and left *inner speech*—predicated action sequences—to assess a semantic, experiential sense of agency and procedure. Social and inner speech are synthesized as *articulatory rehearsal*—sentences that solve problems. Cognition uses the following: right hemisphere *response programs*—"if-then" proposals, and left *action programs*—"first-then" narrative sequences. The procedural self responds, using rules and imitations, which derive from precepts and values. The agent initiates, using operant means to an end, which derive from beliefs.

53

FIGURE 2.2. Social Experiential Loops

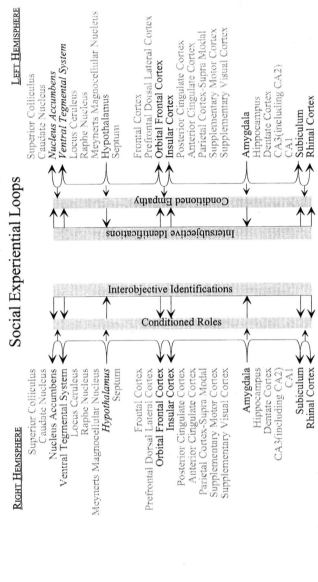

Social Experiential Loops

Bold structures show functional activations, *italicized* show differential increased hemispheric activation.

*Arrows point to and/or from that anatomy in the corresponding horizontal row which participates in the given neural system.

All the loop figures are most useful for suggestive examination after the material in the first three chapters has been studied.

Our social experience rests on a mass of implicitly conditioned associations and explicit long-term memories. We relate both *interobjectively*—to the reality of self and other representations—and *intersubjectively*—empathically. Each hemisphere separately conditions our social experience. Massed conditioned associations form identifications, which structure our social relationships. Our social self's role relates to others' pain and affect. Our social subject relates to others' pleasures and needs. Our social self is structured by *anaclitic* (other-directed) identifications, our social subject by *narcissistic* ones.

FIGURE 2.3. Emotional Experiential Loops

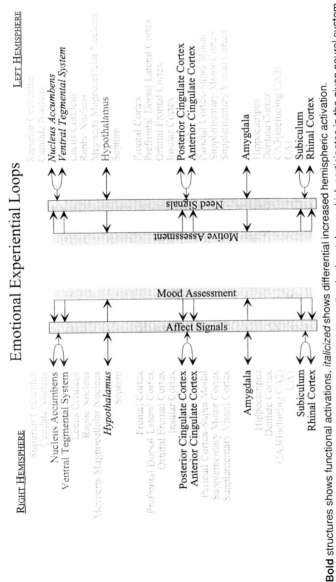

Bold structures shows functional activations, *italicized* shows differential increased hemispheric activation.

*Arrows point to and/or from that anatomy in the corresponding horizontal row which participates in the given neural system.

All the loop figures are most useful for suggestive examination after the material in the first three chapters has been studied.

Our emotional experience derives from somatic signals engendered by the amygdala and the hypothalamus. The rhinal cortex implicitly processes the data that trigger somatic signals. Emotional signals are assessed by anterior and posterior cingulate cortex, which participate in the prefrontal system's identity synthesis. Our emotional system assesses signals of right hemisphere affect pressure and left consummatory—need—pressure. The self assesses our somatic affect pressures and transforms them to moods. The subject assesses our somatic need pressures and transforms them to motives.

speech processing (Amaral et al., 1992). Is that why a picture is worth a thousand words?

TRANSFER LTP

How Long-Term Potentiation Travels

There is a rock formation called "The Labyrinth" at a private resort called the *Mohunk Mountain House.* It is possible to climb in narrow channels among the boulders to get to the top where there is a beautiful mountain view. It is also possible for the unwary to get lost among rock facades that go nowhere. Generations of climbers have left arrows and built small ladders to help those who come later to find their way to the top. Like a generous trail blazer, transfer LTP smooths the paths, makes the signs, and builds the ladders that we use each time we ascend data trails to find our Acropolis.

How does the brain build its multiple networks of coordinated experiential loops? The concept *transfer LTP* explains the formation of extended networks in which associations are multiply stored and, hence, multiply coordinated during data analysis and behavioral preparation. In transfer LTP (or transfer kindling), when LTP occurs in one site, its output tends to produce LTP in other excitatory neurons (Spiller and Racine, 1994). In understanding transfer LTP, we understand how the hippocampus and the amygdala potentiate their outputs to the prefrontal system.

Given that both the amygdala and the rhinal cortex have monosynaptic feedback with insular and orbital frontal assessment cortex (Aggleton, 1992), the existence of transfer LTP explains how limbic LTP can almost immediately cause prefrontal LTP. The prefrontal cortex is very plastic in the sense that it can both undergo local LTP and change its linkages rather easily. Normally, transfer LTP transforms assessment cortex so that it is compatible with limbically conditioned experience. We also see neocortical plasticity manifest in the phantom limb phenomena. After the loss of a limb, the limb's somatosensory cortex changes its linkages so radically that stimulation of other body parts can evoke limb sensations.

FUNCTIONS OF THE PREFRONTAL SYSTEM

One way to understand how our prefrontal cortex unifies sensory, motor, social, and emotional data to solve problems is to extrapolate from its functions in primates. Decisive action is simpler in primates. Their prefrontal cortexes coordinate eye and hand decisions (how to respond to salient and significant visual features), to stop and go and to move left or right (Eichenbaum and Buckingham, 1995). The primate's prefrontal system mediates short-term memory's delayed responses (Goldman-Rakic, 1992). Large parts of both the dorsolateral cortex and the orbital frontal cortex fire after the onset of cues *and* after the onset of responses. Moreover, the whole prefrontal cortex responds strongly to significant or salient qualities of stimuli (Eichenbaum and Buckingham, 1995).[1]

As human beings, we look for data that will sustain or suspend our behavioral programs. When confronted with novel data, we suspend problem solving and evaluate the new data. We recognize the way a new datum fits an old pattern by referring to our visceral response. If the new datum elicits a sense of somatic dread (as it does when the laser printer suddenly tells us to change its drum), we feel it ominously relevant to our problem solving. To understand gut dread, let us see how the amygdala interacts with medial cortex to form anxiety signals rather than fear discharges.

HOW DOES THE AMYGDALA CONDITION THE INFANT'S BRAIN?

The amygdala conditions most heavily in infancy, when its peptide production and LTP peak (Roberts, 1992).

> Plasticity during fear conditioning probably results from a change in synaptic inputs prior to or in the amygdala rather than from a change in its efferent target areas. The ability to produce [LTP] in the amygdala, and the finding that local infusion of NMDA antagonists into the amygdala blocks the retention of fear conditioning is consistent with this hypothesis. (Davis, 1992b, p. 283)

The amygdala is involved in emotional organization throughout the processing cycle. The amygdala is conditioned, and it conditions. Once conditioned by its inputs in infancy, the amygdala transmits emotional data early in its processing cycle. The amygdala performs several functions sequentially.

- It potentiates a startle response (M. Davis, 1992b).
- It discharges into the nearby origin of the cholinergic system, which *arouses* the whole neocortex (Amaral et al., 1992).
- It evokes classical and operant conditioning.
- It discharges to the hypothalamus, producing *somatic signals*.
- It stimulates the hippocampus to process data.
- It affects cingulate, orbital, and insular limbic prefrontal cortices to *assess* emotional signals.
- It affects dorsolateral cortex to assess explicit data.

Distinct central amygdala populations coordinate instinctual responses to vision, audition, somesthesia, multiple modalities, specific objects, and novel objects (Nishijo, Ono, and Nishijo, 1988). Thus, the amygdala conditions and adds emotional and autonomic quality to data of all modalities, including their percept organization. The amygdala's response to objects dovetails with posterior cortical signals of their salience and significance.

Once the amygdala casts a spell of aversive cathexis on data that inputs into it, the fate of that data is like the fate of the baby princess in the story of Sleeping Beauty. The septal nucleus (a limbic system subcortical conditioner), like the good fairy godmother, can only *ameliorate* the amygdala's negative conditioning as it happens. If the amygdala says no to reward, it will take the *ventral tegmental dopaminergic consummation system's* pleasure helpers, which monitor the salient pleasure-promoting qualities of stimuli, a century to undo the amygdala's command. Once we do not like liver, that is it.

We cannot ever completely undo the effects of our amygdala's infant conditioning. The lateral amygdala cannot extinguish its conditioned inputs, so that its outputs no longer evoke somatic signals (Everitt and Robbins, 1992). However, prefrontal cortex overrides amygdalar conditioning with its own conditioned regulation. Because cingulate and orbital frontal cortex can more easily recondition their inputs than the amygdala can, it is easier to adapt to social reward and punishment signals than to biological ones (Rolls, 1992). We can overlay amygdalar conditioning with executive judgment. Of course, we go through a long socialization to become human beings who are partially freed from survival instincts and biologically conditioned experience.

INSTINCT, CONDITIONING, AND DRIVE

How can the amygdala condition the instinctual life of the infant and then relinquish further control of behavior? We know it can. To all appearances, we are still quite human if our amygdalae are destroyed in adult life. To understand a human's ability to dissociate from instinct, we will have to study the fundamental developmental relationship among instinct, conditioning, and drive. I will argue that these emotional determinants operate hemispherically.

Reward and *reactive displeasure* are outcomes of conditioned instincts in the left hemisphere. *Aversion* and *pain relief* are right hemisphere outcomes. Each of us develops social tendencies based on one of these four types of conditioning. For each of us, the mass effect of our conditioned associations determines our development of unique kinds of social relationships, which I will designate *primary transference*. We will call reexperiencing episodic or event-sourced memory on the stage of the present *secondary transference*. Cortazer's Marcello experienced secondary transference.

As I said in Chapter 1, the bulk effect of conditioned social associations gives rise to somatic signals that determine our intermediate zones' social expectations. We each develop a unique *social subject* and a unique *social self* based on the developmental effects of primary transference. Thus, primary transference gives rise to personality tendencies toward expected reward, disappointment, pain, or relief in our social relations.

Let us posit four outcomes of infant conditioning:

- The amygdala causes the ventral tegmental dopamine (VTD) system to *permit pleasure*. This produces *rewarded associations*.
- The amygdala causes the VTD system to *inhibit pleasure*. This produces aversive-type associations and *reactive displeasure*.
- The amygdala causes the hypothalamus to *permit pain*. This produces *aversion* to associations to the pain.
- The amygdala causes the hypothalamus to inhibit pain. This conditions associations to pain *relief*.

Adults have the same range of conditioning, but they can get over the effects easier. To feel good after you stop banging your head on the wall (relief) is a different pleasure from feeling good when you have had a meal (reward). To feel bad when your intercourse fails (reactive displeasure) is not the same kind of pain as feeling bad (aversion) when your printer quits.

How Do Instincts Differ from Drives?

The amygdala links phylogenetically predetermined neural components of instinctual *orientation, vigilance,* and *attention* to each of the four conditions. These three instincts (sets of innately hardwired sensory, motor, and autonomic components) must be tamed in order for us to develop human flexibility. In infancy, instincts are tamed when each component is conditioned again and again by the amygdala, both to ventral tegmental reward and displeasure and to hypothalamic pain and relief.

The three basic instincts found three basic drives:

- The *libidinal drive orients* toward *consummation*.
- The *aggressive drive* induces *vigilance*.
- The *neutral drive* provides *vitality*.

In early infancy, the amygdala transforms instinctual states into *biogenic amine-regulated drive states*. Thereafter, it helps coordinate drive, anxiety, and defense. (See Figure 2.4.)

FIGURE 2.4. Drive, Anxiety, and Defense Loops
Drive, Anxiety, and Defense Loops

RIGHT HEMISPHERE					LEFT HEMISPHERE
Superior Colliculus		↔			Superior Colliculus
Caudate Nucleus		↔			Caudate Nucleus
Nucleus Accumbens		↔			Nucleus Accumbens
Ventral Tegmental System	*Visual Significance*	↔	*Visual Salience*		*Ventral Tegmental System*
Locus Ceruleus	*Aggressive System*	↔	*Libidinal System*		Locus Ceruleus
Raphe Nucleus	*Neutralization*	↔	*Neutralization*		Raphe Nucleus
Meynerts Magnocellular Nucleus	*Vitality*	↔	*Vitality*		Meynerts Magnocellular Nucleus
Hypothalamus	*Anxiety Discharge*	↔	*Anxiety Discharge*		Hypothalamus
Septum	*Discharge Regulation*	↔	*Discharge Regulation*		Septum

RIGHT HEMISPHERE					LEFT HEMISPHERE
Frontal Cortex					Frontal Cortex
Prefrontal Dorsal Lateral Cortex	*Denial*	→	*Repression*	↓	Prefrontal Dorsal Lateral Cortex
Orbital Frontal Cortex	*Isolation*	→	*Suppression*	↓	Orbital Frontal Cortex
Insular Cortex	*Reaction formation*	→	*Inhibition*	↓	Insular Cortex
Posterior Cingulate Cortex					Posterior Cingulate Cortex
Anterior Cingulate Cortex	*Blocking*	→	*Renunciation*	↓	Anterior Cingulate Cortex
Parietal Cortex–Supra Modal					Parietal Cortex–Supra Modal
Supplementary Motor Cortex					Supplementary Motor Cortex
Supplementary Visual Cortex					Supplementary Visual Cortex

RIGHT HEMISPHERE				LEFT HEMISPHERE
Amygdala	↔	*Drive and Anxiety Coordination*	↔	Amygdala
Hippocampus				Hippocampus
Dentate Cortex				Dentate Cortex
CA3(including CA2)				CA3(including CA2)
CA1				CA1
Subiculum				Subiculum
Rhinal Cortex				Rhinal Cortex

Bold structures show functional activations, *italicized* show differential increased hemispheric activation.

*Arrows point to and/or from that anatomy in the corresponding horizontal row which participates in the given neural system.

All the loop figures are most useful for suggestive examination after the material in the first three chapters has been studied.

The amygdala, septum, and hypothalamus regulate the aminergic systems' origins of three drives. The amygdalae's bilateral regulation determines the drives' laterality. The right noradrenergic, aggressive drive promotes vigilance and exploration. It binds—cathects—*signifi-cant* associations. The left, dopaminergic, libidinal drive promotes consummation. It binds—cathects—*salient* associations. The dual serotinergic/cholinergic, neutral drive promotes vitality and attention. They reinforce and integrate—neutralize—the function of the other two. The hypothalamus discharges anxiety.

Diverse amygdaloid populations do the following:

- provide significance and salience to cognitive data
- provide rich peptide resources to their outputs
- access many hypothalamic and limbic paths
- access the nuclear centers of all the biogenic amine systems
- access bilateral connections to each other (Amaral et al., 1992)

The amygdala is in the driver's seat of our instinctual life.

Instinct, conditioning, and *drive* form a hierarchical lacework. The pattern and design, but not the stitching, is apparent to reflection. Our three instincts are the threads of our life. These fates are woven by the amygdala, patterned by our drives, explicitly designed by our hippocampus, and in the end, determined by what our executive does with our portion.

How Does the Amygdala Tame the Instincts?

Instincts are innate social programs that operate before the infant develops cognition. When an animal displays an instinctual behavior such as grooming, the amygdala links the social stimulus with the behavior (Kling and Brothers, 1992). In the human rooting instinct, the nursing infant turns her head from side to side when her mouth is stimulated until she finds the pleasure-giving nipple. Rene Spitz showed how rooting is tamed and turned into the foundation of the yes or no head shaking *gesture* (1957). Thus, the amygdala tames a piece of the consummatory orientation instinct as it links rooting to a libidinized gesture. When the two-month-old perceives a friendly face design, instinct triggers a smiling pleasure release.

The amygdala directs social instincts in phylogenetic paths paved by evolution. Some amygdala populations trigger response to others' facial expressions, e.g., aversion or relief (Aggleton, 1992). Not only does the amygdala respond directly to social signals, its output to the orbital frontal cortex also conditions populations in that cortex to social contexts. Thus, instincts unite seemlessly with emotional development. [2]

Brazelton (1980) describes the infant's emergence into three basic and observable *instinctual states* during the first two months:

- Vigilance is a set of sensory, motor, and autonomic responses to unexpected stimuli. Innate blinking and startle reflexes give way to *vigilant states* of exploratory behavior.
- Orientation is a set of sensory, motor, and autonomic responses to potentially satisfying stimuli. The innate rooting reflex gives way to *consummatory states*, reaching out attitudes.

- Vitality is a set of sensory, motor, and autonomic social responses. Bradycardia—slowed heart rate—and gaze fixation give way to *vital states* of interpersonal interest.

As I said, the bihemispheric organization of conditioning, instincts, and drives gives rise to personality tendencies. For instance, an infant heavily conditioned to a combination of (1) left hemisphere displeasure and (2) right hemisphere pain relief may become an avoidant adult, characterized by vulnerability to shame, sensitivity to rejection, and narcissistic emptiness. In this light, consider our first case history.

The Titan Who Was Doomed

The Greeks thought that Titans roamed the earth before the gods achieved supremacy. Tityus, one of these primitive, monster beings, was a son of Mother Earth and Father Chaos. Nine acres long when stretched from end to end, Tityus attempted to rape Leto, the mother of Artemis and Apollo. Artemis, the huntress, whom this text takes as an icon for the right hemisphere's social self, shot Tityus and had him banished to Hades. Tethered there, Tityus submitted to vultures, who pecked out his liver. The Greeks thought of the liver as an organ made from the earth. Its lobes foretold the course of the passions. Tityus' liver grew back with each full moon. Direct and instinctual, Tityus' act reminds us of an infant's trying—before the reality principle has formed—to wrest hallucinatory gratification from an image of mother. We can understand Tityus as a metaphor for anyone whose life is tethered to infancy's conditioned displeasure and conditioned pain. We may think of him as like a schizoid man ruled by his amygdala.

Titus, the subject of our case history, was the youngest and largest of six children. Titus was born to a chaotic, alcoholic, physically and sexually abusing, philandering father, and a mother who had become psychotically depressed by the time Titus was born. Hiding from his father in his mother's bed, Titus grew up tethered to his mother's pain. By the time her son reached adolescence, Titus's mother stayed awake every night. She studied astrological signs to foretell the future.

Titus had his "first prophetic dream" at the age of seventeen. In this dream, a great erupting, volcanic pain ascended from his abdomen to his mouth. Three weeks after the dream, he felt the pain in waking life. Vomiting, Titus felt he was dying. He drank alcohol heavily to suppress the pain. For the next three years, Titus spent his time drinking and tinkering with cars.

When he was twenty, Titus was arrested for driving while intoxicated. The result of his conviction was enrollment in a course which vividly taught that alcoholics suffer bleeding varices, liver failure, abdominal pain, and death. Sensing Titus's maternal symbiosis, a counselor told Titus that he had a choice between separating from his mother or drinking himself to death. Titus took this routine advice as an oracular pronouncement, and for the next four years, while continuing to live at home, Titus refused to talk to his mother.

The less Titus talked to his mother, the worse his painful eruptions became. Meanwhile, his mother sickened with congestive heart failure, and began to die slowly. Then, Titus had a second "prophetic dream." A huge, blond, moustached man intruded into his basement and started killing him. Titus resumed drinking after this dream. The results were terrible.

Horribly drunk, Titus tried to kill and rape a woman whom he did not know. He struck his victim over the head with a steel pipe from a car he was working on. Instead of dying, the woman fled, and the police arrested her assailant.

In awe, Titus told me that the man who had prosecuted him was the man from his dream. I interpreted, but did not say, that dynamically, the dream man was Titus's father, who had actually sodomized Titus when Titus was five. Titus was identifying with the aggressor who had brutalized him. I also thought that the dream father was punishing Titus for his erupting, symbiotic, oedipal fantasy that had originally shielded Titus from his experience of being sodomized. The repression was returning in Titus' actual atavistic enactment—possessing and killing each parent as he is possessed and killed. I further interpreted, but did not say, that the enormous dream man was Titus, himself. Titus was imprisoned for three years while his mother was dying.

But, of course, I learned all this after the fact, for like Dostoevsky's Raskolnikov, Titus tried to separate himself from entanglement with a dying mother whose pain he could not resist. When I first saw Titus (after his mother's death), he began our session by affectionately saying "kill," to my miniature poodle, who helps me gauge my patients' affect in the consulting room. Titus was like a little boy who spoke the words in all innocence. Titus then complained that his "abdominal pains of unknown origin" were mounting. He felt that they foretold his death. Titus asked me in agony if it were true that he would die if he drank once more.

It should be clear by now that Titus had little sense of himself as an adult and no expectations of life. His identity never differentiated to the point where his prefrontal system could flexibly mediate his decision making. Indeed, it seemed to me that under the influence of alcohol, his prefrontal system lost its minimal capacity to regulate his instincts, drives, and derivative fantasies.

Instead of developing reliable emotional and anxiety signal systems, which regulate the amygdala, Titus was subjected repeatedly to instinctual gut discharges that made him feel that he was facing the pain of death. In truth, whenever he sensed that he was losing his mother or symbiotic object, Titus discharged raw fear into his gut. At these times, he felt what an infant feels, that he would die without his mother. It was inevitable that when a counselor told Titus to give up his mother as a way to stop drinking, the order put Titus in a bind: give up mother and feel as if you are dying, or die equally painfully from alcohol poisoning. Without alcohol or mother, for Titus, prison was a foretaste of Tityus' Hades.

HOW THE AMYGDALA EMBODIES PLEASURE AND PAIN

Let us study the amygdala's role in emotional development, a development that remained primitive in Titus' case. Each amygdala mediates its own hemisphere's emotional processing and effects conditioning in the other hemisphere. The left and right hemisphere's amygdalae provide feedback directly with one another (Aggleton, 1992). The left coordinates pleasure processing. The right coordinates pain processing. The two amygdalae together determine whether pain or pleasure will exert the greatest influence on behavior. How is this mediation exerted? (See Figure 2.4.)

The Pleasure Loop

The left amygdala engages the left ventral tegmental dopamine system to produce hedonic tones and feelings of pleasure during both conditioning and behavior. The left amygdala regulates this dopamine system's septal pleasure nuclei and reward-coordinating *nucleus accumbens*. The nucleus accumbens feeds directly back to the amygdala (Aggleton, 1992) and to the anterior and posterior cingulate assessment cortices. This pleasure loop reinforces all phases of classical and operant conditioning and provides reward signals to ongoing behavioral programs.

Titus could not achieve mature satisfaction. His infantile conditioning to avoiding displeasure and to relieving his mother's pain as well as his own was too strong for him to overcome. Instead of maturing flexibly and reconditioning his prefrontal cortex, Titus developed avoidant and schizoid personality traits which shielded him from feeling humiliated and rejected. When Titus' schizoid defenses worked, he was impervious to the need for pleasure and warmth with others. These needs were fixed to his fantasy of fusing symbiotically with his inner mother. To look outside for satisfaction led Titus to feel betrayed by his inner symbiote. Looking to the outside social world for satisfaction and direction fed Titus' primitive rage responses and wishes to kill.

Sensing his mother's illness brought Titus back to his infantile conditioning, which had been sealed off by his father's rape of him. All hell broke loose when Titus reentered the conditioned world of his infancy without his schizoid defenses. Identified with the introjected persecutor, his father, Titus tried to rape the woman who represented his mother and himself.

The Pain Loop

Diverse amygdaloid populations mediate pain processing. The amygdala's outflow to the hypothalamus is ultimately responsible for conditioning pain. One central amygdalar output regulates instinctual *pain discharges* directly into the hypothalamus.[3] Hypothalamic populations relay the amygdala's basomedial fear discharges to lower autonomic centers.[4] Another central output relays signals of *pain conditioned stimuli* to the medial prefrontal cortex, where they are assessed.[5,6]

Titus' amygdala overly conditioned him to avoid displeasure and to seek relief of pain. He lacked the prefrontal capacity to flexibly regulate his behavior. Because he was so primitively conditioned, Titus was not interested in reading or learning, except about how cars and machines worked, and that was because he perceived cars and machines as extensions of his physical body. For Titus, every part of a car, including the part that he used to club his victim, was an extension of his own body. When Titus felt his mother slipping away, his symbiosis was threatened and he experienced raw discharges of fear and affect in his gut. His infantile conditioning no longer held his amygdala in check.

HOW THE AMYGDALA REGULATES
THE EXECUTIVE'S SIGNAL SYSTEMS

By capitalizing on the first faint autonomic signals of emotion and anxiety, the prefrontal system inhibits full-blown amygdalar discharges. I will refer to the pathways for receiving emotional and anxiety signals and for inhibiting full-blown autonomic discharges as the Drive, Anxiety, and Defense Loops. (See Figure 2.4.)

When the amygdala too heavily conditions orbital frontal associations to another person, it casts shadows of both *narcissistic* and *anaclitic identifications* on the conscious emotional life. When we are overly conditioned to another person, as Titus was to his mother, we cannot shake the shadow of the other. Titus could not stop longing for his mother after her death. As new experience alters this shadow, we ordinarily grieve a loss.

We can grieve and work through a loss because the conditioned social experience of orbital frontal cortex can be extinguished (Rolls, 1992). In grief, we decide to relinquish the object of our conditioning.

Human amygdalotomies for intractable seizures lessen, but do not destroy, the emotional life (Aggleton, 1992). Together with the aminergic systems' drive states, the cingulate, orbital, and insular cortexes continue to produce what, to all appearances, is an emotional existence. Conceivably, the old emotional life continues, while new emotional adaptation disappears. Perhaps the capacity to become traumatized and to profoundly change one's intrapsychic identity is lost with amygdalotomy. After all, we know that when the orbital cortex is damaged, a person cannot adapt to fresh experience.

In the service of problem solving, the prefrontal system tempers instinctual hypothalamic discharges of fight or flight. Instead of full-blown panic initiated by the left hemisphere or terror initiated by the right, all three zones can use defenses to temper these discharges. They do this by signaling an extension of the amygdala called the *bed nucleus of the stria terminalis* to inhibit fear conditioning (Davis, 1995). The amygdala can respond by reducing the drive pressure for problem solving.

Phineas Gage Revisited

Orbital frontal lesions can destroy the ability to use past social experience as a guide to decision making. In the late nineteenth century, the once famous Phineas Gage used explosives to level land for railroad construction. His explosives were contained in pipes called petards. One day, a piece of an exploding petard penetrated Gage's skull and remained imbedded in his orbital frontal cortex. Dazed, Gage walked away from the scene of the explosion, almost as if nothing had happened. In fact, he continued to work with the pipe extruding from his skull. He seemed to be a walking, working, wounded wonder.

Something had happened to Gage though: he left his job and became a ne'er do well. People thought fame had spoiled him. Studying Gage's records (as well as those of other previously normal patients who developed orbital frontal lesions), Damasio, Tramel, and Damasio (1990) concluded, however, that the defect of seeming fecklessness in people with similar injuries:

> is due to an inability to activate somatic states linked to punishment and reward, that were previously experienced in connection with anticipated outcomes of response options. During the processing that follows the perception of a social event, the experience of certain

anticipated outcomes of response options would be marked by the reactivation of an appropriate somatic state. (p. 81)

In other words, social judgment requires an intact orbital frontal cortex to assess socially conditioned somatic signals.

HOW DO WE EVOKE AND SENSE OUR PAST?

A failure to find salience or significance during problem solving feeds back to the amygdala. The amygdala sends anxiety signals to the cingulate cortex. These indicate what is wrong. The amygdala sends emotional signals that indicate the source of difficulty to the intermediate cortex. The executive evaluates these signals verbally, and accesses relevant source memory. From its signals, the executive accesses *events*, processed in the left hemisphere, or *episodes*, processed in the right.

We recall *events* such as taking our qualifying examinations, with *pride* or *shame*. We recall *episodes* with affects such as *distress or relief* that bear on present experience. As I am shaving and thinking of this manuscript, hoping I do not cut myself, two episodes return. My mother says, "Your father should have taught you how to shave." In the same breath, a patient who reminds me of my mother says cuttingly, "Men always miss that part of their face."

Our social past illuminates our social present. The executive integrates our social subject by accessing events, and the executive integrates our social self by accessing episodes. When a neuropsychologist tests a patient's left hemisphere's capacity to narrate events and his right hemisphere's capacity to understand the affect lodged in episodes, he tells the patient a story. Luria, the father of neuropsychology, designed stories to test each hemisphere's capacity to use its past experience.

Luria would tell the patient about the crow, who, in a time of famine noticed that the pigeons were well fed. The crow flew to the pigeons' coop, but he was shooed away with a great beating of wings because of his color. The clever crow thought out what to do. He flew into a pan of whitewash to make himself white. Then he returned to the pigeons' coop. The pigeons attacked him again. The crow smelled wrong. Returning to the crows, our hero found them feasting on a fresh kill. When he tried to join them, they attacked him, believing he was a pigeon.

A patient with damage in his left hemisphere's experiential loops, probably cannot reproduce this sequence of events. The crow's changing tactics cannot be recalled in a meaningful sequence. A patient with damage in his right hemisphere's experiential loops probably cannot understand the crow's affects. The moral of the story evades him. I trust that an analyst who turns to the neuroscientists will receive better treatment.

When a motivated person verbalizes and carries out a new plan of action that accomplishes his goal, the individual extrapolates a *belief* from the sequence of events. First, somatic reward signals attached to verbal associations accompany the formation of motivated plans. Later, memories of the event reenforce motivated, volitional belief/action programs. A belief is an expected outcome that arises from temporal associations.

The following daydream relates to my wishes and beliefs associated with the present book: "If I present this material as a special guest lecturer at the University of British Columbia, then I'll get paid for promoting my own work, and I'll learn a lot from the feedback. Perhaps Dr. Reiser was right when he told me while I was a resident that you have to become known as an expert in one small area of the field. Presenting at Grand Rounds is a good, modern way of becoming known and successful and promoting your ideas. I'm not sure I've convinced myself. I might be a flop and communicate nothing. Well, I'll try it."

Reward signals are *libidinally cathected sensations of discharge*. Pleasure loops attach sensations derived from the body's erogenous zones, including those from the voluntary and involuntary muscles. The muscles of the speech apparatus—of the face and of the eyes—all give rise to the pleasure of cathexis in the formation of associations to events. When we initiate any successful action, including the formation of speech by the articulatory muscles, the feedback sensation is cathected with pleasure, large or small. For example, we often pleasurably remember the first time we successfully used a word or a phrase.

When somatic signals evoke event associations, we remember, in the subjective arrow of time, sequences that were rewarded or that failed. At social gatherings, we find ourselves retelling the same stories. We are willing to repeat ourselves *ad nauseam*, and the strange thing is, we never get tired of the details or leave out a piece of the sequence: *first I did this, then I did that*. This sequencing is the sign of left hemisphere action program formation. Narrations of organizing events are highly charged with motivations and lessons about how to go about getting what we want and need. As we age, particular events seem more important. They imbed personal fantasies and family myths. They become templates for characteristic behaviors.

Episodic memories have an affective epicenter. The center's *visceral signals*—feelings—convey a sense of reality. To give an example, a well-known poet's image of an earthquake evokes the moment his mother had a lobotomy. Neither his reality nor hers was the same after that moment. His poetry became his way of preserving an intact self.

Ordinarily we encode episodes as lessons that reinforce response programs. Episodes are timeless. Their affect returns full force. Freud found that affects cannot be transformed, only expressed or blocked (1900). Some people dissociate, or become anorexic/bulimic to block retraumatizing memories. Another well-known poet of my acquaintance began to write after suffering from posttraumatic stress disorder. He found that writing poetry was a way of neutralizing flashbacks from the Second World War.

HOW CAN EMOTIONAL CONTEXTS BECOME EXPLICIT?

Let us explore how emotional experience can become explicitly verbal and how cognitive experience can lose verbal access. To become explicit, associations enter *configured networks:* "Modulatory relations are ones in which a stimulus takes as its associative object another association" (Rescorla, 1992, p. 68). In modulatory relations, explicit associations can access implicitly conditioned associations. Our prefrontal cognitive networks weave into socially conditioned networks. Thus, a verbal association can root in conditioned data. Like a sunflower, it grows larger if it is planted in compost.

In his clinical study of free associations, Freud discovered that mental *contents* are formed in a temporal sequence within an explicit emotional context. He discovered that the temporal sequence of cognitive associations is determined by their socially conditioned emotional evocations. He found that when a cognitive link is missing, it is because an unpleasant somatic state has evoked defenses against it. At some time in the past, he concluded, repression excluded the unpleasant cognitive link. Implicit, conditioned associations form a bed that helps draw repressed explicit associations into their unconscious realm.

When our executive reflects on the contents of articulatory rehearsal, new data form, and these can be reprocessed. Many mental contents have undergone previous reflection. We have all had the experience of not knowing whether we are remembering an actual event, a later recollection of the event, or being told about the event. This is because we process an experience directly; we also process our reflections about the experience. Reprocessed reflection provides us with an intake of linguistically organized data. Reprocessed reflection, then, provides the foundations of higher-order belief systems.

Acute traumatic stress disorder illustrates the interaction between the amygdala's conditioning of emotional experience, the hippocampus' explicit processing of emotional experience, and the executive's maintenance of identity. During acute stress, a person's attention rivets to her state of reflective identity rather than to usual mental contents. Traumatic, semantic, and perceptual experiences are recycled over and over until they bind to new structures of intrapsychic identity. Unwanted contents infiltrate and undermine premorbid identity. The new identity has a life of its own. Consider a case vignette.

Lida's Trauma

A gang of rapacious teenage boys descended on Lida, a twenty-two-year-old woman. They all but raped her before she could escape. During the attack, Lida felt enclosed in a man trap. She said she felt like a lobster in a pot with no escape but death. In the weeks that followed, Lida felt detached, unreal—a spectator to her body. Even her hands looked alien to her. She stopped caring for herself, and her self-esteem plummeted. Lida felt deeply ashamed. She *knew* she would die in a matter of time.

Lida felt like an automaton during work and other daily activities. During the attack, she felt a helpless child had replaced her self. By night, she dreamed of lying on a table while a gang of youths stuck her with knives. In my office, Lida perceived a picture of an innocent child holding flowers in a garden as an out-of-control child holding a knife. She had no ability to modulate the sense that she would kill or be killed.

Lida mixed old memories with more recent ones. The memory of a man she had known who died of a heroin overdose blended with recollections of a distant friend who had recently taken an overdose without dying. She took an overdose of Xanax, not in an attempt to kill "Lida," but to kill her weak new self.

A week after the attack, Lida began to hallucinate about a gang of male voices. The voices made fun of her and her body. She could not make out exactly what they were saying. It was enough to know that they were laughing at her. Mortified, unable to share this experience, Lida wanted to be alone.

She felt that her new condition was permanent. She could not understand her friends' and therapist's reassurance that it was not. She no longer wanted to see her boyfriend because it made no sense to her that he would want to relate to "Lida," who had already died. She did not feel she could stand to talk about what had happened to "Lida," but she could not stop talking about her strange new state of identity.

Trapped in psychosis, Lida soiled her bed and her room with urine and menstrual blood. Still, she wrote poetry—"Lida's" poetry of damaged identity. Each poem described the experience of abuse without escape:

> I make gastric acid, throw it up, piss on inflamed floors.
> Haunted clean sheets absorb the blood from my numbed pores.
> Get lost languid Lida, there are no fire exit doors.

Trying to master the trauma of entrapment with no exit, Lida used poetry to express her experience of lapsing identity.

As with Titus, Lida's gastric torment brings us to Henke's article on stomach pathology and the amygdala:

> The amygdala (is) associated with threatening conditions . . . and gut reactions . . . this limbic structure plays an important role in gastric stress ulcer modulation . . . the amygdala is a nodal point in . . . temporal lobe circuits (which also include hippocampus and entorrhinal cortex) that modify gastric stress pathologies. (1992, p. 323)

Lida's response to her trauma illustrates how the formation of new conditioning and new emotionally organized source memory can profoundly disrupt identity. Our reliance on a stable sense of identity is built on shifting foundations. The changes that occur in both limbic and prefrontal processing are rapid in acute trauma. This means to me that the LTP that is regulated by the amygdala's cathexis can produce prodigious and ongoing transfer LTP over both brief and extended periods. When masses of newly conditioned associations form after infancy, they are only partly accompanied by explicit cognitive associations. This may be why our belief and value systems sometimes change in ways that we cannot account for by reviewing accessible source memories.

The plasticity of the prefrontal cortex, particularly the orbital frontal cortex, may be a factor in rapid changes of identity during posttraumatic periods. For instance, Lida felt that she had developed a whole new self, that her old self was now a distant friend. She evoked memories of rapid changes in others, like her friend who began to take heroin and then died. She did not recover from her psychosis until several months later. When she did recover, she was able, in therapy, to translate her poetry into a direct, coherent, emotionally complete rendering of her trauma. From this, we may conclude that by engendering beauty and cadencing aggression, poetry provides a prosthesis for identity. It is a vehicle for resynthesizing prefrontal identity, as it recycles our experience, and it performs this function for readers as well as writers.

THE FOUNDATIONS OF COGNITIVE PROCESSING

We are still a long way from understanding what distorts cognitive processing and memory formation in trauma. We can be sure it is not a matter of simply repressing what we cannot stand to know. I think the answer resides in how the hippocampus precognitively processes data. Normally, when the amygdala sends anxiety and emotional reports to the medial and intermediate prefrontal cortex, the data that gives rise to these reports are also cognitively processed, via hippocampal feedbacks to the lateral prefrontal cortex. In mild stress, the amygdala enhances precognitive processing by intensifying rhinal cortical data that enters the CA 1 and subicular fields of the hippocampus.

In mild stress, emotionally organized *source memory* forms and remains accessible. If the reader were to be tested on the data presented in this chapter, the present paragraph could help or harm her learning by presenting a challenge to her identity. Mild stress that has an emotional component increases hippocampal precognitive processing and thereby increases prefrontal cognitive processing. But, if the reader has test anxiety and if her baby is sick, then her stress level could impair her precognitive processing of data as well as her test performance. In order to understand all this, we will have to study some neural systems and their mechanisms of interaction.

The hippocampus' CA 1 field is critical to retrievable source memory formation. When source memory forms, data enters the rhinal cortex, loops unidirectionally to CA 1 neurones, and then exits via the subiculum back to the rhinal cortex (Amaral, 1991). All the prefrontal and frontal zones feed back and forth monosynaptically with the subicular rhinal cortex (Amaral et al., 1992). Thus, potentiation in CA 1/subicular synapses can make explicit associations retrievable by the prefrontal system.

Once formed by potentiation, source memory can be retrieved. But all data that become explicit need not be stored. They may simply be used in ordinary problem solving. This is where the hippocampus' CA 3 field comes into play. The hippocampus' CA 3 field is critical to contextualizing all data during problem solving. We do not have to remember every time and circumstance we unlock our front door. We simply have to unlock it if it is locked. But if something is unusual, or the lock sticks, then we may form new source memory.

During problem solving, we take in so much data that we have to: (1) examine some, (2) merely categorize some, (3) exclude some as too emotionally hot to handle, and (4) keep some on hold without thinking. Data enter these various processing modes, which I will call the four Cs, from the rhinal cortex:

1. *Configuring* explicitly associates data.
2. *Contextualizing* implicitly associates data.
3. *Conditioning* primes novel, emotional data.
4. *Cuing* primes familiar, nonemotional sensory data. (See Figures 2.5 and 2.6.)

FIGURE 2.5. Explicit (Precognitive) Loops

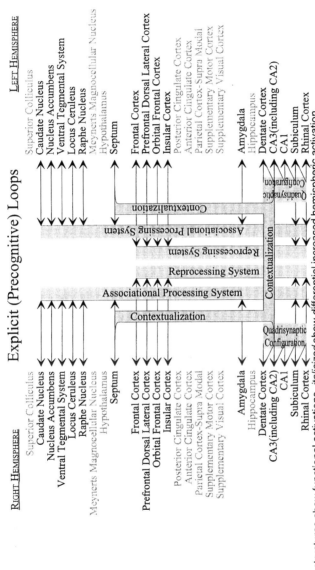

Bold structures show functional activations, *italicized* show differential increased hemispheric activation.

*Arrows point to and/or from that anatomy in the corresponding horizontal row which participates in the given neural system.

All the loop figures are most useful for suggestive examination after the material in the first three chapters has been studied.

To reach verbal consciousness and to form *explicit* memory—verbally associated memory—and long-term memory—consolidated over hours, data must be processed by the "quadrisynaptic hippocampal loop." Passing all the way through the hippocampus, data potentiate—facilitate their synapses—outflow paths. This both *contextualizes* data and gives data *configural association*—a networking matrix of associations. Right hemisphere pictorial data, unlike left verbal data, can reach consciousness only after prefrontal system processing. Data are reprocessed serially by the hippocampus and the prefrontal system as they are cognized.

FIGURE 2.6 Implicit Loops

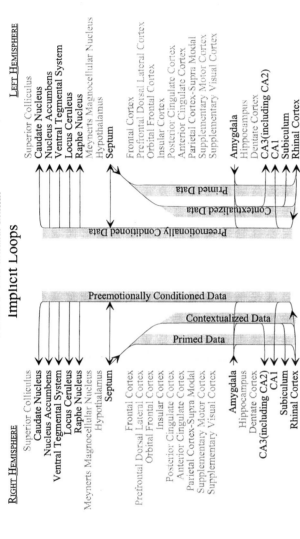

Bold structures show functional activations, *italicized* show differential increased hemispheric activation.

*Arrows point to and/or from that anatomy in the corresponding horizontal row which participates in the given neural system.

All the loop figures are most useful for suggestive examination after the material in the first three chapters has been studied.

There are several ways to use *implicit* data. Rhinal cortex primes pictorial data, the left verbal. The right rhinal cortex primes pictorial data, the left verbal. Rhinal data ramifies its context as it passes directly through the hippocampal CA 3 field. In this way, we can *prime contexts*. When amygdalar-intensified novel data take the short path through the hippocampal CA 1 field, they are *primed emotionally*. Thus, amygdala-charged, *preemotionally conditioned* data can be held for potential use. In this case, we sense that something is going on that will affect us later.

Configuring

Let us consider the anatomy of the hippocampus' precognitive loop in detail. From the rhinal cortex data proceed

1. from the dentate's pyriform mossy fibers to CA 3 and CA 2,
2. then via Schaffer collateral to CA 1, and
3. finally they exit through subicular outflow populations.

The subiculum opens data's door to source memory formation in the parahippocampus and prefrontal cortex. Taking a *quadrisynaptic* path from dentate to subiculum, data ramify their configuration and context, which forms new explicit memory (Eichenbaum and Buckingham, 1995). Data can also traverse the hippocampus via a short path: rhinal cortex/CA 1/subiculum. This path is reenforced by the amygdala during its emotional processing. When data takes both paths and concurrently undergoes amygdalar emotional processing, emotionally organized source memory can form. If the reader's baby is undergoing a developmental advance at the same time she is studying infant development, her study data is both emotionally organized and cognized—a lesson for the generations.

Contextualizing

Some data enter the hippocampus from the rhinal cortex and exits via the CA 3 fields to the septum. These data may be simply and implicitly contextualized. A bedroom chair is different from an identical one in the kitchen. With facilitatory help from a cholinergic system that ordinates in the septum, the septum can feed contextualized data back to the rhinal cortex for explicit processing. The anticholinergic drug, scopolamine, blocks the septum's facilitation of primed visual data (Mishkin, 1994). That is why preanesthetic scopolamine prevents incidental sensory imagery that precedes an operation from entering explicit memory.

Conditioning

The septum, as well as the amygdala, can condition emotional data. Because the septum has reciprocal connections with the rhinal cortex, amygdala, basal ganglia, and the ventral tegmental system, it is able to condition implicit data operantly. Here, conditioning occurs in the basal ganglia when visual or auditory signals acquire *orienting salience*. The basal ganglia combine sensory data with motor impulses to form *habits*. Perhaps I turn my head to the right whenever I hear a sound that could be the dinner bell in a house where I am a guest. Or maybe a dim light down the corridor means another guest has arrived. That may be irrelevant to me now, but later it could be the maestro arriving. The second visual cortex relay (V2) arrives at the the basal ganglia soon after a relay from the primary (V1) visual cortex arrives at the perirhinal cortex. V2 data, joined with motor associations that have been facilitated by the pleasure loop, forms *habit memory* (Mishkin, 1994). Orienting to the right may trigger the action plan that will lead me down the hall to the dining room where I will meet the esteemed guests.

Classical and operant conditioning are both kinds of implicit memory. They set the table for our dinner, but we do not realize the work they have done to make the meal possible. In *operant conditioning*, data are reenforced as they enter the basal ganglia to become *salient* in a way that triggers *habit formation*. The amygdala and septum cause the *ventral tegmental dopaminergic system* to condition motor associations in the basal ganglia.

Cuing: Sensory and Motor Priming

Some data that enter the rhinal cortex are destined to be used later, if at all. The rhinal cortex coordinates *delayed recognition* (sensory priming) by holding sensory data for day-long periods. Cued data can later enter the hippocampus for explicit processing when needed for problem solving. For instance, the first visually relayed data from the occipital cortex (V1) received in perirhinal cortex at 100 milliseconds can be preserved until they are needed by the prefrontal cortex, or they can be discarded (Mishkin, 1994).

In *the Poetzl phenomenon,* subthreshold, nonattended sensory data enter dream imagery. In this form of delayed recognition, neutral data flash on a screen faster than can be perceived. The person is told he will find the data in a dream that night. He does, because suggestion brings the dreamer's attention to them.

CA 1's FIDELITY, CA 3's PROMISCUITY

"Apparently, it is hippocampal neurons that had the highest concentration of corticosteroid receptors which are most vulnerable to dying" (Sapolsky, 1992, p. 119). Neurons have a life, a death, and relationships of their own which impact the person. Episodic and event source memories form in great perturbations as waves of calcium ions move through CA 1 synapses. In neoteny's stage changes, in organic pathology, or in trauma, these waves can unleash excitotoxic energy cascades that destroy postsynaptic neurons as they pervade postsynaptic cytoplasm. Some CA 1 pathways permanently potentiate, becoming dedicated, or hard wired. Others are destroyed.

Why does the microanatomy of CA 1 pathways permit them to make dedicated marriages through excitotoxic selection, while other synaptic relationships in the quadrisynaptic path remain available for ordinary data processing? While CA 3 neurones make promiscuous contact with thousands of other neurons in and out of the hippocampus, which forms *processing contexts*, CA 1 neuron's dendrites can join over and over again to the same Schaffer collateral axons. In this way, they receive dedicated—highly determined—input paths. Conceivably, CA 1's *subicular* output neurons can also dedicate, and these outputs can make their own faithful contacts, all of which forms a long-term memory net. Subicular LTP transcribes genome factors in the parahippocampus when memory consolidation occurs (Kaczmarek, 1992).

Damage to CA 1 and CA 3 populations yields a differential memory effect. In humans with substantial damage confined to bilateral CA 3 output, retrograde memory retrieval is blocked—the context is lost. What good are associations to an object if the object—or its meaning—has no context? Previously learned material cannot be retrieved, and anterograde memory—new memory formation—is impaired. Damage confined to CA 1 output blocks only new memory formation. We can still experience because our CA 3 output can still access our brain's old memory.

THE HIPPOCAMPUS'S MICRO- AND MACROANATOMY

Let us put our hippocampal soul under the microscope. A comparative survey of CA 3, CA 1, and dentate population's synaptic characteristics will concretize how the hippocampus effectuates differential processing of novel data.[7] Dentate, CA 3, and CA 1 populations each undergo unique potentiation. During hippocampal kindling by erratic electrical stimulation (the original experiment that led to the concept that kindling reduces the epileptic threshold), dentate cells are potentiated for two minutes, CA 3 cells for forty minutes, and CA 1 cells for hours (Lothman, 1991; Kuba and Kumamoto, 1990).

During periods of intense experiential stimulation, all three forms of potentiation coexist. I conclude that when all three synapses are potentiated simultaneously during LTP, long-term memory will form. Prolonged CA 1 output through the subiculum will produce multiple parahippocampal and transferred neocortical consolidations. This profusion of associations is one factor that *overdetermines* long-term memory.

CA 1 LTP gives rise to transcription events in the genome of the post-synaptic cell during memory storage (Kandel, 1994). If protein synthesis is blocked in the first hour, no long-term memory storage occurs. Thus, CA 1 outflow though the subiculum lasts the requisite time to form multiple, overdetermined consolidations—long-term memory associations—as CA 1 prolongs its potentiation of subicular routes to the parahippocampus.[8]

HOW ASSOCIATIONS ARE LINKED

As we age, our capacity to form new source memory decreases. The greater the number of segregated CA 1 pathways already dedicated to source memory, the smaller the number available for forming new memory. The older we get, and the more intense experience we have undergone, the greater our reliance on prefrontal semantic and representational networks that have been built up over a lifetime, and the smaller our capacity to form new long-term memory. As we age it is the CA 1 and subicular neurons that show the greatest decrease.

Barnes (1994) confirms this view of hippocampal processing by comparing synaptic function in younger and older rats. Younger rats show a greater overall hippocampal synaptic response to input, whereas older rats show a lessened total synaptic response. Each remaining synapse in older rats is more productive because their CA 3 cells' AMPA receptors upregulate to their mossy fiber input (Barnes, 1994). The decreased overall number of synaptic responses to stimuli in older rats is due to a decreased number of Schaffer collateral inputs into CA 1 cells. From this I infer that excitotoxicity destroyed some CA 1 cells and their presynaptic Schaffer collaterals. I conclude that most CA 1 synapses in older rats are already dedicated to their network outputs, while each Ca 3 synapse carries a greater burden of assessing present context.

CONCLUSION: TRUTH IS BEAUTY, BEAUTY TRUTH

I have observed that Lida and others who have been traumatized in situations of inescapable abuse mobilize a sense of beauty that transfigures their identity. Looking ahead to the rest of this book, we will want to explore how such transfigurations can occur. Our survey of the hippocampus and amygdala allows us to reach some preliminary conclusions. During inescapable trauma, the amygdala reweaves prefrontal associational networks. These moments shape new value systems and new intrapsychic identity.

Humans are unique in being structure-making animals. The necessity for solving problems of survival leads us to weave structures that are compatible with our identity. We cathect successful structures with drive so that they give pleasure, relief, and vitality. The amygdala directs the drives to cathect structures derived from multiple association matrices. The hippocampus is the loom that designs the whole context and configuration of structures from their preliminary data.

The pattern of our libidinal cathexis of our semantic and representational networks determines our aesthetic sense. Our sense of perfection imbues the left hemisphere's prefrontal subjective structures with a sense of elegance. Just as the infant cathects the capacity to crawl or walk with a sense of pleasure, so a human being endows the highest achievements of problem solving with a pleasure cathexis. We enjoy knowing how to solve problems and we enjoy exercising that knowledge.

Our conscious structures of identity are twofold. Aesthetic representations of our identity are narcissistic structures that requite our yearnings for beauty. They are formed in the left hemisphere. Representations of our identity in reality are objectifying structures constructed by the right hemisphere. They discover the truth of our existence. When our highest cognitive structures find the nirvana of solution, feedback from the amygdalar heart and the hippocampal soul of experience produce a synthesis of our humanity, both beautiful and true.

One question becomes preeminent in our survival: "Who am I?" Collectively, the question is, "Who are we?" At the pinnacle of our mind's Acropolis, our executive's identity metafunction can absorb all our energy. When the twenty-five-year old poet, John Keats, was dying of tuberculosis that made every swallow painful, he turned to his muse, Fanny Braun. Feeling that he pursued her eternally in his poetry, like the primal scene image of lovers eternally pursuing nymphs on a Grecian urn, Keats turned back to his infantile source of being. He could face his ongoing trauma if his human identity could resurrect itself eternally in his pursuit of his muse. Similarly, in the story cited at the beginning of this chapter, Marcello pursues his muse, Lina, by giving up the stage to her. When all else fails, we synthesize identity in the illusion of a human kind that lives forever.

As Keats followed the tracery of mythological figures curling in his mind, he simultaneously recreated his identity as a poet and set to rest the pain of his tuberculosis (Harris and Harris, 1981): "Beauty is Truth, truth beauty,—that is all ye know on earth, and all ye need to know." As we saw with the poet whose mother had a lobotomy, poetry sometimes transcends trauma. As we saw with our patient Lida, poetry's way of synthesizing identity can even ameliorate psychosis.

Chapter 3

The Anatomy of Our Being

What . . . occurred to me in the analysis were the Augean stables . . . cleansed by Hercules. This Hercules was I. I had discovered the infantile aetiology of the neuroses, and thus had saved my children from falling ill. (Freud, S., Standard Edition, vol. V, p. 460)

When Freud referred to Hercules' feat of cleansing the stables by diverting the river Peneus, he compared the accomplishment to the reorganization of the drives that occurs in the phallic state of development. (Harris and Harris, 1984, p. 112)

THE STRUGGLE FOR A HIGHER CONSCIOUSNESS

Instead of debunking Freud's Herculean labor of discovering drive development and its expression in individual and collective fantasy and mythology, we should celebrate it. As I see it, contemporary insight into human development and psychopathology has been distorted by oversimplified beliefs in external causes and genetic defects that deny more truth than they reveal.

The belief in external social and cultural causes is a linchpin of postmodern thinking. Modern thinkers use their own associations and responses to a work, buttressed by their own knowledge of relevant social and cultural causes to construct an analysis of a work's relevance. Postmodern structural analysis takes the opposite view than Freud did. For Freud, the meaning of a dream, a work, or a symptom is found in the maker's own associations. I think we are mistaken if we look to our own cultural associations to a work rather than to the author's associations, life experiences, and biological predispositions.

The postmodern movement to find meaning in the eyes of the beholder comes about, I think, because our modern social, cultural, and intellectual world has fallen under the sway of a psychology of trauma. So many people have been physically, sexually, and emotionally abused in our postmodern world that we look to the external world for cause and meaning, rather than into our own inner world.

As postmodern academia has flourished, Freud has been faulted for allegedly reneging on his theory of a traumatic aetiology of psychic conflict. For interest, in a highly publicized dispute, Janet Malcom (1984) reported on Jeffrey Masson's theory that Freud's father had molested the young Freud. According to Masson, Freud discovered, then denied, the significance of trauma to psychopathology. Masson concluded that Freud falsely ascribed his own abuse to fantasy. In truth, Freud repeatedly analyzed the effect of childhood molestation on development. But Freud discovered that universal primal scene constructs and oedipal fantasies are biologically determined to shape development, both in the presence and absence of sexual abuse.

Our inability to take what is useful from Freud's labors was starkly illustrated in the December 1995 *New York Times* report of a protest against a Freud retrospective, which was to have been held at the Library of Congress. Fifty signers contended that the retrospective should be wide enough to include a full range of scholars' views. The retrospective was cancelled because the bulk of protesting scholars believed their postmodern views were left out of account in determining the cultural significance of psychoanalysis.[1] Thus, Gloria Steinem argued that Freud degraded women's experience, and Freud's granddaughter, Sophie, called Freud's drive theory outmoded.

Assaulted now by a steady stream of misrepresentation, as he had been when he dreamed of cleaning the Aegian Stables, Freud must be turning over in his grave. In my reading, Freud's portrait of mental life is biologically rooted, and it reconstructs actual experience. Freud valued each person's life experience by analyzing it. Perhaps, the accuracy of Freud's analytic method can be measured by the fear it inspires in a culture that devalues life experience.

A brief case vignette exemplifies the interaction of sexual abuse with oedipal drive development. A patient of mine was sodomized by his grandfather when the patient was six years old. His grandfather told him he must submit in silence or kill his mother. During the rape the child imagined, as if in a dream, that his mother was a bad woman of the jungle who gave herself to men. To screen out the sodomy, the child imagined he must allow a wound to be created in his own back to "save" his mother from degradation. Then, as the rape was consummated, the child imagined that he was bouncing a basketball higher and higher until it disappeared into a bright sky of beauty. His sexual abuse was experienced within the context of oedipal stage fantasies. What I want the reader to see is that a person must experience sexual trauma—like any other trauma—within his or her developmental stage. One wonders, I should add, if it is possible to process *any* experience outside of one's own developmental context.

Since the 1960s, our social analysis has arisen from a culture of trauma. Traumatized, we collectively detach from the biologically rooted, developmentally complex organization of our drives and our experience. Thus, psychiatry took biogenic amine systems out of their neural system's context *and* out of their human context in order to propose testable hypotheses of syndrome formation. The public mind gladly translated this narrow focus into the proposition that psychiatric syndromes are the result of chemical imbalances, not of biologically determined social and individual experience. Many patients I have consulted with and their therapists want to believe in chemical imbalance at the expense of the relevance of human experience. This chapter labors to reconcile contemporary neuroscience with Freud's drive theory, seen in the context of a developing individual.

THE NEURAL REGULATION OF EXPERIENCE

We are about to examine that odd arena where the neural becomes the mental. The question we will have repeat to ourselves is, how can we move between the two systems without getting dizzy? As we saw in Chapter 2, the evolutionarily ancient amygdalae regulate drives' demands on the prefrontal cortex's behavioral ouput. Augmented by drive, the amygdalae's emotional pressures inaugerate problem solving. This replicates Freud's view that instincts, their attendant drives, and their derivative fantasies place a demand on the brain to solve problems.

We have the same drives that pressure survival in other mammalian species. We can surmise from our intimate acquaintance with our pets that we all have the same basic drives that other mammals do. Cumulative reflection on life, however, shows that our sentient feelings broaden as life goes on. A sexual encounter with a partner of many years, for example, contains the history of that relationship, and it becomes a channel for a multitude of interpersonal feelings. Indeed, all interpersonal relationships grow out of a broadening assimilation of one another's drives. We know our drives as behavioral states of personal identity, experienced within an interpersonal frame. Our drives, therefore, acquire greater higher cortical and dichotomous regulation than exists in other species.

We saw in Chapter 2 that in infancy, the biogenic amines give rise to behavioral states. Indeed, the effect of biogenic amine drive systems on our prefrontal cortex produces consummatory, vigilant, and attentional behavioral states throughout life. Gradually these behavioral states interact with our personality organization, and we become aware of our behavioral states when others respond to them. How does this happen?

Under social and economic pressure what starts as love, and is expressed in lovemaking, can also regress to aggressive, preoedipal power relationships. Family therapists call this the "one-up, one-down" equilibrium. Two abused adults, for instance, often reexpereince both their up and down with each other. Their lovemaking discharges sadomasochistic fantasies. They use their accumulated knowledge of each other's drives to immobilize, rather than to enhance, each other's maturity.

In one couple, the husband, a physician, and his wife, his office manager, have a constantly reversing up/down relationship. Each is terrified of being abandoned by the other. To be in control, the wife tells her husband exactly what he must do in every situation at home and in the office. She insists, moreover, that only he can treat her medical condition. Resentful, always on the edge of anger, the husband responds with passive aggression. They go through icy periods when the wife withholds sex and the husband has fantasies of other women. Battles that replay the childhood of each end in brief exciting sexual encounters that thaw the ice with a blowtorch, and so their equilibrium reestablishes itself. But this couple remains static in time. Neither comes to sense the origins of the other's behavioral states.

How does the human brain get to know itself? We saw in Chapter 2 that experience contains the integration of our amygdalar/emotional heart, our hippocampal/cognitive soul, and our prefrontal/reflective articulation. Moment by moment, however, sentience arises through serial processing epochs.

1. Instinctual registration occurs at seven to eleven milliseconds (msecs).
2. Conditioning occurs at 100 msecs.
3. Cognition occurs at 300 msecs (known as p300).
4. Linguistic assessment and behavior occurs at one to two seconds.

> After multiple neocortical amygdala feedback cycles, the pattern of activated cells in the amygdala would come to reflect those that participate in the distributed neural networks that include both neocortex and amygdala, and that specifically encode the currently experienced event. (Halgren, 1992, p. 215)

The fact that experiential tendencies may be coarsely elicited in an epileptic aura displays each experiential loop's extended net (Gloor, 1992). As a neocortical trigger zone spreads its excitation (aura) to the limbic system, we have an experience. Because the amygdala and hippo-campus form an array of experiential loops that radiate like spokes to the prefrontal cortex's wheel of identity, excitation goes back to the hub. Then, the amygdala and the hippocampus spread epileptic discharge to the whole brain, and tonic/clonic seizures halt consciousness.

Seizures are one price evolution exacts for the flexibly potentiated neocortical working zones that characterize our species. They are a down-side of our fine and flexible working minds. The same may be said of other neuropsychiatric syndromes. They also—and always—compromise our sense of who we are. The sad fact is, our elaborate capacity for prefrontal identity renders us vulnerable to mental and interpersonal breakdowns.

WHAT HAPPENS WHEN OUR IDENTITY IS THREATENED?

Like Hercules, modern-day athletes strive for preeminence. Among male athletes, their phallic narcissism works for or against the individual's talent and his team's success. The outcome depends on the flow of phallic narcissism into derivative fantasies, which determine a player's mutable identity. Athletes' identity conflicts often play out in their athletic perfor-mance. Sometimes it is a question of which hemisphere wins. Consider a well-known, professional basketball player.

On his game, this player spontaneously drives to the basket and makes reverse layups, or he makes three-point shots with uncanny accuracy. Unfor-tunately, his success flows into self-defeating fantasies of heroism, which leads him to overlook his teammates. Once he makes a few bad shots, he cannot stop shooting the ball. He loses his spontaneity, and he starts taking aim. At this point, filled with the anxiety that he has lost his greatness, he cannot do anything right, and he is likely to explode into atavistic rages.

What happens? First, instinct fails. Now, he is consciously taking aim. His right hemisphere is performing imitative procedures. It is as if his coach is looking over his shoulder telling him what to do. His ego ideal, Michael Jordan, is no longer feeding his spontaneity. His left hemisphere no longer initiates the gesture in which the ball is his extension into the hole. His cerebellum no longer synchronizes his caudate nuclei. His inner speech lies to his supplementary cortex about the moment of truth and beauty. His failure resides in his threatened identity.

A FURTHER ANATOMICAL INQUIRY
INTO PROBLEM SOLVING

We will now take an extended look at how the prefrontal cortex, cere-bellum, and caudate work together as teammates in the brain.

Questions at issue here are:

- How does the prefrontal system regulate its networks?
- How the does the caudate balance consciousness, drive, and conditioning during our conduct of action and response programs?
- How does the cerebellum enhance problem solving as it (1) primes motor associations, (2) conditions and compels motor sequencing in the *striatum* (subcortical motor-coordinating centers), and (3) selectively focuses attention?

THE NEOCORTEX'S ANATOMICAL STRUCTURE

Prefrontal identity structure is flexible. As we saw in Chapter 1, it can be remodeled by its form of LTP. This is one good reason why our belief and value systems are not written in stone. Identity continually alters. The structure of our metafunctions is transcribed in ever changing grids.

As we also saw in Chapter 1, when a member of our genus, the monkey, has to learn new fine motor finger skills, his or her somatosensory finger representations change over time (Mersenick, 1994). Experience recomposes associational fields that represent the fingers. The same is true for humans. When our basketball player broke his finger, he had it taped to the next one, and before long, he heroically shot better than ever.

We can conclude from Mersenick's mapping of our relative's cortical finger representations that neocortical LTP is dynamic and fluid. New associational potentiations are formed, and old ones broken. Experience reorganizes frontal and prefrontal motor networks, most easily in the supplementary motor association cortex, which unleashes behavior (Mersenick, 1994).[2]

As the athlete's drive states respond to prevailing fantasies, his sense of identity gradually changes. Will he use bound aggression as a role player, or unbound aggression as a fallen star? This question of identity determines his neural system's reorganization. Biogenic amine systems monitor LTP's formation of the flexible connections that structure neocortical work zones at the same time that they regulate behavioral states. Later in this chapter, we will explore how biogenic amine systems are drive systems. Each biogenic amine system distinctively regulates neocortical glutamate synapses, either enhancing or inhibiting new associative connectivity. Neocortical output neurons either maintain their working flexibility, or potentiate their synapses. Trillions of these synapses make neocortical LTP a mechanism for regulating flexible brain connections.[3]

Our drives have a greater degree of higher cortical and dichotomous regulation than exists in other species because our sense of identity reciprocally regulates the drives. This reciprocity between mind and brain helps to explain why many experimenters have found that *catecholamines* are more unequally distributed in our two hemispheres than in other species.

The catecholamine disparity reflects human evolution toward hemispheric specialization. The left hemisphere's speech and action initiative, for instance, requires a high dopaminergic input throughout its whole domain. Mammals, especially humans, have evolved an increased dopaminergic regulation of the hippocampus, as well as the whole brain (Samson et al., 1990). Thus, both our precognitive and cognitive capacity have evolved consonant with our drives.

HOW DOES THE CAUDATE MEDIATE CONSCIOUSNESS AND DRIVE?

Before each intentional act, we have to decide whether to proceed. We search for drive cathected signs and salients that show the moment to be propitious, and we do this hundreds of times a day in large and small ways. What is the anatomical basis for our social judgement? Judging activates the caudate nuclei, which are subcortical structures that mediate between behavioral programs and these programs' feedback of salient and significant data (Pontius, 1980). Let us consider how the caudatum mediate between our behavior and our drives in a human situation.

Psyche's Mythological Board Examination

We are about to embark on an extended allegory based on the myth of Psyche. In order to understand what the mythological Psyche represents in the development of mind and identity, the reader is directed to Chapter 6. For now, let us say that the reader's friend Psyche is about to be examined on her capacity to conduct a diagnostic interview. Psyche's professional advancement depends on her performance at the Board Exams. At the time of her examination or initiation rite, Psyche is in a consummatory behavioral state and therefore, highly vulnerable to anticipatory anxiety. The stakes are high because Psyche is trying to consolidate her professional identity within a framework of pragmatic ideals that will suit her future.

In her quest, there are many things Psyche needs to know, and prove she knows. She needs to know all the criteria of DSM-IV, an almost mythically difficult sorting task, and she needs to prove that she recognizes the signs and symptoms of syndromes as they are exhibited by her unknown patient. She will have to formulate and prioritize a differential diagnosis as her mental status examination hones in on target signs and symptoms.

As Psyche comes into the cramped examining room, she realizes that she will have to make contact with the overly handsome man who will be her patient for one-half hour. Her two seated examiners are older women, and possibly jealous. She must show the examiners that she understands her patient's transference and be so aware of her own countertransference emotions so that she does no harm. Above all, as a physician, she must show that her diagnostic powers will be used for good rather than ill.

Psyche's patient, Eric, presents a complex diagnostic problem that Psyche finally narrows down: Eric is either a sociopath or he has a frontal lobe syndrome. In her interview, Psyche discerns that like the mythological Eros (Cupid), Eric is a strikingly handsome young man who had been an athletic but rebellious youth. He had often run away. He had been a rogue, sometimes a womanizer, and was always in trouble. For a while, he had overcome his youthful excesses. He had worked for several years as a troubleshooter at a large corporation. Two years before the mental status exam, however, he lost his job, and the woman he had been living with left him because he consorted with prostitutes. As Psyche listens, Eric recounts his story intelligently, in simple sentences without much expression, except sporadic excitement.

At this point, Psyche's senior examiner remarks, "You have five minutes to complete your examination."

He is not manipulative, and he is no longer charming, Psyche thinks to herself as she assesses her own erotic response to the man, so he is probably not sociopathic. "It is almost as if some essential part of him were oddly dead," she thinks. Under time pressure to nail down the diagnosis, Psyche spontaneously poses a new question to further test the patient's social judgment.

"What would you do if someone were to offer you one million dollars to go troubleshooting in Alaska?"

"I would go." Eric answers without hesitation, but Psyche wants to know, "Might it be possible that you were being duped or set up?" When Eric says "Yes," Psyche asks him if he would still go if he thought he were being set up. To this, Eric says, "No."

"Do you want to change your answer to the million-dollar question, then?" Psyche says as she gives her patient a careful look.

Unfazed, Eric says, "Yes."

"That's no sociopath; perhaps he is a phallic narcissist," Psyche says to herself. As Psyche gathers her thoughts to present them to the examiners, she is anxious about whether she has made a mistake in her diagnosis. She is also anxious about her wish to demonstrate her competence to the older female examiners. As the examination has gone on, she has increasingly felt that something is oddly wrong with Eric. His speech is overly simple, and he seems almost apathetic. Psyche concludes that Eric must have suffered some brain damage that is still in the process of creating a frontal lobe syndrome. She concludes this mainly because she senses a contrast between his present state and the vitality and sensuality she knows must have been present earlier in his life. His responses are out of keeping with sociopathic malingering. Perhaps he has a meningioma that has been overlooked. Perhaps it is not too late to intervene. Psyche struggles to bring her heart and soul to her professional identity as it has taken hold during this initiation.

During the last minutes' questioning, Eric shows no anxiety about whether he might make a mistake. He is able to follow the logic of Psyche's questions, and come to a different conclusion about the million dollars than he had at first. Being caught in a contradiction does not seem to bother his sense of self-esteem, nor does he need to explain his change of mind.

In the last minutes, then, both Psyche and Eric have had their social judgments tested more severely tested than they know. The deepest, most fixated wishes of each have been matched against their separate senses of social identity. The whole history of each person's limbic pleasure conditioning has been pitted against her or his social identity as each one's orbital prefrontal cortex assessed it.

When she entered the examination room, Psyche was on the verge of an important step forward in her sense of her professional identity. She needed to allow herself to be spontaneous. Perhaps, this is what led to her creative use of the mental status examination. She had originally heard an analogous million-dollar question in a rather different context. In fact, her question elaborated a joke that her mother had told her in her adolescence: A man asks a woman, "Would you sleep with me for one hundred dollars?" "No!" "For a thousand dollars?" "No!" "For a million dollars?" "Well, maybe yes for a million dollars!" "Okay, now that we've established what you are, let's bargain over the real price for your services." That joke had made Psyche feel unspontaneous, and unaware of her real beauty for all the years since her mother told her the story.

Psyche must have unconsciously associated to that joke as she performed her mental status examination on this handsome, oddly empty man in front of her female examiners. New confidence freed libidinal energy that had been held in abeyance by her mother's joke. She internalized a different metaphor suspended in the joke than she had before: to be true to your own sense of beauty is to be true to your own sense of integrity. In one great synthetic effort, Psyche became spontaneous.

She understood herself, and therefore she was able to assess Eric accurately. It was a relief to know what Freud had meant when he had said that sublimation was the social purpose with which we invest our narcissistic libido. The intersubjective love Psyche had held back from her mother because of enduring hurt had now found its way into an attainable professional ideal. Psyche realized that she need not be diffident about telling her examiners what she thought.

With regard to her diagnosis, Psyche understood herself well enough now to know that if she could not empathize with Eric; it was because something organic was blocking Eric from connecting with her empathy. He felt pleasure inviting him to act, but he was organically unable to make appropriate plans. Eric's supervisory planning and his executive judgment were impaired because a meningioma impinged on his left hemisphere's orbital frontal cortex. When Eric was on the point of making decisions, his assessments of his own social conditioning were disconnected from his sense of salience. His left caudate did not assess the data it needed to mediate a socially appropriate decision.

"That's no sociopath," Psyche said to the examiners. "Maybe he has a left hemisphere meningioma that is impinging on his orbital frontal cortex." Then she told them why she thought so.

Understanding how our caudate nuclei function will help us understand how we translate our conditioned personality tendencies into success or failure. In this regard, the caudate nuclei bring signals of salience or significance to the executive who must decide whether to proceed with action and response programs. Each program is composed of segments that require the presence of significant and salient data to trigger behavior; e.g., "If this, then that." Psyche's mental status examination, for instance, is composed of a series of communication behaviors that must be carried out in a logical sequence. If there is a sign of pathology, such as Eric's emotional dissonance, then she has to pursue a particular line of questioning to further define the pathology encountered.

Psyche's caudate processing has to confirm the presence of significant and salient features required for the successful completion of her mental status communication sequence. One set of caudate populations uses limbic signals to prepare behaviors—*get ready*, another set feeds this data back to system consciousness—*get set*, and a third set activates motor schema that regulate the caudate's striatal efferents (basal ganglia output)—*go*! Let's examine Psyche's caudate functions in turn.

One to Get Ready

The caudate integrates amygdalar and catcholamine regulated (drive-cathected) limbic data prior to behavioral release. Two intrinsic caudate populations mediate the prefrontal system's interaction with the limbic system:

1. enkephalin (endogenous opioid) and substance P *patches*
2. acetylcholine and somatostatin *matrix* (Gerfen, 1984)

Enkephalins damp caudate ouput until patches receive signals that libidinal tension will be relieved. This is one reason why some opioids cause a person to lose interest in satisfaction.

Psyche readied her fateful question at a moment of high drive. Her left hemisphere's caudate patches received signals of salience—potential reward—from two sources. The first was from her pleasure loop. Its *nucleus accumbens* transmitted her left amygdala's operantly reward-conditioned salience to her caudate. The left nucleus accumbens transmits salience signals it receives from activated conditioned associations to the left caudate. During pleasure conditioning, *transcription factors* (which turn on a cell's genetic mechanism for synthesizing proteins) are produced in the lateral septum, amygdala, and parahippocampal cortex, but not in the nucleus accumbens (Brown et al., 1992). While these other populations are conditioned, and therefore change their mode of neuronal functioning, the nucleus accumbens merely *transmits salience to the caudate*.

The executive receives hints of impending pleasure when the caudate transmits broad signals of salience to the social subject's intermediate zone. Thus, in one example, Psyche assesses her own socially conditioned somatic reward signals as she tests Eric. Wondering whether she is on the right track, Psyche uses her source memory of a specific event, her mother's joke, to alter her action program. Her daring question conforms to her reconditioned social subject, which is already nearly integrated into her identity.

Confidence comes from using salience properly. Psyche's nucleus accumbens transmits *confidence* in pursuing her mental status examination creatively to her left caudate. When Eric hears Psyche say "one million dollars," his sense of salience is immediately communicated to his caudate by his pleasure loop, but he cannot judge the social relevance of these signals because his left hemisphere's orbital cortex is impaired. Eric has false confidence. Since Eric's left lateral cortex is unimpaired, he understands that the logic of his decision is faulty when Psyche, by a series of questions, leads him to a different conclusion.

Self-esteem comes from using significance properly. Psyche understands the significance of Eric's organic response, because she is looking for it with eagle eyes. Her right hemisphere's caudate patches receive significance signals from two sources. The first comes from her central amygdala, which transmits the fact that Eric's expressions are not engaging. The second comes from her right intermediate zone's assessment of conditioned somatic signals of potential punishment (Gerfen, 1984). To take unjustified significance from her data may distort reality, cause prolonged mental pain, and lower her self-esteem. This is why Psyche is relieved when Eric's communication pattern coincides with her expectation of an organic response.

Two to Get Set

Before she asked the fateful question, Psyche says to herself, "Now, I'll ask him if he wants to get a lot of pleasure without thinking of the consequences." As she composes her actual question, she inserts verbal images from her source memory ("Would you do it for one million dollars?") into her articulatory rehearsal. This is how we get set to act.

While coordinating her articulatory rehearsal—*getting set*—Psyche scrutinizes Eric carefully. She divines a look of almost apathetic detachment, combined with a longing to awaken. By scanning his face and posture one more time, she concludes that he cannot be manipulating her. This makes sense. We prepare our behaviors as much through visual scanning as we do through verbal analysis. Visual scanning is not passive. it is a visual motor search for salience and significance.

The right hemisphere's preparation for response derives from supplementary visual association (SVA) cortex, motor eye cortex, and the superior colliculus (Hikosaka, Sakamoto, and Usui, 1989): "Visual memory and reward contingent eye movements are correlated with increased activity in superior colliculus neurons" (Gerfen, 1992, p. 134). Using these feedbacks, both hemispheres' caudates integrate visual fixation on features as we get set to act.

Caudate patches monitor limbic data during behavioral preparation, while caudate matrix receives reports on whether action and response programs are set. In the Psyche example, our protagonist's left lateral prefrontal cortex assesses that she was correct about Eric. Her supervisory inner speech tells her supplementary motor cortex, "go ahead, ask!" Her left hemisphere's caudate confirms reward signals. So, Psyche's right hemisphere's neocerebellum shifts her attention to her examiners.

And Three to Go

Finally, the caudate integrates behavioral discharge as fateful communications are made. The caudate's path to the striatum, which are subcortical motor regulators, consists of two consecutive glutamate populations (Dure, Young, and Penney, 1991). For this reason, the caudate's behavioral discharge pathway can undergo the LTP, which makes behavioral discharge reliable. In sum, the caudate is the executive's major subcortical feedback integrator of behavioral discharge.

Postscript: Next time, Psyche will have an easier time acting creatively on the basis of what she has learned. Eric did have a meningioma that was impinging on his left hemisphere's orbital frontal cortex. It was removed, and he was eternally grateful to Psyche; and Psyche's sense of her soul—confidence in the integrity and consistency of her subjective origins—was rendered whole by her contact with Eric.

THE CEREBELLUM'S ROLE AS A MOTOR MEMORY BANK

Just as the rhinal cortex, the amygdala, the septum, and the orbital frontal, anterior cingulate and insular cortex together provide a memory bank of conditioned associations for responding to sensory data, so the cerebellum provides a conditioned memory bank for motor associations. These motor associations are the repository of automatic and habituated procedures, which we conduct in perfected sequences without having to actively accompany our fine motor activity with thought. Let us see how the cerebellum develops these functions and how they are fed into a striatal pathway for motor discharge.

The brain and its spinal extension are full of reflexes. Reflexes are formed from irreversible LTP, which "hardwires" a neural circuit. The cerebellum develops hardwired reflexes both pre- and postnatally. We will begin our study of the cerebellum by considering its *reflex formations*.

I have been saying that reflexes are a rudimentary form of motor memory. Let us refer to this form of motor memory as *motor reflex*. The cerebellum builds other motor control functions on this foundation. In the same way that it is essential that any sensory image maintain its physical definition in different contexts, behavioral stability requires a basis for reliable movements. One motor reflex, the *vestibular-ocular reflex* (VOR) tracks visual stimuli. A conditioned reflex, it coordinates automatic adjustments between head position, eye movements, and the vestibular sense. The VOR fires at eleven msecs and uses an irreversibly potentiated path of "floculus" motor neurons that fire when their purkinje inhibitors are lifted (Lisberger, 1994).

In addition to forming the bedrock reflex coordination of movement, the cerebellum develops flexible, personal adaptations. In reciprocal coordination with the rhinal cortex and the basal ganglia, the cerebellum undergoes operant conditioning and consolidates motor memory (Lalond and Botez, 1990). The way this happens is that the cerebellum's conditioned LTP forms motor association networks. These make up a motor memory bank comparable to the rhinal cortex's sensory memory bank.

Moreover, the cerebellum coordinates microshifts in attention. When an animal *orients* to salient place locations, the rhinal cortex's perirhinal neurons fire as the cerebellum lifts their inhibition (Courschesne et al., 1994). How we orient brings up three related questions:

- Is attention a motor or sensory function?
- Is motor memory an action schema or a serial sensory one?
- Is procedure a motor memory or a visual imitation?

Freud believed attention was a motor quality of consciousness (1900). When we introspect, we actively shift focus to complete a thought. I infer that the cerebellum coordinates executive attention to extended motor and sensory networks by selectively lifting inhibitions on both the basal ganglia's motor images and the rhinal cortex's sensory images. When we learn a motor act such as skiing, the first thing we do is attend to our motor schema in a multisensory context.

By associating visual and somesthetic signals with a variety of sequenced motor schema, and by associating vestibular signals with saccades, the cerebellum provides spatial coordinates to these schema. This is how we recognize the integrity of objects when our head is positioned differently in space. If we cannot, we have a problem. A dyslexic, for example, cannot distinguish the letter "p" from the letter "b", because his cerebellum cannot stabilize the letter position. A dyslexic's rotational difficulty is caused by an inability to associate vestibular and saccadic images in space (Levinson, 1988).

How Does Michael Jordan Do It?

Now let us turn to the cerebellum's role in fine tuning motor procedures. Practice makes perfect. When an athlete focuses on each sensory image and each muscle movement in response to the sensory image, he is training—conditioning—his cerebellum. How does Michael Jordan seem to suspend himself in air and have all the time in the world to decide which maneuver would elude the defense while putting the ball in the basket or passing off?

If you watch Michael Jordan, you will see that there is always a conscious starting point for each series of related maneuvers. He starts driving some fifteen or seventeen feet from the basket. If there is an opening he leaps, transfers the ball to the other hand, or not, scoops toward the basket, or pushes the ball up over outstretched hands into the basket. Alternatively, if he starts to drive in the same way and a defender blocks his path, Michael passes the ball behind his back to the trailing Scottie Pippen, or he suddenly pulls back and deftly arches a shot from a set position that is frozen for just an instant before release.

From this particular starting point, Michael has practiced each move thousands of times until it becomes automatic. Each time a move results in a basket, Michael's cerebellum's fine-tuned coordination is positively conditioned. Each alternative cerebellar motor-sensory schema is conditioned so that it has a life of its own.

As Michael leaps, the salient and significant features his saccades detect on the court determine which move his caudate will select as the discharge behavior. After this determination is made at the set point, the *go* in his discharge action uses the visual, vestibular/positional motor schemata that his cerebellum potentiated. As a gifted athlete who tries harder, Michael has a greater repertory of successful moves and a quicker execution. This is why he can be a star.

Fine tuning our motor acts requires that we potentiate our cerebellar motor schema. Once LTP fixes these schema, they are always potentially available. A potentiated schema is permanent, even if we have not used it for a long time. Once stored in the cerebellum, its functional activity can be freshened at need. An adult who rode a bike as a child will pick up the activity and the pleasure in a few trials.

Michael Jordan tried baseball for a while after his father's murder. Perhaps he felt that his father would have wanted him to succeed in baseball. The skills required for baseball and basketball are different, however, and its hard to refine a new set of motor skills at the age of thirty-two. When Michael decided to come back from baseball, his basketball moves were still almost as fresh as they had been when first he was a star.[4]

As we act, the cerebellar output to the striatum compels motor sequencing. Fine-tuned movements result from sequenced, exquisitely reciprocating excitations and inhibitions. Cerebellar motor memory, whether reflex or conditioned, is always implicit—never available to consciousness. Do not bother to ask Michael for an explanation of how he really does it. I did not.

Finally, the cerebellum has a major role to play in *motor priming*. The lateral cerebellum and its subcortical dentate cortex both enlarged in human evolution are highly activated during verbal predication of ongoing action (Leiner, Leiner, and Dow, 1989). Just as the rhinal cortex primes sensory data so that they are available for inclusion in prefrontal representational networks, so the lateral cerebellum primes verbally induced motor acts. The cerebellum primes prefrontal motor schema so that when the supplementary motor cortex uses inner speech to release behavioral programs the schema are ready to structure behavior.

THE DRIVES ARE BEHAVIORAL STATES

We have said that biogenic amine systems regulate prefrontal behavioral states. In this sense, they are drive systems. I now propose that identity's hemispheric duality determines the dichotomous regulation of the catecholamine drives. Thus, the ventral tegmental system's libidinal drive is regulated by the left hemisphere's *consummatory behavioral state*, and the locus ceruleus's aggressive drive is regulated by the right's *reality-vigilant state*. What is instinctual (orientation, vigilance, and vitality) limbically, is drive-state organized prefrontally.[5]

NEUROBIOLOGICAL MECHANISMS OF ANXIETY REGULATION

Classical analysts agree that (1) aggressive and libidinal drives pressure system consciousness to do work, and (2) that anxiety systems regulate these drive pressures. When neuroleptics (antipsychotic major tranquilizers) block ventral tegmental dopamine reception, they both block libidinal drive and tranquilize anticipatory anxiety. When tricyclics or opioids inhibit the locus ceruleus's norepinephrine output, they reduce both aggressive pressure and novelty anxiety. Thus, biogenic amine systems regulate both drive and anxiety.

Analysts also describe a neutral drive that *fuses* aggression and libido (Hartmann, 1964). I propose that this interregulation is the inhibitory effect of serotonin and the facilitatory effect of acetylcholine on the same modules regulated by the catecholamines. Unlike catecholamines, which induce anxiety with increased drive pressure, serotonin induces anxiety when its pressure reduces. This is because serotonin reenforces our inhibitory capacity. Serotonin deficit in the orbital frontal cortex undermines the executive capacity of judgement to withhold behavior until problem solving is complete. This causes what I have called *identity anxiety*. Obsessive-compulsives (Chapter 8) anxiously doubt their own authenticity when they make decisions.

Each biogenic amine neuron synapses with millions of modules in immediate, working, short-term and metamemory systems. Each drive neuron synapses with anxiety discharge regulating neurons in the amygdala and the hypothalamus. Indeed, each biogenic amine neuron is a system itself. For this reason, a progressive destruction of these neurons during later stages of human neoteny trenchantly effects how the brain talks to itself in middle and old age. Beginning early in adult life, our 40,000 dopamine neurons decrease by a significant percentage yearly (Cooper, Bloom, and Roth, 1991).

Biogenic amine systems have evolved an array of different kinds of receptors, including autoreceptors, each with different regulatory effects. Conceivably, as catecholamine systems lose neurons, autoregulation of each system's output downregulates its drive pressure. This may be why we cannot do as much as we age, and why, after a while, this does not bother us.

I propose that each biogenic amine system is functionally tied to a separate form of anxiety regulation. These regulations determine how we process data and the circumstances under which we effectuate behavior. I further propose that each drive system determines a characteristic behavioral state and is mentally regulated by a characteristic anxiety signal.

Freud (1926) concluded that as we develop, anxiety begins to operate as a signal system. Its warning keeps us from having to undergo the profound mental pain that comes with nasty lessons. Let us consider a neural system's basis for anxiety as a signal system *and* as a discharge system. When we cannot discharge drive pressures, each type of anxiety mobilizes a characteristic, hypothalamically induced somatic discharge orchestrated by the amygdala.

Anxiety moves from signal to discharge in steps.[6]

1. Behavioral discharge relieves drive pressure, but
2. failed behavior increases drive pressure, and
3. reports of mild amygdalar discharges are cognized,
4. defenses are mobilized, behavior is altered, and
5. new feedback inhibits amygdalar discharge, or
6. it fails, and the amygdala discharges to the hypothalamus.

When signal anxiety appears, defenses cannot be far behind.

Failed behavior induces the amygdala to negatively condition data at p300, just before data becomes conscious (Halgren, 1992). We sense signal anxiety when we become conscious of failure or novelty. As we will see in Chapter 6, between working memory's epoch, p300, and behavioral discharge (up to two seconds), we mobilize defenses. In anxiety regulation, the prefrontal cortex feedsback directly upon the amygdala's *bed nucleus*. As we saw in Chapter 2, both medial, cingulate (anxiety looped) and intermediate, orbital frontal (emotionally looped) cortexes are directly linked to the amygdala and the lateral hypothalamus.[7]

To sum up, there are three biological forms of anxiety:

1. *Anticipatory anxiety* is triggered by failed dopaminergic consummation. When we try, but "cannot do it," we have to conclude we are in error. Then, to avoid reactive displeasure, we inhibit our dopamine system's pressure.

2. *Vigilance anxiety* is triggered by norepinephrine pressure that yields alarming signifiers. Unrelenting novelty induces the norepinephrine system to elicit mental pain. To avoid this, we inhibit our norepinephrine system's discharge.

3. *Identity anxiety* is triggered when our vitality lapses. When our serotonin system cannot neutralize catecholamine pressures, we reactively inhibit our central acetylcholine system's facilitatory activity. Anxiety is therefore a form of inhibition.

Each anxiety system has its own feedback regulation. Each biogenic amine nucleus interacts with the amygdala to inhibit further drive pressure. Signals from all three anxiety systems can cause the amygdala's bed nucleus to keep anxiety from fulminating into raw, instinctual discharges.[8]

The Consummatory State: Eros' Libidinal Drive

How does the ventral tegmental dopamine system regulate consummatory behavior? The heavy saturation of dopamine receptors throughout the pleasure loop suggests that dopamine evolved as a consummatory system (Blackburn, Pfaust, and Phillips, 1992). Rewarded behavior diminishes the biological need for further action. There is no need to hunt after a hearty meal. After successful behavior, need pressure relaxes, because the reuptake of dopamine blocks further dopamine production (Cooper, Bloom, and Roth, 1991). Thus, the dopamine system's presynaptic autofeedback regulation enhances its consummatory function.

> Dopamine systems increase an animal's preparedness to act by enhancing the capacity of specific stimuli . . . to elicit active skeletal responses, especially when those stimuli are not associated with specific, well defined, previously acquired responses. (Blackburn, Pfaust, and Phillips, 1992, p. 248)

We use the dopamine system to acquire salience in operant conditioning. Moreover, using dopamine receptors as a signal system, the left hemisphere's medial cortex assesses pleasure feedback (Cooper, Bloom, and Roth, 1991; Goldman-Rakic, 1992). When Psyche prepared to ask her dramatic question, she had to overcome anticipatory anxiety that she might make a mistake. The same system that augmented her consummatory behavioral state also gave her the feedback that she could indeed proceed with her course of action.[9,10]

Comparing pleasure signals induced by the ventral tegmental dopamine system with salience signals from the nucleus accumbens, the left hemisphere's anterior cingulate association cortex activates the supplementary association cortex, which begins voluntary behavior. Anticipatory (error) anxiety is triggered when the nucleus accumbens gives the go-ahead to the caudate, while the anterior cingulate cortex gives an opposing message, which causes conflict. Then, the left hemisphere's anxiety loop interrupts behavior (Thomas, 1988).

Libidinal drive sets the tone for the consummatory state of motivated behavioral discharge. Computerized EEG studies show that the left hemisphere processes pleasure.[11] I define the consummatory pressure promoted by the pleasure loop on all three left hemisphere experiential loops as *libidinal drive*.

When Psyche was fully activated toward the consummation of her action plan, her left hemisphere's pleasure loop fired up as

1. her anterior cingulate cortex gave positive somatic signals,
2. her auditory cortex formed her sense impression of her words,
3. her Broca's cortex formed articuleme motor sequences, and
4. her dorsolateral cortex conducted articulatory rehearsal.

After her examination was over, Psyche could relax.

The Vigilant State: Dionysus' Aggressive Drive

Aggressive drive cathects the world's structure. Aggression binds both our sense of who we are in the world and our sense of who rules the world. Unbinding aggression returns us to a primitive state. What is more, our species needs aggressive types such as Dionysus as well as libidinal types such as Psyche and her counterpart, Eros.

Suppose we could take a trip into mythology. Dionysus, the God of wine, could be brutal. He was, after all, the God of the vine, of strangling growth and of binding. The wandering, singing Maenads served him. These women, from whose activities we take the word manic, tore men limb from limb. They represented unbound aggression, which is what they represent to us today. Back in the days when Eastern cults invaded the

Greek world, Dionysus came to Tyre. Legend has it that King Penthius opposed Dionysus. The King, whose job it was to bind aggression, was naturally the first to be dismembered when he opposed the new God. The King's female relatives struck the first blows.

It seems to me that the Maenads who barely, if ever, encompassed their aggression, represent the right hemisphere's unthrottled affect with their wild cries and melodious singing. The Greeks recognized the difference between political liberty and inebriated freedom from restraint. The moral of the Dionysus myth is not difficult to see: when freedom arises from mania or wine, it licenses uninhibited aggression to break rules.

One is reminded of Janice Joplin's intoxicated wail in "Me and Bobby McGee"—"Freedom is just another word for nothing left to lose. Nothing don't mean nothing if it ain't free." When the right amygdala ceases restraint, the norepinephrine system has nothing left to cathect; when the right hemisphere's self disorganizes, there is nothing left to lose.

The amygdala relaxes in all bacchanals, and we see the absence of social restraints at contemporary solstice festivals, at Mardi Gras, Oktoberfest, and in mania itself. Controlled by the right hemisphere's amygdala, the power of aggression restrains or releases pleasure. The social occasions liberate affect symbolically; in war, unbinding goes further than a liberation of affect. The aggression that structures the bond between self and object is released. When combatants see men torn limb from limb or head from body, the battle grows intoxicating. To avoid the pain of rending human bonds, combatants want to savor the blood of those who die. Inquisitions, reigns of terror, and bloodthirsty atavistic warriors are familiar to students of history.

Affect signals the fate of our aggressive cathexis. The stronger our affect, the greater our attempt to both restrain and express our aggression. If affect is unleashed, unheeded, and unabsorbed by self, our self's structure will be dismembered by pain laden with affects. If our affects guide us to be at one with our world, we feel relief and openness to pleasure.

It is not the pathological unbinding of the aggressive drive, however, but its binding—its cathexis of structures and contexts of reality—that interests us here. In this sense, the aim of the aggressive drive is to explore reality, to adapt to its variety, and to form new structures through which to relate to reality. Chief among the structures that we adaptively reorganize is our own affect-assessing, self-representation.

Character adaptation is the aggressive drive's permanent form of stress reduction. By reconditioning ourselves when the demands of reality change, and then by forming new viable structures of self, social self, object representations, and new adaptive procedures, we bind our aggression to new intrapsychic structures. When they work, we are free of stress.

If dopamine autoregulation *decreases* consummatory pressure after need satisfaction, norepinephrine autoregulation *increases* stress response during reality threats (Cooper, Bloom, and Roth, 1991). At the beginning of a stress response, before opioids and other neuromodulators dampen it, the norepinephrine system enhances its own capacity to mediate stress. By prolonging our adaptive responses, a self-regulating stress system enhances our survival. The norepinephrine system regulates the following:

- the spatial location of objects
- classical pain conditioning
- the stress response to novelty

The norepinephrine system increases our vigilant capacity to adaptively explore reality more thoroughly.

Novel data are potentially painful. They stimulate the self to bind affect. Computer EEG studies show the right hemisphere activated, whenever we process painful stimuli or expect punishment. During stress, we have to adaptively find procedures with which to respond to reality. Norepinephrine binds self, social self, and procedural self to their three networks.[12,13,14,15] I define the locus ceruleus' effects on the right hemisphere's three experiential loops as *aggressive drive*.

The Vitality State: Apollo's Neutral Drive

Contrary to popular belief, the Apollonian and Dionysian principles are not opposed. We modulate our affect as much through the auspices of serotonin, which powers the inhibitory force of the neutral drive, and acetylcholine, which powers its facilitatory force, as we do through norepinephrine which binds aggression. Consider seasonal depression in which the dying of the light infiltrates neural systems and promotes depression. There is reason to believe that this effect is mediated by the serotonin system.

The Greeks considered Apollo to be the giver of light, the healer, the truth-teller, and the beneficent soother. He also brought plague and heat-related disease. He symbolized higher consciousness. Driving his fiery steeds through all the disasters the signs of the Zodiac portend, Apollo kept a straight course from dawn to dusk, where others would be consumed. Apollo was the sun. In the present context, he embodies serotonin's power to neutralize our catecholamine drives, which would otherwise lose regulation.

Dylan Thomas urged his dying father to hold on to vitality: "Rage, rage against the dying of the light." The sense of indwelling vitality centers our identity. I will maintain at greater length in Chapter 4 that neutral drive reinforces our sense of vitality. This is what we may intuitively understand about serotonin's contribution to our brains' organization: Apollo must balance Dionysus if adaptation is to be effective.

The raphe nucleus' serotonin (5-HT) system evolved as a diurnal pacemaker. Its helps us sleep at night and be vital in the day. Perhaps because serotonin's precursor, tryptamine, is more highly absorbed after feeding, a big meal promotes sleep. Tryptamine's absorption enhances sleep, and increase serotonin's availability the following day (Cooper, Bloom, and Roth, 1991).

Serotonin, then, is the essence of vitality: it facilitates motivated motor responses and damps distracting sensory and emotional stimuli during high activity periods (Cooper, Bloom, and Roth, 1991). Serotonin enhances the capacity for selective inhibition during attentional states when the executive unifies items of consciousness that are essential for problem solving. Serotonin increases the attentive capacity to evaluate salients and signifiers during both consummatory and vigilant states. Thus, serotonin is necessary for focused behavior.[16]

Serotonin density is high in the emotion-binding, socially conditioned, orbital frontal association cortex (Arato et al., 1991). Serotonin levels are also relatively high synoptically within the whole amygdaloid complex (Amaral, 1992). Serotonin also regulates hippocampal formation onstream processing, since destruction of the brain's serotonin receptors causes more data entry (Ehlers, Wall, and Chaplin, 1991). This means that serotonin mobilizes perceptual defense. Thus, while the executive reflects on the social relevance of its orbital frontal data assessment, serotonin selectively effects that data's access to processing. I define the raphe system's enhancement of the left hemisphere's response to salience—combined with its stabilizing effect on the right's affect and percept processing—as the *neutral drive*.

PSYCHOANALYTIC DRIVE REGULATION: A NEURAL SYSTEMS PERSPECTIVE

To gather our conclusions in psychoanalytic terms: as they operate together, the left hemisphere's consummation and the right's pain relief make up the "nirvana principle" of drive regulation (Freud, 1915). Drive pressures system consciousness to process data in order to solve problems of need and response. Effective problem solving discharges action or response programs, which reduces drive pressures. At the same time, the aggressive and libidinal drives are regulated by anticipatory and vigilant signal anxiety systems.

The neutral drive balances the emotional systems. The left hemisphere's emotional system exerts motivational pressure; the right's exerts affect pressure. Neutralization is the bilateral orbital frontal association cortex's capacity to evaluate somatic emotional signals in the context of conditioned associations that are relevant to behavior's past results.

Hartmann believed that drive neutralization is an adaptive function (1954). The adaptive function may be seen in its neural context as the capacity to use past emotional and social experience in the service of present-day problem solving. The fact that the serotonin system balances response and need makes it a stabilizing factor in adaptation.

While norepinephrine contributes to LTP induction in the hippocampus, and while dopamine is sometimes inhibitory and sometimes facilitatory (Kuba and Kumamoto, 1990), serotonin inhibits hippocampal LTP (Corradetti et al., 1992). Thus, adequate serotonin ensures that we can solve problems without resorting to the formation of new source memory. Serotonin, therefore, promotes stable emotional processing in the present, and it preserves the value of past emotional experience. This is, in large measure, what we mean by the neutralizing function.

STRESS REGULATION

Sapolsky echoes Hartmann's conception of maladaptation in a brain mediated, psychological stress mechanism: "Critical factors . . . for psychological stress . . . *include loss of control, loss of predictability, loss of outlets for frustration, and a perception of things worsening*" (1992, p. 296, italics in original).

What happens when the drives and their anxiety systems cannot regulate the brain's experiential loops in (1) stress, (2) neoteny, and (3) syndrome formation? When neural systems destabilize, biogenic amine systems and neurohormonal peptides release LTP rather than restrain it. During severe stress, the amygdala prodigiously produces neurohormones which directly and indirectly cause the hippocampus to trigger the formation of massive new event and episode source memory. Therefore, it seems to me that when up and down regulation of biogenic amine systems and peptide receptors fail to regulate experience, LTP increases until distributed systems can be reregulated by the drives.

THE ROOTS OF EMOTIONAL ORGANIZATION

The scale of new conditioning and new memory formation can become massive, hence emotionally organizing during trauma or fixation. The mass conditioning effect is even greater during developmental stage changes, which are the topic of the next chapter. Then, it is the neural systems themselves, and new somatic and hormonal sources of stimulation, that provide the impetus for LTP. Stage changes evoke massive LTP, necessary and sufficient to reorganize succeeding periods of life.

In the next chapter, I will argue that recurrent bursts of LTP in development, trauma, fixation, or in syndrome formation permanently condition amygdaloid pathways and modify hippocampal quadrisynaptic loop pathways, and that all information processing systems adapt reciprocally. We can take an example from ordinary psychopathology to show how *repetition* of trauma is the key to reorganized perceptual representation.

Freud said that for a preoedipal boy who has a symbiotic relationship with his mother's body, traumatic, repeated perception of the fact that the mother does not have a penis induces fetishism (1927). The most innocent detail associated with the traumatic perception—such as the foot— becomes the overdetermined signifier and salient for the missing penis. Reifying a nonentity (a special form of perceptual denial) becomes the prototype for the formation of other symbolic constructs that can hide painful reality. During the first episode of trauma, the amygdala conditions the images of trauma. In later episodes, the orbital frontal cortex cannot accommodate to the induction of traumatic perceptions and affects. Fetishists and perverts are profoundly fixated to infantile conditioning.

The narcissism men hold for their most prized possession can also undergo a characterological fate. When the little boy sees his father's penis and compares it with his own, the strongest wish for seeing his own penis in the father's mold can give rise to the phallic narcissism of the athlete. Forever after, the little boy as man may play at performances meant to show his prowess. In order not to believe he might be superman, Michael Jordan, or some other heroic father imago, the little boy has to realize that he will gradually grow into his manhood. As I said at the beginning of this chapter, athletes who are fixated on trying to force the issue are likely to fail.

Chapter 4

How We Become Who We Are:
Incarnating Psychoanalysis

As a . . . common feature of neural apoptosis, there is considerable
overproduction of the primary neurons of the nervous system . . .
there emerges a competition for synaptic connections with neighbor-
ing neurons, and those less connected are eliminated. Such develop-
mental pruning is viewed as an adaptive means of shaping, selecting
for optimal wiring of the nervous system, and correcting errors.
(Sapolsky, 1992, p. 147)

INTRODUCTION:
A NEURAL VIEW OF THE STAGES OF LIFE

During the prolonged maturation that we call *development,* neural systems stage periodic advances that we call neoteny. Neoteny unfolds through
periodic advances induced by high frequency LTP. At the advent of a new
stage, high frequency LTP massively reconditions the limbic system. Then,
during consecutive periods of slow consolidation, from medial to lateral,
prefrontal synaptogenesis coordinates the capacity to deal with new forms
and structures of experience. Each rapid stage advance and its slow periodic
consolidation brings volumes of experience into the parallel processing,
prefrontal associational networks.

While it is awe inspiring to realize that each brain records decades of
experience, it is more amazing that separate volumes of experience talk to
each other within a single brain. Coordinating our development is a life's
work. The job entails successive reorganization of neural systems triggered by:

- the corpus callosum's maturation at eighteen to thirty-six months,
  which synthesizes a *bilaterally* coordinated prefrontal system;
- neocortical maturation in the oedipal and latency stages;
- preadolescent and adolescent neurohormonal maturation;

- adult adaptation to experience; and
- loss of biogenic amine and hippocampal glutamate neurons during aging.

While all of these neural forces normally reorganize intrapsychic identity in their proper sequence, neuro- and psychopathological syndromes can reorganize identity in any stage of life.

In the language of animal studies, *imprinting* is one-time learning soon after birth. For a long time now, scientists who study animal behavior have wondered how imprinting works. LTP and imprinting have much in common. If the reader will make me his leader, as the motherless duckling follows the little boy who happens on him at the critical moment, we will start an adventure.

Imprinting is nothing less than the formation of fixed neural pathways. The duckling imprints a leader when excitotoxicity destroys the access of all other images to his following system. Using neural Darwinism as his buttress, Greenough (1994) argues that imprinting's programmed excitotoxicity (apoptosis) is a form of LTP that determines permanent neural pathways by excluding all but the functionally viable. Imprinting fixes the intake of experience over functional neural pathways that can not vary after they have been established.

I am going to argue here that *excitotoxicity determines neoteny.* There is cogent evidence that we will look at presently, and which parents know intuitively, that the infant's neural systems' organization is jolted almost daily by the neural induction of excitotoxic LTP. The infant's life is definitely more complex than the duckling's.

During infancy, new bursts of LTP come fast and furiously. Parents watch their infants undergo neurally generated advances every day. Biogenic amine systems regulate these advances. Experience coordinates potentiation in lateral, medial, and intermediate prefrontal networks with thalamic, limbic, basal ganglia, and cerebellar conditioning. In this way, the infant integrates behavioral states with autonomic ones.

LONG-TERM POTENTIATION
AS A DEVELOPMENTAL MECHANISM

As we will see, LTP-induced neuron selection in the fetal stage creates neural structures. Postnatal, experientially regulated selection determines the neural foundations of explicit, associational memory. What is excluded from explicit memory is as important as what is included. Early life experience determines that we will not hear some sounds, see some sights, taste some tastes, smell some smells, feel some potential feelings, and ever understand some potential meanings. Most of us will never pronounce the guttural *gh*, see the shades of gray in an eskimo landscape, or understand the world like a Renaissance man.

A sample of converging research into hippocampal excitotoxicity shows that LTP forms functional connections.[1] I propose that both high and low amounts of LTP prune neural connections.

As a general rule of hippocampal neural development, overstimulated excitatory synapses lead to apoptosis—programmed neuron death, while understimulated ones lead the presynaptic neuron to relinquish its link with the postsynaptic neuron. Thus, functional excitatory system neural linkages depend on optimal LTP. Only functionally appropriate glutamate synapses structure a particular brain's development (Sapolsky, 1992).

The development of vertebrate visual systems illustrates how LTP determines the functional connection of modules: "an activity-dependent competition between axonal inputs for . . . postsynaptic neurons is respon-sible . . . for the establishment of orderly sets of connections" (Shatz, 1991, pp. 734-735). LTP makes activity-dependent connections permanent, when pre- and postsynaptic neurons are coupled through NMDA receptor activation in critical periods of development (Slater et al., 1992).

Thus in the dense changes of infant development, LTP determines the formation of viable neural links. High production of NMDA receptors during periods of rapid synaptic growth correlate with LTP quantity, increased neuronal plasticity, and functional readiness (McDonald and John-ston, 1990). Glutamate populations account for the volumetric evolutionary increase in the human brain's prefrontal cortex, supplementary association cortex, supplementary visual cortex, and in the phylogenetically older hip-pocampal formation, orbital frontal association cortex, and anterior cingu-late association cortex (Rapoport, 1990). This supports my thesis that ample assessment cortex provides the foundation for reflective consciousness.

Glutamate populations provide the experientially triggered, expanded memory networks that characterize human mental activity. Hippocampal glutamate transmission peaks at twelve to eighteen months to levels three times that found in adults (Slater et al., 1992). The volume of NMDA receptors and vulnerability to hypoxia and epileptogenesis both peak at this time. The surplus indicates that functional memory networks are forming and that overactive LTP prunes exuberant links (Slater et al., 1992).

STRESS

Sustained and severe stress can damage the primate hippocampus. Moreover, glucocorticoids alone can damage both the fetal and adult hip-pocampus (Sapolsky, 1992, p. 314). Stress is another concept, like drive, that straddles mind and brain. We will consider questions about how stress affects the following:

- neural systems development
- experiential processing
- the formation of emotionally organized source memory
- personality development
- vulnerability to syndrome formation

In Chapters 1 through 3, we concluded that biogenic amines systems, amygdala, hippocampal formation, and prefrontal cortex together determine the formation of working neural networks. We learned that the degree of stress determines whether the hippocampus and the prefrontal system can develop ample networks for explicit processing, or whether large portions of neural resources succumb to the formation of conditioned implicit networks that remain forever inaccessible. We also learned that some individuals are destined to become fine cognitive thinkers and others, such as Titus, to remain more primitive, conditioned beings. Now, we will ask, how does each individual develop a tendency toward maturation or regression?

In concert with the hypothalamic pituitary axis (HPA), the amygdala controls the hippocampus' response to stress by regulating the hippocampus' local neurohormonal milieu. The hippocampus, in turn, modulates our cognitive response to stress through its rich fields of glucocorticoid and other intracellular receptors. To see this, we must remember that stress is not only a mechanism that determines our physiological response to life's duress; it is involved in the formation and reformation of neural structures, particularly in the hippocampus.[2]

The stress system, adaptive hippocampal circuits, and memory formation are linked from the beginning. It follows that good enough—sufficiently stimulating, but not overstimulating—infant experience induces the development of a flexible, hippocampal stress system. Appropriate development of the infant's hippocampal glutamate systems enables the stress system to bind experience through explicit, reliable memory formation.

If stress regulation through corticosteroid effects on receptors within hippocampal excitatory neurons determines how memory forms, then memory is an experiential record of the revision of neural structure. Explicit memory forms after hippocampal CA 3 and CA 1 fields' glucorticoid receptors have developed the capacity to absorb stress signals without inducing excitotoxicity. When hippocampal glucocorticoid receptors cannot absorb stress effects, hippocampal overpotentiation can transfer potentiation to prefrontal networks.

Transfer potentiation induces primitive identity formation in prefrontal networks, which is hard to modify by later experience. Object relations theorists are right to say, then, that high infant stress determines the formation of highly conditioned introjects that have a life of their own.

Animal studies show that restraint stress (no escape) profoundly decreases limbic processing. If there is absolutely no escape, then there is no point in learning a lesson. The best thing is just to lay low, which is what happens when an animal stops processing new experience. The animal becomes depressed.

I believe that beginning in infancy, social subordination acts as restraint stress. A person who is abandoned by authority, helpless and hopeless economically, and subordinated in his family and social relations undergoes restraint stress. If these deprivations render the use of identity to solve problems futile, the hippocampus neurophysiologically inhibits ongoing cognitive processing.

As the research cited in Chapters 2 and 3 shows, in infancy, developing amygdaloid paths coordinate (1) mild, (2) moderate, (3) prolonged, and (4) severe stress responses. Each stress response characteristically effects the formation of new memory.

Mild Stress

Mild stress stimulates our adaptation to novelty. It increases both the HPA output of cortisone releasing factor (CRF) and the local amygdalar output of CRF. In addition to releasing pituitary cortisone, CRF also induces new learning by activating the locus ceruleus. Activating the norepinephrine system, in turn, facilitates explicit hippocampal processing and pressures the prefrontal system to explore novelty.[3]

Acute Stress

Acute stress, in contrast to mild, damps explicit processing. This ensures that during acute trauma, CA 1 neurons will not form source memory. In acute stress, amygdalar, aversive conditioning increases while new learning decreases. A second, similar bout of acute stress, however, will increase explicit processing and promote nasty lessons. *"Don't you ever put that bobby pin in the electric socket again!"* The first episode just conditions us.

Prolonged Moderate Stress

Prolonged moderate stress downregulates CA 3 processing so that less data can be processed. The mossy fibers that lead to the CA 3 fields respond to cortisone by developing a presynaptic glutamate inhibition

(McEwen et al., 1992). These fibers simply stop signaling the CA 3 fields to contextualize data. This inhibition can even cause the CA 3 dendrites to undergo atrophy. This mechanism can affect the clinical course of post-traumatic stress disorder and chronic depression.[4]

Severe Stress

Severe stress induces a genome-activating, hypercortisol response that triggers massive LTP in the hippocampus (McEwen et al., 1992). Unlike the damping of CA 1 neurones by their glucocorticoid receptors in single episodes of moderate stress, in severe stress cortisone effects the genome to increase glutamate production. Thus, severe stress sets the stage for increased hippocampal LTP:

> . . . glucocorticoids exacerbate the (glutamate)/NMDA/calcium cascade of degeneration . . . disrupt hippocampal energetics, most plausibly by inhibiting glucose transport. This produces a mild energy deficit in neurons, one that is readily survived under normal circumstances. However, when this deficit occurs at the time of an insult . . . steps of the cascade are augmented because of the energy deficit. (Sapolsky, 1992, p. 256)

Just as experimenters induced kindling (a locally lowered seizure thresh-old) through erratic electrical stimulation of the hippocampus, so, I conceive, prolonged or repeated severe stress induces CA 1 LTP that forms profuse source memory. As we saw in Chapter 2, novel, highly charged data induce high frequency input into both the deep and the superficial route to the hippocampus. This intense activation overcomes GABA and peptide inhibitions and induces LTP in the *quadrisynaptic loop* of dentate, CA 3, CA 1, and subiculum (Jones, 1993).

How Do We Reconcile the Oedipal Stage with Neoteny?

A developing *second signal system* during early and middle childhood superimposes a second, hierarchical, prefrontal assessment system on the first experiential system. Neglecting this neural determinant, psychoanalysis understands the oedipal reorganization and its socialization in latency as the building of a first, living floor over the foundations of young childhood and the basement of infancy. Because this living floor has its own multimodal networks that facilitate cognition, the child is partly protected from frequent floods in the basement. Those floods excited the limbic system and forced neural systems to advance at a rapid pace in infancy and young childhood.

The advent of the second signal system is a revolution within an evolution. The movement from young childhood to childhood per se is a dysjunction, comparable to the effect of the computer information revolution on a still evolving industrial revolution. It is as if the brain's system of transporting data by train or car, had added an airlink with computerized centers of operations. After the oedipal advent, we only need the train or car to get to the airport. By this I mean the prefrontal cortex, with its distributed neocortical networks, needs less input from the hippocampus. Thus, around age four, after the maturation of neocortex, higher cortical functions maintain their autonomy, despite brain damage (Luria, 1980).

While object relations theorists emphasize the continuity of development, orthodox Freudians emphasize the discontinuity. For them, the oedipal fantasies completely revamp the previous instinctual life. This disagreement, more that the dispute about a trauma- versus a fantasy-based theory of psychopathology separates these two subdisciplines. I think both perspectives are correct, but the Freudian perspective, staying closer to neural development, is closer to the truth.

Childhood development is punctuated by periodic developments of new semantically organized cognitive operations. In latency, the brain synthesizes semantic networks, which generate abstract generalization. Creating a linguistically organized identity, the second signal system forms a socialized vehicle for identity. Social language informs the executive how to proceed with minimal danger and failure. Social communication—one executive's language to the other's—becomes the medium of problem solving.

The second signal system's executive develops the capacity for *reflection*, a hierarchical structure for consciousness. This doubling of assessment—the assessment of assessments—is further amplified in adolescence when neurohormonal development extends the range of prefrontal assessment synapses. Evolution left our brains vulnerable to epilepsy and syndrome formation. But it also built plasticity into our higher cortical metafunctions. Plasticity provides the capacity to bridge troubled waters.

TERMS FOR HOW WE BECOME WHO WE ARE

Social and cognitive scientists, neuroscientists, and psychoanalysts have each produced a terminology that serves their own disciplines. Indeed, subdisciplines in each field have developed their own special vocabularies. By understanding that we are all dealing with different manifestations of brain structure, we can develop a shared terminology that can enrich each field. In this connection, I note that ego psychologists who study child development, traditionally integrate neural system's concepts with cognitive and psychoanalytic concepts.

D.W. Winnicott, Rene Spitz, Jean Piaget, Anna Freud, Margaret Mahler, Heinz Kohut, and Dan Stern exemplify this tradition in ego psychology. The terms for metafunctions and for identity zones presented in my structural functional model, which I call the Acropolis of the Mind (see Figure 1.1) are culled from their work and from the current literature. Many of the terms are translated from Mahler's and Stern's terms for ego development. My terms are consistent with the following:

- Winnicott's (1965) *true and false self* contrasts subjective identity (left hemisphere) with objective identity (right hemisphere).
- Spitz's embryological concept, *neurobiological unfolding* (1957), sees identity unfold in innate, progressive stages.
- Piaget's *assimilative and accommodative* periods (1954) of cognitive development contrast subjective data intake (left hemisphere) with objective reality-imitation (right).
- Kohut's *self-object* (1971) sees narcissistic identity as based on inter-subjective identifications (left hemisphere).

These psychological theories add to the cumulative framework for understanding each hemisphere's forms of identity organization.

Descartes' Dream of Identity

How do we achieve a new sense of identity in moments of epiphany? How do we access the Acropolis of our Mind? The iconography of this book is more than a set of monuments to mythology: It is a guide to the accessible roots of our identity. In traumatic identity crises, we have to rebuild our identity in order to face our future. At crisis points in our lives, we reflect on our identity, and consciously decide whether we can undertake the monumental change required to recreate ourselves.

"I think, therefore I am," Descartes' famous reflection on his identity, is a watershed in our collective sense of who we are. Let us take an interlude and explore how it might be that Descartes came to his crucial realization. Descartes recreates himself in what Freud (1900) called *a dream from above . . .* what I will call *a dream of identity.*

Then, during the night, when all was fever, thunderstorms, panic, phantoms rose before the dreamer. He tried to get up to drive them away. But he fell back, ashamed of himself, feeling troubled by a great weakness in his right side. All at once a window in the room opened. Terrified, he felt himself carried away by the gusts of a violent wind, which made him whirl around several times on his left foot . . .

Dragging himself staggering along, he reached the buildings of the college in which he had been educated. He tried desperately to enter the chapel to make his devotions. At that moment, some people passed by. He wanted to stop in order to speak to them; he noticed that one of them was carrying a melon . . .

Then Descartes awoke and fell back to sleep, dreaming, "*Quod vitae sectabor iter?*" A man appeared and made him read "Est et non" (it is and is not). Descartes persuaded himself "that it was the Spirit of Truth which had chosen to open all the treasures of science to him by this dream. (Editor's note, *Freud's Collected Works*, vol. XXI, pp. 200-201)

An allegory from the Acropolis of the Mind is an apt metaphor for Descartes' dream. Zeus hurls bolts of identity realization. Athena marshalls semantic reasoning to find pleasure. Artemis focuses objectified representations to relieve pain. Wrestling with the left and right of his identity in *a dream from above*—an identity synthesis while falling asleep and waking—Descartes':

- subject (Aphrodite) integrates his body's pleasure (in salience of a melon), which signals libidinal discharge,
- self (Perseus) integrates his body's pain as he whirls and staggers on his left foot and tries to assess his affect signals while he discharges aggression,
- social subject (Psyche) integrates his source memories of devotion as he assesses his past social pleasures,
- social self (Dionysus and Maenads) integrates his phantom past selves into a realization of the truth of his existence,
- agent (Hermes) integrates his search for semantic reason,
- procedural self (Arachne) integrates the percepts that hold the treasures of science.

Each of these six integrations contributes to a unified statement of identity. "I—am—knowing—me—myself—exists." Of course, Descartes' need to avoid solitude and address others creates a more elegant sentence: "I think, therefore I am." Only then could Descarte fall asleep. We are all insomniacs when we fear we will lose ourselves in a darkness we equate with chaos.

"Est et non"—it is and it is not—is the cogent thesis of Descartes' reflections on his identity, and perhaps it relates to his struggle to define geometric functions. We see from his dream of right-sided devotions and left-sided sinning that Descartes attempts to regulate his body's emotional signals through the formation of pure reason. Descartes' dream from above is a dream of his newly revised identity holding back chaos.

The hypnogogue states of falling asleep and the pompnogogue states of waking open a window into the flux of identity. Through it, we watch the imagery of our intrapsychic identity fall apart with the onset of sleep and coalesce as we wake up. The entrance to sleep is paved with the cognition that yields its content to sleep. When a person invests his whole identity in solving a problem, sleep remains suspended in a hypnogogue.

Not unlike Descartes' hypnogogue as he is wrestling with his identity and with a scientific problem, only half falling asleep by the fire, Kekule, the discoverer of the carbon ring, blended his hypnogogic imagery with his preoccupying problem. In this state, Kekule saw the image of six carbon molecules align themselves in a ring—a ring of fire—that reawakened him with his solution.

Dreams from above, then, are images of identity wrestling with problems that suspend the entrance into slow wave sleep. One recalls Jacob falling asleep in great turmoil and struggling to wrest his consciousness from the angel of death. The traumatized fall into identity fluxes and flashbacks in their hypnogogues. They relive their trauma as they struggle with insomnia even as they succumb to slow wave sleep. Indeed our hypnogogic and hypnopompic states pervade our later dream sleep. Freud (1900) noted that these states are incorporated into our dream imagery, a phenomenon he called "the Silberer phenomenon," after its discoverer.

For us all, identity synthesizes reflection, and reflection synthesizes identity in every sentence. For the brain's inner communication, each sentence is solipsistic. Each sentence we compose informs our executive of the state of each of our identity regulating zones; uttered, it communicates the same to others. We continually renarrate our identity as we go along in life. As we go along, Descartes' identity storm can serve as a paradigm for the experience of changing one's identity, whether in neoteny, psychotic restitution, or in creative pursuits.

PSYCHOANALYTIC STRUCTURAL THEORY

The study of the neural systems' development after birth is the royal road to psychoanalytic structural theory. As students of psychoanalysis know, Freud (1900) tried to reconcile mind and brain in his *topographic model* of structured data processing. This model shows how data becomes explicit as they progress from subconscious to preconscious to conscious. In this model

- data enters the brain through the sensory apparatus, and discharges behaviorally through the motor apparatus;
- system-consciousness is a (prefrontal) sense organ for neural assessment of other neurons' functions; and
- system-consciousness mediates between sensory assessment and motor (behavioral) preparation.

Surrendering to a *clinical* science of the mind, as he became preoccupied with the cancer of his jaw in 1921, Freud produced his well-known *structural theory:* id, ego, and superego (1923).

We will incarnate topographic and structural theory in the present model. I think Freud would have approved this project.

Let us consider the brain's *vertical* (limbic to prefrontal) and *horizontal* (by zones) organization. Vertically, the four data-processing systems—*immediate memory, working memory, short-term memory,* and *metamemory*—replicate data processing in Freud's topographic model: *unconscious, preconscious, attentive,* then *conscious.* Horizontal structure analyzes data in parallel emotional, social, and cognitive neural loops in each hemisphere. The neuroscience literature yields the following terms for *metafunctions* that horizontally regulate the prefrontal zones:

- *Executive functions* perform transcallosal syntheses.
- *Supervisory functions* integrate the left hemisphere's zones.
- *Observing functions* integrate the right hemisphere's zones.

Thus, the executive, supervisory, and observing metafunctions supraordinately organize reflective intrapsychic identity. Together, they generate a sense of reflection on assessment: being outside the mind in the social world and within the mind.

HOW ID, SUPEREGO, AND EGO FIT
INTO A NEURAL SYSTEM'S MODEL

Metafunctions are assessed assessments—reflective, cognitive structures—infused with a sense of identity rather than a sense of direct experience. There are metafunctions that assess identity states in each horizontal zone. The medial zones reflect on emotional and affect signals and on anxiety signals: "I feel good." The intermediate zones reflect on socially conditioned signals: "I am ashamed of myself," or "You should feel guilty." The lateral zones reflect on states of agency or procedure: "I want to buy that," or "How do I find your house?" The executive metafunction unifies all the assessments. Thus, the executive supraordinately responds to anxiety and emotional signals and to signals of shame and guilt by mobilizing defenses that modulate data processing and behavior.

The persistence of amygdala-conditioned intermediate zone, discharge tendencies gives the *id* its power. A libidinal, *fixated* tendency leads to *acting out*, while an aggressive *traumatized* tendency ends in *repetition compulsion*. Acting out and repetition compulsion are fixated and traumatized behaviors that evade executive regulation. All this is to say that when the executive cannot assess data's relevance, the id has its way.

I posit a *dual hemisphere superego: a left ego ideal and a right superego proper*. I call these *Type 1 and Type 2 superego functions,* respectively. Because the superego regulates the id's activated mass of conditioned pleasure and pain associations, the superego senses the state of our pleasure and pain. Because our left hemisphere anticipates, the *ego ideal* pulls us toward a *perfectible future*. Because the right hemisphere realizes, the *superego proper* rules us from the experience of the *past's pain.*

Identifications are the residue of social conditioning. From massive social identifications, the superego forms a hierarchical emotional regulatory system. When the superego signals shame (Type 1) or guilt (Type 2), we experience somatic signals, such as shame's blush or guilt's clench, as if they arose from an external, socially prohibiting source. The common experience of childhood tells us that the superego gives rise to somatic signals whenever our intentions (to act sexually) or responses (to the temptation to cheat or steal) are felt to be in conflict with the social requirements of external authority.

The superego uses emotional feedback from ongoing problem solving to regulate mood states. When subjective confidence diminishes, shame inhibits intentions. When self-esteem wanes, guilt inhibits social responses. The superego prolongs the inhibition of drive pressure.

For many people, the superego's social mediation remains ambiguously inside and outside the mind. Thus, shame or guilt are easily projected onto others. Many people choose friends or mates who have qualities disowned by the person's own identity. The interpersonal reciprocity of superego functions is intrinsic to couples' and families' equilibria. For instance, one "moral patient" chose a dishonest business partner. His partner kept the books. At a certain point in his therapy, the patient looked at the books and found that his partner had cheated both the IRS and himself. It was easier for him to break up with the friend than it was to own up to his own impulses to cheat.

The ego is a set of lateralized higher cortical functions that enable problem solving. The ego's way is assessment of cathexis—the salience or significance of associations. Distributed perceptual links in each modality convey the cathexis that signals the quantity and quality of drive pressures that we have to consider in prioritizing behaviors. My dog, for instance, begs for chocolate chips until she is sated. Then the chips lose their salience. Their conditioned latent cathexis—the nucleus accumben's orienting response to their smell and to the associated crinkle of cellophane—lasts forever.

From infancy onward, every problem we try to solve requires the assessment of cathexis. The formation of cathexis increases when neural capacities come into the developmental stream. For instance, my six-month-old granddaughter tried and tried to crawl, and she cathected her crawling movements with pleasure as she reached for salient objects. In adult life too, libidinal drive continues to create salience and to animate motivation during problem solving. Consider Kekule's sense of beauty and pleasure in the solution of his scientific problem.

Because lateral metafunctions reflect on cognitive identity, when we *apperceive*, we *know* we perceive. When we reflect, we know we are thinking, and when we experience volition, we know we will act. *"We know"* implies the reflective synthesis that shows that cognitive metafunctions are identity functions.

DYNAMICS: HOW NEURAL SYSTEMS CONFLICT

We become aware of another person's conflict when that person makes inconsistent statements. Therapists know that *confronting* inconsistency arouses defenses, annoyance, and rationales. The patient reacts like a traveler who pulls his coat more closely around him when the wind blows. By suspending disbelief, but following each inconsistency to its emotional core, the therapist inevitably finds the patient conflicted about his own identity. If the patient wants the feeling of freedom that goes with being coatless, but he is insecure about getting sick, then two renderings of his identity are in conflict. Only then can the therapist make an interpretation that helps the person take off his coat and become a patient, e.g., "You need to depend on yourself when there is no one to be warm to you."

Freud thought conflict inevitable when psychosexual development abuts social regulation. Oral, anal, urethral, and genital zones progressively produce somatic pressures in alternating libidinal (left hemisphere) and aggressive (right) phases (1901). These somatic pressures inevitably conflict with social and interpersonal forces, as well as with one another. They become socially conditioned. The pressures reduce when

- lovemaking recapitulates and resolves them,
- they are sublimated in social participation,
- they animate character traits, and
- they enter the dynamics of symptom formation.

The previously mentioned physician, who made love out of duty rather than desire, adhered to anal, rather than to genital, organization of his drives. His wife sensed she was a burden, and her lovemaking reciprocated the anal pattern. The couple engaged in a power struggle and in mutual sadomasochistic acting out in place of genital sexuality. The aggressive cathexes of the anal period of each drove a wedge in the relationship and into each person's own sense of integrity.

This dynamic view of psychosexual maturation is anathema to social fundamentalists. For instance, believing that conflict is socially, politically, or economically motivated, dogmatic communists rejected the view that intrapsychic conflicts are biologically inevitable. As a result, the great investigator of higher cortical functions, A. R. Luria, hid his psychoanalytic view of dynamics behind a thick layer of Pavlovian social conditioning. Ironically, many Eastern European nations are undergoing a rebirth of psychoanalytic belief in the biological determination of conflict, while these beliefs wane in the West.

HORIZONTAL AND VERTICAL CONFLICTS

The neural system's dynamic view of conflicts includes: (1) vertical conflicts between limbic and prefrontal systems, and (2) horizontal conflicts among parallel processing zones. Both the prefrontal and the limbic system are socially and neurobiologically regulated. The prefrontal system is regulated by the drives and by belief systems, while the limbic system is socially conditioned.

Vertical conflicts between system consciousness and earlier processing systems are regulated by the defenses of *denial and repression*, which keep unwanted emotions and cognitions out of articulatory preparation for behavior. Here the anxiety systems automatically respond to the pressures for behavior with signals that mobilize defenses to channel behaviors in familiar patterns. We will see later that these defenses begin at p300 (300 msecs), when data becomes potentially conscious.

Horizontal conflict is experienced in identity. The caveat "this is not me" or "I cannot do that," often precedes the onset of *identity anxiety.* Freud called the signal system that protects the integrity of intrapsychic identity *superego anxiety* (1923). The feeling of being abandoned by one's own indwelling superego is ineffably dreadful chaos. Thus, the second signal system's superego comes to hierarchically regulate the primary system's emotional and anxiety signal systems.

To illustrate horizontal conflict consider the case of a man who has cancer, which is denied by his *social self*, because to accept it would undermine his sense of *self-esteem* and his patriarchal family authority. At the same time, his *self* receives distressing *affect signals*, which even make their way into his dreams, without recruiting wakeful self-observation. Here, the self and the social self are in conflict, and the observer mediates by promoting partial denial.

Horizontal, intrapsychic identity conflicts are now the province of two specialized forms of psychoanalytic theory:

- *Self-psychology* (I would call it *subject-psychology*) deals with left hemisphere conflicts. These narcissistic conflicts are the province of self-psychology. They undermine the left hemisphere's realm of ambition, talent, and fixity of goals.
- *Object-relations* theory deals with conflict between self and object representations: Right hemisphere conflicts induce interpersonal boundary issues, identity diffusion, and identifications with the aggressor, all of which destabilize the personality.

Thus, horizontal identity conflicts manifest incompatibility among parallel identity zones or between the two hemispheres.

Luria noticed that when one is talking, the energy available for acting is reduced. He deduced that different brain systems share energy resources. Because the drive energy deployed in the ego's initiating, thinking, expressing, reacting, imitating and emoting is limited and must be equilibrated among zones, horizontal conflicts arise between hemispheres or among working zones. *Horizontal conflicts* mediated by the superego, induce primitive defenses that save aggressive energy. Thus, *projection and projective identification, displacement, condensation, splitting, and fragmentation* exclude large bodies of data from assessment. One deploys less bound aggression by concluding, "The devil made me do it."

The Case of Echo

Let us explore vertical *and* horizontal conflicts in a case vignette, using compatible neural systems' and psychoanalytic terms. The reader has to be mindful that in the brain horizontal and vertical conflicts are inextricably linked. This exercise will enhance the reader's use of the text's terms. The case reverberates to the myth of Echo, the daughter of Juno. Echo was fated by her mother's envy to love a narcissistic man.

The present-day case of "Echo and Juno" is classic in the sense that it illustrates a psychological reality. Many women feel they cannot express themselves because their relationships with their mothers train them in diffidence. We approached this concept when we described Psyche's imaginary board exam. Like Psyche, Echo could not speak for herself. She had been made diffident by Juno's infernal reproaches. Because her supervisory function was weak, Echo lacked narcissistic integrity.

In the background of this story, Juno had grown up with the sense that her own mother did not love her. When Juno was seventeen, she allowed a successful older man to impregnate her with Echo so that he would marry her, and give her social standing in the community. That would put Juno's mother to shame. When Echo was five years old and in school, Juno repudiated her husband. He left her although he tried to maintain contact with Echo. Juno would not allow Echo to say she loved her father. Indeed, Juno blamed Echo for Juno's miserable condition. She said she rid herself of her husband for Echo's sake. Juno insisted that Echo must love only her, no man, and in this way make up to Juno, Juno's own lack of mothering. Juno constantly complained about her own mother's rejection of her and she was angry when Echo seemed to love her grandmother.

When Echo was ten, Juno married another older man. He too tried to be a father to Echo, but Juno did not want that. Juno would confuse Echo by · telling her daughter that she (Echo) did not love her stepfather. When Echo developed a relationship with a boyfriend, Juno claimed the stepfather opposed it. So far as Juno was concerned, this was a sufficient rationale for leaving her second husband.

As an adolescent, Echo suffered from intense anxiety and shame. Juno was anxiety-ridden herself, and she advised Echo to stay close to home, away from men, and to keep her mouth and body shut. When Echo went to the same college as her boyfriend, Juno moved far away, so that Echo had no home. In college, Echo tried to please the man who became her husband. When Echo married and moved back to her home town, Juno moved back too.

Echo came to therapy when she found that her husband was having an affair. Juno insisted that Echo's husband was no good. She thought Echo should show her loyalty to her mother by divorcing her husband. Meanwhile, Echo's narcissistic husband would brook no opposition from Echo or Juno about his affair. He felt entitled. During a session of couple's therapy—not with me—Echo and her husband were advised that Echo's lack of a father had rendered her unable to satisfy her husband. That is when Echo dropped the couple's therapy and began individual therapy.

Incurring Juno's wrath, Echo and her husband moved to a new state in order to save their marriage. Echo's mother, naturally, would not talk to her, except in terms of reproach. Echo felt shame. She did not know how to appease both her husband and her mother. She was doing her best to be a good mother to her own daughter, who seemed to love Juno as much as she loved Echo. Because of these conflicts, Echo began a second course of individual therapy with me.

After the move, Echo called her mother repeatedly and against her own better adult judgment. Juno rebuffed Echo every time, which made Echo feel ashamed about moving. The deadly part of the interaction was that Juno made sure to let Echo know that Echo was diffident and that she lacked spunk. "Why don't you speak up and admit that you hate me," her mother would say. Finally, taking Juno's reproof as an interpretation, Echo did say "I hate you." In the following session, she remembered times of hating her mother. She realized that these experiences of hate and rage had led her to believe she was a bad girl, unworthy of her mother's love.

Echo felt shamed by her mother's rebuff because she retained a sense of her childhood identity as an extension of her mother's. If her mother derogated her being, then Echo felt shame. Echo's adult executive knew what to expect from her mother, but her childhood habit of longing for understanding undermined her adult confidence in her own emotional insight. Her childhood ego ideal continued to make her feel unworthy of her mother's love. Her immature sense of identity undermined her executive judgment that she would have to stop idealizing her mother.

Echo's husband had been raised to believe he could do no wrong. He would tell his wife, "Why don't you just ignore your mother? When you talk to her, you become miserable." Echo would agree with him, but then her shame about cutting Juno off would build, and she would feel that she was cutting her daughter off from Juno, depriving her daughter as she had been deprived of her grandmother, whom Juno hated. When Echo's husband told her to stop phoning her mother, she tried. But she responded to her husband's advice as if it were her mother's. She was diffident with her husband. Echo felt she could not do anything right.

As Echo learned that she would never have an understanding mother, she felt her adult sense of identity mature along with her confidence—until some event such as her daughter's birthday would lead to another feeble attempt at finding Juno's mirroring reassurance and love.

Despite a talent for art and a surprisingly successful career as a decorator before she had children, Echo inhibited her ambitions. The truth is that Echo's mother fancied herself tasteful, but Echo's eye for the aesthetic surpassed hers. After she had children, Echo deferred to her husband's career.

In her therapy, Echo realized that when she had childhood rages directed against her mother, she felt out of control. In their aftermath, when her mother would banish her, Echo would feel ashamed. She felt as if something were fundamentally wrong with her and that this was the reason for her mother's refusal to give her any emotional nourishment.

In her childhood, Echo learned to subdue her rage responses and her impulse to run away to her father or to her grandmother. Those impulses and feelings seemed proof of her unworthiness. In states of enduring shame, she at least felt that she was loyal to her mother by subduing herself.

Echo suffered from ego-ideal prohibitions. She grew up lacking confidence. In the aftermath of her outbreaks of rage and hatred and impulses to leave, she felt that she was ugly, stupid, and bad. Even when she felt mild resentment, she became quiet and helpless. Echo sensed, at these times, that her identity fragmented.

As Echo tried to relinquish her mother, she felt herself becoming more like her mother. In therapy, Echo discovered that she could not release herself from her childhood sense of being her mother's extension. In therapy, Echo did not know whether she was saying what she meant, or what her mother would mean. Even when her adult executive identity came to different conclusions, she could not turn these conclusions into her own articulatory rehearsal. She constantly needed the therapist to phrase her potential mature utterances. Then she would repeat them.

Taking benzodiazepines for her anxiety and a selective serotonin reuptake inhibitor (SSRI) for emotional stress, Echo was able to make increasing use of her therapy. Her mature identity as a mother and a wife coalesced as she nurtured her daughter's capacity to express herself freely. She realized that she could disagree with her husband because he was not her mother. His phallic aggressive teasing responses had a less recalcitrant tone than her mother's refusal to see things her way. Echo began to educate her husband about their family's emotional life and about how husband and wife mature together.

To sum up what we have seen so far, Echo suffered from narcissistic depletion and a generalized anxiety disorder. Her character formation was deformed by her attempts to deal with outbreaks of rage and hatred. In order to subdue her identity disrupting instinctual discharges of rage she reinforced her defenses with ego-ideal identifications with her mother. How did her neural systems mediate this development?

During Echo's childhood states of profound anxiety, her hypothalamus proceeded beyond its signalling function to induce deep instinctual fight responses. Fight is accompanied by both rage and panic. In her instinctualized states, Echo's sense of identity was overwhelmed and disorganized.

Even in her adult life, she would become perplexed about what she was really feeling. In order to avoid the chaos of confusion, Echo's love for her mother was joined by hatred, and the hatred was secondarily linked to the strongest ego-ideal prohibitions.

HOW CAN THERAPY INDUCE CHANGE?

How can therapy help a person to mature as an adult when she was stultified as a child? There are many forms of therapy, and they can all be effective under some circumstances. For any therapy to work, the patient has to use it to undergo a change in her sense of whom she is, and to whom she must answer. Let us further elaborate the neural system's horizontal and vertical approaches to the structure of dynamics as they effect identity formation. This will help us make some preliminary answers to the question of how therapy mediates intrapsychic change. (See Chapter 13 for a complete description of *structural therapy.*)

Echo's shame kept the wounded child suspended in time. It was the work of therapy to repair Echo's shattered narcissism by reuniting the shamed child she was with the mature adult she was becoming. In order for this work to succeed, Echo had to grieve for the lost illusion of her mother's loving her. This working through took many months.

Echo experienced therapy as permission to express herself. The therapist provided new cognitive models for how a mature person evaluates her feelings and experience. Echo identified with the empathy and instruction she received, and gradually she internalized this new mode as she practiced it. The medications reduced the emotional pressure and anxiety that had fixed her in her old, child's way of processing her experience. Echo was not completely cured, however, until she formed her own theory of how an adult mind works. She tailored her therapy to suit her own ongoing maturation.

Echo's *theory of mind* was partly determined by her reading popular books on developmental psychology. An overeater, she read that women who eat too much are starving for maternal, emotional nourishment. So far so good. But Echo also read about the fixating effects of sexual abuse on wounded children. Echo's unquestioning application of this theory to herself formed a brief but intense source of resistance. For Echo, believing that her father had abused her was a way of keeping the illusion of her mother's love for her alive. If he had, then Echo's mother was right to have divorced him for Echo's good.

How can communication with a therapist change neural systems from the top down? We judge each potential behavior, including interpersonal communication, according to whether it is compatible with our identity, e.g., with our aspirations and our reputation. When we are in conflict, our behavior is inconsistent with our sense of intrapsychic identity. When we acknowledge conflict, our mutable prefrontal cortex begins to change. Here is how.

Because every new behavioral decision plumbs childhood development, the brain's past is available to reorganization at a higher level. To give a brief explanation: to be assessed for relevance for adult problem solving, emotional data enter a conditioned limbic network. Then, the prefrontal system's medial and intermediate networks judge the signal quality and relevance of the data to problem solving. When we encounter conflict, we plumb source memory to explicitly process events and episodes to see what lessons we can learn from the past. It is at this point that the therapist can shed a new cognitive light on the relevance of childhood experience to adult decision making.

In normal development, identifications mediate between emotional assessment and the formation of new cognitive structures. They internalize know-how. When a person cannot establish a relationship that is needed for intrapsychic maturation during childhood, a *pathological* identification replaces that relationship. A pathological identification is one that conditions a person to become like the other, rather than learning how to resolve needs or avoid hurt.

Echo's identification with her mother illustrates a left-hemisphere, intersubjective pathological identification. A pathological narcissistic identification is always paired with the necessary illusion that a nurturing relationship actually exists. Such identifications cannot be relinquished easily, because they are rigid structures that are incapable of internalization. Pathological narcissistic identifications keep the child suspended in time. Echo felt that only Juno knew how to find satisfaction. Reinterpreting childhood experience allows the therapeutic relationship to become reparative as it gradually replaces the pathological identification.

Another case also illustrates this process. A forty-year-old man with an eccentric, self-absorbed father found himself recreating the pattern of his father's life. His father had used his son as a vehicle for proving his own self-worth. The father tried to teach his son everything he knew about selling electronic equipment. The problem was, he wanted his son to admire him, more than showing any concern for his son's feelings.

The son did admire his father, and he did become an electronics salesman as his father had been. In therapy, the patient realized that others saw his father as bombastic. Seeing his huge, ungainly, father gradually failing and diabetic, left him with a sense that he had unwisely invested too much in becoming his father. As an adult, when this patient felt himself becoming fat, his child self that was suspended in the time of his conditioning was pleased at this proof of becoming like his father. His adult sense of subjective social being had no sense of taking over his own life. He lived to please the "Darth Vaders" in his commercial world of selling electronic equipment. All men were either figures to be admired or feared.

Like Echo, this patient used a pathological identification with a parent to replace a missing parental, warm, and mirroring relationship. This patient too, has to undergo the tedious process of relinquishing a relationship that froze his maturation rather than enhancing it. The work of his therapy requires him to acknowledge his sense of futility and shame in a thousand situations that flow out of his pathological identification with his father. Like his father, he devalues women: he lets women make all the emotional decisions; he uses masturbation and food to assuage his sense of futility; he works seventy hours a week to justify and balance his shame about his inadequacy. Of course, this is just an abbreviated vignette.

Echo's working through will go on forever. Every time she expresses herself according to her adult needs and overcomes reticence based on identification with her mother, she grieves a little more for the loss of the illusion of her mother's love. Echo can identify with herself as a mature woman to the extent that she continues to work these issues through long after her contact with me is over. In order to understand how the adult's neural systems relate to those of the child, we must now study how we become who we are (see Figure 4.1).

HOW THE BRAIN STRUCTURES INTRAPSYCHIC DEVELOPMENT

Delineating life stages is a human preoccupation. The present neural systems' approach illuminates, well-documented observational approaches to development, i.e., the psychoanalytic, ego psychological, cognitive, and family systems. Because stages of life repeat developmental patterns, we will look carefully at the formation of infant foundations of identity.

The Spiral Synthesis Model of Development

What follows is my neural systems' model for intrapsychic development. I invite the reader to refer to *Spiral Synthesis* for an organizational grid of neural systems' development that correlates with ego psychology's child observation. The Spiral Synthesis model depicts identity going forward in cycles and stages that move from hemisphere to hemisphere in alternating developmental steps. Chapter 5 follows this progress in detail.

FIGURE 4.1. Prefrontal Cortex Development: Spiral Synthesis (SS)

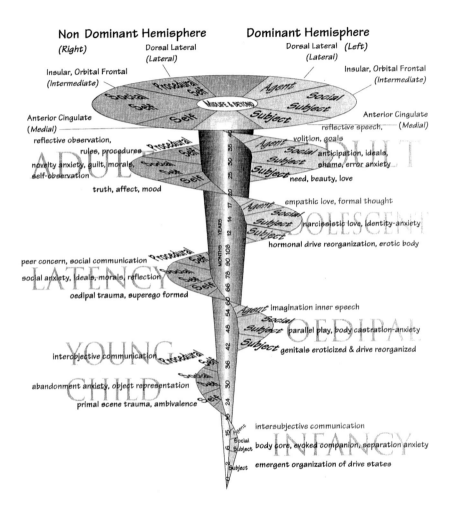

To begin: the corpus callosum myelinates and becomes a structural brain system organizer at eighteen to twenty-four-months (Rapoport, 1990). This myelination allows transcortical associations to form. As we discussed in Chapter 1, each hemisphere contributes equally to the formation of higher cortical functions in childhood. Luria concluded that after the corpus callosum becomes functional, one hemisphere develops the foreground for a particular higher cortical function while the other develops its background. Thus, the right hand gestures expressively, while the left hand draws a pictograph of the limits of the communication. Higher cortical functions' organization "involves the participation of a dynamic 'constellation' of collectively working parts of the brain and areas of the cortex" (Luria, 1980, p. 375).

As we saw in the introduction, quantitative EEG reveals that neocortical networks increase their power cyclically, from lateral to medial, and from the left hemisphere to the right three times before adult life begins (Thatcher, 1992). Thatcher's findings support my conclusion that developmental stages spiral (Harris, 1986). In spiral development, one hemisphere, then the other leads in forming new higher cortical functions and metafunctions. The left and right hemispheres alternately develop the foreground of identity. Identity is synthesized in layers.

In spiral development, each hemisphere organizes its own characteristic identity. The left hemisphere integrates a subjective sense that coalesces needs, motives, purposes, and goals. The right integrates an objective sense of identity that coalesces responses, reactions, and explorations of reality. Each new stage characteristically redistributes the drives, which we experience in deeply personal ways. Increased libido disposes us to new *egocentric* pleasure experience. Increased aggression disposes us to new *self-centered* ways of owning reality. *We cycle from stages of left hemisphere, egocentrically rooted, identity to right self-centered, identity.* Each *stage* of life develops in consecutive *periods* of:

- *emotional* development,
- *social* identificatory development, e.g., subject and self linked in associative networks with others' representations, and
- *cognitive* development.

These periods correspond to the development of new *medial, intermediate*, and *lateral* prefrontal networks respectively. The first period of each stage anchors an emotional framework that is quite private, either subjectively egocentric, or objectively self-centered. The second elaborates this framework in social identifications. The third translates identifications into pragmatic language structures that enhance behavioral competence.

From what I have concluded in preceding chapters, I pose the following model for periodic development within each stage:

- In the initial medial period, new drive pressure induces the amygdala to recondition the instincts and drives. This period redeploys somatic signals of affect and expression.
- In the intermediate period, orbital frontal and insular cortex recondition our socialization and the basis of our social relationships. This provides the foundations for identificatory development. As new source memory forms, the amygdala and the hippocampus bring this memory into associative conjunction with conditioned orbital frontal and insular association cortex.
- In the lateral period, prefrontal networks expand their links to anterior posterior data analysis in the left hemisphere, or for integrating data holistically in the right.

To sum up the Spiral Synthesis model:

- Left hemisphere libidinal and right hemisphere aggressive periods each serially integrate medial, intermediate, and lateral networks.
- We progress from stages of newly defined needs and motives to stages of newly defined adaptations to reality.
- A whole cycle consists of two stages: a libidinal egocentric one and an aggressive self-centered one.
- Each time the prefrontal system synthesizes a transcallosal network, it completes a new layer of intrapsychic identity that has its origins in the limbic system.
- Social reenforcement of our identity stabilizes each stage's cognitive development. We are who we think.

THE DEVELOPMENT OF PRIMARY NARCISSISM

To continue our psychoanalytic incarnation, what can we learn about the infantile origins of primary egocentrism, narcissism, and intersubjective communication from the Spiral Synthesis Model? We move from egocentric to narcissistic to intersubjective communication in specifiable periods during each libidinal stage. This movement recapitulates the process of falling in love, and it develops neurally from medial to intermediate to lateral in the left hemisphere. Thus, we fall in love with "body chemistry," melt into the other's eyes, and know we have bonded.

In *On Narcissism* (1914). Freud described narcissistic relating as serial periods of falling in love. In the initial, egocentric period, one's own somatic signals *are* the love object. One falls in love with one's own body. Next, according to Freud, the libidinal cathexis attaches to the other person when the narcissistic relator senses mirroring of his own somatic signals. In this state of *identity,* one who is falling in love says empathically to the other, "I know just how you feel." Freud's use of the term *identity* in this paper refers both to a feeling of symbiotic bonding and to intrapsychic identity.

The experience of *identity* invites narcissistic love. If someone stands next to you mirrors your gestures and posture, as the mythical Echo did with Narcissus, you feel you are falling in love. Some therapists purposely mirror in this way to calm an agitated patient, or to invite "positive" transference. This is how the mythological Echo tried to make Narcissus fall in love with her instead of with his own image.

Could we say that the infant falls in love with her mother? Of course we could. Later, falling in love recapitulates periods of infantile libidinal development. There is one exception to this development. Sandra Harris (personal communication) has observed that the autist never moves emotionally beyond the egocentric period of any stage. The autist develops cognitive functions that are used for entirely egocentric purposes. Autism always shows up in infancy as the failure to go through the maturation of narcissistic development.

INFANT DEVELOPMENT: AN OVERVIEW

Infants cannot tell us about their experience. Even if they had language, they lack the equipment to reflect on it. We have to infer what their experience is like and how it coalesces in ways that provide the foundations of the experience we all come to know that is integrated in our sense of intrapsychic identity. Let us call the neural structures that provide the foundations of identity experience *integers.* Dan Stern (1985) infers from his careful observations that infants sense the organizing integers of their identity as these integers are forming.

Stern describes the following chronology (1985):

1. Between 0 and 2 months, consciousness is *emergent.*
2. Between 2 and 6 months, a *core* consciousness develops.
3. Between 7 and 15 months, consciousness is *intersubjective.*
4. Between 15 and 24 months, consciousness becomes *verbal.*

Emergent consciousness, core consciousness, intersubjective consciousness, and *verbal consciousness* are Stern's way of describing the infant's experience of consciousness. Like Stern, Margaret Mahler divides infant consciousness into four periods. Her periods are identical to Stern's. She calls them (1) *autistic*, (2) *symbiotic*, (3) *practicing*, and (4) *rapprochement*. The reason for the parallel is not hard to see: the progression of periods follows the maturation of neural systems.

These terms are well and good, but how does consciousness manifest before the two hemispheres have differentiated their higher cortical functions at eighteen months? In the beginning, consciousness appears to be purely subjective. As students of cognitive psychology know, Piaget characterized infancy as an *egocentric sensorimotor period* (1954). "I" rather than "me" tends to hold the foreground throughout infancy. The term egocentric in this sense means "self-centered."

Despite the infant's necessary illusion of creating life and maternal love that reciprocates her own, it is important for us to realize that each hemisphere has the innate capacity to process both subjective and objective forms of data. Thus, in infancy and early childhood, each hemisphere is undifferentiated enough to compensate for the other's deficits. This is why persons born with only one hemisphere or with corpus callosal agenesis still develop both egocentricity and self-centeredness.

What causes differential processing to develop in the two hemispheres? As we have already discussed, the dopaminergic system more highly innervates the speech, motor, and need-processing associational cortices in the left hemisphere than it does the right hemisphere's visual association cortex. The left hemisphere's consummatory and the right's vigilant states of consciousness gradually lateralize. Norepinephrine innervates the spatial processing visual association areas, which causes the right hemisphere to enhance vigilance. Norepinephrine does not innervate the basal ganglia. Thus, as I see it, the libidinal and aggressive drives reenforce distinct behavioral states.

In the emergent period, infants stabilize their autonomic systems with the help of parental interventions. Brazelton (1980) describes emergent infants' manifesting three kinds of states of consciousness: one is consummatory, one is vigilant, and one attentional. Each state has a distinctive autonomic accompaniment that emerges from one of the three instinctual organizations. Infants shift back and forth among these states. As we saw in Chapter 3, consummatory states are dopamine driven; and vigilant states, which involve exploring the world with eye and head movements, are norepinephrine driven. Finally, serotonin drives attentional states where the infant's gaze locks in mutual bonding with the caretaker. Autistic infants do not develop mutual gaze.

It follows that the infant has quite a different set of experiences in each drive state. As we saw in Chapter 3, the amygdala parcels out libidinal and aggressive cathexes as it processes the salience and novelty of new stimuli. As the amygdala mobilizes drive states in response to endogenous and exogenous stimuli, it sets up corresponding autonomic states through its hypothalamic outflow pathways. Once autonomic states stabilize, they remain stabilized for life. The polygraph, for instance, works on the principle that emotionally relevant stimuli trigger characteristic, measurable autonomic discharges.

CONCLUSION

As our consciousness develops hierarchically in stages, reflection adds ever increasing dimensions to our organized sense of experience. Infants can reflect little on experience, and, indeed, experience per se remains alien from the adult's consciousness because adults cannot have experience without reflecting on it. This is because experience per se, as we have defined it, is primarily a property of the limbic system. Conceivably, direct experience determines which data will endure as limbic associations and which will not. Clearly animals have direct experience that forms associations, and we ascribe very little capacity for reflection to them.

Most infants' associations are probably limbic ones, whereas those associations that are available to a nascent sense of identity are neocortical. The infants' behavioral states produce clusters of both limbic and identity associations. If we agree that drive, as we have previously defined it, determines behavioral states, then we can begin to intuit the sense of nascent organization that accompanies the formation of combined limbic and prefrontal experiential loops.

Chapter 5

The Stages of Life

Yes, I will be thy priest, and build a fane [temple]
In some untrodden region of my mind,
Where branched thoughts, new grown with pleasant pain,
Instead of pines shall murmur in the wind:
Far, far around shall these dark clustered trees
Fledge the wild ridged mountains steep by steep . . .
And in the midst of this wide quietness
A rosy sanctuary will I dress
With the wreathed trellis of a working brain . . .

—John Keats,
"Ode to Psyche"

A solid person is familiar with her drives. There is knowledge beyond familiarity, though. Our children lead us to it. While they are depleting our narcissism, children show us how their drives develop. You could say that they reacquaint us with our souls—unpleasant parts included. Maybe the general level of turmoil keeps us from being perfect observers. What, in an ideal world, could we learn from observing our children?

Imagine, if you will, an Olympian Psyche. In the narrative conceit of this chapter, Psyche is no longer a graduating psychiatrist plagued by intrusive older women. She is the Psyche of myth. Legend, the reader will recall, has it that Psyche overcomes many trials precipitated by envious older sisters. Ovid tells us that Psyche marries Eros (Cupid) and gives birth to a daughter, Voluptua (Pleasure).

Gentle reader, now a goddess, Psyche finds herself in an ideal world. Here is a mother able to learn *ab initio* how the drives develop. The goddess of psychology will follow her child's growth. Picking up where Ovid left off, this chapter trails after Psyche, who studies Voluptua's spiral synthesis. To complete the allegory, Voluptua's working brain is a garden.

Look at it this way. We will see the country with a native guide. Dante needed Virgil to guide him through Hell. Beatrice guided him through Heaven. Some two millennia after Ovid's death, new things are happening on Olympus.

When the pregnant goddess Psyche looks down from Olympus, she remembers the desires of her whole human life, which culminated in her creation of Voluptua. Perhaps with help from Keats, Psyche's memories of overcoming her life's pain joined in the development of her daughter's brain. Psyche knows she will have to use her own maturation to guide her daughter until Voluptua develops her own identity.

Once we take pleasure in knowing our own identity and it takes root in our drives, we anticipate a higher level of pleasure if we proceed with our staged development and maturation. From the beginning, we take pleasure in the illusion that we alone animate all things that exist in our infant mind. Out of that illusion, as much as anything else, we develop a soul. Like any mother, Psyche prepares to know the growing soul of her future daughter.

SPIRAL SYNTHESIS:
THE BRAIN'S GROWING GARDEN OF THE MIND

Spiral synthesis is a comprehensive neural system's model for both cognitive and psychoanalytic development. The model follows; it does not lead the way to understanding the functional communication among the brain's working structures. Nandor Balazs, to whom this book is dedicated, once told me that at Cornell, after new academic buildings have been constructed, the administration lets students make their own paths to the new buildings from existing structures. Later, the administration paves walkways among garden beds and trees by following the already established pragmatic paths. This metaphor for neural Darwinism shows how neural systems establish new paths for communication after neoteny builds new structures.

As we learned in Chapter 4, infants cycle among three drive states: consummatory, vigilant, and vital. Utilizing different cries, my two-month-old granddaughter said things such as "I'm hungry," "What's going on?" and "Let's play." Her amygdala—like everyone else's—coordinated the formation of these three drive states as it promoted the functional attachment of the biogenic amines to instinctually organized sensory and motor behaviors. *The basic principle is that dopaminergic consummation states arouse the infant to her subjective needs, noradrenergic vigilant states arouse her to explore her objective world, and serotonergic/acetycholinergic states arouse her to feel alive.*

As conditioned socialization tames instincts during the first two months, the nascent assessor senses the birth of identity. *Intrapsychic coherence* arises from a sense that we know the drives that animate our intercourse with the world. Satisfaction and desire, and relief and frustration exemplify polar states of our libidinal and aggressive drives, respectively.

The waning of attention presages sleep. Naturally, before sleep we do not need vitality for problem solving. When vital attention is missing or gets numbed during problem solving, however, we sense an inner state of death. Throughout life, being attentively alive differs from sensing libidinal need, or recognizing the aggression that wants to explore. Vitality is the medium between libido and aggression, which is why, as those who are impelled to write know, prolonged attentive vitality decays into states of desire or frustration.

Instincts flower in their beds of conditioned associations, but the beds are only accessible to one who follows the neural trails that lead from stage to stage. As Psyche contemplates the soul of Pleasure, she reassesses this human garden. Let us look down from the Acropolis of Our Minds with Psyche, as she makes her spiral path in time through paths between the beds. Psyche sees six growing identity zones, with paths among them. She sees the following:

- medial emotional, drive paths (subject and self)
- intermediate bonding paths (social subject and social self)
- lateral cognitive paths (agent and procedural self)

INFANCY (ZERO TO TWENTY-FOUR MONTHS)

Dan Stern, stopping just short of a neural system's view, saw the same three paths. He emphasized their: (1) psychoanalytic, (2) ego-psychological (interpersonal), and (3) cognitive effects on the infant's nascent mental organization.

Stern (1985) infers that emergent infants

> take sensations, perceptions, actions, cognitions, internal states of motivation . . . and experience them directly in . . . intensities, shapes, temporal patterns, vitality affects (e.g., surging or fleeting life rhythms), categorical affects (e.g., happy or sad), and hedonic tones. (p. 67)

Thus, the baby associates instinctual orientation, vigilance, and vitality with (1) hedonic tones, (2) categorical affects, and (3) vitality affects, respectively. The baby binds each identity integer when each instinct develops its own *drive associations*.

The baby's first problem is to claim life from the pressures of need and affect states. As she monitors waxing and waning drive pressures, the infant feels a vital "surging and fleeting" life rhythm. Her urgent drive to refocus attention manifests life's vitality. When do adults feel the urge to vitality in a way that recalls the infant's? Waking from anaesthesia, we wrest vitality back from the force of darkness, like Jacob struggling with the angel of death.

Now, with help from Dan Stern, Margaret Mahler, and other ego psychologists, let us methodically survey Psyche's growing baby garden. In the first two months, social instincts give rise to emerging emotions. In the next four months, emotions sprout a core of conditioned associations. In the next nine months, cognitive stems emerge from their compost. At eighteen months, a flowering individual reaches toward the sun of young childhood.

DRIVE BINDS

When dopamine binds (cathects) motor schema, the infant senses a hedonically toned sense of subject. A good example of this can be seen in the cases of congenitally blind infants. At six months, when neural readiness coordinates crawling and visual processing, most infants take pleasure in learning how to crawl. The congenitally blind infant, however, cannot keep crawling because objects block her path. Her crawling gets mired in rocking movements, which manifest both excess pleasure cathexis and its failure to bind an unfolding skill (Fraiberg, 1977).

When norepinephrine binds percepts, the infant senses an affective sense of self, which is originally good (pain relieving) or bad (painful). The infant's aggressive drive to explore what exists links perception to reality. The infant obviously feels good when she discovers the features of new objects. When percepts do not bind aggression, the frustrated infant obviously feels bad. When the external world yields answers, the infant binds new percepts with significance, and experiences relief. As Otto Kernberg theorizes, self-images affectively link clusters of associations to others (1975).

When serotonin (and central acetycholine) bind sensory and motor associations, a coherent sense of intrapsychic identity arises. As we have said before, serotonin steadies resolve and enhances sensory intake as we pay attention. Serotonin neutralizes—interregulates—the libidinal and aggressive drives in this way. Serotonergic states help the amygdala tame the cholinergic flow of vitality. As the mother reciprocates the infant's gaze, she provides an open window between two brains. Together they experience life's vitality in symbiosis.

The Emergent (Autistic) Infant (Zero to Two Months)

In the emergent period, the infant senses a *subject* in signals of visceral pleasure, and a *self* in signals of visceral pain. But, when orienting responses for consummation are associated with failed pleasure, the strongest negative conditioning occurs. According to Freud, intense psychic pain occurs when the infant hallucinates the breast, but the mother fails to appear. This pain conditions vigilant associations to reality, so that the infant forms what Freud called the *reality principle*. Pleasure binding and relief binding cathexis attach the baby to reality. These cathexes only lead to conditioned pain without salient and significant associations.

Instinctual conditioning in the first two months stabilizes the drive systems. As we will see later, the failure to stabilize instinct and catecholamine drive systems in the first two months can lead, later in life, to the autonomic instability of psychosomatic illness. This failure can be life threatening in marasmus (wasting away in infancy), since effective consummation is necessary for survival.

The Core (Symbiotic) Infant (Two to Six Months)

The core period begins at two months with the reality principle. The real, as opposed to the hallucinated, object arouses the infant's vitality. In the core period, the infant compares conditioned social associations (Stern's *evoked companion*) with the presence or absence of a real person. If the breast or mother's face and eyes are part objects, then the presence of the mother is a whole object, much to be desired.

The *vitality state*, really gazing into the mother's eyes, stabilizes the infant's sense of social being. Conceivably, serotonin mediates progress from the emergent to the core period by regulating the orbital frontal LTP of clusters of conditioned social associations. With the help of serotonin, clusters of part object associations are fused into the prototype whole object in the infant's core period. In Chapter 3, we concluded that serotonin promotes stable emotional processing in the present and preserves the value of past emotional experience.

At two months, then, in a movement from *autism* to *symbiosis,* the infant coalesces a sense of a *social subject* out of visceral states associated with the presence of a global entity, *the companion*. The social subject's sense of what Stern calls *history,* develops from the prefrontal system's developing capacity to assess the companion's socially conditioned autonomic signals of pleasure, displeasure, pain, and pain relief. The baby begins to remember being burped, rocked, held, and changed. The core infant assesses the results of different contacts in her serotonin-rich, orbital and insular cortices.

Thus, when the infant is two months old, her intermediate experiential loops support the formation of emotionally organized long-term memory. Social companionship is its first content. Stern observed that social companionship develops during attention states. Imbued with vitality while attentive, the infant maintains eye contact, to the delight of adults. Also, the baby returns the vitality in her mother's eyes. Attention states prolong in the two-to-three-month period as mother and baby engage in social experiences that are welded in each brain by the baby's instinctive smile. In vitality states, infant and mother record social bonding.

The *symbiotic infant* rapidly expands emotionally organized memory contents, which are a visceral associations gathered together under the rubric of "the companion." The baby has to bond socially in order to evoke appropriate parental responses to her drive pressures. It is in states of attentive vitality that social binding coalesces. Thus, this period is characterized by the formation of the social subject and the social self. Bringing images of the companion into conformity with the presence of the real companion during attention states, the infant mediates both her need and vigilance states.

Stern observed that the symbiotic infant's instinctive sociability is reciprocated by emphatic social patterning, which he calls *companionship* (1985). Companionship during the three-to-six-month period supports symbiotic vitality. Stern surmises that source memory evokes a reassuring sense of bonding when an infant is alone, but attentive. The evoked companion, in other words, is the mediator of the infant's sense of vitality. This symbiotic progenitor of fantasy may be the prototype for transitional objects, and later, of imaginary companions.

The Intersubjective (Practicing) Infant (Six to Fifteen Months)

In the practicing period, Stern's infant develops a sense of coherent identity by linking a sense of her history with a sense of her body's *cohesion*. Freud's rock-bottom ego (I/me) is a body ego. Unifying visceral feelings, needs, *and* feedback from the senses and movements, the infant centers her ego in her body.

Stern's terms for the practicing infant's cognitive integers (motor-sensory and sensory-motor associations) are the same ones I proposed in the introduction:

- *Agency* links the infant's sense of volition with predictable motor results.
- *Procedure* is the infant's capacity to realize that a moving object, including itself, maintains its integrity as an object.

During the six-to-fifteen-month practicing period, as visual feature detection is integrated with the developing motor capacity to navigate the world, the infant learns procedures by initiatory experimentation and by imitation. Now, *agency plus procedure gives rise to body coherence*. This means that the infant senses the "body-ego" in its imitative, as well as its initiatory schema. When an infant imitatively places one block on top of another, she fuses her gesture with her perception of the other's procedure, and she fuses her own gesture with her perception of what she has accomplished.

Imitating other's movements yields an objectified procedural self. We can see this when watching modern dance groups such as Momix or Philobolus mime the contours of an object as they reproduce the sense of the object within their own procedural body ego, and show the whole gestalt to the audience. Showing contours reminds us that the eyes' motor palpation of objects integrates visual features and forms the right hemisphere's object representations.

ANXIETY REGULATION IN INFANCY

In the core period, the amygdala conditions instinctual autonomic discharges. In the emergent period, as prefrontally assessed data recirculates through amygdaloid nuclei, panic and terror replace fight and flight. This produces clusters of social/somatic associations to these total anxiety discharges. As we saw in Chapter 2, anxiety regulation begins with prefrontal modulation of amygdalar fight or flight discharges through the hypothalamus. Thus, at about five months, separation and stranger anxiety become cognition's anxiety signal systems.

Viewed as behavioral state regulators, anxiety systems form consummatory series in the left hemisphere and a vigilance series in the right. This series is a developmental progression from (1) instinct to (2) conditioned fear to (3) signal anxiety. Thus, fight, panicky rage, and error anxiety consecutively develop and regulate consummation as infant development moves from medial to intermediate to lateral zones. Similarly, flight, terror, and novelty anxiety form a right hemisphere series from medial to intermediate to lateral zones, respectively.

Now let us consider the infant's development of separation (error) and stranger (novelty) anxiety as a cognitive signal anxiety system in the practicing period. *Separation anxiety* develops as a signal system for protecting the agent's and social subject's integrity at five to six months. When the infant sees her mother disappearing, she experiences a loss of that sense of pleasurable initiation and vitality that maintains the egocentric illusion of creating her companion's presence. Separation anxiety signals the imminent loss of intersubjective cohesion. This means that serotonin modulation fails to enhance the libidinal cathexis of the evoked source memory of the companion.

At five to six months, then, awareness of the evoked companion in the absence of the companion induces the lament: "Where are you when I need you?" When separation anxiety erupts, the infant is desperate until the mother returns. Faced with outbreaks of separation anxiety, many a baby-sitter feels she will never become an adequate mother. I recall mind-ing my five-month-old daughter when my wife was out. She screamed continuously until my wife returned.

Error anxiety erupts when agency fails. When crawling fails to reach the salient object, the infant wriggles anxiously. Error anxiety is a biological regulation that protects every animal from initiating behavior that can threaten its survival. For humans, separation anxiety is the precursor of anticipatory anxiety.

Stranger anxiety develops around seven months. At this point, the infant develops a sense that the real world is a container of persons. A stranger's novelty overwhelms the infant's capacity to bind an expectable companionship, and vigilance anxiety erupts.

Novelty anxiety develops along with stranger anxiety. The whole field of reality becomes filled with signifiers. My infant granddaughter became extremely anxious when she watched the umbrella she knew open and appear to turn into another object. Objects should be reliable.

Once the infant is able to regulate the effects of both separation and stranger anxiety, the world is her oyster. It is there for the taking and the toddler is a brave and fearless explorer (Mahler, Pine, and Bergman, 1975). At fifteen months my granddaughter began to play with putting objects such as umbrellas up and down. She changed their context, while verifying they were the same entity. I watched her do this with my dog's "bed," while shaking her head like the dog and putting her head on the dog's bed. As this shook her sense of identity, she got her mother to move the dog's bed to different places in the room.

My granddaughter's sudden anxiety after making the dog's bed hers, for an instant, exemplifies a new, more comprehensive *identity-anxiety* system. This vitality anxiety develops at fifteen to eighteen months during what Mahler called a *rapprochement period*. Suddenly, separation and stranger anxiety and error and novelty anxiety all reappear together, and reenforce an imminent loss of identity, all at the same time that exploration is rapidly contextualizing the procedural self's world of objects.

The Early Verbal (Rapprochement) Infant (Fifteen to Eighteen Months)

Each stage of identity synthesis is cemented cognitively. As cognition solidifies all of an identity zone's assessments, a sense of the whole mind emerges. Then, a new stage begins.

In *rapprochement*, at the interstage between infancy and young childhood, the infant's mind darts into and out of being. The executive sense of mind is developing, however, and at this point the infant can sense his mother's separate mind. Stern says that *we-ness* (intersubjectivity) and *you-ness* (interobjectivity) advance the infant's emotional *and* cognitive communications.

Now the infant's cognitive capacity for *mutuality* expands:

- We-ness forms mutual understanding via reciprocal gestures.
- You-ness joins the baby with the mother through imitative affect attunement. The mother matches the infant's behavior in modality, intensity, rhythm, vitality, feeling tone, and duration, while purposely introducing novelty. The baby does the same for the mother.
- We-ness and you-ness join cognitively when babies and mothers acknowledge the significance of objects which are pointed out. The expansion of three instincts and three drives into the three forms of mutuality (gesture, affect attunement, and pointing) contributes to language development.

Libidinal needs are communicated by gesture. The infant *supervisor* links subject, social subject, and agency through gestural requests. Affect atunement binds aggression as the infant *observer* links self, social self, and procedural self through imitative affect engagements. The infant is led to bind new procedures—learning a new way to deal with objects—with categories of affect. To the mother's delight, the infant can also undertake affect attunement in which she teaches the mother. Pointing brings gesture and affect attunement into concert. As the infant's executive develops, it links the prefrontal assessment zones together in higher cortical, speech mediated functions.

In autism, the infant never develops an intersubjective sense of others' minds. There is no possibility of empathy and no language for it. In Asperger's Disorder, however, "we-ness" and language for it may develop, but the social objectification of mind, "you-ness," does not develop.

COGNITIVE ADVANCES IN THE TRANSITION TO YOUNG CHILDHOOD

Noam Chomsky is well known for arguing that our brains develop an innate grammar (1980). Following this line of thought, Steven Pinker, who was Chomsky's student at MIT, observed that a diverse group of immigrants spontaneously developed a form of Pidgin English to work together. Their young children who were exposed to the grammarless Pidgin (1994) collectively turned their parent's *ad hoc* dialect into a creole language, complete with its own inherent grammar. From this, we can conclude that the prefrontal cortex is disposed to organize word order and grammatical patterns. How does this happen?

At twenty months, my granddaughter repeated the language patterns she heard. Her mother's cadenced, *affect-attuned* phrases provided a template for similar phrases. When stimulated to fill in phrases with words that rhymed, she could do it easily and in a grammatically correct way. She responds to her mother's "*see* the frog/*see* the . . . " with her own "see the dog."

Affect-attuned, cadenced language makes idioms—phrases that contain templates for syntax and grammar. Rules are imbedded in the templates. The baby experiences words as living entities, which are introjected and organized by young childhood's semantic rules. "Dog" or "frog" denotes a concrete association between gesture and entity. When a baby says "raisin," a set of experiences is condensed in the word. Similarly, my granddaughter's "dog" contained a gestural equivalent of what a dog might be.

PERCEPTUAL ADVANCES IN THE TRANSITION TO YOUNG CHILDHOOD

Perceptual representation also manifests the brain's innate developmental organization. My younger daughter recalls that when she was about eighteen months old, she suddenly became aware of her own face as hers in the mirror. She was right on time. Stern, Mahler, and Piaget all observed the eighteen-month-old infant recognizing that the mirror self belongs both to the world *me*, and to the subject *I*. Before this, the infant relies on transitional objects to mediate the world. As Winnicott observed, a transitional object serves both as a subjective extension and as a real object in the world (1965). When the infant becomes her own transitional object, willing herself into a world reflected in the mirror, she synthesizes herself.

Synthesis, as I define it, is the formation of trancallosal networks that unify (1) *cognitive,* (2) *social,* and (3) *emotional identity integers.* Synthesis unifies the infant's subjectivity with the young child's objectivity. The young child's left hemisphere's subjective identity integers fade into the background as synthesis redistributes identity functions to an objectified right hemisphere foreground. According to Piaget, the infant's *sensory motor period* ends when the *preoperational* young child realizes *and* verbalizes that out of sight is neither out of mind, nor out of existence.

Soon after she recognized herself in the mirror, my daughter recalls a sense of seeing detailed features in her parents' faces as both frightening and reassuring. She saw her parents' features in a context of cheeks covered with minute pores. She was afraid she had aggressively caused these pores.

Thus, in objectified representation, details dot features. This, then, is the hallmark of right hemisphere processing: aggressive feature inspection and saccadic exploration forms right hemisphere percepts. Meaningful details can appear only after the corpus callosum links semantic and perceptual associations. This is the essence of denotation.

THE PRIMAL SCENE'S REORGANIZATION
OF INTRAPSYCHIC IDENTITY

"Oh no! It can't be! But it is!"

Surely I dreamt to-day, or did I see
The winged Psyche with awakened eyes?
I wandered in a forest thoughtlessly,
And, on the sudden, fainting with surprise,
Saw two fair creatures, couched sided by side . . .

They lay calm-breathing on the bedded grass;
their arms embraced, and their pinions, too;
Their lips touched not, but had not bid adieu,
As if disjoined by soft-handed slumber,
And ready still past kisses to outnumber
At tender eye-dawn of Aurorean love: The winged boy I knew:
But who wast thou, O happy, happy dove?
His Psyche true!

—John Keats,
"Ode to Psyche"

And from this union came Pleasure.

What is the point of Keats' poetic prose? Why all this surprise and ostensibly fluctuating consciousness? Working within a long convention of dream visions, Keats commits an act of perfect mimesis. Although Keats knew very well that he was writing about sex and the birth of consciousness, the possibly unconscious object of his imitation is the infant's surprised waking to the primal scene.

We know that at the time of writing, Keats suffered from the pain of tuberculosis, and he had every reason to try to summon beauty to quash his terror of pain and death. As we have seen (in Lida's Case, and in the case of the boy who was raped by his grandfather, and as we shall see in Sam's case and in the case of the contemporary painter), in moments of trauma, right before we experience the terror of imminent catastrophe, we mobilize all the beauty at our disposal to keep from being overwhelmed. This aesthetic reaction begins in the infant's response to the primal scene.

Can the reader believe that *each pleasure stage ends, and a new reality-based stage begins when endogenous trauma triggers massive excitoxicity in the limbic system?* Trauma changes us. It is a vehicle for change. We are genetically programmed, I believe, to suffer universal endogenous traumata through which we mature. To say this another way, *endogenous trauma is an innate mechanism that produces the massive reorganization of neural systems necessary to forming new linkages in neural networks.*

The primal scene is the first endogenous trauma. Freud (1918) reconstructed the eighteen-month-old infant's engagement with a *universal, psychologically organizing primal scene,* which we may define as a scene in reality that is incompatible with the infant's egocentric organization. The experience of the primal scene necessarily induces young childhood.

To clear up a possible misunderstanding, let me say that although Freud identified the primal scene as witnessed coitus between the parents, I do not use the term precisely as Freud did. As I see it, the primal scene that inaugurates young childhood is any exclusive engagement between the parents that the nascent young child cannot deny. The necessary endogenous trauma does not require the infant to witness a sexual act.

In his "Wolf Man" case (1918), Freud observed that the infant greets the primal scene with extended temper tantrums and defecation. The defecation expresses overwhelming drive and affect. Anal discharge of affect demarcates a new development in the somatic basis of the aggressive drive. I surmise that the amygdala conditions anal discharge during primal scene trauma.

In this scenario, the young child's self is brought to the foreground by the following mechanism: an overwhelming sense of novel reality induces the amygdala and hippocampus to respond to this event as a trauma. This is to say that, as maturation reaches a critical level and more neural systems than usual are already on the brink of excitotoxicity, the primal scene pushes a whole mass of them over the edge at the same time. Many amygdalar nuclei, and many hippocampal paths induce massive transfer LTP in their experiential loops. Consequently, new, emotionally organized memory forms in the right parahippocampus, and new affect assessment cortex is potentiated in the right cingulate cortex. Massed affect signals and their assessment bring a new right hemisphere self to the foreground.

Freud's theory of psychosexual development teaches us that new somatic signals are imbued with both libidinal and aggressive drive. The capacity to restrain and release the anal sphincter forms the basis for newly conditioned associations, which become available to structure experience. Now, the right cingulate cortex assesses new affect signals. They form the nidus for new self-organization. The aggression bound by new self tames the primal scene's endogenous and traumatic novelty, which had suffused the infant with a display of experience that was beyond his integrative capacity.

THE EFFECT OF TRAUMA
ON DEVELOPMENTAL STAGE CHANGE

At the onset of young childhood, *endogenous trauma* provides the impetus for psychological *progression*. *Exogenous trauma*, however, can both freeze current psychic organization and cause a *regression* from the recently acquired advances. A child of any age is particularly vulnerable to stasis or regression when neural systems are in the process of rapid change.

Consider a case vignette that illustrates how a single trauma during the onset of young childhood gave rise to regressive, long-lingering fixation and repetition/compulsion. Sam, a twenty-two-month-old child, regressed after trauma to typical rapprochement behavior. He would dart away, then avidly seek reassurance by clinging. Sam clung to consciousness at all costs. Instead of relinquishing consciousness at bedtime, Sam incessantly called his parents into his room during the next three years. When he did fall asleep, he had to remember every dream as if it had a real event's importance.

At twenty-two months, a family friend forced Sam to perform fellatio. Throughout childhood, Sam tended to run away instead of seeking security. Yet, he wanted to be confined in small, safe spaces where the world could not intrude. He became a vegetarian, rather than eating the meat that was offered to him as fellatio. The perpetrator's hairy facial and genital image became a terrifying screen that was ameliorated by the fuzzy images of a special bear. Sam never wanted to see anything directly as it was. Instead, he remained suffused with the sense of beauty of objects coming into being that is characteristic of the period of rapprochement, and in adolescence, he became a poet.

Twenty months old and traveling by sea to a new world, the United States, a now successful abstract painter witnessed his parent's lovemaking. After that, he felt the world arbitrary and changeable. He began to do artwork in early childhood. From then on, he compulsively painted and pieced experience together. Each painting and collage turned into a voyage of self-discovery, a vehicle for overcoming personal fragmentation. A long first marriage dissolved when he had collated sufficient coherent self to look for identity in another. After his divorce, he took a new lover. Her young child came into the room while he made love to his partner. Terrified, he immediately ended that relationship. Even in later life, his paintings always included collage. In analysis, we saw that his images remained disorganized and that he always illustrated a disorganized world. Talking about the pictures, which he brought into sessions, we saw that he longed to recreate the security of his old infantile world.

In this budding artist, exogenous trauma had combined with endogenous trauma. While the primal scene triggered a change to the world of young childhood, the exogenous trauma of losing his old world forced this painter to compulsively repeat the moment of new consciousness. He regressively fixated on the old world by marrying a frigid woman, who represented an empty vision of a nonsexual mother. Unable to relinquish that vision, he was never satisfied in a new relationship.

YOUNG CHILDHOOD
(TWENTY-FOUR TO FORTY-TWO MONTHS)

Developmental observation tells us that: the aggressive drive gains prominence in early childhood. The infant's libidinal binding of the interpersonal world does not disappear in young childhood, aggressive binding supersedes it. A mass of newly conditioned associations changes the young child's interpersonal responses. I infer that after the corpus callosum develops myelin sheaths and becomes functional, libidinal and aggressive drives rebind redistributed prefrontal associations. How does prominent aggression develop the young child's interpersonal/social self?

TWO TYPES OF AMBIVALENCE

Ambivalence is another concept, such as drive and stress, that straddles mind and brain. Moreover, many people mistake the cognitive term *ambiguity* for the relational term *ambivalence*. Neurally, *ambivalence is a mass of conditioned associations that promote divergent interpersonal responses.* We tend to think of ambivalence as an unpleasant condition, and we dislike being its object. Psychoanalytically, however, ambivalence indicates that the drives have reorganized a person's emotional relationships.

Arising in infancy, what I will call *libidinal ambivalence* is an alternation between love and hate. Hate, in other words, is a libidinal, not an aggressive emotion. If, for the infant, love manifests as oral incorporation and hate as spitting and biting, as Freud said, then hate is displeasure, a painfully conditioned expectation of satisfaction. Deeply narcissistic people characteristically oscillate between love and hate. They are easily wounded—bitten—and they employ sarcasm—biting flesh—in retaliation. Let us say, libidinal ambivalence results from pleasurable and unpleasurable amygdalar conditioning and results in idealized and degraded versions of people.

What I will call *aggressive ambivalence* emerges in young childhood. Aggressive ambivalence joins pain-relieving and painful amygdalar conditioning of anal aggressive associations. Here, the key issue is the binding of aggression. When the young child binds her aggression, she senses self and other as good. Unbound aggression yields a sense of bad self and object.

Modern analysts tend to conceptualize ambivalence as coexistent, *fused* love and aggression. *Fusion* is a psychoanalytic concept that describes the development of *multiple drive cathexes* for the same person. A young child may both libidinally love and hate a parent, and also aggressively experience the parent as a source of pain and of pain relief all in different contexts. I think it is accurate to say that libidinal ambivalence takes the background in young childhood, while aggressive ambivalence takes the foreground.

Sam clung to his libidinal ambivalence. As a child, Sam showed sarcastic, biting wit. His aggressive ambivalence was also exaggerated, but unfused and split from his libidinal ambivalence. He mocked the affect tone of his teachers and friends in ways that destroyed their authenticity in the world. In his artwork, Sam drew cartoons that lambasted his teachers and friends. In his play with children, he stayed on the fringe, a watching wounded, wishing he could be popular.

When one of my daughters was two and one-half years old, she expressed fused ambivalence about her beloved aunt. "I love Aunt Minnie, but when she pinches my cheek, I do not like her!" For ambivalence to mature into a complex set of affective responses, the infant's loved and hated imagoes—massed, positive social images—the young child's aggressive and pain relieving images, and all of the attendant conditioned association networks, must be rechannelled by long-term potentiation for inclusion in a new web of episodic memory.

The young child's social self consolidates when aggressive ambivalence reorganizes episodic memory. Now, *screen memories* can block reverberations from the primal scene. Our painter, for example, used the screen of his art to block the pain of his primal scene while he moved to a geographic and psychological new world. In the pathology of young childhood, the person who has suffered an exogenous trauma can suffer reimmersion in the primal scene, with floods of chaotic pain. This fate can also befall a child with organic incapacity to form a screening social self. In general, however, the newly integrated social self can control this chaotic pain and form new, episodic memories of being a socially good or bad child.

ABANDONMENT ANXIETY:
THE REGULATION OF AMBIVALENCE

Because reexperiencing the primal scene is overwhelming, retraumatiz-ing, and disorganizing to the self and social self, I believe the aggressive system realigns its anxiety signal system. *Abandonment anxiety* replaces *stranger anxiety.* Freud (1926) pointed out that abandonment anxiety in young childhood differs from either separation anxiety or stranger anxiety. In separation anxiety, one's libidinal narcissism is threatened. In stranger anxiety, as the binding of signifiers fails, one's sense of order and predict-ability in the world is threatened.

> I will show you something different from either your shadow at morning striding behind you or your shadow at evening rising to meet you; I will show you fear in a handful of dust.

> —T. S. Eliot,
> *The Waste Land*

When you have a shadow, you have a self. Your past is a shadow that follows you; your future, a shadow that goes before. When you lose your shadow, you become a lost boy, Peter Pan, and you live nowhere, in *Neverland.* To find yourself, you need a mother to sew your shadow back on. Otherwise, when you reach down to find your shadow, you know fear in a handful of dust.

Realizing that he exists alone in the real world, the young child knows that he exists at his parents' pleasure. The young child wants to find the source of his parents' power, and he wants to take it into his own social self. Until he can, abandonment anxiety hinges on a threat to the continuity of care.

- A twenty-seven-year-old female mathematician with severe agora-phobic anxiety when she leaves home in the morning, recalls that as a young child she could not leave her mother to go to a play group. As an adult, she hovers around her home, lest her aging mother die. When she immerses herself compulsively in mathematics, her aban-donment anxiety dwindles.
- A thirty-five-year-old agoraphobic diplomat stations himself in the far reaches of the world away from his brilliant fianceé, lest she know him too well and forsake him before marriage. As he returns to her, his abandonment anxiety increases. Relating like a two-year-old to his fianceé, he fears her aggressive power, as well as that of her powerful family. What he is most anxious about is that if she knows him too well, she will see what a bad boy he is and abandon him.

"Fear death by water" (Eliot, 1922). The child is a sailor clinging to a life raft. In a storm of abandonment anxiety, he mobilizes a detached consciousness of his social self and hopes the gods will intervene. Think of a young child left alone in the bathtub when the water goes down the drain. What will he do? The young child's procedural self, which develops in this era, defends against the *universal construct* of the self's disappearing into reality's toilet—the wasteland—and falling into the primal scene's disorganization. This is when the child learns to do things the right way.

The young child's self and social self are structured by a mechanism called *identification with the aggressor.* When my wife was a young child, she continually pulled the tub's plug in delight whenever her mother went out of the bathroom. In this way she formed a repetition-compulsion that turned her abandonment anxiety into a joke. She identified with the aggressor's power by taking matters into her own hands.

COGNITIVE DEVELOPMENT IN YOUNG CHILDHOOD

In young childhood, a new higher cortical function, *thought,* synthesizes the representational network's visual working memory with the semantic network's phonological, verbal working memory. The newly organized networks absorb the infant's icons and gestures into percepts and words. Thus, Kernberg (1975) sees iconic images coalesce as cognitive *representations* in this period. Transcallosal synthesis of prefrontal networks provides an expanded repertoire of procedures, because, with the onset of *delayed imitation* around twenty-four months (Stern, 1985), the young child can translate her procedures into mediating social speech.

Protosentences, in which objects are still extensions of verbal gesture, develop in the last stage of infancy, while complete sentences inaugerate and expand the young child's cognition. *Sentence formation* provides the young child's budding executive with a verbally encoded capacity to coordinate the hemispheres' synthesis of new higher cortical functions. Forming sentences bridges each hemisphere's assessments. Sentences combine the left hemisphere's *pleasure will* with the right hemisphere's; *aggression will not.*

As all parents know, the two-year-old aggresively labels objects constantly, and learns to proceed with their use in a social way, asking, "Wha's this? Wha's dat?" Moreover, as parents can observe, when the slightly older child is falling asleep, he reels off language heard during the day at a prodigious clip, exactly emphasizing intonation, cadence, and affect markers. He *introjects* the right hemisphere's social language and procedures.

By age three, the procedural self's individuation should be supported by introjected—partially assimilated—dialogue. Cognitive constancy emerges when a conscious *thought process* can be inferred from observation (Piaget, 1954). Using Piagetian *preoperational capacity*, the young child manipulates material objects with limited knowledge of the consequences. The young child's right hemisphere's capacity to make a reality foreground and to manipulate it with the help of introjected social language depends on his capacity to follow commands as they are given. The primal power commandment is *no*.

What effect does exogenous trauma before the age of two have on the young child's cognitive development? We know from object relations analysts that introjects interfere with social development. It seems to me that they interfere with cognitive development as well. Between the ages of two and three, Sam parroted and parodied what he heard, but the content did not belong to him.

Later, in latency, when Sam studied unfamiliar material, he became anxious, and appeared to have an attention deficit disorder. He clung to private semantic formulations of how he thought things should be organized in the world. He could not accept any explanations that were dissonant with his own worldview. Sam could not internalize social speech because it remained, like his perpetrator's genitals, a foreign introject. "In the early period of the child's development, the right hemisphere exerts a much greater influence on the course of speech processes" (Luria, 1980, p. 100). Luria noted that under the influence of the right hemisphere, the young child's speech develops *prosody, cadence,* and *affect*.

The young child invests language with the outside world's power, imitating and weighing it according to the power of the message sender. Psychoanalysts know that *superego precursors* draw their power of prohibition from this preoedipal period of development. Superego precursors introjected at this time are invested with raw aggression and cadence. They can come back to socially haunt in the psychotic depressive's or alcoholic's forbidding and demeaning auditory hallucinations.

THE OEDIPAL PERIOD
(FORTY-TWO TO SEVENTY-TWO MONTHS)

Psyche can still view infancy through the new growth of young childhood. But not for long, since new spiral trails of drive, bonding, and language integration will occlude her backward view as they twist forward. "The flowers of young childhood are mulch for the oedipal period," she thinks. By the age of four, a second signal system superimposes a new layer of neocortical assessment upon the first. Prefrontal and parietal neocortex engender massive new associational fields.

Spiral synthesis (see Figure 4.1) depicts the second signal system's reorganization of identity in the oedipal period. As I said in Chapter 4, in any libidinal stage, we move from periods of *egocentricity,* to *narcissism,* through *empathy.* In the oedipal stage, the second signal system:

- realigns libidinal drive and redistributes subjectivity,
- ushers in universal fantasy fixations that induce and reorganize Type 1 memory, and
- reintegrates the expressive speech system.

New instincts, drives, conditioned associations, and event memory reintegrate experiential loops. The expanded prefrontal system synthesizes meta-functions that subordinate the old systems.

Psychosexual theory sees a new somatic basis for generating libidinal pleasure in the oedipal period. The genitals' pleasure signals induce intense wishes for comprehensive gratification (Freud, 1901). The new mass of egocentric conditioned associations infuses *universal oedipal fantasies.* These aim to possess the parents' sources of gratification. The oedipal child directs the following wish toward his or her parents: "I have you here, inside my fantasy!"

In the egocentric period, the capacity to build excitement accompanies fantasy play. The old "I'll pee later" syndrome often ends in symptomatic urinary release, sometimes during dream sleep. Urethral, clitoral, or glans penis excitation attaches to fantasy. Libidinal excitement charges the capacity for fantasy itself. Now, fantasy and libido go glove and hand.

This period builds the capacity for orgasm, but only under conditions of extreme overstimulation. Greenacre (1971) reports the case of a three-and-a-half-year-old girl, very attached to her mother, who orgasmically discharged the painful stimulation of her physical illness. Does orgasm alternately release urethral and anal sphincter excitation (Ferenczi, 1938)?

HOW OEDIPAL FANTASY TRANSFORMS THE SOCIAL SUBJECT

If new libidinal pressure transforms the subject in the egocentric period, then a new form of narcissistic relating—fantasy play—transforms the social subject around the age of four. During this *period of parallel play,* children inhabit a fantasy world of their own making (Piaget, 1954). When four-year-olds play together, their fantasies intersect, but do not interpenetrate. A legacy of this period is that fantasy remains narcissism's preserve throughout life. We see this, for example, in the case of phallic narcissists and their female counterparts. Fixated on fantasies that intersect, but do not interpenetrate, these people *perform* their lovemaking.

What are the libidinized oedipal wishes? What fantasies accompany them, contain them, and shape their aims? How does the social subject develop *secondary narcissism?* What fantasies shape bisexuality and what Freud called *polymorphous perversity?* How do these fantasies extend into most artistic productions?

The libidinal, narcissistic wishes of the oedipal period give rise to a wish to possess all of the qualities of need gratification each parent possesses. Freud (1923) called the three-year-old's oedipal fantasy *negative,* and the four-year-old's oedipal fantasy *positive.* The three-year-old boy's sense of fusing his egocentric prowess with his father's leads to a wish to be encompassed by the father. The four-year-old boy's phallic narcissism leads to a wish to penetrate the mother and fuse inside her body with her qualities of need satisfying. The three-year-old girl wishes to fuse with the mother's qualities of need satisfying. The four-year-old girl wishes to be encompassed by the father.

In the oedipal stage, Freud made quite clear, these wishes join a *primary process* misunderstanding of the body, body parts, body products, and babies. Primary process is a residual infant mulch of conditioned instincts and drives where products of later development can still take root. The oedipal child can easily imagine fusing with a baby, a penis, or feces inside the mother's or father's body. The same child can as easily imagine that he or she can make babies or that the stork brings them.

Education at this age is irrelevant to fantasy formation. An exasperated father, trying to convince his four-year-old son to relinquish cuddling with the boy's mother in the parents' bed every night, told his son that he should sleep with his teddy bear, who was lonely and needed cuddling and warmth all night. The boy tried for about two minutes and then announced that he was going to get into bed with his mother because the teddy bear "takes up too much room."

We can all see how primary process images of the phallic mother or the pregnant father give birth to the fantasy of monsters. Immersed in fantasy, during a time of reorganizing body imagery, the oedipal child imagines that monsters exist. Those of us who revisit the reservoir of scary dinosaurs, sharks, mastodons, and their ilk immerse in a replay of old masturbatory pleasure . . . and of castration anxiety.

To complicate matters, the oedipal child lives in a world of cuts and bruises. He/she knows the body can be torn apart. If the knee can get a booboo, what will happen if the important part, the genitals are mutilated?

A form of anticipatory body anxiety that Freud called *castration anxiety* necessarily monitors primary process wishes and their derivative fantasies. Otherwise, the sense of body integrity is unprotected. Take the case of a thirty-eight-year-old man, whose castration anxiety failed to preserve his adult integrity. He donned a superman cape and tried to fly from his roof by leaping toward a tree. He missed and became hemiparetic.

Thus, castration anxiety—body anxiety—has to limit the expression of fantasy. The narcissistic period of the oedipal stage produces a reorganization of defenses that are mobilized by body anxiety. The social subject is reorganized by what Edith Jacobson called *selective identifications* (1954). These identifications seek out qualities of the parents, upon which to remodel the social subject's attributes.

COGNITIVE DEVELOPMENT IN THE OEDIPAL PERIOD

Vygotsky (1962) observed that during parallel play:

> egocentric speech develops . . . a tendency toward a . . . specific form of abbreviation: omitting the subject of a sentence and all words connected with it while preserving the predicate . . . the basic syntactic form of inner speech. (p. 139)

Inner speech predicates action. The subject, "I," is implicit.

As in infancy, inner speech assumes a wishful quality. Back then, objects were expected to comply with gestural needs. Now, the oedipal child tells the object, "Stop . . . Go!" He tells his rolling marble, "Go left! Go right! Find!"

The advantage of this new inner speech, I believe, is that it simplifies motor schema. That is, it contracts semantic schemes by deleting what the brain needs for communication with others. Instead of guiding one's action with a remark such as, "Now I will get into the car, but first I must open its door," inner speech says, "Get the car door." Thus, the agent's volition links inner speech's *operatives* (preschematized action sequences) to planned behaviors (Leudar, 1992). Inner speech conveys ongoing intentional planning to the agent, and its operatives link to the formation of extended action plans. This motor set continues throughout life. When an adult uses inner speech while undergoing a PET scan, the left dorsolateral association cortex shows increased functional activation (Damasio and Damasio, 1992).

Thought is trial action. Anticipatory body anxiety monitors the second signal system's capacity to delay action. This cognitive anxiety system regulates the *agent's* initiative in the left hemisphere. At age five, plans are conspicuously defective. The child needs adult interventions to complete them. For instance, given a balsa wood model airplane that needs just a few insertions of wings and tail to body, the oedipal child will go swooping himself, holding the parts, or he will place the wings in the tail section. The fantasy abruptly ends in body anxiety, when the airplane refuses to comply.

Psychoanalysis tells us that repression begins in this period. Repression makes delayed behavior possible by selectively inhibiting intentions, or parts of intentions. An intention contains more than its inner speech and its operatives; it contains motive as well. To give an example of repression forming in the earliest stages, we see children practicing repression on others while playing cops and robbers. "Don't move! Don't dare move, or I will plug you!" Consider also games such as "Captain May I?" or "Mother May I?", also known as "Giant Steps" East of the Mississippi. The line we all remember is, "Go back! You didn't say may I!" The point of "Captain May I" and other such games is to induce frozen motion. When we are dealing with slightly older players, the frozen kids enjoy planning how they will unfreeze and sneak along.

SOCIAL SPEECH: THE COGNITIVE FOUNDATIONS OF SOCIAL ROLES

Toward the end of the oedipal stage, social roles begin to pervade play.[1] The five-year-old develops what Vygotsky called *social speech*. Not part of a conversation in the present, this kind of social speech evokes a previous dialogue. The child asks himself, "How do I put this model airplane together?" He answers himself: "First, put the wings in the body, then the tail in the body, then the glue." The answer replays procedural instruction from a previous dialogue with the father. The revisited paternal answer is social speech. In other words, *social speech is a precursor of what we call internalization.*

Increasingly, the child interrupts play to seek procedural instruction. It is new that the child leaves his inner speech's action operatives in the left hemisphere and shifts to the right hemisphere in order to successfully complete a plan. The child internalizes the dialogue that frames the help, and in the process, develops revised *procedural self* based on role-playing.

The six-year-old-child synthesizes—internalizes—social instruction with inner speech sequences. The result is articulatory rehearsal—"first this, then that, and if this, then that." The five-year-old's left hemisphere's inner speech and the six-year-old's right hemisphere's social speech reweave transcortical associations. These syntheses provide articulatory rehearsal with reflective verbalization. The child can summon internalized dialogue when faced with procedural questions.

Social speech can internalize completely, so that social speech's linguistic structures and imperatives can be completely at the agent's disposal. Toward age six, the child's impulsive fantasy yields to socially mediated planning, as inner speech yields to social speech. Castration anxiety, repression, and internalized social speech pit reality testing against fantasy.

Latency (Ages Six to Eleven)

Moving her attention away from the left path through the oedipal child garden, Psyche looks right. In the foreground, she sees cupolas and small buildings that look to her like fanes. "Kindergarten," she thinks, "is the garden where the child's mind begins to grow toward maturity. On the left path, my Pleasure will be free to dream of me and Eros; on the right, she will be instructed. Oh, Athena, teach my Pleasure the wisdom to supervise her own love's development. Artemis, teach my Pleasure how to self-observe rather than denying the pain that some gods or mortals will inflict on her."

Descending now for a closer look, Psyche enters the latency world, like Alice entering the Queen's croquet ground. A great fanfare erupts. Banners proclaim: "Fairness and Justice in Utopia," but signs of dissension immediately materialize. The latency players interrupt the games with cries of "That's not fair!"; "You always cheat!"; "I do not!" For good or ill, everything in this garden has to do with structure and boundary.

In latency, spiral synthesis brings aggression's structuring power to the foreground of the child's newly objectified social identity. Latency begins as a self-centered aggressive period, gradually becomes a socially centered, social self-building period, and ends with the formation of the procedural self's character structure. Above all, the latency child binds aggression into indwelling, socialized intrapsychic identity. Her mental boundaries requires well-structured reflection.

To understand how latency builds the mind's boundaries, let us review the mind's earlier development: the infant senses shared minds. The young child objectifies other's minds. The oedipal child senses that mind and body can shatter. In latency, the child who once saw herself in the mirror for the first time now see herself as a social person for the first time.

When my older daughter was five, she thought that God was infinite. But, she asked over and over whether infinite firemen could put out the sun. We see in this vignette a mind that is boundless, anxious about losing its vitality, in contact with its drives, and extending its cognitive scope to new context.

Just as the eighteen-month primal scene endogenously traumatized the infant, so does the endogenously shattering of the Oedipal Complex traumatize the child again. Just as the young child clings to the life raft of new autonomy when transitional object thinking melts, the latency child clings to a newly solidified, socially bounded mind when his fantasy world evaporates like the childhood belief in Santa Claus.

The latency child knows that his mind is private and bounded. He can lie because his mental process is not transparent. In latency, the child develops a new form of identity anxiety—*superego anxiety*. Superego anxiety triggers somatic signals of shame and guilt to reenforce the sense of a continent, socially bounded mind. Shame and guilt restrict lying, and they banish fantasy from reality. Basing intrapsychic identity on socialized identifications, latency consolidates character. From now on, a person's character is defined in its social context.

Latency completes the second signal system's doubling of assessment. Consolidating intrapsychic identity, the latency child subordinates higher cortical ego functions to identity-based metafunctions. Latency reflection produces *continuous self-observation*. Freud remarked that the latency child knows that he has a continuous past. Source memory socializes as the latency child tells stories that keep track of source memories.

Freud discovered that when the child relinquishes his investment in his oedipal fantasies, he identifies with both parents, and the identifications structure the superego (1923). In the preoedipal period, parental identifications remained imbedded in the young child's mind as *imagoes*—massed, positively conditioned social images—that impel, or *introject*—massed negatively conditioned social images that rebuke. In latency, parental identifications flow into character. They are *internalized*. The child now finds that like his parents, he personally possesses ideals and moral rules. This child possesses an ability to perceive, deduce, and elaborate social behavior with principals subscribed to by members of his peer group.

The left hemisphere's prefrontal system reorganizes preoedipal and oedipal libidinal identifications as ideals that provide a sense of socially perfected action programs. This is why Robinson Crusoe's ability to build a life from detritus makes alluring reading. The child absorbs himself, intersubjectively, into the biography of his hero, Amelia Earhart, Robinson Crusoe, or Babe Ruth. By absorbing social know-how, ideals provide alternatives for perfecting one's plans/action programs.

The right hemisphere's intermediate prefrontal networks reorganize via identifications with the parent's social power. These identifications socialize self-observation, which becomes one's conscience. In its turn, conscience provides socialized procedural rules for alternative response programs.

This is why the latency child is fascinated with Utopias and perfect justice. This child understands that her parents exist in a social world not of their making. This realization makes the power of the club or gang equivalent to the outside world's power. I remember that during the years of World War II, which coincided with my latency in Minnesota, we habitually broke into two groups, made snow forts, and defended our strongholds with a bombardment of snowballs.

As I will show in Chapter 6, Piaget's *operational cognition*—the latency child's capacity to abstract physical qualities and quantities—follows from the neural developments that provide the procedural self's capacity for making cognitive categories from social speech.

Adolescence (Ages Twelve to Twenty-One)

Psyche leaves behind the right hemisphere's neatly structured region of latency truths. Spiraling upward to the left hemisphere's garden, where beauty dwells, Psyche sees that Voluptua, like all of our daughters, will sexually flower in bewilderment. Voluptua's eyes will glaze in her mirror. The pubescent girl can only see beauty in other girls or women. Like Snow White, she is vulnerable to her mother's narcissistic envy, and to her father's repudiation of his own attraction to his daughter's sexuality. No matter how the parents act and feel, biology mandates this confusion.

Puberty inaugurates a third libidinal stage. Beginning in the latency and increasingly in prepuberty, the cortisone, and then the thyroid system become more active. Hormonal maturation induces an enormous expansion of synaptic networks: "Estrogens, androgens, and adrenal steroids are potent trophic and growth factors that surge in adolescence . . . associated with lengthening of dendritic spines in CA 1 and CA. . . ." (Stevens, 1992, p. 241). For reasons presented in Chapter 3, this causes hippocampal populations to undergo the LTP that initiates pubertal identity.

Follow neoteny's slow, experience-intensive trail, adolescents move from (1) an egocentric, body-centered phase, to (2) a narcissistic, self-love phase, to (3) an intersubjective, falling in love phase, to (4) an object-related phase that begins in an identity crisis and ends in the beginning of adulthood (Harris, 1986). Once again, the subject, the social subject, and the agent develop in a biologically mandated sequence. Adult onset shifts identity's foreground equally to the right hemisphere.

The pubertal adolescent feels as if her body is a new body. The nimble latency girl who can pick up ten jacks quicker than a wink, gives way to the awkward adolescent, longing for grace. Much like the four-year-olds who engage in intersecting parallel play, egocentric eleven- to fourteen-year-olds see others as subject extensions. In early adolescence, the body's emergent sexuality takes the foreground. Pubertal adolescents have to see other's as like or unlike their own subjective "I." They stare at their hair, faces, and bodies for hours. Never out of the mirror, they cannot stop comparing themselves to their friends.

Fifteen- to sixteen-year-olds develop an emotionally organizing masturbation fantasy that gives rise to narcissistic epiphanies of love (Lauffer, 1976). The adolescent's social subject develops overt narcissism. Love is experienced in the mirror, and in being mirrored. For boys, the girl is an extension of his masturbation fantasy, not much removed from the centerfold of *Playboy*. For girls, the boy enters her dreams, with no life of his own. When that life intrudes, it is a bother.

When the boy and the girl fuse their narcissistic longings, they experience love's epiphany. The whole world becomes an extension of their own dreams and fantasies. Puppy loves are eternally fixating. When Freud says, in his article, "On Narcissism," that men love women who love themselves, he is describing the love of midadolescence (1914).

Seventeen- to eighteen-year-olds develop empathic, intersubjective love. While the emotionally organizing masturbation fantasy continues to determine object choice, the chosen one is granted a subjective life of his or her own. The other is granted a center of initiative and sexuality. At this time, other's minds are grist for narcissistic identifications that can pattern one's own life expectations, directions, and goals. Thus, college kids constantly bounce their changing plans off one another.

But, what's this? As Psyche finally prepares to exit childhood's garden, she foresees that her daughter will have to undergo a crisis of passage before Voluptua will be ready to inhabit Olympia, as a human ideal that will give hope to marriage. Nineteen- to twenty-one-year-olds have an identity crisis when their love encounters the whole truth of their beloved's personality. In the same way that people do not fully know what they are getting into when they are making a contract, in the same way that wishful, greedy, narcissistic, and intersubjective yearnings lead to the moment of truth when a contract is defined, the identity crisis produces a crisis of confidence when objective terms of the interpersonal agreement have to be spelled out. The adult *world* demands that the young adult engage in a binding contract with it. Stability is mandatory now.

ADOLESCENT COGNITION

In midadolescence, sexual metaphor leads the way to what Piaget termed *formal thought*. A *third signal system* confers the capacity to extend our assessments to yet another level—to feel what we are feeling, to realize what is significant about our memory as we remember, to think about thinking as we think.

Reflecting about thinking and feeling leads to *metalanguage,* a supra-ordinate synthesis of reflection. "Metalanguage is precisely the form that self-consciousness takes in the realm of language: it is language speaking of itself" (Jameson, 1972, p 207). When we speak of adult executive functions, we are speaking of the metalanguage of identity synthesis. Formal thought synthesizes *metaidentity,* which is who we are intrapsychi-cally, socially and linguistically at the moment of synthesis.

When a person reflects on his own, whole, synthesized identity, he forms *an adult theory of mind.* Once framed in formal thought, we know who we are, and our identity crisis resolves. Once formed, personal adult identity stabilizes the present. It is the container for all childhood experience. We include childhood explicitly or implicitly in every moment of decision. Thus, metaknowledge is always framed in a personal theory of identity—our personal executive's belief system.

Being the most general container of identity, *executive identity makes metaphor of every experience.* It is the source of humor. When you have lost your money, your health has gone bad, your children desert you, and you have become the neighborhood pariah, it is still possible to say, "Things could be worse; I could cease to exist." Or, as Freud said when the Nazi Gestapo finally let him leave for England without any of his possessions, "I would recommend the Gestapo to anyone!" Thus, we can use the intact state of our forward-looking, self-observant identity to ameliorate any episodes that befall us. Perhaps it is in this sense that, turning her back to lament what had already befallen her, Lot's wife turned to stone.

Formal identity metaphors produce personal theories of mind to which every artist and scientist clings. James Joyce's epiphanies gradually built to a personal theory of mind and aesthetics, to which he clung during his writing life. Joyce documents his egocentric adolescent journey toward writing in *Portrait of the Artist as a Young Man.* Freud's late adolescent researches on the bisexuality of the eel became, for him, a personal identity metaphor and a basic tenet in his theory of mind, to which he would cling in the later pursuit of his science of psychoanalysis (Harris and Harris, 1986).

Examples are legion. The adolescent Piaget investigated the flora and fauna of his local Swiss pond to find out if evolution produces new species that accommodate life's changing conditions. The adolescent Luria, marooned by the Russian revolution, used an old hand dynanometer he found to compare hand strength during periods of pure motor effort versus periods where the brain entertained itself with thought. These adolescent theories became the source of adult research.

Indeed, every adolescent's theory of mind peers back into a mythology of personal origins and forward to a romance of adult destination. The mythology is both fantasy and screen. It accounts for personal historical events and family, economic, and ethnic grievances. It is fabricated with socially available materials. The late adolescent harbors a romance with life in order to force the world he is entering to conform to his mythology. Either he strives to redress his family's misfortunes, or he strives to make his own fortune.

Neoteny spirals to adulthood. (See Figure 1.)

Chapter 6

How Adults Solve Problems

We use language against a background of shared beliefs about things and within the framework of . . . social institutions. The study of language use must be concerned with the place of language in a system of cognitive structures embodying pragmatic competence. . . . (Chomsky, 1980, pp. 247-248)

Adults cannot transcend the social language in their minds: Semantic and iconic, language rules us like indwelling gods.

INTRODUCTION: MYTHOPOIESIS IN THE BRAIN

How does the brain build cognitive and linguistic resources from raw data? Each cycle of the brain's structural development builds new data organizers, which we have called neuropsychological functions, ego functions, and metafunctions. The adult's working brain uses all three to gather, integrate, and synthesize raw data. To solve problems, the two hemispheres form a cognitive synthesis by linguistically analyzing the organized data.

Let us clarify these terms from the top down before we go on:

1. *Metafunctions* derive from the adult brain's coherent intrapsychic identity. They imbed identity in a person's social framework. The social framework itself is subject to the family, social, and historical forces that formed it. We recognize these forces as *mythopoiesis*. Mythopoiesis engenders a transgenerational social template for each person's identity.

2. *Ego functions* (higher cortical functions) determine the working constellation of neural systems. Consider it a traffic system that coordinates trillions of synapses in microseconds. To solve problems, the working brain has to synchronize its data gathering, analysis, integration, and synthesis. When the brain talks to itself in millisecond epochs, it creates ego functions.

3. Even before we know it, *neuropsychological functions* encode pre-cognitive data in primitive linguistic forms. Encoded by ego functions and gathered by metapsychological functions, these forms are the brain's inner language. On the brink of action, we transform that language so that it communicates socially. This chapter looks at how neuropsychological functions, ego functions, and metafunctions use inner language to solve adult problems.

THE MYTHOPOIESIS OF COPING AND ADAPTING

In adult life, each hemisphere solves problems differently. The left copes; the right adapts. Coping initiates. Adaptation responds. An early coping ancestor invents a stone tool; an adaptive progenitor moves on to greener pastures. During a local recession, a coping family forms a new business. An adaptive one holds onto old skills and moves to a new location.

We will say that those who cope belong to Type 1, those who adapt to Type 2. The coping left hemisphere finds alternatives to unsatisfactory *action programs*, while the adapting right hemisphere locates alternatives to superannuated *response programs.* Although each person copes more or adapts more, we all cope and adapt.

Adding two more definitions, *confidence* arises from successful coping, while *self-esteem* arises when one is positively responded to in social situations. In stressful times, a confident person plumbs left hemisphere source memory for earlier coping methods. He invents new strategies if necessary. A person with high self-esteem, on the other hand, mines the right hemisphere's repertoire of earlier adaptive responses. If necessary, he combines old elements in a compromise solution.

USING MYTHS AND LEGENDS AS SURVIVAL STRATEGIES

Emerging from the animal into the consciously human, man became consciously social rather than instinctively social: identity became capable of socialization. Jumping over the vast time that followed our descent from the trees, we come to a phase of primitive psychobiography that took the form of myth.

Limiting ourselves to a vein of core myths for Western culture, we see that the Greeks described man as a monstrous being who emerged from *chaos* into a primitively cognized world. The *gods* initially embodied humankind's sense of personal identity. The Olympians idealized the body and had comprehensible human desires. The comic book precis of the Olympians' initial position begins in a state of all-out war. On one side, we have the Olympians; on the other, monsters. Over time, individual gods emerged to represent disparate, but prototypically human survival strategies. Prometheus (forethought), a Titan, embodied the left hemisphere's capacity for planning. Sacrificing himself by giving fire to humans, Prometheus, elevated mankind to a level nearly divine. Since then, you might say, we have relied on our initiatory collaboration to protect us from regressing back into chaos.

Myths are social narratives, among other things. Semantic and iconic, and true to the brain's way of communicating with itself as it solves vital problems, they record survival strategies. Their method is a mythopoeisis of history.

The old mythopoietic framework is increasingly inaccessible. Nevertheless, let us rely on Freud's intuition that myths embody a coherent picture of the cognitive, social, and emotional life. This intuition seems particularly attractive in a contemporary culture that deliberately practices fragmentation and dissonance. As we will see, Freud's mythologically inspired, quasi-biological theories can help provide a present-day context for a neural system's approach to coping and adaptation.

The essential point is that the myths we will look at are simply classic tellings of the personal and family myths that we develop in early childhood, socialize in latency, codify in adolescence, and use as adults. Personal or culturally updated myths orchestrate our problem solving. The individual who relies on a myth does not think of it as familial, an artifact of contemporary culture, a product of historical or religious tradition, or part of the Greco-Roman arsenal. His goal is to organize adult action and response programs.

A myth is valuable, therefore, because it is a template. I will be arguing that:

1. *Type 1, libidinal templates* organize plans by projecting goals and ordering the steps needed to fulfill them, and
2. *Type 2, aggressive templates* organize affective responses to realities beyond the individual's control. The gist of what follows is that the executive uses myth's hemispherically divided templates to stabilize adult and transgenerational identity. In other words, every act of coping or adaptation is filtered through the templates of myth.

The Myth of Coping: Type 1 Psyche

Virgil's story of Psyche recapitulates what we know about the left hemisphere's maturation. To review, from infancy on, the left hippocampus explicitly encodes experiences of love that the amygdala simultaneously conditions. The sense of a soul, or Psyche, gathers the subjective continuity inhering in this explicit encoding. Put developmentally, consciousness arises when the infant embodies a sense of love in gestures or in words as verbal gestures. To generate libidinal experience, the infant invests every entity with salience that gives it luster. The salience with which the infant invests the object is the lustre that attracts her attention (Chapter 5). These roots of meaning and salience eventually generate the sense of perfection and beauty that adults equate with their own narcissistic integrity. Now, in our myth, Psyche is the youngest of three princesses, and Aphrodite is the mother of a grown son. Envying Psyche's surpassing beauty, the goddess of love orders Eros to wound Psyche with love's arrow. Aphrodite wants Psyche to fall in love with a lowlife, but Aphrodite gets what she does not want. Enchanted with Psyche's beauty, Eros unwittingly pierces himself. This is how Cupid falls in love with Psyche.

Now an oracle declares that no *man* will fall in love with Psyche. Believing that a mysterious fate awaits her, the young woman's family abandons Psyche on a mountaintop. A Zephyr lifts her to beautiful gardens that surround a palace where every item's luster matches her own. A godlike, invisible lover comes to Psyche at night. He fills her with sexual beauty, on the condition that she never see him.

Psyche longs to tell her family what has happened. Granting her wish, Psyche's invisible lover has Zephyr transport her sisters to Psyche's mountain valley. Poor Psyche gets her wish. The sisters envy Psyche. They are so envious and frenzied by the celestial decor that they are ready to kill. The sisters convince Psyche that if she cannot see her lover, he cannot be real.

Credulous, Psyche goes to Eros's bed with a lamp. As she sees him, a drop of hot wax from the mortal world falls upon him and wounds him more deeply than he immediately knows. Eros flies away in an aura of light. Declaring that Psyche betrayed their pact, he decrees that she must live without love.

Envious singles, Psyche's sisters seize this opportunity to search for Eros. They ascend Psyche's mountain, offer themselves to Zephyr, who is not kind, and fall to their deaths.

When Eros falls sick with his wound, Aphrodite discovers his love for Psyche. Aphrodite wants to destroy the girl, but Hera and Demeter convince her that Psyche should be tried with impossible tasks. To earn her unearthly love, Psyche will have to sort hordes of mixed grains, gather the golden fleece, carry the deathly water of the river Styx, and finally bring Aphrodite Proserpine's box of eternal cosmetics. These will restore the beauty Aphrodite has lost in her worry over Eros.

Psyche performs the first three tasks with the fairy tale help of creatures. Then, as any woman would, Psyche gives in to the wish to make herself permanently beautiful for Eros, if in eternal sleep. Psyche partakes of the cosmetics, and falls into a death-like sleep. At this point, Eros recovers and returns to Psyche, restores her to wakefulness, and helps her fulfill the task of bringing Proserpine's cosmetics back to Aphrodite. Then Eros gains Zeus's support for his marriage to Psyche. Zeus intervenes on Eros' behalf so that the raging mother can relinquish her son and accept his eternal marriage with Psyche.

In the myth, Psyche uses all her libidinal, coping effort to extend her subjective integrity—her healthy narcissism—into the intersubjective space where she unites with Eros. At first, Psyche enjoys Eros' physical and vocal passion, but in needing to see him as a god, she overreaches. In addition, Psyche has to cope with her sisters' envy and with Aphrodite's. We learn from watching Aphrodite and the sisters that envy is one residue of immature narcissism. Those who retain too much envy cannot achieve intersubjectivity—the concomitants of which are the ability to love and take pleasure in another. To achieve her own goal, Psyche has to relinquish her own immature narcissism.

Before she can unite with Eros, Psyche has to reallocate her libidinal drive. At first, her libido is bound to a mental tool that is insufficient for the job of loving Eros. She begins by being bound to all the salience that lends objects their luster. Then, however, she is forced to relinquish her magic palace and all it contains. Psyche, unlike her sisters, lets go of salience in order to sublimate her libido to a higher purpose.

Psyche's tasks are of increasing use to the gods. Challenged to sort the grains, Psyche is stupefied and mute. Although she has the will, Psyche can not complete any of the tasks without accepting help from her soul-mate and fairy tale helpers who represent the ability to form intricate and articulated plans. Thus, Eros gets the ants to do the sorting, the harmonious reeds whisper instructions about how to avoid the fierce rams, a voice from a tower instructs her how to cross the river Styx. Psyche internalizes the help so that it becomes her own mental tool, included within her own articulatory rehearsal. Psyche's strength is in her willingness to adopt coping skills. Psyche is validated by the intensity of her love. Resisting the pathological narcissism to which her sisters yielded, she was able to become Eros' wife. Psyche's is the romance of coping.

The myth leaves room for narcissistic foibles. On one hand, Psyche did have to see her lover in his godlike radiance, and did have to succumb to the wish to make herself eternally beautiful. Aphrodite, on the other hand, was an envious mother who wanted to hold on to her son as an eternal youth, which guaranteed their relationship, her own juvenility, and her family-encompassing narcissism. Like Psyche, Aphrodite had to accept direction—in her case, from other gods—and relinquish some of her own narcissism. This is a familiar human story. In it, we see the interactive equilibrium among gods, families, and individuals, as is the interaction between the superego, ego, and id.

The Myth of Adaptation: Type 2 Cadmus

Cadmus' is a myth of adaptation. Brother of Europa, whom Zeus carried off in the guise of a bull, Cadmus, searching for her, becomes a wanderer and explorer. Cadmus adaptively binds his aggression. He follows Apollo's direction to pursue a white ox that has never been bound to a plow. The god orders Cadmus to build a city, Thebes, in Boeotia (meaning ox—oxford) at her resting place. In the course of events, a dragon slays Cadmus's original Phoenician followers. But, the dragon is sacred to Ares (Mars), the god of war. Inspired by Athena to superhuman force and pinpoint accuracy, Cadmus spears the raging dragon to a tree through its blood-foaming mouth. Following Athena's advice, Cadmus seeds the Boeotian field with dragon's teeth.

Two armies spring from the dragon's teeth. Not participating in their battle, Cadmus watches the armies neutralize each other. A remnant of five survivors become the original Boeotians, and with them, Cadmus founds his city—but only after eight years penitential service with Ares. Because he binds his aggression, the gods give Cadmus the goddess Harmonia in marriage. She is the daughter of Ares and Aphrodite.

We might look at this as a marriage of hemispheres. Ares and Aphrodite represent the source of *love unbound* as vengeful war and the source of *love fulfilled*, both intrinsic to the left hemisphere. Harmonia is a left hemisphere goddess. Cadmus, however, personifies the right hemisphere's capacity to bind its aggressive drive in service of adaption/exploration. Having married a goddess, Cadmus' human progeny are nearly divine.

Children of the right hemisphere, Cadmus' five offspring are doomed by unbinding aggression. Cadmus' daughter Semele, for instance, was impregnated by Zeus and bore Dionysus. Tricked by Aphrodite, who was jealous of Semele's beauty, Semele was granted her wish to see Zeus in his splendor. Semele was incinerated as he materialized. Dionysus and his Maenads bring relief and joy (binding) or dismemberment (unbinding). Cadmus' line ends with Oedipus.

FROM MYTH TO THEORY

Freud used a variety of myths to penetrate his own libidinal and aggressive themes and to restructure his identity. Freud derived his dual drive theory from a comparison of daily human experience with prototypes in myth. During the first half of his life, Freud's knowing and avoiding Oedipus's fate engendered coping. Playing Hercules against Thanatos (death) helped him adapt in the second. In the first part of his life, Freud pitted an instinct for survival of the species against an instinct for personal survival. During World War I and after his cancer took hold, he opposed libidinal and death instincts.

Although most of us merely cope or adapt as best we can, when neither coping nor adaptation are effective survival mechanisms, some of us, like Psyche, Cadmus, or Freud, are able to turn up the strength of our drives. What does this mean? To offer an animal analogy, in the animal herd, the leader's succumbing to age, illness, or defeat in sexual competition causes another animal to step forth. That animal upregulates his previously dampened neurophysiological repertoire. To do this, he raises the level of his catecholamines and cortisol. Now, so far as Freud was concerned, the old *weltanschauung* (worldview) had lost its potency. For a while, he naively used cocaine to upregulate his socially damped neurophysiological repertoire. In the end, he became so attuned to his drives and their derivatives that he was able to see how dynamics create a worldview. This made him a leader of others.

To the extent that we all lead ourselves, we all step up our drives and change our neural systems when coping and adaptation fail. In preceding chapters, we concluded that when confronting volumes of new experience a person remodels her prefrontal identity. Her amygdala stimulates biogenic amine availability and, in concert with the hippocampus, induces a cascade of long-term potentiation that rededicates experiential loops to the new exigencies of life. In this sense, Psyche and Cadmus illustrate more than libidinal coping or aggressive adaptation: they represent intrapsychic change.

THE BRAIN'S ORGANIC UNIVERSE

Q: Why have I selected gods and mythic characters to represent brain functions in the illustrated *Acropolis of the Mind*?
A: The collective recorded consciousness of our civilization has always externalized these functions under these or other names.

The Greeks, for example, thought that four humors—black bile, yellow bile, phlegm, and blood—created the melancholic, bilious, phlegmatic, and sanguine personality types. These types codified personality organization, psychopathology, and an arcana of physical disorders. Brain functions were understood as secretions from the spleen, liver, mucosa, and bone marrow. A depressed person suffered from black bile and exhibited melancholy. A bilious one had a vented spleen. A phlegmatic one remained calm, probably to stave off asthma. A sanguine person showed sturdiness, high color, and good cheer. The theory of humors thus mythologized the relationship of body and mind.

These humorous terms and others derived from similar mythologies are snippets, which, when spliced together, form a linguistic code (a submerged, metaphoric system) that signifies how the body and mind function together. This linguistic legacy insidiously determines how we put together our theories of mind. In contemporary culture, for instance, one's food, mind, and body are bound in a loose mythopoeisis of health. The theory of mind implied by this code is more than insidious, it is pervasive.

I contend this all happens because the brain externalizes its working structure. We all collaborate in these externalizations. We use the social field to enact (or challenge) the externalized, submerged values we share, as well as our overtly held beliefs. Certainly, in their relation to mythologies, shrines, oracles, forms of worship, etc., social institutions present us with an image of the brain's structure. The Acropolis of the Mind is my representation of the brain's prefrontal identity zones. Let us take another look at these zones' iconography (see Figure 1.1).

Dividing the brain into two spheres, we uncover diverse metafunctions and identity functions amenable to linguistic and social externalization. Imagine the brain's organic universe as the observer sees it from the right hemisphere's vantage point:

> I am the eye with which the universe
> Beholds itself and knows itself divine;
> All harmony of instrument or verse,
> All prophecy, all medicines are mine . . .

> —From "Hymn to Apollo,"
> Percy Bysshe Shelley

On Apollo's temples were inscribed the following:

> Know thyself; Nothing in excess; Curb your spirit; Observe the limit; Hate hubris; Keep a reverent tongue; Fear authority; Bow before the divine; Glory not in strength; and keep women under rule.

> —*Bullfinch's Mythology*, p. 21

These claims and precepts sum up the right hemisphere's self-observant metafunctions as personified by Apollo and by Diana, who stands for modesty, grace, and virgin vigor. They display socially watchful, well cadenced, bound aggression.

Both Apollo and Diana also preside over the unbinding of aggression. In the Greek mythos, Apollo, the god of the sun, brings sunstroke, pestilence, and malaria. When Diana's metafunctions lose their bound quality, the huntress uses the moon's arc as her bow, and the rays of the moon as shafts that wound or kill.

Ben Jonson approaches Diana in typical male fashion:

> Lay thy bow of pearl apart,
> And thy crystal-shining quiver;
> Give unto the flying hart
> Space to breathe, how short soever;
> Thou that mak'st a day of night,
> Goddess excellently bright.

> —*Hymn to Cynthia*

It is important to note here that in the Greek mythos, women tend to purvey aggression. In our present culture, the opposite is usually true. It is the men whose aggression unbinds, and the women who develop moral control. Wanting simply to ascribe bound and unbound aggression to the observer, in the Acropolis of the Mind, I take the twins Apollo/Diana as a single figure that represents the right hemisphere's observing function.

On the left side, Athena represents the supervisor. Standing for left hemisphere metafunctions, she parallels Apollo/Diana. Having sprung from Zeus's head as his brain child in the Greek mythos, in the Acropolis of the Mind, Athena oversees the left hemisphere's inner speech and she counsels action. In *The Iliad* and *The Odyssey,* Athena deploys cunning and craft. Protecting Odysseus, Athena endows her protege with strategic survival skills, hallmark of the coping left hemisphere's metafunctions.

Moving down to the bottom row where the identity functions are depicted, imagine that Hermes, the Greek messenger of the gods, is our agent. The agent is a left hemisphere function. It conveys semantic data to the supervisor (Athena) where it inaugurates inner speech, and to the executive (Zeus), where it engenders articulatory rehearsal. Hermes is a spellbinder. In myth, his caduceus is a magic scepter. He charms like a sociopath or an impostor. Hermes' persuasive narration spins such a yarn that he is the patron of commerce, rogues, and gamblers. Like Hermes, the agent animates myths and fantasies. Its repeated narration seems to immortalize human experience. The agent's magic wand can also hypnotically transform consciousness from attentiveness to fantasy states that merge with sleep.

I selected Arachne, the weaver, to represent the procedural self. She portrays our prolific capacity to imitate and render what we perceive. The tale of Arachne follows.

Hearing about Arachne's vaunted skill in weaving and embroidery, Athena comes to Arachne in the guise of an old woman. Athena warns Arachne that she may challenge mortals, but not the gods. Arachne tells the goddess to keep her counsel to herself. With that, Athena weaves a divine and lively soul:

> Among these leaves she made a Butterfly,
> With excellent device and wondrous slight,
> Fluttering among the olives wantonly,
> That seemed to live, so like was it in sight;
> The velvet nap which on its wings doth lie,
> The silken down with which his back is dight,
> His broad outstretched horns, his hairy thighs,
> His glorious colors, and his glistening eyes.
> Which when Arachne saw, as overlaid
> And mastered with workmanship so rare,
> She stood astonished long, ne aught gainsaid;
> And with fast-fixed eyes on her did stare,
> And by her silence, sign of one dismayed,
> The victory did yield her as her share;
> Yet did she inly fret and felly burn,
> And all her blood to poisonous rancor turn.

> —From Spenser's *Muiopotmos*

Unheeding, Arachne takes up the challenge. She weaves lifelike images of Zeus's misdeeds: Danae Zeus's golden shower [of semen], Europa deceived by Zeus's guise as a bull, and Leda and the Swan. But, perfect as her imitation is, Arachne is railing against Zeus's power to create, wanton as it is, and against Athena's power to carry out Zeus's will.

> Being so caught up,
> So mastered by the brute blood of the air,
> Did she put on his knowledge with his power
> Before the indifferent beak could let her drop?

> —From W.B. Yeats' *Leda and the Swan*

As her truth is only mortal, and as Athena rents her woven web, Arachne hangs herself, and is transformed into a hanging spider. Imitation is not creation. That is why the right procedural self is represented as a human, while the left agent, Hermes, is represented as a god. The left hemisphere's capacity to spin a tail seems divine, while the right's abides by human limitations. We see the war between the hemispheres, between gods and the human, in Athena's spinning bout with Arachne.

Remaining in the right hemisphere, I selected Perseus to represent the self's endurance. As Freud (1922) said, Perseus overcomes men's great terror, castration, which the Gorgon, Medusa, represents in Greek mythology. Graea and Gorgons, Medusa's old-maid cronies, parallel Diana's troop of virgins as they guard Medusa:

> They lament in dreary song,
> That they should live so long.
> Medusa turns the men to stone,
> Who see her snaky crown.
>
> —Jay Harris

Athena and Hermes help the hero steal the single eye and tooth the Graea share. Defanged and robbed of gaze, these three hags (Medusa's sisters) lose their power to terrorize Perseus. Then, equipped with winged sandals by the Graea, Perseus flies to the shore of Oceanus, where he finds Medusa asleep. With his face turned away, Perseus decapitates Medusa while Athena reveals the Gorgon in the mirror of his shield. Athena guides Perseus's hand for the blow. From Medusa's body springs the phallic winged horse Pegasus, powerful and divine.

Riding Pegasus, Perseus flies to Atlas's realm of the golden apples, where he wishes to rest and eat. Atlas refuses to credit Perseus's introduction of himself as Zeus's son. Fearing for his golden apples, Atlas tries to expel Perseus. Not to be frustrated, Perseus shows Atlas Medusa's head, which creates the Atlas mountains, the stone foundation of heaven.

In the Acropolis of the Mind, Perseus represents the right hemisphere's capacity to prevail over petrifying terror. For men, the terror of castration represents the death of the self. For us all, to turn to stone is to be dehumanized and permanently detached, a fate of those who, like Lot's wife, yield to trauma.

Reviewing the Greek myths represented in the Acropolis of the Mind, we can imagine that the Greek world was patriarchal. Collectively, the mythopoiesis provides a metaphor for social and family conduct. In the myths, women prototypes of the left hemisphere tolerate male infidelity, and they are jealous of their rivals. They portray an encompassing narcissism that defines family boundaries. Women prototypes of the right hemisphere are virginal, and they threaten male potency.

These prototypes still provide a metaphor for marital, family, and interpersonal equilibria. As we saw in the case of Echo, a person's dynamics discharge unstable marital and family equilibria. They discharge the emotional energy that cannot be contained by the templates of mythopoiesis. That is why people reexperience their past relationships in transference in therapy.

MYTHOPOIESIS IN THE ADULT'S SYSTEM-CONSCIOUSNESS

When emotional disturbance and cognitive dissonance threaten the executive's ability to do work and coordinate metafunctions, the left hemisphere uses fantasies and the right hemisphere uses constructs to maintain the coherence of identity under duress. Problem solving requires prefrontal decision making that is consistent with the executive's framework of beliefs and values. When Mars' sons, Terror, Trembling, Panic, and Fear, and his sister Discord (mother of Strife), violate our beliefs and values, the executive has to avert chaos. Coping, adaptation, and intrapsychic change restore the prefrontal system's equilibrium.

Fantasies bind and hold imaginary satisfaction and inhibit disillusionment. On the threshold of adult life, we consolidate a personalized Janus-faced myth that spawns fantasies that narrate the future of our identity (Chapter 5). The way this works is by the left hemisphere fabricating living events that wishfully recreate and romanticize family myths. The adult executive's goal is to profit from the lesson of the past.

The mature executive *consciously* fantasizes to promote an array of trial actions. Each fantasy is a *compromise formation* among:

- *libidinal drive*
- *available action programs*
- *acting out fixations*
- *action ideals*
- *selective repression of intentions*
- *social pressure*

Fantasies protect supervisory metafunctions from being overwhelmed with libidinal pressure.

Freud, for instance, embraced a family romance mythology in his latency, which gave rise to a love of reading and narration. In *The Interpretation of Dreams,* he traced his love of reading to having been enthralled by the history of Massena, the Jewish marshall who helped Napoleon cross the Alps and conquer Europe as Hannibal had done (1900). As he read, he ambitiously fantasized that he was with Massena. In later years, self-analysis taught him that his identifications with Massena and later, Moses, originated in a latency family romance: he was really the son of a great hero or king and was meant to fulfill a great destiny (Harris and Harris, 1984).

What was the source of Freud's family romance? Harris and Harris (1984) showed that Freud was deeply affected by his family doctor and by his nursemaid. When Freud was twenty months old, his younger brother, Julius, died. The family doctor presided over Julius's death. Freud never did completely synthesize an identity for himself that excluded Julius as a symbiote. While the family was recovering from this tragedy, however, little Sigmund asked his nurse what happens to babies when they die. She told him about limbo and hell—interesting news for a Jewish child.

The nurse and family doctor became prototypes of alternative, Christian parents. They seemed to represent an irrational but compelling world, deeply rooted in the past. Sadly, the beloved nurse left the house after being identified as a thief. At the same time, the father's business failed. The family left Fraiberg for Leipzig. During the train journey, Freud recalled seeing gas jets burning. They seemed to confirm hell's flames.

All that and devouring classical mythology shaped Freud's latency family romance. Mythologizing his own origins and sublimating the fantasies which derived from them, Freud struggled to unify disparate worldviews: the Greco/Christian *and* the Jewish world (Harris and Harris, 1984). It is now needless to say that Freud wished to redress his father's failure in the Christian world.

Freud wanted to understand what we are calling the executive metafunction. For him, climbing mountains and seeing vistas sublimated a fantasy of omniscience. He tried to understand consciousness by analyzing its associations and finding the rules that govern their coherent patterns. At the core of his fantasy was a Mosaic desire to bring these discoveries to the people. This is to say, Freud saw contemporary psychology as primitive or erroneous, and he wanted (and in his mountaineering expressed) to bring revelation from the mountaintop.

The right hemisphere forms perceptual, affective constructs. Some of these are familiar to us as cartoons: simplified, affect-laden percepts that span deleted aspects of reality. Cartoons, like fairy tales, establish a primitive iconography that binds aggression. Planted by our parents in front of TV or computer screens from early childhood, we absorb cultural icons as building blocks in our value system. The effect is confusing.

Constructed with powerful idealism, *Sesame Street* characters, for instance, lead the young viewer to imagine that prejudice does not pervade our multicultural society. The possible benefits of this positive social propaganda are secondary to the unconsciously deleterious effects of aiming idealistic, parenting propaganda at an audience of children. Here, ethnic tolerance ceases to be the issue. These scripts favor interpersonal resolution, nonviolent solutions, and a nurturing environment mediated by eminently decent adults. Children do not need parenting propaganda; parents do. Although *Sesame Street*'s adult characters can screen family violence or deficits in parenting, they do not allow the child protagonist to triumph over real trauma. This is because the scripts represent problems amenable to logic rather than traumata, which are the staple of fairy tales, which are amenable to emotional resolution.

What did I see when I opened my eyes this morning to the business report? Kermit the Frog was giving a commencement address to the graduates of Southampton University. This icon of the graduates' youth exhorted these future participants in the economy to go forth and improve the marine environment.

I have had patients who got married in Disneyland to screen out childhood trauma. In one couple, both partners had endured childhood physical and sexual abuse. At their wedding, they took movies of the ceremony, with Mickey and Minnie in attendance. This couple planned to show the movies to their children to pass along the cultural mythology that screened their own childhood traumata. Think of Disneyland's mythology covering the world! Its castles, characters, and icons flash in our imaginations, and even on some adult citizens' computer screen savers.

Another patient, a paramedic, who is terrified of children's death, experienced the sudden loss of his teenage son. At the time, the boy and his eight-year-old sister were visiting their grandparents in Florida. Because the sister felt deprived of the fun she had with her brother, the parents decided to make it up to her by taking her to Disneyland. The parents too, felt that Disneyland might compensate them for the loss of their son.

People defend their social selves against violent trauma by using television characters, movie characters, or cartoons as screens. Witness the popularity of Japanese comic books, still defending the population from the trauma of World War II. Old-fashioned cartoons such as "Tom and Jerry" and modern-day computer robot cartoons dehumanize aggression, elevate perceptual denial to an extreme, and make experience timeless.

Constructs respond to trauma by altering painful, episodic memories to block the return of pain. To give an example, our patient, Echo (Chapter 5), believed her mother cared about her. Without this construct, she would have lacked a template for maturation. In therapy, Echo had to relinquish and work through the loss of her false mother construct. Constructs such as Echo's span the gaps in identity that denial and other defense mechanisms create. They can promote emotional growth and stability as well as syndrome formation.

We have studied how three kinds of anxiety protect identity's coherence (Chapters 3 and 5). When dopamine's pressure for satisfaction is unfulfilled, anticipatory anxiety elicits repression, a Type 1 defense. When norepinephrine's exploratory pressure produces unrelenting novelty, vigilance anxiety elicits denial, which is a Type 2 defense. When serotonin's synthesis fails, identity-anxiety elicits a detachment from vitality, a bilateral defense. Repression, denial, or detachment can be exerted against whole streams of amygdaloid and hippocampal data.

Repression with detachment promotes *fantasy immersion states.* Fantasy states suspend *action initiation,* just as dream sleep does (Freud, 1900). When anxiety signals persist during problem solving, we immerse. We have all immersed in fantasy while studying for a difficult examination. In examination of dreams and fantasies, we return to earlier bouts of difficult problem solving that we resolved after much anxiety.

Denial and detachment promote *screen-memory immersion states.* These states suspend *responses to reality.* Thus, abused persons detach, and their responses are paralyzed. Immersion states end when anxiety recurs, or when the source memories that pervade fantasy and screens suggest adaptation or coping strategies.

ALTERED CONSCIOUSNESS

Dissociative disorders are immersion states' syndromatic fulminations. Multiple traumas and/or fixations in successive periods of development may induce dissociative disorders. Complexly interacting fantasies and screen memories compromise the executive mediation of states of consciousness. In Type 1, people act out impulse disorders, "I didn't do it on purpose" shows Type 1 dissociation (subjective abrogation). Perversion, gambling, or kleptomania exemplify shattered identity. Type 2 dissociation, "the devil made me do it," splits the self. Multiple selves can organize disparate identity states. Fragmented—crazed—identity dehumanizes a person.

The mythological Psyche averted pathological narcissism, but the mythological Echo did not. When Echo fell in love with Narcissis, her identity shattered. Our patient, Echo, averted shattering. Another clinical vignette will illustrate shattering.

The patient is a forty-year-old virgin. Her mother had died when the patient was five, and her father blamed her for it. The patient lived a fantasy of being an obedient son. She could not find a mother in herself with whom to identify. Her therapist became her transference mother, as well as the intrusive, bad father.

When hormonal and emotional signals of menopause stimulated the patient's latent wish to bear the child she would not have, her sense of cohesion repeatedly shattered. She felt that if she could not become a mother, there could never be a woman in herself. Her long-standing, emotionally organizing fantasy of being an obedient son, and her desire to become a mature woman conflicted. She raged that she had no center, that her therapist had not helped her mature as a woman. She then panicked about losing the mother/father bond with her therapist. This *identity pros-thesis* maintained her fragile emotional equilibrium.

Identity prosthesis manifests in the phenomenon of hypnotism. One who can disassociate allows the hypnotist to temporarily assume the executive role. To relinquish ones executive identity renders a person vulnerable to many psychopathological syndromes. Some people become psychotic when their identity prosthesis (whether therapist, friend, or relative) disappears.

The supervisor and executive protect subjective integrity from shatter-ing (from anticipatory-anxiety lifted to panic) by maintaining the organiz-ing fantasies which configure repression's selective inhibition. The supervi-sor selectively inhibits intentions arising from wishes. The supervisor admits only pragmatically meaningful semantic data from working memory.

People vulnerable to Type 1 dissociation experience overloads of unex-pected, conditioned pleasure. Psychoanalytically, each dissociated *fixation* is acted out. Immature people, with fantasy-based identity, can develop *Type 1 character distortions:* narcissistic, narcissistic sociopathilogical, hysterical, avoidant, paranoid, schizoid, or schizotypal personality disor-ders. These people often try to compel others to enable their acting out.

Often, a mother fabricates family history to conform with her need for narcissistic integrity. I have seen many patients who became schizophrenic when they renounced their family's mythology. Their renunciation brings on such an identity altering flux of transference that their identities cannot cohere. They then reinstate the family mythology delusionally. These patients may live a family romance, delusional "American-dream" of wealth that insulates them in their rags. One patient lived on the streets of Jersey City, looking across the water at "his" Manhattan, which he called his "bubble world." Delusionally, he regained his family's lost fortune.

MYTHOPOIETIC SOURCES OF ADULT IDENTITY

We had better not build our castles in the air. The Acropolis of the Mind crumbles on imaginary foundations. Those who live too exclusively in family or social mythologies are vulnerable to the vicissitudes of every social and economic upheaval that effects our families' fortunes. Without flexible intrapsychic identity that can absorb new data, we fall ill.

Ordinarily, executive identity synthesis paces the brain's progression through life. When the executive's maturity falters, pathological narcissism or mood disorders can erupt. In other words, when essential problems of life remain insoluble, and when adaptation and coping fail, then intrapsychic identity itself must change. Earlier, we concluded that identity zones and their metafunctions alter in response to adult life changes.

Many people cling to outmoded (subjective or objective) structures of identity. Sleeping Beauty, Psyche's fairy tale counterpart, could not emerge into adult life as a woman until she survived a long, sleeping metamorphosis. Unable to face the challenge to mature, our amygdaloid conditioning and our hippocampal associations and contexts lock in childhood patterns.

One woman took PCP (phencyclidine—angel dust) daily from age eighteen to twenty-eight. She felt like a sleepwalking cartoon. At twenty-eight, her emotional and cognitive maturity remained as they had been when she was eighteen. The combination of PCP's retarding the formation of new, dedicated amygdaloid, hippocampal, and prefrontal circuits, and shutting out experience produced emotional and cognitive stasis. Neither Cupid nor a prince enabled her capacity to become a loving woman. Instead, she had to struggle daily to find herself—with minimal help from a drug program. To wake each day to find herself a twenty-eight-year-old was to find a void in her identity that only constant eating seemed to fill. She entered college wanting to study psychology in order to try to mature.

Source memories of abuse can be disenfranchised when family mythology opposes recognition of the abuse. In Chapter 7, I will argue that after the second signal system becomes operational, the prefrontal system absorbs both true and false memories of infancy and young childhood into belief and value systems that are buttressed by fantasies and constructs. These belief and value systems conform to social and family mythology.

False memories are the *bête noir* of those who dare to treat traumatized people. How can we tell whether a child has been sexually abused? Perhaps she has been convinced it happened by repeated narration of a false event, embellished and encouraged, or even planted by a "well-meaning" examiner. Investigators find that socially reenforced false memories are easy to come by (Kihlstrom, 1995) In Chapter 7, we will learn how to distinguish true from false source memory.

How can we distinguish organic from functional amnesia? People who develop *transient global amnesia* cannot process new data because their hippocampus becomes dysfunctional. They show retrograde amnesia for decades of sourced memory, but they do not lose their childhood's emotionally organized memories. People with *paramnesia*—functional amnesia—show normal hippocampal processing, but they "lose" their sense of who they are *and* their sources memories (Kritchevsky et al., 1995).

Trauma freezes source memory. One unfortunate patient found his sister's body, minutes after she had been murdered by his cousin. An instant later, he realized that his cousin's brain was splattered over the wall. For months on end, his detached mind lived in the moments leading up to the crime, in search of explanation. With detective help from friends and a therapist, he reconstructed the following scenario: his cousin had been set that night to revenge himself against a mobster who had beaten the cousin's younger brother. Drunk and frightened, mistaking the patient's sister for the one on whom revenge was to be exacted, the cousin shot her, and then he shot himself in the head as he realized his mistake.

Whether true or false, this reconstruction was necessary to this patient's social self's integrity. He had to preserve the integrity of his premorbid identity, to keep from identifying with the aggressor and becoming a criminal himself. Aggression unbound leads to *splitting*, a terror of reality that detaches observation, and pathologically changes personality organization. The timeless search for detailed explanation of trauma may underlie the popular murder and detective genre. The urbane omniscience of a sherlock remedies the trauma. Is validating reconstruction the work of the detective genre?

AN OVERVIEW OF EVENT-RELATED POTENTIAL (ERP) STUDIES

We have considered how the adult brain organizes its emotional life.[1] Now let us see how it weaves cognitive data with brilliant speed, as the two hemispheres shuttle data back and forth, right and left, between percept and word. Event-related potential studies help us follow *cognitive epochs*. Entrained data are:

- *registered* (100 milliseconds—msecs),
- *processed* (300 msecs),
- *discriminated* (400-700 msecs),
- *assessed* (700-1200 msecs), and
- *reflected* (1.2 to 5 seconds).

In a moment, then, data are prefiltered, selectively registered, multiply associated, redistributed, itemized, and enter the self-observing, reflective domain of the executive's identity.

In most ERP studies, the subject attends to a particular sensory or verbal stimulus and makes a simple response when it is presented. Even uninstructed or demented subjects attend to novel stimuli.[2] During stimulation, a computer EEG (CEEG) records the brain's activations and inhibitions, by area, in msecs. Activations and inhibitions reflect synaptically generated positive and negative waves.

Testers identify particular waves in timed epochs. Positive *P-waves* report facilitation. Negative *N-waves* report inhibition. p300, for instance, is a processing wave generated some 300 msecs after the presentation of the stimulus; and the *contingent negative variation wave (CNV)*, that follows p300, selectively inhibits brain regions that are about to discriminate features.

When we are confronted with novelty, a reorientation reflex causes our frontal/prefrontal system to inhibit brain processing. This makes a level playing field in which all new data are potentially important. Then, as the executive renews problem solving, higher cortical functions selectively inhibit brain areas that will receive and code data. This inhibition in the amygdala, hippocampus, basal ganglia, cerebellum, in the speech encoding Broca's and Wernicke's cortex, as well as other sites records as N waves. While actually registering and coding data, the brain generates facilitatory P waves in distributed matrices. The data analyzing rule is, N waves precede P waves.

As an adult analyzes data, his attention generates serial N1, N2 (CNV), and sometimes N3 (prolonged CNV) waves. The capacity to generate each N wave matures with frontal development (Shibisaki and Myazaki, 1992). Thus, CNV development corresponds to a capacity to delay response while complex data are being analyzed. The brain develops cyclically. Inhibitory capacity hones in on fresh processing areas while others functionally differentiate.

The Development of Data Analysis: An Overview

By four months, infants generate characteristic ERP responses to familiar faces (Nelson and Collins, 1992). Face data is processed preemotionally in the amygdala and precognitively in the rhinal cortex (Chapter 2). As much of our lifelong data processing has to do with recognizing faces and detecting their expressive play as it does with semantics. From infancy, visual processing precedes phonological processing (Johnson, 1989).

Working memory functions before the corpus callosum matures at eighteen months; however, its dual visual and phonological processing systems mature after the corpus callosum myelinates. Visual processing's precedence over phonological processing tells us something fundamental about consciousness: we attend percepts before we cognize them. Preconsciously then, we know an entity exists and how it makes us feel before we encode it semantically.

As the corpus callosum matures, the right hemisphere makes a foreground for higher cortical functions (Chapter 5), and face processing shifts toward the right hemisphere's parahippocampus (Sergent, 1992). Face processing requires "Perceptual mechanisms capable of detecting subtle differences among faces. . . . Each representation must then be stored reliably . . . further operations . . . make contact between perceived and stored facial information" (Sergent, 1992, p. 16).

The eighteen-month-old girl who noticed her parents' facial pores also read her parent's faces to see if her behavior could lead to abandonment. Since *panic disorders* (terrors) activate the right parahippocampus (Reiman et al., 1989), and since they come out of the blue, I wonder if face processing of abandonment signifiers remains a nonverbal function throughout life.

Before eighteen months of age, the infant's visual memory is a rolling scroll that imprints a vast reservoir of affect cartoons. Some artists can find and reproduce these cartoons. Arachne's *visual sketch pad* in the right hemisphere forms *iconic gestalts—percepts—*that fill sensory gaps and delete nonfunctional data (Baddeley, 1986). Arachne's sketching from life is illustrated by a study that flashes different colored dots in a person's visual field. The person's working memory fuses them into a moving, unicolored entity (Dennet and Kinsbourne, 1992).

As working memory finishes its lightning sketch, Hermes' *phonological processing unit* in the left hemisphere schematizes morphemes and sequences articulemes, deletes meaningless sounds, and fills in missing auditory data (Baddeley, 1986). The twenty-four-month-old child's capacity to form a sentence requires that working memory select, delete, and integrate both phonological and visual data. By matching words with visual images, the young child brings details out of the cartoon. Young childhood's *denotation* is concretely cognitive.

Because the second signal system begins to mature at forty-two months, *iconic and phonological buffering* (N2) also mature at that time. Buffering selectively maintains facilitation in prefrontal modules during delayed responses, as one searches for data relevant to problem solving (Goldman-Racik, 1992).[3]

Cognition's advance to *operational thinking* in early latency can be studied in mismatched and oddball ERP paradigms. Despite the name "mismatch," the subject is asked to respond only to *expected* data. In "oddball" paradigms, a person is asked to respond when a sound, word, picture, or meaning is unusual. P300, oddball, auditory discriminations can be evoked at six years, but *oddball semantic* responses usually cannot be evoked until age ten (Shibasaki and Myazaki, 1992). Oddball capacity develops later than mismatch.

On hearing a word ambiguously, even adults ascribe an expected meaning to it before asking, "What did you say?" Latency's frontal and prefrontal maturation provides the capacity to recheck meaning. The CNV wave matures throughout latency, but p300 does not fully mature until puberty (Johnson, 1989).

What ERP Adds to a Neural System's View of Adult Cognition

Working memory has interdigitating but separate visual and phonological processing units. In this way, each hemisphere makes a distinctive contribution to consciousness. In our discussion of mythological templates for identity, we spoke of the war of the hemispheres. Sometimes, each hemisphere may come to a different conclusion about data's salience or significance. This can produce odd effects in our sense of identity.

Analyzing such a linguistic, aesthetic phenomenon in a paper he called *The Uncanny* (1919), Freud related the *heimlich* (familiar), to the *unheimlich* (unfamiliar). When we think about the antithetical sense of primal words such as familiar/unfamiliar, the psychological emphasis falls on the prefix, *un-*. The right hemisphere creates *un-* by establishing a construct for the unknowable—which is to say for a quality (the familiar) deprived of itself (the unfamiliar). Because the right hemisphere processes the left side of our body's experience, the right hemisphere produces "sinister," terrifying images of novelty, which may leave us uncertain whether an entity is alive.

As we discussed earlier in the chapter, Perseus represents the self's capacity to overcome the castrating Gorgon, Medusa. Medusa turns men to stone, if they meet her gaze. Freud equated that particular uncanny image of being turned into a nonentity with castration anxiety. He also equated the uncanny image of *nothing* (no-thing) with the little boy's sense of a woman's missing penis. In *The Uncanny*, Freud equates uncanniness with the castrating sense of the eyes being torn out. When the right hemisphere lacks vision, we cannot observe self.

What do you as reader need to know to recreate your mind and your identity out of your functioning brain systems, each moment? Keep this question in mind as we use ERP to evaluate how your brain builds experience and recreates identity from sense impressions and their semantic transformations. Now, to make things really interesting, also keep the concept of the *unheimlich* in mind while we try to imagine what happened when, while riding in a train, Sigmund Freud felt his compartment lurch. A door opened and the father of psychoanalysis had to implicitly ask the following questions.

"Is Something There?"

Registration happens at 100 msecs in the rhinal cortex, hippocampus, amygdala, cerebellum, and basal ganglia—all areas where LTP forms extensive associational networks (Bruder et al., 1992).

"What and Where Is It?"

Processing occurs at 300 msecs as rhinal cortex, parietal cortex, basal ganglia, and other matrices generate N1 (n200). N1 deletes irrelevant sensory data. P300 forms preconscious items in areas that N1 prepared for selective data processing.[4] processing explicit data, working memory determines what entities exist and where. As p300 facilitates visual gestalts, Freud sees a person framed in the doorway and produces the word, "someone."

"What Kind Is That?"

Discrimination takes place at 400 to 700 msecs. Discrimination tells us about data's salience or significance.[5] During discrimination, processing networks separate wheat from chaff. Working memory's discriminative epoch detects:

- features in context, e.g., "traveling hat, dressing gown." His N2 stabilizes and prolongs feature and semantic detection.
- face detection begins and Freud implicitly asks, "Who is that? What expression does he have?" CNV is higher in the right hemisphere (Barret and Rugg, 1989), and now P3 (p500) detects simple oddball variations (Stuss et al., 1992). Freud begins to implicitly ask, "What's wrong with this picture?"
- Complex features appear as unfamiliar data elicits right hemisphere N3—prolonged CNV—and then, Freud attempts a
- verbal transformation, as N3 prolongs the left hemisphere's P3 discrimination up to 700 msecs. Staring at the person who had revealed himself, Freud is startled by an "uncanny intruder."

Thus, working memory's discrimination epoch turns data into items of which we are conscious. Parietal networks provide an associational context for these items. The right parietal networks provide spatial gestalts for body images. Those on the left create a temporal sequence for semantic items. *Extended working memory* turns data into items held in short-term memory (Kounios and Holcomb, 1992). (You, the reader, resolve my discordant syntax at P3 [p500], but you resolve my discordant meaning at p750.) Resolving syntax before meaning, we use syntax to provide a template for meaning. We process simple sentences before complicated ones (Ruchkin et al., 1992). Some people cannot enjoy complex sentences. They prefer Hemingway to Faulkner.

Having seen the uncanny intruder, Freud has to assess the situation. His internal assessor, his Perseus, implicitly asks a question about the new item in consciousness.

"Will It Help or Harm?"

Assessment takes place at 700 to 1200 msecs. Sometime later, reflecting in tranquility, Freud remembered his clear assessment. "I can still recall that I thoroughly disliked his appearance" (Freud, 1919, p. 248).

During prefrontal assessment, consistent and meaningful short-term memory items are absorbed by articulatory rehearsal. Unsure about data's meaning or familiarity, we repeatedly backtrack to working memory. There is a window of opportunity here: Short-term memory may merge with working memory for up to three to five seconds (Elbert et al., 1991).

As working memory and short-term memory alternate, we become subjectively aware of prolonged assessment. This awareness accompanies prolongation of left hemisphere CNV (Ruchkin et al., 1992). As the executive gathers items into articulatory rehearsal, the supervisor assesses how long that gathering takes. Looking at this evidence, Freud would say that the sense of time is contingent on the ego's observation of its own process.[6]

Mental status examinations and common sense show that adults absorb about seven short-term memory items into articulatory rehearsal, which is why telephone numbers have seven digits. Complexity, however, decreases the number of items that can be held (Belleville, Peretez, and Arguin, 1992). Emotional pressure and anxiety signals also decrease short-term memory's capacity.

What happens during a long assessment interval, such as reading this paragraph? Prolonged semantic or syntactic errors elicit anxiety signals. How many times has my wife told me that prolonged syntax requires a shaped argument? "Begin," she says, "with a topic sentence, provide examples, and come to a conclusion."

Prolonged novelty can also elicit anxiety signals that force a perceptual reorientation. In the case at hand, Freud's train phobia may have frozen his right hemisphere's perception, because unfamiliarity with the familiar threatens our sense of objective identity. I posit that prolonged CNV waves accompany repression and denial. Repression and denial manifest the prefrontal system's selective inhibition of the left hemisphere's motivational inconsistencies and the right's affective threats.

ERP data on phobic patients adds to this description of the effect of defenses on adult processing. Phobic patient's working memory damps p300 responses to visual or verbal references to the phobic object, it even damps responses to symbolic or dynamically related ones (Kushwaha, Williams, and Shevrin, 1992). When data have already been processed and are conscious, however, their p300 effect cannot be damped by defenses (Farwell and Donchin, 1991). This tells us that repression works during or before working memory, suppression after it. After we are conscious of an item we may repress, but we cannot lie to ourselves.

But, back to Freud. Having assessed the intruder as unlikeable and probably harmful, Freud has a problem. The implicit question for him is,

"What Should I Do?

Reflection takes place at 1.2 to 5 secs.

> Jumping up with the intention of putting him right, I at once realized to my dismay that the intruder was nothing but my own reflection in the looking-glass on the open door. (Freud, 1919, p. 248)

Quick judgement is at issue here. Simple behavior occurs at 1.0 to 1.5 secs (Pfurtscheller and Berghold, 1988). Supplementary motor cortex uses inner speech to trigger behavior (Chapter 1): Inner speech says, "Jump up!" Freud jumps up.

In more prolonged data evaluation, *articulatory rehearsal* makes an explicit sentence the prelude to behavior. Then, the executive exercises judgment to determine whether the proposed behavior or communication is socially and personally appropriate. We can delay behavior, because the "articulatory loop" that links working memory and short-term memory can extend short-term memory indefinitely (Paulescu, Frith, and Fracko-wiak, 1993). During *prolonged reassessment,* we constantly reshape the sentence of the moment. As far as short-term memory is concerned, pro-longed reassessment is like musical chairs played with the same number of chairs, but variable numbers of players. The items under analysis change and repeat. The items that keep finding a chair undergo associative ramification on their way to inclusion in a spoken sentence.

A state of identity awareness between assessment and behavior, *extended executive reflection,* monitors signal anxiety and redeploys defenses. When identity anxiety persists, the executive extends articulatory rehearsal to include further associations to events and episodes. Frequently, this memory data emerges in fantasies or screens. Like dreams, fantasies block access to voluntary behavior so that the individual can take an imaginative "time out." Some people enter spells of great permeability in which any image might inspire a creative solution. During prolonged reassessment, visual imaging and spontaneous emotional imaging reenforce and modify short-term memory. Then, the executive may change plans.[7]

Given to creative spells, repeatedly prolonged over weeks or months, during which he produced his identity-altering works, Freud (1919) used his train experience as a source memory for his paper, *The Uncanny*. He tied the sense of the uncanny double to defenses against castration anxiety. It remained for a later work, *A Disturbance of Memory on the Acropolis* (1933), to bring the psychology of aggression into the analysis of his identity disturbances. With help from Arachne, we will pick up the thread of Freud's identity disturbance in Chapter 7. We will see that identity disturbances are often triggered by an aggressive conflict that is mediated by the right hemisphere.

To conclude, articulatory rehearsal synthesizes the content of the prefrontal system's parallel assessment zones. When the executive forms one of Chomsky's (1980) infinite, possible sentences, that sentence is structured by reflection. Reflection is a hierarchical prefrontal synthesis that creates a psychologically whole person. The creation of reflective consciousness is the emergence of mind from brain.

If you, the reader, understand how time's arrow pierces the successive epochs of the brain's cognitive universe, you too are a changed person. If so, something new exists in your mind and brain that you can use to better understand how your brain talks to itself. If not, I suggest you read the above data set again.

THE THREE LAYERS OF SYSTEM-CONSCIOUSNESS

The functional hierarchy of cognition recapitulates the brain's neoteny. By this I mean that to analyze data, we use three functions successively. First we use the *neuropsychological functions*, which comprise the associated products of neural systems. Then we use the *ego functions*, i.e., prefrontally organized higher cortical functions. Finally, we use the *metafunctions*, which are supraordinate prefrontal identity functions. We filter consciousness through this functional hierarchy in the moment of multiply processing new data. To see how the brain talks to itself, we need to think about these functions serially.

Neuropsychological Functions in Infancy and Young Childhood

In the rudimentary first speech system, socialized babbling forms *protolanguage* (Werner, 1940). Protolanguage is the language of infancy. It fuses vocal gestures with multiple primary objects. Object cartoons begin global shapes, that we can call iconic prototypes. In English proto-language, *Da* is "daddy," "duck," or "that." Protolanguage is made of single morphemes/articulemes. Each utterance condenses a protosentence. Thus, *da* does nicely for "Daddy, come here," "Give me the duck," and "I want that." Vocal intonation makes protocommunications effective. Parents hear the intoned differences and understand protosentences as complete communications. The linguistic miracle of adulthood is that you understand that while the baby wants to fuse with the object, the baby is also simply identifying it as a member of a global class.

The baby's protolanguage invites the parents to fuse intersubjectively with the baby's intent. Protolanguage is the glue that holds all later sentences together. If a sentence were a piece of bread, protolanguage would be the gluten inside a kernel of wheat.

More basic than protolanguage, neuropsychological phenomena illustrate the left hemisphere's innate tendency to produce semantic meaning and express libidinal themes. Laughing is a sudden release of libidinal pressures for satisfaction. In *cataplexy*, the libidinal release can be so sudden that the whole motor system loses its tone, often after a belly laugh. "To die laughing" has its origin in this neuropsychological phenomenon.

Infants laugh with an infectious release of libidinal drive. Like every other neural development, the original formation of consonant utterances is libidinally cathected. Laughing releases babbling from its libidinal cathexis, in the same way that Freud (1905) said that verbal jokes release libido. Discharging libido, laughing is the prototype of expression. The sounds of h-h-h or ha- ha- ha- convey the release of consummatory pressure.

When an adult refinds her own protolanguage, laughter always follows. Our baby words and our baby gestures make us laugh with pleasure when they slip out and are recognized for what they are. In this way, laughter also relieves the pressure of our adult determination to be goal oriented. When we feel a surplus of too many goals that we cannot achieve all at once, we sometimes throw up our hands and laugh.

I remember studying for both finals and boards in medical school with a friend. At 2:00 a.m. on the night before the neurology final, we were trying to learn the names and locations of all the autonomic ganglia in the head. Having taken thirty-one tests in the sixteen previous days, and confronting as novices a complexity of strange morpheme strings, our task seemed so ridiculous we almost died laughing.

The left hemisphere receives *aural phonemes,* the receptive building blocks of meaning in Wernicke's superior temporal area; and it forms vocal motor schema known as *articulemes,* and *serial articulemes*, known as morphemes in Broca's lateral frontal area. Phonemes associate auditory and kinaesthetic sensory images. Morphemes express meaning because they are building blocks of vocal gesture. The left hemisphere's dorsolateral frontal cortex strings morphemes to form speech.

What linguists have missed is the dopaminergic cathexis of these building blocks of expressive speech. A good example is found in the sn-group of articulemes: snort, sniff, snout, sneer, etc. In this onomatopoetic group, the gesture of the tongue pushes libidinized consonants out of the nose. Here, consonants convey gestural meaning, and they contain libidinal pressures like the explosive h-h-h of laughing, which discharges libido in a grand exhalation. But, if we grunt, groan, growl, grouse, or just say grr, watch out, our libidinal initiative is being stifled, and that is no laughing matter. Thus, even consonant groups can be differently conditioned.

If consonants are libidinally cathected, vowels are aggressively cathected. Vowels hold aggression, and release it as affect. Crying is the prototypical affect explosion. Crying vents unrestrained affects as vowels. "Aieee— OH Me —Oi Vay—Oi Yoy Yoy." Examples of the right hemisphere's conveying affect in vowels are endless. There is a rhythmic beat of aggressive rhythm in crying too. Consider sobbing.

We have been talking about the drive cathexis of simple neuropsychological functions. Considering how catecholamines modify their neural receptors, I realize that the modifications last for intervals that correspond to short-term memory. Norepinephrine, the carrier of the aggressive drive, modulates its targets for up to a few seconds. There is an inherent rhythmicity in the aggressive cathexis of prosody and rhythm.

While vowels contain affect, the beat contains the underlying rhythm of aggression. Primitive rhythms accompany aggressive discharges later in life. Think about rap cadence or the grunts of the bayoneter or athlete. Drums beat aggression as troops go into battle. Parade music celebrates their success or failure. To offer another example of aggression losing its bound quality, dismemberment murderers regress deeply and rapidly. Some described a drum beat of aggression as they carried out their ritual slaughter (Harris and Pontius, 1975).

Thus, I hypothesize that the brain's catecholamine systems infuse their neuropsychological functions with drive for the second or two required for behavioral discharge. How do we bind and regulate the drive that cathects simple neuropsychological language functions? Let us explore how the development of social language comes to regulate the brain's functional state.

Our spiral synthesis model shows that as the corpus callosum matures, it synthesizes introjected social language with gestural speech. Thereafter, formulating *sentences* binds our drive pressures and limits acting out. A sentence unifies the brain's whole neural, cognitive, and emotional analysis. In this way, language controls the brain's functional state.

Beginning in young childhood, affect attunement inculcates social language. The right hemisphere infuses vowels with affect, and it instills affect and cadence into social language (Luria, 1980). In the heavily stressed syllables of affect attunement, the mother and others repeat the infant's protowords as well as the young child's imitations of adult phrases.

Meanwhile, the young child imitates social language while naming objects. At the neuropsychological level, he cathects his crossmodal associations with cadenced aggression and affect. In other words, naming and labeling are language functions that emerge from affect-attuned, social language.

When the parents aggressively demand that the young child handle objects obediently, the young child heavily introjects their language. *Introjection* is a psychoanalytic term. It means that the young child feels he is being forced to "throw" the words into his mental space. Introjection therefore refers to the aggression binding, neuropsychological process of throwing the power of language inside where it can be redeployed.

Projection reverses introjection. Every parent gets to have the cry of "no" thrown back in his or her face. In the three-party system of mother, father, and young child, or parent, sibling, and young child, identification with the aggressor arises as introjection and projection form a new interpersonal mechanism. When, for example, the young child hears the father call the mother a bitch, the young child is soon deploying the same weapon. Identification with the aggressor is one of the less pleasant building blocks of character structure.

It takes work for both the young child and the parent to tame the aggression inherent in the young child's introjected social language. The young child's love for the parents and fear of abandonment enter into the process of verbal introjection. We can see this work going on as we listen to what the young child repeats as he falls asleep. The day's experience enters long-term memory as the day's introjected language is recited.

Ego Functions in Childhood

Ego functions deploy language to arrange higher cortical functions. Let us review the brain's expansion of ego functions in the oedipal stage and latency. Inner speech is the left hemisphere's oedipal version of libidinized protolanguage. Inner speech is egocentric. It is subjectively conceived for the purpose of the subject's telling the agent of action to do something such as "Go find!" or "Jump up!" Inner speech need not specify reality signifiers or use syntax.

Inner speech inaugurates a new way for the brain to talk to itself. The libidinal voice of child's play—inner speech—invokes action on the brink. Athletes use inner speech to effectuate their immediate action plans. The golfer says "Go left! Roll! Stop!" This is because inner speech contains the *operatives* for behavior. Vygotsky saw residual inner speech in the action language of lovers (1962). Lovers need not articulate a whole sentence to each other. They need only indicate how their wishes coincide, intersubjectively. They can develop a shared inner speech. "Do it. Do it more." They incorporate the protolanguage of infancy in their endearments. They call each other pet names from infancy, "Do it, baby. Love you, duck."

Towards latency, the child begins to use social speech to internalize instruction. While the three-year-old is commanded and controlled by aggressively conditioned social language, the six-year-old takes social instruction from the outside and turns it into flexible action plans of his own making. *Internalization* turns heard social speech into inner speech. Internalized social speech turns into *volitional* speech as *reflexive sentences* that tell the brain how to organize procedures. "He made himself sit down." Attention disordered kids cannot use reflexive language very well. "Can't you make yourself sit down?" asks the exasperated teacher.

The latency kid begins to *internalize entire dialogues*. He begins to tell stories of his conversations to his friends and family. He refreshes the dialogue in narratives: "I said this, and he said that." Sometimes, early in latency, kids have imaginary companions who get to play the role of the social other. Imaginary dialogues take off from the internalized ones.

If *internalized dialogue* is boiled down to a linguistic sauce (*espagnol* or *glace de viand*); that sauce is *articulatory rehearsal*. Articulatory rehearsal has two types of ingredients—inner speech and social speech—which can be recombined and reformulated as many possible sentences. Pragmatically, articulatory rehearsal is the recipe of items necessary to formulate a problem-solving sentence. Each problem-solving sentence unifies elements of cognition, social relationship, anxiety and emotional signals, and defense. Thus, as each sentence unifies the integers of identity, the brain practices new combination of ego functions—its working constellations.

Articulatory rehearsal synthesizes inner speech and social speech while absorbing the data held in short-term memory. Distinguishing between short-term memory and articulatory rehearsal is difficult because when we hold items in short-term memory, we tend to imbed them in sentence fragments that articulatory rehearsal deploys. When we make an attempt to remember items for a few minutes, the items are not in our consciousness, but they are potentially there. The networks of associations upon which they depend remain facilitated (buffered), so that the items can be reconstituted if needed in consciousness. I am going to ask you, the reader, to briefly repeat this point after you read the next paragraph.

The three-year-old's sentences are simple and concrete. The latency child's sentences achieve syntactic and semantic complexity, formulating abstractions that prepare for a greater range of behaviors. Latency planning carries over to the next day. Before going to sleep, the latency age child uses reflexive sentences to record surplus intentions into his source memory. That is a fancy way of saying that turning out the light, Johnny thinks, "Tomorrow, I will remind myself, my father promised to take me to the Knicks' game."

What is buffering? Do you remember?

Metapsychological Functions in Adolescence and Adulthood

Language's self-observing quality reinforces identity. In fact, our formal sense of coherent identity is imbedded in every reflection. Adolescence is when every thought comes to have the reflective quality that Piaget called formal thought. Thus, metalanguage structures adolescent formal thought—thinking about thinking (Chapter 6). Formal thought is metalanguage that conveys self-observing reflection about identity.

Language's reflexive metafunction operates in the right hemisphere (Luria, 1980). Anosagnosia—inability to self-observe—occurs when a right hemisphere stroke destroys language's reflexive capacity. Right hemisphere damage disorganizes our capacity to use language to self-observe because that hemisphere "reads between the lines," between the words, so to speak. If we ask someone, "what does the saying, 'the grass is always greener on the other side of the fence' mean to you?" and the person says it means "someone else has it better than I do, but they do not necessarily," you can know that the person's right hemisphere is able to use metaphor to communicate in a socially appropriate way. More than this, the person is showing a capacity to self-observe, and to use images that go beyond simple words to come to a social conclusion. The right hemisphere makes sense of more than what is said.

Indeed, *the right hemisphere contextualizes the whole social field.* Metalanguage locates the communication within the social field in which its content is meant to have an impact, and then it conveys instructions about how a message is to be taken. Put another way, metalanguage conveys the sender's identity state to the receiver's identity state. The injunction, "Listen to me carefully" promises dire repercussions to both the speaker and the listener if unheeded.

The adult has to try to understand the social consequences of every behavior before discharging it in words or deeds. Every behavior has social consequences. As we solve problems, we not only process information and prepare to act, we also modify our behavior through reciprocal social communication. The reciprocity includes more that the meaning of the spoken words, gestures, and emotional expression. It also includes the communication of images and metaphors that speak more directly and comprehensively about each person's identity state. Identity communication is imbedded in reflexive metalanguage such as idiom. Saying "You're a dick" to someone sends a pungent identity message.

Metalanguage tells us who we are in relation to others. When we internalize metalanguage, we provide ourselves with social rules and goals for social behavior. Advertising's effect on our immediate behavior illustrates metalanguage's effect. The media panders to our needs for social identity. Appealing advertising writing offers us a vehicle for feeling good about our social participation: "drink X-beer" (because you'll have a life with your peers that they approve). We give money to a good cause when it is presented to us in metalanguage that gets to the guts of our social identity. "This is Officer Constable. The Police Athletic League needs . . . "

Like protosentences, early concrete sentences, and simple articulatory rehearsal, metalanguage binds the drive energy that pressures us to solve problems. Metafunctions distribute both our higher cortical functions and our neuropsychological functions as we analyze data and prepare to behave. The executive's meta-analysis proactively selects earlier processing modes that will be activated and inhibited during the problem-solving analysis of data. Thus, metafunctions determine which distributed links will be used for any particular task.

Even our metalangauge is mastered by our drives. The superego regulates the id's mass of conditioned associations. In that sense, by analyzing every problem's social repercussions, we automatically bring the proper mix of drive pressures to bear on its solution. When our solutions are maladaptive or poorly coped, or when our extended networks cannot validate our data analysis, then we must change our identities or become immersed in syndromes. That is the topic of the next chapter.

Chapter 7

The Source of Brain Syndromes

Various stressors trigger the endocrine and neural adaptations that constitute the stress response . . . While glucocorticoids are vital for surviving acute physical stressors, prolonged glucocorticoid exposure . . . can cause a variety of diseases. (Sapolsky, 1992, p. 299)

Picking up the thread from Sapolsky, we can view stress as a general mechanism of adaptation that contributes to the formation of many psychiatric and neuropsychiatric syndromes, as well as a specific mechanism that can lead directly to post-traumatic stress disorder (which we will consider in Chapter 8). A major mediator of stress, glucocorticoids produce effects on various hippocampal glutamate populations ranging from:

- excitotoxicity, to
- increased long-term potentiation, to
- decreased long-term potentiation, to
- dendritic atrophy with vastly decreased activity.[1]

Since each effect has long-term cognitive consequences, we will need to understand which effects are most instrumental in the formation of a particular cognitive or psychiatric disorder.

What adaptive function can syndromes serve? We partially answered this question when we concluded that epilepsy is the price we pay for the brain's evolutionary capacity to flexibly change its neural pathways through its LTP mechanism. In response to exogenous or endogenous stress, the brain undergoes periods of either rapid change or slow accommodation. Its rapid change reorganizes its biochemistry, neural systems, neural networks, and identity, as well as its social representations. A syndrome accommodates to rapid change, or inflexible stasis in any of these structural levels. Incompatibility between our prefrontal networks and their parallel processing networks that assess cognitive, social, and emotional data, can trigger experiential dissonance that leads to syndrome formation.

We have to distinguish between individual stress mechanisms of adaptation and coping, and a species-wide, collectively evolved gene-pool which contributes to survival. I argued in Chapter 6 that our brains evolved collectively to preserve our species. In this Darwinian sense, family, social, political, and economic institutions are (1) historical extensions of collective identity metafunctions and (2) contemporary determinants of what our brains deal with as we solve problems.

In Chapter 6, I argued that mythopoiesis is a collective historical narration that preserves mechanisms of coping and adaptation. Thus, our species survives better over the long run if some, like Psyche, are genetically determined to cope creatively, and others, like Cadmus, are genetically determined to adaptively explore. Even now, this difference manifests in disagreements between those who think we should spend our collective monies on pure, creative research, and those who want to adapt by exploring the frontiers of space. Some think we should spend NIMH (National Institute of Mental Health) monies on basic neuroscientific research, and others prefer pragmatically adaptive clinical research.

This chapter uses the neurobiological and phenomenological findings in neuropsychiatric syndromes to more firmly ground the hypotheses presented in the first half of this book. In Chapters 4 and 5, I argued that endogenous excitotoxicity ushers in neurally ready developmental stage changes. In following the process of the brain's developmental spiral synthesis, I posited that both endogenous and exogenous excitotoxicity play a major role in determining each hemisphere's capacity to organize experience. What mechanisms account for the formation of both psychiatric and neuropsychiatric syndromes? Psychopathology results from:

- a disassociation between overall prefrontal assessment and particular networks's data processing, and/or
- a disassociation between hippocampal precognitive processing and amygdalar emotional processing.

Either disassociation can occur in organic or nonorganic conditions. Both distort identity coherence. Both defend against traumatic excitotoxicity. The aftermath of trauma dampens hippocampal, precognitive processing; intensifies amygdalar, emotional processing; and interferes with identity coherence.

NEUROPSYCHIATRIC SYNDROMES

We will discuss a variety of neuropsychiatric syndromes in order to further clarify how excitotoxicity and the brain's natural defenses against excitotoxicity lead to syndrome formation. Later in the chapter, we will distinguish syndromes according to which hemisphere in most impacted by excitotoxicity and its defenses. We will want to keep in mind the question of how to reestablish a natural equilibrium in the brain's excitatory processes.

Strokes

Let us study the excitotoxicity that leads to neural death in more detail. The reader may elect to follow the process of preprogrammed neuron death by apoptosis without learning all the particulars involved. The biochemical changes underlying various types of LTP are a specialist's domain. In either case, we will approach the topic by looking at strokes. Strokes provide one model of the excitotoxic process that leads to spreading neuronal dysfunction in neurons some distance from the stroke.

Thus, it is not so much acute bleeding damage or ischemic lack of blood supply—hypoxia—that causes neural damage in strokes, but the aftermath—the excitotoxic process that the stroke triggers. Presently there is a search for medications capable of interrupting excitotoxicity that can minimize stroke damage. Essential to our argument, however, is that neural damage secondary to excitotoxicity proceeds in stages (Choi, 1990).

The neurons most vulnerable to strokes are also most vulnerable to LTP, kindling, and excitotoxicity (Choi, 1990). Choi's most vulnerable list includes CA 1 hippocampal, neocortical pyramidal, and cerebellar purkinje neurons. These are all glutamate populations essential to the formation of distributed links. As a result, strokes' excitotoxicity undermine our most essential distributed data processing systems.

Excitotoxicity proceeds in three stages (Choi, 1990):

1. *Induction* caused by hypoxia is an energizing biochemical process triggered by a high postsynaptic influx of calcium ions. The influx lasts for more than thirty minutes.[2]
2. *Amplification* takes place after the thirty minutes. During amplification, LTP transfers to other neuron populations.[3]
3. *Expression* lasts up to three days after acute hypoxia in a *penumbra* area surrounding the acute damage.[4]

Alzheimer's Dementia

The major dementias—microinfarct, Alzheimer's, closed head injury, Pick's, and those associated with Huntington's and Parkinson's syndromes— also involve excitotoxicity. Once these dementias begin, excitotoxicity may carry out much of the neural destruction. The functional type of dementia depends on (1) which glutamate populations are effected first, and (2) the consequences of their destruction on the brain's communication.

Alzheimer's heavily affects the hippocampal formation and neocortical association areas, Pick's the frontal and prefrontal association cortex, Huntington's the caudate connections, and Parkinson's the basal ganglia—all areas high in glutamate populations (Morrison and Hof, 1991). Apoptosis normally increases with aging. In Alzheimer's, the brain's housekeeping function of clearing cellular debris appears to be genetically undermined.[5]

Temporal Lobe Epilepsy

Temporal lobe epilepsy and its antecedent, *kindling*—which lowers the seizure *threshold*—provides another window into mechanisms of excitotoxic spread. Volumetric studies of brains that have undergone temporal lobe epilepsy often show hippocampal formation shrinkage (Cook et al., 1992). *Status epilepticus* is a condition of repeated seizures persisting for over thirty minutes and leading to death in fifty percent of cases. Those who survive develop hippocampal sclerosis (Lothman, 1990). Thus, repeated temporal lobe seizures, even widely spaced in time, lead to cellular destruction in the hippocampal formation.

As we discussed in Chapter 1, ubiquitous gabaminergic (GABA) systems ordinarily limit neural excitability to levels consistent with functional transmission. After a seizure, GABA activity characteristically spreads neural depression, but this damping becomes exhausted after thirty minutes. The fact that GABA inhibition limits the spread of a seizure is seen in the EEG spike and wave phenomenon of *absence seizures*. The downwards spike corresponds to GABA inhibition, the upward wave corresponds to glutamate transmission (Gloor, 1989). GABA exhaustion releases the excitotoxic process, which causes hippocampal sclerosis.

Lothman (1990) presents an experimental seizure model for the excitotoxic process. Repeated application of excitotoxic NMDA activating agents in the baboon hippocampus induces status epilepticus, which becomes self-activating in thirty minutes. As GABA inhibition deteriorates, kindled neurons generalize their seizure activity. Eventually, the baboons show excitotoxicity in the neocerebellum and the middle neocortex as well as the hippocampus.

Lothman's work confirms that prolonged potentiation damages those glutamate systems that comprise experiential loops. The lack of excitotoxicity in the amygdala means that the amygdala is mostly hard wired by its fetal and infantile LTP, so that it merely transmits neural intensity to the major experiential networks. The spread of kindling to these networks substantiates our model for the "transfer" process: the march of controlled LTP reorganizes distributed networks.

The Effects of Exogenous Stimulation of the Limbic System

We can have profound, sometimes traumatic, experiences during organic duress to the brain. Dysfunction in any of the parallel processing experiential loops distorts our experience of reflective identity. To feel coherent, every experience has to find a place in our intrapsychic identity. Therefore, when we have repeated or profound, organically induced experiences, we develop syndromes that accommodate our identity to our condition.

To take an innocent example from everyday life, people like coffee because it blocks the presynaptic, adenosine-mediated inhibition of glutamate populations' excitation. This fosters controlled excitation, which facilitates ordinary processing. Matching their syndromes to their identities, some people become addicted to caffeine, either because they cannot stand to process their experience in an ordinary way, or because they want to process every minute of it. One patient told me that she loves coffee. The trouble is, it bothers her stomach two days later. Conceivably, coffee stimulates her amygdala to push her mass of infantile conditioned associations, and her stress level goes up. We can conceive of this situation as one in which stress levels do not reach traumatic proportions.

To take a more morbid example, a twenty-year-old man smoked crack for twenty-four hours straight. He smoked large amounts of marijuana at the same time. Perhaps it goes without saying that at the end of that period, he felt as though he was dying. With an irregular heartbeat and sharply brightened visual experience, he experienced panicky terror, and his appetite for food stopped dead.

Consulting with me two weeks later, his vision was foggy, his short-term memory capacity was faulty, and he suffered panic attacks. I placed him on a benzodiazepine to limit the vicious circle of his traumatically induced anxiety.

Two weeks after the initial consultation, when I saw him again, he said that he could never be the same person he was before the episode. He felt forced to see everything with new eyes, and to experience himself as a new person. He longed to find his old sense of identity, but that, he knew, was impossible. The day before our second consultation, this young man dreamed that I had told him he was of sound mind. In the same dream, he won the lottery. During our session, I reassured my patient that he would again become of sound mind. On the other hand, I did not think it any more likely that he would win the lottery than that he could repeat his drug experience with impunity.

This young man was pharmacologically and traumatically forced to adapt to a whole set of alien experiences. Some of his drug-induced experiences contained elements of what we will see later in this chapter as *near-death experience*. Fortunately, he was sufficiently impressed by his trauma that his altered sense of himself will probably protect him from drug use in the future.

Direct information on organically induced experience comes from electrical stimulation of the brain in conscious patients. This information has been gleaned from cases in which doctors probe for the source of intractable seizures. When doctors electrically stimulated the patients' right hemispheres' amygdalar and rhinal cortical regions, patients reexperienced trauma, trauma-related memory, and compelling ancillary images (Gloor et al., 1982). The electrically evoked experience corresponds to what we have called *episodic source memory.*

As Chapter 2 discussed, the right hemisphere's rhinal cortex stores aversively conditioned and affect-laden, episodic memory. When damage kindles this area, source memories of becoming brain damaged recur. These source memories can trigger epileptic discharge when retraumatization experience occurs. Even imagery distant to the psychic trauma may induce seizures.

Gloor's group found that most of the thirty-five patients they stimulated electrically had evoked experiential phenomena, most often when the right amygdala was stimulated, and almost as frequently when the right hippocampus or rhinal cortex was stimulated. These patients experienced fear or terror, often a sense of compelling familiarity, sometimes complex visual hallucinations, and sometimes a compelling sense of a visual and spatial world that seemed ineluctably connected with this one.

A Case of Epilepsy Induced by Post-Traumatic Water Imagery

These experiences are significantly similar to near-death experiences, although as compared to near-death experiences they are incomplete. Indeed, Gloor's group reported that electrical stimulation sometimes revivified actual near-death experiences. In one case, upon stimulation, a twenty-two-year-old man recounted with terror a traumatic episode from his eighth year when a larger boy pushed him and held him under water. This episode, which took place at a pool, occurred just prior to the onset of the young man's seizures. Conceivably, that hypoxic episode gave rise to his temporal lobe epilepsy. Further stimulation of this man's right amygdala gave rise to a sense of falling off a cliff into the water, then into "a world away," then again into a world of rain and terror. Then, right parahippocampal stimulation brought the patient to the edge of a fountain, and, as the stimulation spontaneously spread to his right amygdala, he visualized a place of "storybook" familiarity.

As we concluded earlier, old experience is recreated when the amygdala is heavily excited and activates associational networks in distributed experiential loops. In Gloor's young man, the evoked affective connection of terror with water imagery shows how an amygdaloid-induced, hypothalamic discharge of terror can facilitate a whole associational network that conveys the force of a traumatic, emotionally organizing, episodic memory. The young man's sense of falling (originally the traumatic experience of being pushed under the water) seems to have been associatively linked to his loss of consciousness during seizures.

There is another lesson to be learned from this rich material: *negative transference is the direct reexperiencing of a past trauma on the stage of the present.* The hippocampus and amygdala continue to process fresh experience, even as the past traumatic experience is being evoked. Meanwhile, the prefrontal cortex's executive takes the whole constellation as unitary experience. In the psychology of the Gloor case, the doctor is the revenant of the evil boy who pushed the patient under the water. The image of trauma fuses with the image of being electrically stimulated to find the source of seizures. Researchers who come to conclusions on the basis of externally applied brain stimulation have to be aware that transference—the past experienced as present—inevitably causes the experimental situation to be equated with a right hemisphere source memory.

To experience an emotionally organized source memory, be it mechanically or naturally evoked, is to experience that memory within the executive's context of the present, which is why evoked memory cannot evade the analysis that data undergo on their way to reflection and voluntary communication. The anticipation of an operation that may or may not relieve intractable epilepsy evokes a sense of inescapable retraumatization sufficient to induce traumatic images and defensive screens.

How Does the Limbic System Record Trauma?

I argued in Chapter 3 that during trauma neurophysiological mechanisms block intense sensory registrations, while amygdalar input enhances the most innocent impressions. This is one source of the *screen images* that the observer uses to fill in experiential gaps. I concluded that the observer forms screen images from innocent impressions to inform the executive of the consequences of painful emotional experience.

What function does this response to trauma serve? Excluding too much data from explicit processing is maladaptive. We have to learn our lessons. But, during trauma, the executive has to compromise on what we can know, lest we become psychotic and dysfunctional as Lida did. Thus, Gloor's patient experienced fascinating images and scenes in place of his original terror. Pleasanter images of water replaced those of the drowning-pool. In more deliberate ways, cognitive and behavioral therapists use the brain's own technique of using pleasant images to reduce stress and anxiety. Asking the patient to imagine pleasant scenes during heightened periods of stress can reduce seizure frequency. I conclude that we use imagery to protect ourselves against the retraumatizing recycling of painful experience.

Images and symbols, which are fodder for mythopoesis, help to maintain a neural equilibrium after the mind and brain have been traumatized. In post-traumatic stress disorder, we regularly see the traumatic episode give rise to compelling images and screens, a never ending stream, that pervades ongoing experience, dreams, and identity. Freud (1899) pointed out that we can use source memories to screen out present traumata. This right hemisphere mechanism is, moreover, ubiquitous. Freud knew that in dream formation, the dreamer uses *innocent day residues* to bind the displaced emotional charge of experience. Artists know that symbolism condenses images to replace unbearable experience.

Cases of sexual and physical abuse, show us that the route to recalling the source of trauma is through associations that do not make sense without filling in the blanks of experience through reconstruction. When reconstruction elicits credible source memories, we find many of the harsher elements untranscribed. Massive conditioning, without the formation of very much explicit memory, alters our social identity without our being able to cognize why. We saw this in Lida's case (see Chapter 2). Traumatic disruption of the seamless web of experience requires us to form screens that fill the gaps until we own the original experience.

Psychotic Trigger Reactions

There is a delicate balance between limbic processing and prefrontal assessment in cases of both endogenous and exogenous trauma. The balance may become dysfunctional and syndromatic leading to (1) behavioral discharge, (2) psychosis, (3) autonomic discharge or epilepsy, (4) character distortion, or (5) some combination of the above. The outcome can depend on both exogenous and endogenous events.

Pontius (1987) described a syndrome of "psychotic trigger reactions" that overlaps PTSD, impulsivity, and temporal lobe epilepsy (TLE). She described a series of eighteen cases in which early life trauma evoked a latter day psychotic, murderous behavior, accompanied by prolonged autonomic discharge, when a cognitively compelling sense of repetition occurred. Her patients were moved to unexpected violence when scenes in their present lives presented them with an all-pervasive, albeit innocent imagery, apparently identical with incidental imagery that surrounded them during traumata earlier in life. Pontius's patients acted out past, dynamically significant trauma in the present, albeit in affectless states. In other words, their violent reenactments of past scenes were carried out during consciously affectless states, despite the occurrence of prolonged autonomic discharge.

Most cases showed nonspecific EEG abnormalities. Pontius concluded that early trauma had potentiated limbic responses that were released by situational cognitive approximations of the earlier episodes. For these patients, cognitive reliving consonant with earlier trauma gives rise to behavioral and autonomic discharges that completely evade executive regulation. Apparently, these patients' prefrontal assessment of their experiential neural loops became temporarily impaired.

I have seen similar autonomic and behavioral releases in patients who had smoked phencyclidine (PCP—angel dust). They believed, when they acted, that they were living a past trauma. In these cases, the patients tried to remove themselves from present stressful reality situations, only to find themselves entering into the worst prototypes of the present. One tripping man sitting on a park bench tried to kill a passerby whom he thought was a friend from the past who had betrayed him.

PCP shuts out explicit processing as it blocks the ionic NMDA receptors in the hippocampus. Yet, like cocaine, it liberates traumatic memories and stimulates the amygdala's input into experiential loops by liberating biogenic amines which increases, then decreases pleasure processing of compelled experience. The anticholinergic effect of PCP can also produce a delirium, which compromises executive metafunctions. Thus, in bad angel dust trips, processing, assessment, and reflection are all compromised at a time when the drives and emotionally organized memory are intensely stimulated.

Consciousness During Stress and Trauma: Near-Death Experience

Public understanding of the near-death experience is shrouded in a mystical belief that afflicted persons sample death and an afterlife. The mysticism may arise from the executive's interpretation of the near-death experience. Indeed, we may ask whether, and to what extent, in the history of man's social evolution, the near-death experience gave rise to the mythologies of the gods? Mysticism is reified near death.

Nemesia: A Case of a Hispanic Woman Who Escaped Death

Nemesia was born to poverty. Her mother was illiterate and full of denial, and her crippled father would suddenly lash out with his cane when he was displeased. One night he died, and the family did not know what to do with his body. A bill collector came to the door the next morning. Nemesia was only eight years old. The bill collector said, "I want to see your father." Nemesia calmly said, "You can't. He's dead." "Don't tell me that little girl," the bill collector said, "take me to your father." So, she did. Her dead father was sitting in his chair, bolt upright and dead.

Thereafter, Nemesia was the head of the family, despite the fact that she had older brothers and sisters. They were not as smart and determined as she was. When she was ten years old, a bully in the neighborhood attacked her older brother, who came whimpering into the apartment. Nemesia calmly went outside, and in a complete fury thrashed the bully into devastated submission. She became known as the neighborhood fury and so, when she was twelve years old, her mother sent her to Puerto Rico to live with her uncle, the sheriff of a town in the mountains.

Her teenage cousin attempted to rape her, and his fate was the same as the bully's. She knew that when her uncle returned she would be beaten. Therefore, she got her uncle's gun. When the uncle returned and her aunt and cousin ganged up on her, she calmly threatened to kill them all. She took the gun and went off to live in the mountains. A month later, she called her uncle, and explained what happened. He believed her. Sent back to New York, Nemesia continued her retributive behavior toward anyone who harmed her or her family. When she was thirteen years old, she was labeled *oppositional defiant* and placed in a "home."

She promptly escaped from the home, became pregnant, and married the eighteen-year-old father of her child. They lived on the street. By the time she came to the hospital to give birth, she was dying of eclampsia and malnutrition. As she was giving birth to her dead baby, dying herself, she felt herself going into a dark tunnel of perpetual night, and then she was miraculously lifted onto a shining white star. She remained comatose for twelve days. Ascending, she resolved with peace and clarity that if she lived, she would lift herself out of her dark poverty of night into the bright world of decency.

Returning to her husband, she later gave birth to two children. The first, a boy, became a lawyer, the second, a girl, became a teacher. She came into therapy when her daughter betrayed her. Her daughter and her daughter's fiancé, also a teacher, whom the patient had taken into her own house to raise, walked away from the altar, leaving Nemesia with the wedding debts. She felt that her daughter was descending into the depths she had left behind. Because of an almost irresistible impulse to kill the daughter's fiancé, Nemesia came for therapy.

Before she came, however, she destroyed her daughter's fiancé's car with a bat, and attempted to destroy his career. She went to the principal of the school where her daughter's fiancé worked, and told the tale. She also printed up a description of what he had done and distributed leaflets.

Nemesia could hardly control her fury. Her only revenge was to damage the fianceé to let him know how she felt, while holding onto the sense that was so necessary to her own identity cohesion, that her daughter was an extension of her. Nemesia lamented that she had been *so* close to her daughter, that they had fantasized together, during the wedding rehearsal about what a pleasure it would be for them both when her daughter gave birth.

As Nemesia's therapist, I confirmed her feeling that she had been betrayed, but I used my authority to help her control her rage. She narrated volumes of stories about growing up without any legitimate authority that she could count on. In every story, she wrought revenge and justice. I soothed her by confirming how hard it is to grow up as a child who knows more about the world than any one else in the family.

Nemesia's near-death experience had transformed her life. Clearly, her near-death experience of coming through the tunnel into the light was equated with a sense of being reborn herself, even though her baby died. Subsequently, each new birth was a rebirth of her own self. She vested her hopes for decency in each child, to the point that each became a narcissistic extension, mythologized within her own family structure, which was segregated in her mind from her family or origin. Betrayed by her daughter, Nemesia lost control of her emotional life.

This case illustrates how profoundly near-death experience effects intrapsychic identity organization. After her near-death experience, Nemesia fervently believed her ascent into the afterlife had given her special survival powers. Her sense of identity had been permanently transformed, but her identity was fragile and grandiosely narcissistic. Nemesis, thy name is woman.

WHAT IS THE NEAR-DEATH EXPERIENCE?

Near-death experience quintessentially exemplifies exogenous, traumatic effects on the brain's organization. What we know about long-term potentiation helps us understand the neural causes of near-death experience. Inescapable, life-threatening trauma induces neurophsysiological mechanisms so extreme, that the amygdala stops inducing hypothalamic panic and terror responses, and the amygdala's neurohormones suppress hippocampal processing.

Jansen's *Neuroscience and the Near-Death Experience* (1990) provides a model for how near-death experience alters limbic processing. He proposes that the peptide blockade of NMDA receptors during the near-death experience is similar to the ketamine or phencyclidine blockade of this receptor, and that it induces similar experiences. Ketamine is an anaesthetic that induces a twilight state of numbed, detached, and transformed experience. Jansen details a five-stage continuum in near-death experience: (1) peacefulness, (2) body detachment, (3) entering the dark, (4) moving through a tunnel, and (5) entering the light.

As I understand the near-death experience, it is an acute, intense, trauma that first leads to an almost complete blockade of hippocampal glutamate transmission. The early stages of the near-death experience can be attributed to this blockade. If the experience persists long enough, the blockade gives way and massive hippocampal LTP begins. *Authentic—* almost died—near-death experiences are more likely to produce the end-stage experience of intense light, and cognitive beauty and truth, the harbingers of identity change (Owen, Cook, and Stevenson, 1990).

From what we know about how the brain registers, processes assesses and reflects data, we can dissect the anatomy of near-death consciousness. At first, the executive works full tilt on all the assessment zones because the drives pressure the prefrontal system with intense arousal and alertness. At the same time, explicit processing is extremely diminished. This is a highly unusual combination to analyze: all that urgency with nothing there, except conditioned limbic quality—no content.

The experience of timelessness (slow-motion assessment) is probably determined by a left hemisphere poverty of assessable cognitive signals. The young man who traumatized himself with cocaine and marijuana still felt, a month later, that time was passing in a slow-motion dream that made his trauma seem like it had occurred only yesterday. We surmised from ERP data in Chapter 6 that the left parietal cortex forms a subjective assessment of time. The poverty of salient incoming signals to this cortex gives rise to the supervisor's sense that nothing is happening in subjective time. There is meaning and clarity of thought with no basis for forming an action plan. There is nothing to do or say.

Near death, our right hemisphere's observer, has nothing to go on either. The procedural self assesses intense familiarity, despite a poverty of inferotemporal visual associational data. The intensification of conditioned social associations for the orbital and insular cortex to assess, gives way to a poverty of new conditioning. The social subject and self respond with detachment. Without signals to assess, the right parietal cortex lacks a reality context for the body's image, which gives rise to depersonalization and derealization.

Near death, the medial experiential loops contribute little emotional assessment to the executive. Somatic signals of anxiety and emotion are dampened. Anxiety is gone. Affect is quiet. The executive reflects on peacefulness without tension.

Early elements of the near-death experience may correspond, then, to the assessment of contentless limbic qualities. When the NMDA channel blockade gives way, LTP flares dramatically. Content becomes pervasive, all-encompassing, and condensed. All the prefrontal networks flare into experience. Peacefulness, clarity, timelessness, and dark give way to chaotic flooding. Thus, the darkness corresponds to damped sensory stimuli, the tunnel to transition to LTP, and light to massive LTP. Nemesia migrated to a blinding star.

Flooding begins with intense sensory stimulation, accompanied by comprehensive, emotional source memory. Those who are really near death for some time may find themselves in the spotlight with all of their emotionally organizing memories dancing before them. As we saw in the case of the young man who abused drugs, and Nemesia, who almost died, the near-death experience stimulates a reorganization of the executive's beliefs, values, goals, and identity in its aftermath.

SCREEN MEMORIES

The neural system's approach to screen memory phenomena answers a question that puzzled Freud. Freud (1899) detected a detached self-as-observer imbedded in screen memories' supernaturally clear, innocent details. In a screen memory, bright, neutral, and extremely clear imagery replace the traumata that psychoanalysis reconstructs. It is reasonable to think that Freud's screen memories are the executive's take on traumatic experiences. Are not the muted, innocent qualities of screen memories, such as those in near-death experiences, renditions of traumatic data experienced amidst intense drive?

FREUD'S "DÈJÁ VU" IN THE ACROPOLIS OF HIS MIND

Like screen memory, *dèjá vu* is a phenomenon in which a person experiences the sense of having previously experienced an identical reality of perception, without conscious memory of that experience. Freud illustrated a *dèjá vu*-type phenomenon in his paper, *A Disturbance of Memory on the Acropolis* (1936). For much of his life, Freud had wanted to ascend the Acropolis to see the vistas that animated the Greek's construction of their civilization, and to personally absorb their devotion to the gods of Olympus. He waited until he was a relatively old man, because it always seemed that he did not yet deserve to be there.

When he ascended the Acropolis as an old man, he had the dèjá vu experience that he had been there before, and that he could not really be there in the present. His self-analysis of this phenomenon related it to a time in his adolescence when he had looked at pictures of the Acropolis with his brother, Alexander, who was ten years younger. It was not until Sigmund was an old man, and Alexander also had survived to old age, that he could bring the moment of earlier wishing into fruition.

Sigmund, not Alexander, had been his mother's special child. His family had sacrificed much so that Sigmund could use his genius to study and to bring credit to the family. In his adolescence, no one in the family was allowed to interfere with his studies; no one was even allowed to play music, because Sigmund was studying. In his adolescence, Freud denied his wish to ascend the Acropolis because it had aroused aggressive, self-centered wishes to surpass Alexander, to make him disappear as his first brother Julius had, by dying, when Freud was eighteen months old.

Freud's wish to ascend the Acropolis was not only a deep childhood wish; it was a dynamically overdetermined image of his identity as a special man, who could, like Moses, bring unified truth down from the heights of consciousness. Freud's identity was split between his sense of a family romance origin, in which the Christian doctor of his childhood and his Christian nurse represented alternative parents, parents who could provide a Greco-Christian legacy of greatness.

In dèjá vu, I believe, there is always an aggressive wish that is screened from view by the observer because one's identity integration is threatened by the fulfillment of the wish. The infant Sigmund's loss of Julius accompanied his primal scene's endogenous trauma when he was ascending out of infancy into self-consciousness. He must have sensed that his surpassing consciousness came at the expense of his infant brother's loss.

Freud's way of writing papers betrayed his tendency to intellectually destroy those who would pretend that they could ascend to his height of intellectual truth. In his writing style, Freud usually set up a straw man, whose views he would destroy whenever he needed to overcome the irrational and reach a higher level of truth (Harris and Harris, 1984). Ascending the Acropolis then, represented Freud's wish to rid himself of all revenants who could challenge his uniqueness.

SCREENS IN PANIC DISORDER

The blockade of affective source memory is complete in panic disorder. In panic disorder, an acute terror of dying and losing one's mind appears to come out of the blue. The observer senses disintegrating mind and body. Right parahippocampal activation accompanies these phenomena (Reiman et al., 1989). The lack of present-day content during the panic may indicate a revival of contentless, traumatic Type 2 memory. The limbic quality remains, but the data is eliminated by the observer's need to form a complete screen in order to adapt to an untenable present.

The reader will recall that facial processing matures around the time of the primal scene, just before verbal recollection comes on stream. The right parahippocampus processes faces. The processing yields a sense of how one is being responded to socially. Thus, the right parahippocampus processes the deepest sense of how we stand in reality. If our social position is threatened, and we have a pervasive anxiety of being overwhelmed and abandoned, then we are set for panic—or terror—disorder. I posit that panic disorder's content is too primitive and pervasive to be known. Clinically, I find that patients with panic disorder have a pervasive sense of potential abandonment.

The above spectrum of clinical phenomena suggest that we are able to screen out the *content* of traumatic memory, but not its limbic *quality*. We cannot screen out the limbic component because limbic activation is instinctual and conditioned. However, the executive avoids retraumatization by defending against source content. The executive fills in the gaps brought about by trauma by using symbols, images, and metaphors to construct fantasies and screen memories in a way that is consistent with identity structure at the time of trauma.

OTHER CLINICAL PHENOMENA RELATED TO SCREENS

We will continue to examine clinical phenomena that can be modeled on trauma, and its extreme, the near-death experience. If the prototype of early stage near-death experience is dampening, then the prototype of end-stage near-death experience is intensification. Psychosis or mania may be experienced as near death, or even psychological death. End-stage phenomena develop from massive LTP's *intensification* of experience.

Consider, for example, the *switch mechanism*, an intensely bright, but blank, sometimes orgasmic, dream occurring at the onset of acute mania (Bunney et al., 1972). If excessive LTP induces mania, then intense amygdalar stimulation produces the intensified drive states that accompany the onset of mania. The bright, blank quality may indicate that dampening is giving way to intense stimulation. Psychoanalysts describe a golden aura that often accompanies a woman's revival of traumatic memories of the "awesome paternal phallus." Condensed screen images make the perception into a symbol. One female patient who had been sexually abused by her father describes her mission to find the golden ideal of perfecting herself. A male, fetishistic search for the Holy Grail, in place of the Medusa's head—missing phallus—also symbolizes an awesome view of the father's genitals.

Freud (1900) observed that intense light in a dream indicates a highly condensed set of past experiences and their associations. He indicates that because of the intense condensation, it is unlikely that associations relevant to the present can be expected from analysis of this dream element. Intense light in a dream, then, like symbolism, screens out the latent content of recent experience. Thus, intensity-related clinical phenomena can be understood in the same frame as the light at the end of a near-death tunnel. There is too much intensity to bear.

THE ORGANIC THEORY OF PSYCHOSIS

Our theory of psychosis begins at the point of disassociation between executive reflection and data processing. In his paper, "Does Kindling Model Anything Clinically Relevant?" Adamac argues that "forced normalization" (prolonged damping) in the interictal (seizure-free) period of temporal lobe epilepsy produces clinical syndromes (1990). While clinical *phenomena* are predicated on the brain's defenses against seizures, clinical *syndromes* appears to result from alternating excitotoxicity and forced normalization.

In the early years of partial complex seizures, temporal lobe epileptics show increased anxiety, irritable defensive avoidance, and distrust, phenomena that Adamac correlates with excessive amygdalar discharge (Adamac, 1990). Conceivably, high levels of amygdalar LTP can induce character change in these patients. In later years, about one-third of these patients become syndromatic: left hemisphere temporal lobe epileptics develop a chronic schizophreniform psychosis or paranoia, and right hemisphere temporal lobe epileptics develop a mood disorder.

Let us distinguish *acute psychosis,* which I suggest follows from excessive LTP, from *chronic psychosis*, which follows from a series of accommodations to recurrent periods of excessive LTP. If *forced normalization* produces compensatory changes in the ventral tegmental dopamine system that leads to chronic psychosis as Caldecott-Hazard (1987) and Adamac (1990) say, then:

1. the amygdala's increased output to the left hemisphere's ventral tegmental dopamine system upregulates dopamine receptors,
2. the caudate upregulates its dopaminergic activity,
3. increased dopamine stimulates prefrontal behavioral pressure,
4. and finally the amygdala decreases its prefrontal output as its opioid receptors become supersensitive.

These are all relevant research findings in schizophrenia.

Given what we have learned about the ventral tegmental dopamine system's role in stimulating consummation and signaling salience, increased dopamine reception in the ventral tegmental dopamine system would cause subjectively conceived false signals of salience. In other words, when no satisfaction is really at hand, false signals of salience produce a feeling of humiliation. When this experience is repeated over and over, the executive concludes that others promise false satisfaction. This leads to distrust, paranoia, or schizophreniform psychosis.

A series of patients with partial complex seizures triggered in the left hemisphere manifested religiosity, hypergraphia, decreased sexuality, and paranoid delusions in the interictal period. Undoubtedly, these patients have a neural basis for their paranoia. Conceivably, these phenomena result from the executive's response to the nucleus accumbens' false salience signals (Bear, 1979). A parallel group with right hemisphere partial complex seizures developed interictal mood disorders. If you are always on the verge of something big, but it never happens, you may get paranoid or hypomanic.

Paranoid Schizophrenia or Temporal Lobe Epilepsy?

Conceivably, altered hippocampal output leads to paranoid schizo-phrenic's cognitive disorder.

> Extensive postmortem histological examination of the brains of many schizophrenics reveals not only loss of some hippocampal neurons . . . but also inappropriate connections, cell disarray, and misalignment of . . . pyramidal cell layers CA 3 and CA 1. (Kreik-haus, Donahoe, and Morgan, 1992, p. 561)

Kriekhaus and colleagues (1992) conjecture that

1. increased dopamine stimulation overactivates CA 1 cells,
2. CA 1 outflow increases new memory formation, and
3. dopamine's forced pressure of satisfaction produces a delusional over-estimation of the new memory's salience.

The Case of the Man Who Dropped His Tray

A forty-two-year-old man returned to therapy with puzzling symptoms suggestive of partial complex seizures, dissociative disorder, and psycho-sis. He had no verified seizure history. He complained of *dèjà raconte,* of being unaware of whether he had told me and many other people about events in his life.

He narrated an incident of being asked how he felt a moment after he dropped a lunch tray at his feet during a noon work conference. He could not remember the event then. Moreover, he was not sure whether he had already told me about it. In another incident, he was to meet someone in a restaurant. Arriving early, he went into the restroom. When he came out, he found himself in a different restaurant. When driving, he found that cars were suddenly closer to him or in different lanes.

EEG showed left temporal slow waves with spiking activity. Magnetic resonance imaging (MRI) showed left temporal lobe shrinkage and increased ventricular size. This is where diagnosis can become ambiguous. These changes are consistent with both schizophrenia and temporal lobe epilepsy. Paranoid schizophrenia can produce left hemisphere hippocampal formation shrinkage (Kriekhaus, Donahoe, and Morgan, 1992) or sclerosis (Stevens, 1992). Excitotoxicity triggered by epilepsy or by schizophrenia may be morphologically indistinguishable.

This patient's left hemisphere's temporal lobe pathology developed in a life context of intense humiliation. He narrated his whole life as a series of humiliating events. When he was nine years old, the patient's older half-brother would shoot or hang an animal as a pointed demonstration of what he would later do to the patient. Subsequently, he would tie the patient to a chair and blindfold him. The brother would then tell the patient that the brother was playing Russian roulette. Holding the gun against the patient's head, the brother would pull the trigger. Then the brother would laugh at the patient. The patient's next older brother would emulate the half-brother in making fun of the patient's panicky responses. Thus, the patient was in much the same position as the famous paranoid, Schreber, whose father would tie the child Schreber to a chair to morally stiffen him.

As an adult, my patient would hear a voice saying, "shoot me." This often happened at work when the patient found himself embroiled in the politics of his workplace. He believed that he was being persecuted by a conspiracy of fellow workers because he had taken a different political position on controversial work issues. The feeling of persecution was much like what he experienced with his brothers in the episodes of sibling politics. He was so involved in thoughts of persecution that he would find himself in timeless states in which hours would go by before he could continue with his work. In these states, he was unsure about whether he had committed himself to a work project or what he had communicated about his work or his personal life.

The patient felt intense rage, and he did not know whether or not to act on the basis of the rage. When he had rages, he pounded on his head and felt his sense of identity shatter. I believe that this patient's symptoms comprised a left hemisphere syndrome of delusional disorder. I conceived the following brain/mind interactions in this patient:

- His rage, humiliation, and panic induced left hemisphere limbic excitotoxicity, and then forced normalization.

- His endogenous, excitotoxicity proceeded to actual kindling and temporal lobe epilepsy.
- His sense of disappearing subjective time related to left hemisphere forced normalization.
- He experienced the workplace politics as retraumatizing.

Years before the discovery of his hippocampal shrinkage, the patient developed a classical paranoid delusional transference psychosis. He believed that I purposely misconstrued what he said in order to persecute him. He projected his own self-persecution onto me. He attributed to me things that he himself had said to humiliate himself. I placed him on neuroleptic medication. Then I interpreted the effect on him of his feelings of love and need for me. I told him that his love for me had made him feel so vulnerable to rejection that he had lost his sense of boundaries between us. Consequently, he stopped feeling that I was persecuting him. Years later, after this therapy, the patient became so detached from his own incompatible behaviors, that he was diagnosed as a multiple personality, and hospitalized.

In this case, childhood trauma leads to the adult formation of an emotionally, cognitively, and organically organized syndrome. The patient's cognitive and emotional deficits arose because he did not know the source of his humiliation. His brothers' malevolent tricks confused him. These tricks became templates for delusions of reference which recurred in many later relationships and in the transference psychosis.

It is tempting to think that this patient's paranoia gradually developed an excitotoxic trigger. In this view, new humiliations cycled faster as limbic LTP became excitotoxic. Thus, each new humiliation induced new bouts of excitotoxicity in his left hemisphere's hippocampal formation. This thesis is comparable to Post's belief that local kindling, instead of inducing epilepsy, induces rapid cycling in bipolar disorder.

This case shows us how difficult it can be to parcel out causes of syndrome formation in any particular case. Genetic tendencies toward mental illness, for instance, can only be statistically configured by making the assumption that official diagnoses represent definable single syndromes. In this case, the patient did not have a unitary syndrome. The patient's father had the symptoms of a delusional disorder off and on throughout the father's life. Delusional disorder is believed to show some genetic concordance.

The concept that genetically induced overpermeability to stimuli—oversensitivity—leads toward psychosis is an old one in psychiatry. Oversensitivity means that a person is more easily traumatized by stress, with all the neural sequelae. As so often happens, the sensitive one in the family becomes the designated "sick one" who carries the family's pathology.

In a *family systems* approach, this patient's sensitivity to stimuli and his vulnerability led him to become the family scapegoat, and the designated carrier of his family's need to redeem itself financially and socially. The delusional father was seen as a poor breadwinner. The mother had lost her battle to compete with her siblings. The mother's family of origin degraded the mother's new family. The mother's sister went so far as to wash out the patient's mouth with soap when, as a boy, he tried to defend his family's honor.

The patient's mother invested this particular son with her need for redemption. She wanted to prove her own narcissistic integrity by proving that her three sons were better than her sister's. Her oldest son, the one who attacked the patient sadistically and tortured him, had been illegitimate. Indeed, the mother's extended maternal family designed a mythology to cover up the fact that this son had been fathered by the husband of the mother's sister. His being a bastard led the older brother to attack the patient, whom he saw as the favored son. We may conclude in this case that genetic, neural, developmental, familial, traumatic, and dynamic determinants all coincided to produce this patient's symptoms and syndromes.

CONCLUSION:
DOES PTSD CONFER SURVIVAL ADVANTAGE?

The innate, genetic predisposition to use one hemisphere's mechanisms more than the other's is a major factor in our tendency to develop syndromes. Syndromes exaggerate the predisposition to process experience in extreme ways. During times of intense social repression, the Type 2 adapter may have an advantage. During times of great social disorganization and transgenerational abuse, the Type 1 person with a will to innovate survives better in the long run.

In Freud's socially repressed time, Type 1 neuroses were, perhaps, the most common syndromes. In my opinion, our *fin de siècle* social disorganization breeds Type 2 post-traumatic stress disorder, amoral sociopathy, and borderline adaptation. Indeed, the capacity to develop a degree of borderline adaptation may help a person to rise in the bureaucracy (a Type 2 institution).

If it is true that we now evolve in response to the social world we create, then the stochastic array of different types of people who can more easily modify particular neural systems always turns up types who are better able to survive at a given time through their particular syndromes. In our own time, the borderline or amoral sociopath has an easy time detaching from other people's pain during social disorganization. Borderlines and sociopaths can cut to the bottom line—their own—when people have to be laid off to benefit bureaucracies or corporations.

I posit the anti-intuitive proposition that PTSD, the focal syndrome considered in this book, confers a survival advantage to some persons and some social, political groups during periods of social chaos. Periods of social chaos induce transgenerational tendencies toward wars and revolutions on one hand, toward identification with the dictator on the other. Afflicted persons are more ready to become heroes, lose their lives, or become terrorists. Perhaps this tendency enhances social change at the expense of social stability.

Chapter 8

The Origins
of Psychiatric Syndromes

*When, after passing through a narrow defile, we suddenly emerge
upon a piece of high ground where the path divides and the finest
prospects open up on every side, we may pause for a moment and
consider in which direction we shall turn our steps.*

—Sigmund Freud,
The Interpretation of Dreams, p. 122

So said Freud, as he invited his readers to explore the vistas opened by
his first dream interpretation. Having ascended the Acropolis of the Mind,
we may now explore the many vistas opened by our study of neural
system's organization: the *Diagnostic and Statistical Manual of Mental
Disorders IV* (DSM-IV) syndromes.

The successive versions of the DSMs for psychiatric diagnosis portray
a search for biological causes of psychiatric disorders. Over time, the DSMs
have increasingly recognized neurobiological factors—including stress effects
on neural systems—as forming a backdrop for syndrome formation. Indeed,
stress and trauma play a major role in the chronological unfolding of many
syndromes. Chapter 8 asks the following: How do genetic predisposition,
stress, trauma, conflict, source memory, and experience collectively find their
way to the prefrontal zones' syndrome-producing flash points?

Like the vista that opens up on either side, *The Origin of Syndromes*
(Figures 8.1 through 8.6) depicts syndromes' origination in each prefrontal zone. The terrain divides into distinctive Type 1 and Type 2 syndromes
in the brain's left and right hemispheres. Each syndrome:

- is distinguished by its origin in separate zones,
- distorts identity that the executive integrates in that zone, and
- distorts that prefrontal zone's higher cortical functions.

Thus, syndromes bias the executive's way of solving problems.

FIGURE 8.1. The Origin of Syndromes: Dominant Hemisphere Agent—Lateral Zone

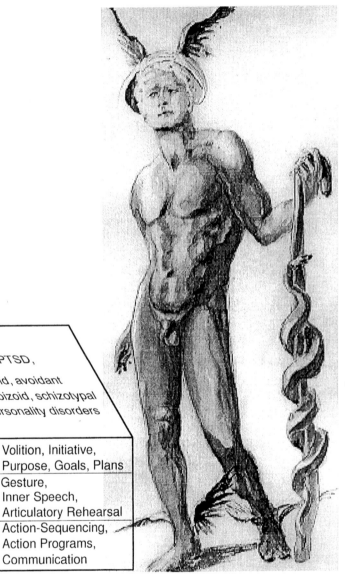

Hysteria,

Numbed PTSD,

Paranoid, avoidant schoizoid, schizotypal personality disorders

Metafunction

Ego Function

Neoropsychological Function

Volition, Initiative, Purpose, Goals, Plans

Gesture, Inner Speech, Articulatory Rehearsal

Action-Sequencing, Action Programs, Communication

FIGURE 8.2. The Origin of Syndromes: Nondominant Hemisphere
Procedural Self—Lateral Zone

FIGURE 8.3. The Origin of Syndromes: Nondominant Hemisphere
Social Self—Intermediate Zone

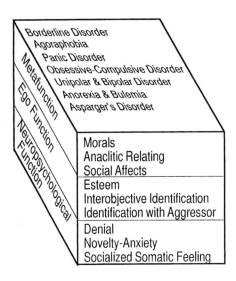

FIGURE 8.4. The Origin of Syndromes: Dominant Hemisphere
Social Subject—Intermediate Zone

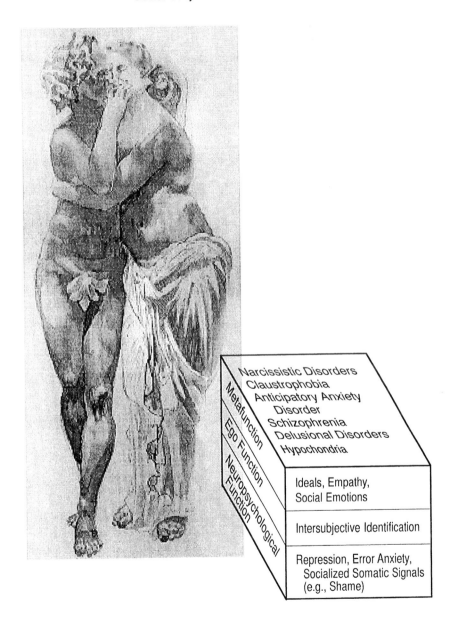

FIGURE 8.5. The Origin of Syndromes: Nondominant Hemisphere
Self—Medial Zone

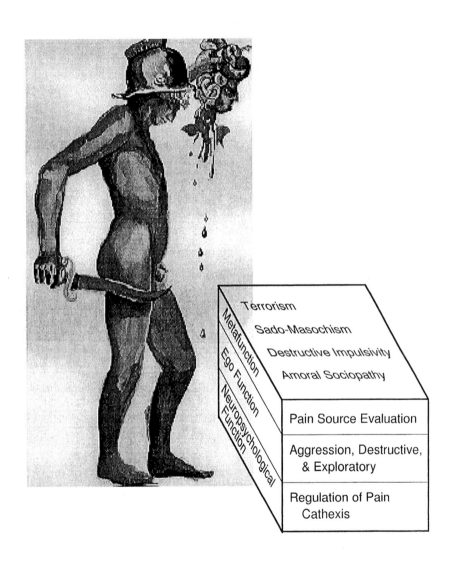

FIGURE 8.6. The Origin of Syndromes: Dominant Hemisphere
Subject—Medial Zone

Acting-Out Disorders
Perversion
Wishful Impulse
Disorders
Narcissistic
Sociopathy

Metafunction
Ego Function
Neuropsychological
Function

Wish & Need
Evaluation

Libidinal, Erotic,
& Tender Love

Regulation of
Pleasure Cathexis

HOW STRESS AFFECTS SYNDROME FORMATION

In our present social, political, and economic environment of dissonant authority, stress-related disorders have replaced fantasy and conflict-based disorders as the major cause of psychopathology. This view amplifies when we consider that drug-induced pathology is often caused by PTSD patients' self-medication with drugs. Each type of drug induces a brain response that characteristically enters an equilibrium cycle with episodes of retraumatization. Moreover, early life physical and sexual abuse, parental neglect, and social disregard induce many persons with PTSD to develop sociopathy, narcissistic depletion, and borderline-type identifications with the aggressor.

This chapter continues Chapter 7's comprehensive examination of the induction and development of post-traumatic stress disorders (PTSD). Understanding PTSD's mechanisms provides a template for understanding other syndromes that ultimately derive from PTSD, and leads us toward clinical applications in PTSD and these other syndromes. Many individuals with PTSD, for example, develop psychotic disorders, and those individuals are treated as schizophrenics or bipolar psychotic patients.

In Chapter 7 we studied the disassociation between prefrontal identity and limbic experience that occurs in the near-death episode. The neurophysiological mechanisms that the near-death episode unleashes provide a model for how, acute inescapable trauma triggers the formation of PTSD. We saw that both massive long-term potentiation (LTP) and neurobiological defenses against LTP produced characteristic clinical phenomenology. Now we will undertake a more systematic appraisal of these mechanisms.

Using a psychoanalytic and cognitive approach, Mardi Horowitz (1982) emphasized the changes in identity that occur in PTSD, when intrusive, painful, source memories alternate with clinical numbing. He described the reintroduction of earlier self and object representations when trauma fragments more mature identity structures. Using Horowitz's cognitive terms: when personal identity regresses in PTSD, the patient's *belief-schema* fail. A new stabilization for problem solving's cognition cannot reach *completion* until altered identity representations stop invading posttraumatic metafunctions. Lida could not learn, or even believe in learning when her identity was in flux.

PTSD in a Fireman

Consider a case vignette of a fireman who was in the throes of forming PTSD. Dino, a thirty-year-old West Coast firefighter, lost his one and only buddy in a subcellar tenement fire soon after major rioting. Dino and his buddy had gone into a subcellar that was filled with two feet of water because the sprinkler system was functioning so strongly. There were no lights. They set guidelines to return after finding the source of the blaze. Dino's oxygen supply was used up and he had to go back out. His friend did not follow him. Outside, other firefighters were standing around. In a panic, Dino got another mask to go back in to find his friend. As soon as he got inside, his new mask's vibrating alarm went on, but Dino knew, or thought he knew, that he had enough air for several minutes.

Back inside, it was totally dark. The guideline was gone. Water was roaring down so that he could not hear. The emergency vibrations from his mask were shaking his head. He had to crawl in chest-deep water in the direction he had left his buddy. As minutes passed, his air supply gave out. Then, he saw the glint of his buddy's head light shining up, and his buddy face up in the water. He tore off his mask and dragged his buddy to the small window he saw, and helped to get him out the window. His own leg was stuck, bringing him closer to the sense of an encounter with death. Finally, after what seemed an interminable half minute more, he was pulled out himself. He watched someone do mouth-to-mouth resuscitation and his buddy's heart started to beat, briefly, but then he died.

In the weeks that followed, Dino could not sleep. As soon as he would fall asleep, he would begin to shake with anxiety and reliving. He told his wife what had happened, and she said she would leave him if he ever fought fires again. He tried to talk about what happened with counselors, but he felt that no one heard him. It made him sick and furious when they said, "I understand," but did not. He felt that no one in authority cared about the safety of the firefighters. He felt that the new breed of firefighters were unwilling to risk their lives. Finally, the only way he could sleep was by drinking enough alcohol and taking enough drugs to put him out.

After nearly three months, when he was finally receiving some psychotherapy and medication, Dino was able to sleep. Then it rained hard one evening. He suddenly found himself in a deep sweat, and gasping for air he ran out of the house. Afterward, he took a lot of sedatives and alcohol and slept for fifteen hours. He only realized the next day, with the help of his therapist, that the drumbeat of rain was the trigger experience that brought him back into the subcellar where the sprinkler was inundating his being. Then he realized he had recently had the same trigger experience in a small elevator, where he felt trapped. As he talked about returning to light duty, he was overcome with sweaty, heart-racing, gasping panic.

Dino's PTSD was made worse by the sense that he had been abandoned by authority. His friend had been the only person other than his wife whom he trusted. He felt that he could trust no one else, certainly not the authorities in the fire department who wanted to get him back to the front lines, nor his fellow firefighters who had just stood around. Since the riots, Dino believed that other firefighters just wanted to stand around until they could get their pensions.

Dino was a large and powerful man who had to take care of himself from the time he was seventeen years old, when his parents told him that they were moving to Hawaii, and that he was on his own. He had never again wanted to feel as helpless as he did then. During his acute trauma, Dino risked death to avoid abandoning his friend. Since he himself had been abandoned in his adolescence, he could not abandon his friend without betraying himself, because he identified so closely with his friend.

The classic helplessness that Dino experienced in his acute traumatic stress endured and merged with anxiety in the posttraumatic period. When he had reliving experiences, the manifestations of anxiety itself were retraumatizing. Dino had been shut out of or overwhelmed in all of his sensory modalities. The roar in his ears, the vibrations in his head, the lack of ordinary somesthetic cues, the total darkness, the lack of oxygen, the acrid smell, his heart beating like a drum—all made him vulnerable to the posttraumatic effects of anxiety. In the flashbacks, anxiety itself reminded him of the trauma all over. In Dino's case, the return of panic and terror in reliving led him to try to withdraw into drugs and alcohol to quiet himself. In PTSD, panic comes on like a runaway train.

Dino's helpless anxiety and sensory inundation immobilized his sense of adult identity. His belief systems were shattered. He returned to an earlier state of adolescent and childhood abandonment anxiety. His capacity to make decisions about continuing to work as a firefighter lapsed into perplexed rage.

NEUROBIOLOGICAL CHANGES IN PTSD

Like peat fires in a marsh that produce smoky phantoms, PTSD builds on buried, flammable materials. To understand PTSD's silent generation, we will first review the regulating interactions among the amygdala, hippocampus, and prefrontal networks in a *developmental context*. In infancy, hippocampal glucocorticoid receptors located in memory-inducing neurons determine the formation of experiential networks.

We surmised in Chapter 3 that when erratic parental response accompanies the infant's hippocampal glucocorticoid receptor development, this experience engenders vulnerability to PTSD, panic disorder, generalized anxiety disorder, psychosomatic disorders, and, as we will see later in this chapter, borderline disorder. Early life dysregulation of stress responses may be one factor that accounts for some people's developing PTSD or panic disorder, while others, under similar circumstances do not.

What happens in the brain during the interval between trauma and PTSD? As we explore the changes, let us keep in mind how these changes (which both enhance and block LTP) also offer proof for our neural systems model of The Origin of Syndromes. I will consider the evidence that van der Kolk (1994) reviewed, which manifests the neurobiological reorganization that accompanies the formation of PTSD, and I will annotate my own comments.

- People with PTSD show *intensified autonomic response* to stimuli associated with the trauma, such as an increased, poorly habituated, acoustic startle response. (This response is mediated by excitatory [amygdalar and septal] paths that can be permanently potentiated by severe trauma.)
- PTSD permanently alters *biogenic amine and neuromodulatory responses* to stimuli, particularly exaggerating noradrenergic vigilance responses. A pharmacological *yohimbine challenge* to the norepinephrine system induced panic in an astounding 70 percent of veterans with PTSD as compared with 20 percent of controls (Southwick et al., 1993). (As we have seen, abundant norepinephrine release both lowers the kindling threshold, and mobilizes the novelty anxiety that accompanies aggression.)
- PTSD patients produce *higher than normal endogenous opioids* in response to novelty. (Endogenous opioids inhibit the locus ceruleus's central ouput of norepinephrine. PTSD patients' response to opioids dampens norepinephrine-driven upsurges in their aggressive drive, and blocks their vigilance anxiety. That is why some traumatized people are addicted to opioids.)
- *Serotonin activity is markedly decreased in animals that undergo inescapable trauma.* Serotonin "plays a role in the capacity to monitor the environment flexibly, and to respond with behaviors that are situation appropriate, rather than reacting to internal stimuli that are irrelevant. . . ." (van der Kolk, 1994, p. 257). (Serotonin neutralizes aggression, modulates affect, and facilitates hippocampal populations' glutamate autofeedback receptors. This autofeedback can block LTP. Conversely, serotonin depletion lowers the threshold for hippocampal LTP. This causes trauma to induce overly intense source memories.)
- Patients with PTSD show both *amnesia and hypermnesia.* They remember too much that is extraneous and too little that is relevant, and they form too much and too little source memory. Exogenous norepinephrine stimulation produces a flood of flashbacks and reliving, body sensations, and sensorimotor arousal. (Numbing, withdrawal, and amnesia accompanying an underactive physiological state of arousal are a neurobiological mechanism for laying low.)

- *Flashbacks occur during Stage II or III sleep.* Thus, intense reliving intrudes into developing slow-wave sleep. (Since flashbacks occur outside of REM sleep, people with PTSD can enact their trauma outside of dream sleep's paralysis.)
- PTSD patients' *brittle stress response* shows up in *a lower level of endogenous cortisone production, a down-regulation of hippocampal glucocorticoid receptors, and a hyperactive stress response to exogenous cortisone.* (PTSD patients either underreact to mild stress or overreact to moderate stress, producing excess LTP and increased source memory formation—retraumatization.)
- There is *decreased hippocampal formation volume in patients with PTSD* (Bremner, Seibyl, and Scott, 1992). (Neural shrinkage supports the hypothesis that PTSD can become excitotoxic, cause atrophy in the hippocampus, or both.)

The collective neurobiological changes in PTSD manifest a neural process of syndrome formation. The fact that flashbacks and states of numbness and vigilance may begin weeks or months after the traumatic event, as they did in Dino, indicates that PTSD undergoes a silent organization until it emerges clinically. I posit the following sequential organization of PTSD:

1. Trauma induces amygdalar LTP and excitotoxic hippocampal LTP.
2. CA 1 forms excessive source memory.
3. Transfer LTP induces changes in prefrontal identity.
4. Corticosteroid-induced atrophy in CA 3 reduces data processing.
5. New stimuli retraumatize, which restarts the vicious cycle.

In this view, to reexperience the original trauma in waking and sleeping flashbacks, and in reliving, endogenously rekindles the LTP that originally induced the syndrome. This neurally defines *retraumatization.* I posit that in PTSD's progression, excited periods of limbic LTP alternate with periods of reduced limbic excitability. Each period is clinically observable. In PTSD, excitement alternates with withdrawal.

The alternation model is supported by event-related potential (ERP) studies. Compared to controls, a significant proportion of veterans with PTSD show reduced amplitude ERPs (Paige et al., 1990). In this event-related potential study, veterans *initially* inhibited evoked response to auditory tones, but physiological parameters of vigilance and plasma norepinephrine increased with repetition of the tones. Thus, veterans with PTSD attempt to avoid stimulation because stimulation is overarousing.[1] Eventually, the hyperarousal fades.

How does the brain deal with acute trauma in order to avoid PTSD induction? An increase in all the drive systems helps in the short run. We saw in Chapter 4 that a reactive increase in dopaminergic pleasure can stave off the sense of trauma. A person can process novel and intense data as long as he maintains a sense of intrigue. By accepting the norepinephrine system's exploratory pressure, one can also mitigate trauma. Trauma is better tolerated if one feels that it is a learning experience.

Serotonin reduces hippocampal LTP in situations of severe stress. Increased serotonin sharpens the capacity to selectively process data and diminishes the executive's pressure for quick solutions to libidinal and aggressive pressures. With inadequate serotonin modulation, one may withdraw from stimulation to preserve identity and stave off psychosis. Impulsivity increases when serotonin resources diminish. For this reason, the physician prescribed a serotonin reuptake inhibitor for Dino.

TWO HEMISPHERIC TYPES OF PTSD

In their review of Hendin and Haas's *Wounds of War* (1984), Harris and Newman (1986) distinguished Type 1 left hemisphere from Type 2, right hemisphere forms of PTSD, although individuals may show both forms. Type 1 veterans' inability to relate corresponds to a severe inhibition of narcissistic integrity. Type 1 veterans experienced their original trauma as a failure to protect buddies whom they experienced as narcissistic extensions. These vulnerable men were teenagers at the time of trauma. They related in an age-appropriate narcissistic way to their buddies. After their friends died, PTSD impaired these veterans' intersubjective capacity to relate. They could no longer love.

Similarly, Dino's failure to save his friend led to numbness, which defended him against overwhelming shame and helplessness. His numbness led to an inability to relate intersubjectively. He blamed the other firefighters, whom he saw standing around, for their failure to respond to his buddy's danger. He felt he could no longer trust them. Despite the truth in his feelings, his sense of betrayal extended indiscriminately to all of his comrades.

In Type 2 PTSD, veterans' loss of control over their aggression and destructive acts led to (1) vigilance anxiety, (2) flashbacks—pathological episodic source memory, (3) repetition-compulsion, (4) the Dionysian resorting to drugs and alcohol as self-induced "treatment," and (5) an identification with the aggressor that culminated in criminalized behavior.

Identification with the aggressor results in pathological identity changes. After witnessing destruction of people and their bodies, many veterans took on the persona of a sociopathic addict, when that had not been the case previously. Presumably their new destructive behaviors were induced by repetitive bouts of LTP that required the formation of new social self-identity structure to control the terror of reliving.

IDENTITY DYSREGULATION IN PTSD

Clinically, persons suffering from PTSD manifest severely impaired identity regulation. When the executive's metamemory fails to enhance problem solving, when flashbacks and intense anxiety intrude, cognition fails. During retraumatization, the executive is in the position of the man who has a tiger by the tail. The more he tries to keep the beast still, so as not to have his whole being swallowed, the more the danger increases.

We are all familiar with the image of the traumatized Vietnam veteran who, while trying to keep a low profile, finds himself overcome by fresh images of the past that turn the present into the same living hell. In PTSD, the brain talks to itself in the language of source experience. How do PTSD patients regulate their identity during the periodic increases in drive pressures on the prefrontal system?

One World War II veteran found a unique form of identity stabilization that almost destroyed his daughter. He was beset by reliving flashback experiences in which he was killing "Japs." His youngest daughter remained attached to him, while her older sisters and mother cowered as he raged and relived. As a young teenager, the youngest daughter was sent by her mother to the bar to bring her father home. She would sit next to him at the bar, engage him and others in conversation for hours, and then bring her father home when he was calm.

When her father had his flashbacks, the youngest daughter became his partner in reenacting the killing dramas. "I have to shoot them!" he would scream in agony. The daughter would say, "Go ahead, Dad, you have to. It is them or you. You have no choice." The daughter would suspend disbelief for hours of reenactments until her father calmed down. During her later teen years, her father stopped abusing alcohol. However, through a process of intersubjective identification, his daughter replicated his symptoms in her own identity. When he died, she came for therapy, because a part of herself that she could not grieve had been torn away. Her form of psychotherapy on her father is not for the fainthearted.

In PTSD, there is a continuum of biopsychosocial defenses from (1) social detachment, to (2) personal detachment, to (3) dissociation, to (4) identity fragmentation. Dino experienced social detachment. Personal detachment often occurs during severe, acute, inescapable trauma. Consider the case, well-publicized some years ago, of the kidnapper who cut off his victim's ears and sent them to his parents as proof of the need for ransom. Interviewed later, the victim said that he had found the event "interesting." The detachment response becomes part of the trauma. Detachment itself is recorded with the source memory. As retraumatization occurs, it becomes progressively harder not to detach. This is because sensitization to retraumatization evokes detachment more easily.

Indeed, detached self in screen memories is a hallmark of trauma (Freud, 1899). If a person says, "In my dream, I was watching myself with other people," if a persons says, "In my memory, I am watching myself watching my mother cook dinner," if a person refers to herself in the third person so that she says, "She is always like that," instead of "I am always like that," we can be almost sure that trauma is imbedded in the allusion.

In my clinical experience, a person with a poverty of childhood memories that includes just a few, innocent memories has surely been traumatized. Moreover, a woman who does not feel she inhabits her body has probably undergone trauma. Detachment is the executive's last bastion of defense against dissociation or identity fragmentation. Lida went through all the stages of this continuum. As it happens all too often, Lida's identity fragmentation proceeded to psychosis.

SOCIAL FACTORS IN PTSD

The dual hemisphere model of PTSD extends into the social realm. I propose that left hemisphere social ideals regulate ethnic integrity and right hemisphere moral values regulate bureaucratic relationships. Freud (1921) theorized that our libidinal investment in ego ideals (belief systems) determines our narcissistic relationship with social groups. Similarly, our aggressive investment in the superego's morals (value systems) determines our relationship with the laws of our social and political groups. In collective PTSD, beliefs and values are not available to internalization. Without relevant social authority during collective trauma, the populace regresses emotionally and cognitively, passing trauma transgenerationally.

Especially in natural disasters or internecine wars, where the authorities are as helpless as the population, PTSD leads to prolonged feelings of helplessness and the return of emotionally organized earlier states of identity. In PTSD, the regression in identity can easily become collective when whole populations feel helpless, and the social and political authority structure breaks down. When their ego ideals weaken, ethnic groups can become engaged in regressive revenge motifs—narcissistic vendettas.

For example, the internecine war in the former Yugoslavia caused old ethnic antagonisms to reemerge. Similarly, in Rwanda, whole ethnic populations regressed under collective trauma. Thus, old ethnic animosities can give rise to collective left hemisphere traumatized, narcissistic responses: "those who are not with us are against us." Those of different ethnic background are considered nonhuman, and are treated accordingly.

Collective right hemisphere, Dionysian PTSD can occur when a social group's superegos lose their regulatory function. Gangs emerge. Identifying with the social aggressor, gangs perpetrate acts that induce a further collective regression and further social retraumatization. Plundering during the Los Angeles riots illustrates how ethnic and racial animosity and identifications with the aggressor lead segments of the populace to indulge in regressive, Dionysian, plundering rampages.

DEVELOPMENTAL IDENTITY DISRUPTION IN STRESS DISORDERS

In the aftermath of physical abuse, *unassimilated introjects* compromise the executive's capacity to reliably integrate identity. Many syndromes share the right hemisphere's mechanism of forming unassimilated, nonself-observing introjects through identification with the aggressor. The nature of the syndrome depends very much on the stage of life during which the trauma occurs. The stage determines which identity integration functions—which self and object representations—undergoing consolidation will be rendered inflexible by the trauma.

Identity regression is especially marked in children, who lose ego functions that have recently been acquired. Sam, who had resolved the darting away behavior that characterizes rapprochement development, began to run away in spurts of false autonomy after his abuse, and his pleasure in trying new foods regressed to eating mainly pasta. Clinical observation shows that the integration and synthesis of identity is compromised by abuse. Condensed with identifications with the aggressor and with the victim, earlier, more primitive identity states reemerge.

Most traumatized children cannot separate themselves from attachments to others whom they feel are victims. This is one reason a perpetrator may continue to have power over his victim—by pleading his own pain. The Long Island girl who was locked in her tormentor's underground cell, told him, "Take care of yourself, Uncle," as she was being rescued. Induced splits in identity may become permanent. In Sam's case, the adolescent period of renewed separation-individuation conflict allowed further analytic work on his boundary issues. A day care center owner, who had been abused in childhood and traumatized in her adult life, illustrates the abused person's need to care for others and to feel sorry for the abuser.

BORDERLINE DEVELOPMENT

Borderline disorder illuminates all right hemisphere trauma-related disorders. Borderlines compensate for traumatically induced, entrenched feelings of abandonment and helplessness. The borderline aggressively blames to try to force the caretaker to compensate for his hidden helplessness. Consequently, mature self and object representations are contrived—falsely conceived.

Jerome Kroll highlights the association between PTSD and the borderline condition (1993). He concludes that 70 to 80 percent of borderline patients suffered physical or sexual abuse in childhood. In my clinical experience, borderline development is often a result of physical or emotional abuse occurring in the first two years of life. I infer that given such abuse, the right orbital frontal cortex forms overly rigid, painfully conditioned, social representations of self and object that lack the plasticity to be reconditioned in later life experience. Socialized affect signals continue in their infantile patterns.

Object relations psychoanalysts have developed an extensive literature on the results of trauma in the first two years of life. This literature sees introjects develop a segregated life of their own within overall personality development. Thus, segregated, conditioned social associations split painful bad objects and pain relieving good objects. This reasoning supports Kernberg's clinical hypothesis that the formation of pathogenic introjects in infancy causes splitting during the eighteen- to twenty-four-month period, which causes borderline development. Splitting stultifies identity development, because self and object representations cannot assimilate. It is like having a secret room in the basement inhabited by ghosts.

Borderlines illustrate that a traumatically induced syndrome can begin in infancy. Normally, hippocampal glucocorticoid receptor formation in infancy stabilizes stress response, so that source memory can provide the foundations of social identity in young childhood and beyond. Lacking stabilization, limbic conditioning maintains a lifelong tendency to discharge affect instinctually, rather than in a regulated assessable way. The borderline's social self cannot bind affect.

In my clinical experience, mothers who verbally or physically attack their infants produce children who become borderlines. These attacks deform the eighteen- to twenty-four-month-old's identity synthesis. The two-year-old does not develop an intact, self-observing, social self. This is why borderline patients lack reliable self-observation. Characterologically split, the borderline exhibits a lack of reliable self-observation, which impairs her capacity to inhibit projective identification. She projects her bad and good introject precursors of self into the object—and the therapist. She blames those around her.

In one borderline case I treated, the patient's mother had despised her from birth, and the mother made no bones about it. Her mother only cared for her when she was sick. After several years of insight-oriented psychotherapy, the patient's transference crystallized. She felt, and expressed nothing but contempt for me, but she also felt that if she left me, she would inevitably become a "bag woman," sicken, and die.

As the mother transference clarified, the patient's blame and need intensified further, sessions became stormy, and the transference reached psychotic proportions. Paradoxically, at this time the patient became very successful in the business world, as her father had been. Her positive identification with her father blossomed. As she synthesized the blame and the need, the patient self-observantly acknowledged what her father (who had paid for the sessions) had given her.

As her therapist, I had been unable to enjoy a single session with the patient over many years. In every session, she blamed me for her misery and her lack of a sense of identity. She felt and believed that like her mother, I would not help her. After we worked through the transference, which took about three more years, the patient recovered from her borderline condition.

Undoubtedly, some borderline patients have organic deficits that impair their capacities for integrating self and object representations that can bind affect. Affect is unregulated. These deficits may increase mothers' angry responses to potentially unmanageable infants. Consider the interaction between mothers who have taken cocaine during pregnancy and their unsatisfiable, unreachable, hyperactive babies. In some cases, an emotionally unavailable or abusive father contributes to the mother's angry response to the baby. In any case, borderline development is a result of organic incapacity and/or psychic trauma that prevents the normal development of affect regulation and personality integration.

Borderlines' introjects are by and large preverbal and inaccessible to verbal reconciliation. To synthesize a whole identity violates the sanctity of the separate introjects, which have developed a life of their own, as well as an interactive life with one another. If the ghosts in the basement have their way in the light of the day, all hell breaks loose. Object relations theorists are all too familiar with this scene.

The borderline preserves the integrity of introjects through projective identification with others in order to prevent the development of affective psychosis. As therapists who work with borderline patients know, when splitting and projective identification give way, the borderline person has to face her need for the therapy and for the therapist. When the therapist and the therapy become more important than the preservation of the intro-jects in their preternatural state, a transference psychosis develops. Indeed, Kernberg states, and my patient illustrates, that the borderline disorder cannot resolve without the emergence and resolution of a transference psychosis (1974).

This study of borderline development allows us to take the neural systems model a little further. If socially conditioned associations remain segregated in the borderline condition, and if particular episodes form explicit source memory that justifies the conditioned bad and good objects, then normally conditioned associations cannot be absorbed by mature identity structures. Normally, this unification occurs in the prefrontal system during latency and late adolescence. Normally, the right orbital frontal cortex develops a flexible capacity to absorb the socially reconditioned affect signals of a mature social self.

DISSOCIATIVE IDENTITY DISORDER

Dissociative identity disorder develops when fixation, trauma, abuse, or some combination of them all occurs in childhood. *As a result of identification with the perpetrator, introjects develop a life of their own. In multiple personality, (1) the victimized child, (2) the tormentor, and (3) the central executive develop a life of their own.* These lives, called *multiples,* may coexist in segregated neural organizations.

Since physical or emotional abuse and incest or rape often recur in different stages of childhood, multiple personality may be multiply formed. Then multiples from different stages have to coexist and compete with each other for access to the executive. Multiples compete with each other for access to data analysis and emotional source memory that behavioral discharge requires.

During monitoring of a patient with multiple personality disorder, as each multiple appears, it is distinguished by:

> changes in cerebral electrical activity, cerebral blood flow, galvanic skin response, skin temperature, event-related potentials, neuroendocrine profiles, thyroid function, response to medication, perception, visual functioning, visual evoked potentials, and in voice, posture, and . . . behavior. (Miller and Triggiano, 1992, p. 47)

How can this be?

We may take the development of multiples as another buttress of the neural systems model. If the executive cannot synthesize the left hemisphere's supervision with the right's observation, personality organization will be disrupted. Identification with the victim, then, disrupts narcissistic integration of the social subject. Identification with the aggressor disrupts anaclitic—object supported—integration of the social self. Conceivably, right hemisphere introjects maintain separate access to divided masses of conditioned associations, which results in their regulation of distinct neurophysiologic and autonomic states.

Eurynome: The Woman Who Bathed in the Sea During a Hurricane

Like an Oceanid with multiple forms, often called a mermaid, Eurynome consciously devoted herself to serving God and caring for youth. Eurynome suffered multiple syndromes: a mild multiple personality disorder, major depression, a mushroom phobia, and borderline traits. By *mild*, I mean she was sometimes able to own and source experiences that she had in primitive states, different from her usual consciousness.

Eurynome was the second of four children, the oldest girl. Her mother had not wanted this pregnancy because she felt trapped in a marriage where her powerful husband had other women. She felt that having Eurynome sealed her own fate. Nothing Eurynome could do as a little girl pleased her mother, but she kept trying. Indeed, she tried to keep everyone happy and united.

When she was five, her maternal uncle began to take advantage of the maternally starved little girl by bathing her tenderly when she visited her aunt's oceanside home during the summers. During prolonged bathing episodes, the uncle repeatedly forced fellatio on Eurynome, and she would vomit his semen. Eurynome developed a lifelong mushroom phobia. Her siblings made her the butt of their teasing, and they would often chase her down the beach by brandishing mushrooms or toadstools.

When Eurynome was twelve, her uncle raped her after he bathed her. He urged her to open up, and as she did she said that she felt ripped apart, but ashamed of her love-starved acquiescence. Late at night, after the rape, Eurynome turned on the gas stove. She fantasized that when she lit a match, everyone would die. An explosion would spread her experience of being ripped apart to her whole family. In the end, however, she succumbed to the gas fumes and fell asleep without lighting the match. Animating the fantasy was the fact that Eurynome knew she could not talk to her mother or anyone else about the rape.

In the morning, everyone woke up with a headache. They found Eurynome next to the stove, with the gas on. She could not answer why she had turned on the gas. In the ensuing months, as she remained dumb, she was considered to have become retarded by the gas. She was placed in a special school for retarded children. Despite her cognitive gifts, she continued to be unresponsive and dumb.

A minister took an interest in Eurynome, and he spoke to her in a code that only the two of them, and perhaps God, could understand. This communication drew her out and encouraged her to attend a regular high school and to go on to college and theological school. In theological school, Eurynome became a radical feminist with poor judgment about expending her efforts on social change. She trumpeted her lesbianism in ways that made her the victim of social misunderstanding among other homosexuals. She unwittingly fomented social splitting.

When she challenged the paternal authority structures of the church, Eurynome was made a pariah. She blamed herself and decided that her mother had been right to neglect her. She concluded that she herself had a fatal flaw that would prevent her from becoming a minister of the She-God. Her recourse was in teaching Sunday school, and becoming a Girl Scout leader.

Eurynome's Therapy

Eurynome was referred to me after she had badly frightened her female therapist. Her treatment had foundered on the rocks of maternal transference hatred. She experienced her therapist's pregnancy as an unforgivable betrayal of her love. Her maternal transference love turned to hate as she reexperienced herself as an infant about to be replaced by another infant. When the frightened therapist could not deal with Eurynome's transference, the patient's hatred turned into homicidal impulses. Eurynome proposed to bring a gun into the session to possibly shoot her therapist. She wanted the therapist to know what it was like to be ripped apart.

When the patient entered the present therapy, she suffered from a shaky reality sense. She felt walls shimmer and turn into the sea. Because of these symptoms, she had been placed on a major tranquilizer, but her reality sense, and the distinction between her inner life and her life with others, remained unreliable. In her initial consultation, Eurynome could not say whether she would shoot herself or her therapist.

Eurynome's history revealed that she had often enacted dangerous scenarios that symbolized her trauma. She was highly suicidal. On separate occasions, she bathed in the sea during a hurricane, went whitewater canoeing in a storm, and overheated her lake cabin to an incendiary point.

She spoke of a "kamikaze" woman, a multiple personality who attempted to right social wrongs regardless of consequences to herself, and who had a life of her own.

She brought a doll that she had made into her sessions. It embodied two multiples: the mature executive of her identity, and the helpless child. The doll was as large as a five-year-old. As far as Eurynome was concerned, the doll was absolutely vested with life, a condition that the patient expected me to accept without question. She and her doll were very interested to learn that her doll had the qualities of a transitional object. As I explained to them what those qualities were, the doll matured further. In response to her doll's needs for contact, Eurynome made a small menagerie of other humanoids. On her doll's birthday, she, the doll, and the other humanoids had a party. She presented me with a polaroid picture of the whole ensemble, with the doll glowing in her new outfit.

In the therapy sessions, I would speak to the doll, asking the doll to evaluate the dangerous, self-defeating situations the patient had placed herself in. The doll always had a clear, mature perspective on Eurynome's situation and on what Eurynome should do to protect herself—and to protect the life of the doll as well. After a grave social disappointment brought about by her kamikaze woman persona, the patient felt so depressed and her self-esteem was so low that she was determined to shoot herself. She felt unable to deal with the kamikaze woman. Eurynome wanted to leave the doll in my care, so that she could freely kill herself.

Tactfully refusing this charge, I placed her on a selective serotonin reuptake inhibitor (SSRI). I believed that this medication would increase the availability of serotonin as a drive neutralizer, so that Eurynome would be better able to assess the effects of her traumatic experiences. On this medication, she was able to expect that she deserved responses from others, so that she was not so frequently thrown into fits of dejected loss of confidence. The SSRI helped Eurynome absorb reconstructions about her abuse and to use the reconstructions to synthesize her identity. She needed to own and command the same judgment that her doll had.

In this, the patient's first therapy with a male therapist, Eurynome imaginatively turned me into a mermaid as I sat on my chair with my feet crossed on a hassock. By experiencing me as a mermaid, we could fuse. I was sexually neutered, as well as associated with the fixated bathing, which came up in repeated poetic and artistic renderings. Often, the sessions were much like play therapy sessions. As she began to improve, the patient internalized the other humanoid doll personas with her executive doll, and with a sense of herself.

Eurynome's borderline tendencies arose in response to her overt rejection as an infant. In her first two years of life, her mother's rejection led to a lack of basic confidence, a lack of self-esteem, and a lack of affect regulation. Her seduction and rape led to her development of PTSD and multiple personality. Moreover, Eurynome would become deeply depressed and suicidal when she felt unwanted. Her depression surfaced as feelings that her love destroyed, and consequently, that she was unworthy to live.

We can tease apart the sources of Eurynome's multiples. She had a left hemisphere's numbed response to seduction and rape. Her supervisory, semantic function regressed after her rape. She could not recapture her sense of subjective integrity and she became almost mute. Later, she invested her doll with empathic love and good, well verbalized, reflective judgment. This investment, the capacity of her friends to suspend disbelief about the doll's animation, and the therapist's understanding of the doll as a mediating object allowed her to recapture her dignity and mature capacity for reflection.

Eurynome had a right hemisphere response to abuse. She identified with the aggressor when she "raped" another woman, in an incident that seemed to me one of mutual consent. The kamikaze woman was a partially autonomous, aggressive introject. The kamikaze multiple treated men as the pain-giving enemy.

In her therapy, Eurynome reexperienced her trauma over and over, in dreams, imagery, artistic productions, and transference. Like so many traumatized people, Eurynome kept reworking the imagery of her trauma in various artistic productions. These included poetry, art, plays, and essays. Although she verged on psychosis, her ability to maintain her executive function through her doll saved her from identity disintegration, and it allowed her to resynthensize her identity and resume her maturation.

EXECUTIVE DESYNTHESIS IN PSYCHOSIS

I now propose that *executive desynthesis* triggers psychosis. By desynthesis, I mean the executive's incapacity to join each hemisphere's identity-regulating zones in verbal reflection. Executive desynthesis occurs when unmanageable endogenous or exogenous experience triggers severe identity anxiety and floods of emotionally sourced memory. The prefrontal system's networks show compromised data processing. Depending on the flash point, I postulate left or right hemisphere psychosis.

Put simply, in schizophrenia, the left hemisphere's capacity for love is compromised. In affective psychosis, the right's ability to relate affectively is impaired. In either case, compromised problem solving and identity confusion lead to states of severe panic and terror, which can induce psychotic regression and prolonged functional impairment. As I have already posited, this state of endogenous trauma gives rise to either excito-toxicity or stringent defenses against excitotoxicity, which translate experientially into deadened vitality.

How do we reconcile the present explanation for psychosis with standard biogenic amine hypotheses? As we concluded earlier, prefrontal and amygdaloid regulation both determine the hemispheric allocation of the biogenic amine system's drive resources. Given the amygdala's input into prefrontal modules, biogenic amine regulation hypotheses of syndrome formation have to account for each prefrontal hemisphere's identity regulation.

For example, the dopamine hypothesis of schizophrenia holds that dysregulation of the left ventral tegmental dopamine system impairs emotional and motivational processing. This hypothesis receives support from the finding that neuroleptics blockade many dopamine receptors in this system and relieve many schizophrenic symptoms. The left hemisphere's medial prefrontal region regulates dopamine (Glowinski, 1979). Thus, left hemisphere regulation of identity *and* dopamine allocation effects psychosis.

The supervisor's regulation of (1) the agent's planning, (2) the social subject's event sequencing, and (3) the subject's capacity to deal with humiliation and panic, all effect dopamine regulation. When the schizophrenic expects his pursuit of work and love to fail, he *de facto* lowers his motivated goals to avoid humiliation. This inertia becomes schizophrenic chronicity.

Freud (1915) defined drive (instinct at the time of writing):

> as a concept . . . between the mental and the somatic, as the psychical representative of the stimuli originating within the organism and reaching the mind, as a measure of the demand made upon the mind for work in consequence of its connection with the body. (pp. 121-122)

Thus, libidinal drive pressures the supervisor to initiate consummatory behaviors. When the supervisor cannot, because such behaviors are outside of the repertory of possibilities, then conditions are ripe for a psychotic process to begin.

SELF-OBSERVATION DISINTEGRATES
IN PSYCHOTIC MOOD DISORDERS

How does psychosis develop in the right hemisphere? When the observer's reflection on its right hemisphere's data networks falters, one's affect response to reality becomes dysfunctional. The executive loses capacity to find adaptive solutions. Because norepinephrine and serotonin are dysregulated in psychotic mood disorders, we will need to understand how right experiential loops lose their capacity to regulate these biogenic amines.

A case vignette illustrates the phenomenology and dynamics involved in the onset of psychotic mood disorder. A thirty-seven-year-old woman, married for three years, had devoted her life to caring for her family of origin. Her two male siblings had bipolar disorder. She went to her mother's home daily to help manage them. She also worked as a rehab counsellor. She smoked three packs of cigarettes a day to mitigate her feeling of emptying herself out for her family and clients. One month earlier, she stopped smoking (tobacco is an antidepressant) because her breathing was difficult and she wanted to become pregnant. Her two younger married sisters already had children.

Unfortunately, she could not become pregnant. She came for consultation, accompanied by her husband, because she had begun to sob uncontrollably for no apparent reason, and she was unable to sleep because of persistent anxiety. She also had brief periods of high energy, alternating with an agoraphobic seclusion in bed. She began sobbing when I suggested that she felt taken advantage of by her mother and her family, and there seemed no way out unless she became pregnant. But she still did not know why she was crying because she lacked self-observation.

Given her mixed bipolar symptoms and her family history of bipolar illness, I decided to try her on a mood-stabilizing agent, depakote, and a benzodiazepine—clonazepam—which is sometimes effective in bipolar illness with anxiety. Despite this intervention, her symptoms became worse. Since the patient was unable to work, her mother seized the opportunity to ask her to care for a nephew. When her mother asked her to do her hair, the patient became violent, throwing the hair dryer at the wall. However, this unbinding aggression did not generate any insight in the patient about her chronic anger toward her mother.

When I brought up possible hospitalization, she immersed in memories of her brothers' violent declines to becoming state hospital victims. She said that doctors and other mental health workers did not know what they were doing, and that they did not care about patients. When her husband called me to arrange for a hospitalization, the patient felt her family, including her husband, were plotting to get rid of her and to discredit her. She was afraid her phone was bugged. She said that if she were unable to care for others, she did not deserve to live. At this point, she was hospitalized.

This patient illustrates how a person with a genetic tendency for bipolar disorder is vulnerable to disintegration of her right hemisphere's identity.

Her capacity for self-observation, and subsequently for insight into her condition, was limited. When she lost her identity as a caretaker, her superego abandoned her. In a week, she lost her ability to care for her home, clients, husband, family, and self. She could not say what was wrong. Indeed, in sessions, she had to ask her husband to recount what was happening in her life.

How did this patient's right hemisphere trigger psychosis? Freud (1923) observed that the feeling of being abandoned by one's self-evaluating conscience (superego) induces the most powerful adult anxiety. Self and object representations, the pinions of the social self, lose integration. Feeling abandoned by her social world made this patient suicidal. Conceivably, her unbinding aggression and terror induced her amygdala to painfully recondition her social self.

When reactive increase in norepinephrine unbinds the aggressive drive, and when intolerable stress heightens hippocampal LTP, source memory reorganizes. Post (1992) argues that bipolar disorder is a progressive syndrome that accelerates as excitotoxicity stimulates episodes of pathology at ever greater frequencies. This means that each bipolar episode begins with a bout of pathological excitotoxicity; that makes the next episode of excitotoxicity easier to incite. To Post, this process is like epileptic kindling.

As we have seen, forced normalization ends kindling, and excitotoxicity is replaced by sluggishness in the same excitatory systems. It is therefore inviting to hypothesize that each manic episode ends with neurally induced depression. In Post's analysis, emotional and situational factors play less of a role as the syndrome progresses, while episodes of the disorder itself endogenously trigger further episodes (1992).

In their manic phase, many bipolar patients become psychotic. Drive pressures are so severe that manic persons usually refuse to morally self-observe. Right hemisphere triggered manic psychosis often begins with unbridled claims of social freedom. Expansive identification with a superior social power (God) provides a prosthesis for a disintegrating superego and social self. This produces a quasidelusional social self. One manic patient changed her religion, to identify herself with a religious group that was more exalted in her mind. In the depressive phase which followed, she lamely maintained the new religious identity.

What causes the presumed excitotoxicity and forced normalization in bipolar illness? Theoretically, amygdalar responses during manic and depressed phases heavily reconditions medial and intermediate cortex, dysregulating the self and the social self. Hippocampal excitation, producing new source memory provides false rationales for problem solving. Prolonged elevated cortisol levels in bipolar disorder effect the genome of hippocampal glutamate neurons to increase their ouput, increasing the likelihood of excitotoxicity (McEwen et al., 1992).

Prolonged stress can exhaust the cortisol feedback inhibition mechanism, so that cortisol levels remain high. In bipolar disorder, each episode of mania or depression increases the general life stress because of the dysfunctional consequences to the person's life. Each episode of mania and depression adds to the feeling of being behind the eight ball—of losing the high stakes gamble of a good life.

Kraepelin observed that patients with bipolar disorder cannot grieve sufficiently. Consequently, they deny losses (Post, 1992). To me, this indicates a genetic tendency for impaired aggressive binding of self and object representations. The patient I presented could not wait to have a baby. Nor could she grieve the lack of a real mothering relationship in her own life.

Like gamblers, bipolar patients think they must make up for lost time. It is as if they could eradicate losses by larger gains. The grieving difficulty in bipolar patients includes the incapacity to acknowledge the ravages of their mental illness as well as the incapacity to give up dead relationships. It seems to me that the inability to grieve is a phenomenological marker that betrays a source of pathology in the right hemisphere.

Severe manic episodes show several forms of right hemisphere phenomenology. The manic incapacity for self-observation reaches complete denial. As moral judgement and insight diminish, the manic throws off her clothes as she throws off all rules and authority, including that of her own superego. Identity flies apart. The denial of reality, the flight of ideas, the lack of a reality-orienting basis for behavior, the disintegration of episodic memory, and affective dysregulation all manifest a lack of integration by the right hemisphere's prefrontal system. In their depressive phase, bipolars manifest this disintegration as they lose the sense that their self can function in the world. They just want to sleep and shut out the source of all affects.

MELANCHOLIC DEPRESSION

An obsessive, deeply moral lawyer married to a borderline woman was the butt of her projectively identified bad self for all the years of their marriage. When his wife decided to divorce him, he did not question her evaluation of him as worthless. Instead, he took all the force of his own unconscious resentment and directed it against his own self. He developed a severe melancholic depression. When he became suicidal, his wife encouraged him to kill himself. Severely depressed, he bought a gun, drove to a lonely motel, and prepared to kill himself. Instead, he called his brother, who brought him to my office.

When he consulted with me, every piece of self-evaluation reflected his wife's version of him, lock, stock, and barrel. He believed he was an inadequate lawyer. He believed he would be fired from his job because of his suicidal episode. He believed he was an alcoholic (which he was not). He believed he was a bad father, when it was he who had raised the children, while his wife partied. When I called his wife on the phone, she was overtly disappointed that he was still alive.

This patient eventually did well on a regime of high doses of a mono-amine oxidase inhibitor and psychotherapy directed toward understanding why he had been unable to see his wife's projection into him. We learned that she had projected the persona of her alcoholic wrathful father onto him. She had identified with her alcoholic father who was the aggressor in her family, and projected that identification onto her husband. The patient had to develop a whole theory of mind in order to learn how to evaluate both his wife and himself in an appropriate context. Eventually he learned, and he relinquished the pathological relationship.

Freud (1917) posited that melancholia (suspended grief) displays a pathological identification with the lost object. Like the abused person's split-off identification with the aggressor, the melancholic is unable to integrate identifications with the lost object into the reflective structure of his personality. Having to relinquish his wife, the lawyer first pathologi-cally released the aggression that bound this relationship, onto his own social self.

Grieving is the work of weakening conditioned memories that relate the social self to nonviable or dead relationships. The grieving process has to induce plastic changes in the networks of associations (some conditioned, some explicit) to the no-longer significant other. Freud discovered that *melancholic* grieving is blocked until the aggressive part of the ambivalent relationship with the lost object becomes conscious. As I see it, when part of a relationship remains unconscious, the relationship is mired in condi-tioned associations rather than in explicit ones.

Until the lawyer developed his theory of mind and accepted his own authority and morality as legitimate, he was unable to evaluate the source memories from his marriage. The lawyer realized that his wife had made her son the projectively identified "good object." He had become a socio-path, who used his mother to siphon off his father's money for his own purposes. The patient had used his wife as a source of stimulation, because he himself had been unable to enjoy life on his own.

The work of therapy is to create an explicit channel to understanding the pain that the lost object has caused. Dependent, masochistic, and obsessive personality traits all inhibit the emergence of conscious anger and resentment to the lost object. When these traits color a relationship, features of the other person are attributed to the social self. When the social self and its object of dependency lack definite intrapsychic boundaries, the object's loss can lead to the development of melancholic depression.

PSYCHOTIC DEPRESSION

In "Letter 125" to Fliess, Freud noted that in some forms of paranoia, the ego unravels lifetime identifications that it had integrated in the process of character formation (1899, pp. 279-280). A projective mechanism returns these identification figures to the outside world where they are experienced as critically commenting on the person. Subsequently, Freud often noted that a self-critical agency judges the ego. In mood-congruent psychotic depression, delusions and hallucinations show the release of disintegrating childhood identifications.

I think these self-critical, primitive comments reveal the presence of conditioned verbal associations—superego precursors—that are unavailable to the executive function. These associations remain imbedded in painfully conditioned "bad self and object representations." In psychotic depression, there is often a paranoid trend, which indicates the ease of projecting primitive self and object representations, that have never been assimilated in a mature social self.

WHAT FOSTERS ADDICTION?

We have seen that the ventral tegmental dopamine system, which includes the septum and the nucleus accumbens, conveys libidinal drive force. By inserting electrodes into the septum of ambulant patients and delivering stimulation through the electrodes, Heath (1972) broke into the experiential pleasure loop. His patients' electrically stimulated pleasure was equivalent to real life's, and some became addicted to electrical self-stimulation.

Addiction is neurally multidetermined, because pleasure inheres in a left hemisphere loop that includes the ventral tegmental system, the amygdala, the septum, and the medial prefrontal cortex. Pleasure can be induced anywhere in this loop. The mere anticipation of cocaine induces an overflow of dopamine in the nucleus accumbens of addicts as salience builds toward pleasure (Fontana, Post, and Pert, 1991). Operantly conditioned stimuli, like the presence of drug buddies, or the presence of drug paraphernalia triggers dopamine outpouring in the nucleus accumbens. Obviously, then, sending an addict back to his environment resumes the addiction.

The left nucleus accumbens signal its caudate that salience is present. This signal, pleasurable in itself, is comparable to the pleasure that foreplay generates when a person knows that orgasm will be achieved. The satisfaction induced by mouthwatering anticipation answers Freud's question about why foreplay does not painfully increase tension, but instead begins the discharge process. Given the right hemisphere's overall inhibitory regulation of the left hemisphere's behavior, the right hemisphere also promotes the pleasure of addiction and orgasm. The right amygdala releases the left's inhibition of the left nucleus accumbens.

Opiates are highly addictive because their neuromodulation lasts for long periods and because multiple opiate receptors regulate both left and right hemisphere processes. Some opiates such as methadone inhibit aggressive pressures through their dampening of the locus ceruleus. Clinical observation reveals that patients who have come off methadone may become psychotically depressed. Other opiates such as heroin produce prolonged outpouring of dopamine that provide pleasure far greater than any interpersonal or orgasmic pleasure.

CONCLUSION

In this chapter, we have reviewed research findings and clinical evidence that point to the seminal role of trauma in the formation of psychiatric syndromes. Presently, we will explore the concept that trauma, whether endogenous or exogenous, is a mechanism that induces excitotoxicity in PTSD, as well as all forms of chronic psychosis. Just as epilepsy may begin with a focus in the cerebral cortex, and eventually kindle the limbic system, so psychosis may begin with prefrontal disturbances of identity regulation that induces excitotoxicity in the limbic system. In this view, the experience of psychosis is an endogenous trauma that usually induces syndrome formation.

Chapter 9

Mental Syndromes: Unifying Hypotheses

Just as my fingers on these keys
Make music, so the selfsame sounds
On my spirit make a music too.

—From *Peter Quince at the Clavier,*
Wallace Stevens

Just as my fingers on the keys of this computer strive to render how my brain talks to itself, so do my meaning, feeling, and identity strive to reach out to the reader too. Informing our communications with feelings enriches our relationships, but as we will see later in this chapter, when the music of feeling is suppressed by the brain, right hemisphere syndromes can develop.

How does the brain form its myriad syndromes? So far, we have said: when excitotoxicity forges and breaks links in the neural chain, severe syndromes arise. Now we will add a corollary: *less severe syndromes defend against the onset of excitotoxicity.* In less severe syndromes such as dysthymia or the character disorders, intrapsychic identity regulates the biogenic amine systems. *By regulating our drive state's biogenic amine systems, our sense of identity can inhibit potential excitotoxicity.*

I suggest that less severe syndromes form when:

- a genetic tendency increases one hemisphere's processing at the expense of the other,
- the executive alters identity to accommodate experience that has been distorted in particular assessment zones,
- the executive values data assessed in one of a hemisphere's assessment zones over others, and when
- an emergent neural equilibrium among all the experiental loops compensates for these distortions.

Biases in consciousness manifest as *syndromes* triggered in the left hemisphere or right hemisphere. Distortions in assessment appear as personality styles.

Consider the interpersonal dimension: left hemisphere types relate narcissistically. They form intersubjective relationships at the expense of interobjective ones. They crave understanding, mirroring, and admiration. They can form mutually empathic relationships if they feel understood. If they do not, they feel no impact on the world, their social subject is threatened with humiliation or shattering, and they replace empathy with entitlement. All of the Type 1 people listed in The Origin of Syndromes illustrations show distinctive intersubjective dysfunctions.

Right hemisphere types form anaclitic (interobjective) relationships at the expense of intersubjective ones. These relationships can be distorted and dysfunctional. Individuals with these syndromes are concerned about how they come across in public. They relate to others' painful affect as if their own, but others shy away, because Type 2 people preempt others' pain. Type 2 personalities cannot refuse a request, nor can they stand to be refused. They cannot tolerate their own grief, because they cannot separate their own social self from others'. All of the Type 2 people listed in The Origin of Syndromes illustrations manifest interobjective dysfunctions.

EIGHT FACTORS IN DESCRIBING SYNDROMES

Pragmatically, any syndrome is a relatively enduring working constellation of experiential loops that persistently slants consciousness toward a recognizable, abnormal equilibrium. A complete description of a syndrome must:

- reconcile with standard nosology,
- explain how signs and symptoms develop,
- recognize biogenic amine's effects on distributed systems,
- dovetail with event-related potential EEG studies and functional brain imaging when these studies are available,
- suit reasonable dynamic formulations,
- clarify intrapsychic and interpersonal styles,
- enhance treatment decisions, and
- show how the individual fits into special social niches.

THE THEORY OF MAJOR DEPRESSION AND DYSTHYMIA

What follows is a unifying hypothesis for understanding the development of both unipolar major depression and dysthymia. These syndromes defend against the right hemisphere's ever-forming excitotoxicity. The difference between bipolar and unipolar depression is this: depression in bipolar disorders defends against excitotoxicity after it has happened. Bipolar depressives try to lock the barn door after the horse has bolted. Unipolars and dysthymics do not ever let the painfully hobbled horse out of the barn.

Depression is triggered in the right hemisphere. Its course impairs the right hemisphere's hierarchy of functions. The observer establishes a new equilibrium among its various identity metafunctions. In depression, our observer inhibits reality assessment, self-observation, and stress responses. Because the executive must equilibrate all identity functions, it secondarily curtails left hemisphere functions, such as the will to love.

There are cases of *atypical depression* in which the left hemisphere is the first to be compromised. Narcissistic losses, such as creative enterprises going badly, research foundering, or the loss of beauty, entail subjective disillusionment and numbing. If atypical depression begins in the left hemisphere, perhaps it should not be included under the rubric of depression. In my experience, treatment of atypical depression requires a distinctly different therapeutic and psychopharmacological approach than is needed in treating "true depression." Atypical depression calls for the use of therapeutic mirroring and monoamine oxidase inhibitors (MAOs). Cognitive therapy and tricyclic drugs work better in Type 2 depression.

A person with major depression is consistently sad for at least two weeks, and this sadness is accompanied by decreased energy for all activities of daily living. A loss of self-esteem and confidence progresses beyond understandable dynamic issues to states of unfathomable helplessness and hopelessness. Major depression can become so severe, that the autonomic system decreases its facilitation of physiological functions that support normal life. Appetite, sleep, emotion, and sexuality all falter. The autonomic slowdown has been compared to hibernation, presaging up to two years of conserved energy.

The dysthymic feels depressed more often than not for at least two years. His personality accommodates to depression as he pessimistically appraises his experience. His cognitive and behavioral accommodations prevent the development of autonomic dysfunction. However, in *double depression*, intervals of major depression can erupt within a context of lifetime dysthymia.

The image of adaptive or maladaptive hibernation (i.e., of reducing stimulation from and response to exigency) illuminates depressive syndromes. Many of my depressed patients have compared their depressions with being in a deep hole, where any effort to dig out results in sinking deeper. There is no light in depression, because in depression, the executive analyzes a poverty of data.

The depressive's withdrawal affects all three experiential loops in the right hemisphere:

1. The medial zone's affect signals painfully renew the self's sad mood.
2. The intermediate zone's social self, which assesses socially conditioned somatic states, elicits source memories of painful, angry, sad, and frustrated episodes. The depressed individual's immersion in unhappy past episodes *proves* to her that fresh experience will be fruitless.
3. The lateral zone's *procedural self* pessimistically accepts restricted response options as cognitive adaptation narrows.

Thus, the depressed person accepts mental pain, denies its specific origins, and concludes that there is nothing to be done about it, except avoid life. Because all stimuli are painful and evoke painful episodes, the depressed executive institutes perceptual defenses which reduces sensory registration.

Major unipolar depressives show deeper responses to stress than dysthymics. In major depression, the neurophysiological response to stress damps hippocampal cognitive processing. In chronic stress, the CA 3 fields show atrophy of the apical dendrites that receive glutamate from their mossy fiber inputs. As we said in Chapter 2, this is because glucocorticoid receptors in the mossy fibers downregulate glutamate production. Moreover, the mossy fiber's presynaptic glutamate autoreceptors inhibit glutamate release. When CA 3 fields reduce their transmission, less data is processed, and less explicit memory forms. A person with major depression recycles old and painful source memory.

The Woman Who Could Not Bear Her Parents' Faces

An able woman in her mid-thirties, who had built a very successful day care center, developed major depression after she was accused of not reporting a case of child abuse by one of the children's parents. My patient had, in fact, reported the episode. Vengefully, however, a paranoid female employee reported that she had not. The disgruntled employee, it seems, had been passed over for promotion and subsequently fired. Having been fired, this woman terrorized my patient by sending oddly threatening, primitive messages. At one point, she sent a thug to intimidate the patient.

By the time she arrived at her first session, the patient was tearful, her thinking was slowed, and she felt life had become unbearable. She wanted to rid herself of her business, but could not decide to do that because her niece attended her day care center. The patient could barely fall asleep at night; and when she did, she would wake at three in the morning, as if electrified by a jolt of vigilance. This very petite woman had already lost ten pounds over the past month. I placed her on a tricyclic antidepressant because I think this type of medication works well in patients who have developed autonomic dysfunction.

In her reactive major depression, the patient felt that everything she did was wrong, and that she should "just go away somewhere for a long time." In our discussions, I learned that the patient had a childhood history of having been physically and sexually abused. Under siege, she turned a sense of blame and wrongdoing against herself, as abused persons are prone to do. Characteristically, this abused person had dedicated herself to taking care of children.

The patient could not appreciate the visual beauty of the springtime, although she wanted to. When she tried to think about saving her business, she lost focus and returned to memories of trying to overcome her father's tyranny by working hard. She longed for a father to tell her what she should do and a mother to turn to for protection, but she kept concluding that it was as useless to try to seek help in the present as it had been in her childhood. In fact, she could not bear to see her parents' faces.

When major depressives are asked to recount happy and sad past experiences, their responses are slow and overgeneralized, with gaps in cognitive and affective specificity, as this patient's were (Williams and Scott, 1988). In major depression, but not dysthymia, working memory shows increased latency of posticonic integration (N2, P2, P3) in response to visual stimuli (Bruder et al., 1992). Slowed visal working memory lessens the impact of others' disapproving facial expressions, and the right hemisphere's slowed working memory interferes with the prefrontal system's capacity for reflective self-observation. That is why this patient could not enjoy visual stimuli or stand to look at her parents' faces.

Another patient, a fifty-year-old woman in remission from a double depression (dysthymia and recurrent major depressions) of many years' duration, reports that she regularly sees images of faces when she closes her eyes. The faces begin small. Then they get larger and larger until they go beyond the boundaries of her imaging space. Before sleep, this imaging is accompanied by gritty oral sensations. This phenomenon is known to analysts, who see in it a return of the nursing phenomenon: seeing the maternal face while having a gritty feeling in the mouth.

Conceivably, those who are vulnerable to depression avidly scrutinize their parents' faces for approval, beginning in their infancy. Visual facial memory appears to be important in the life history of depressives. Many depressed patients have reported to me that their choice of love objects depends on finding similar facial features to their parents'. I have known many severely depressed patients who begin to have lingering dream images of loved one's faces as they go into and out of major depressive episodes.

Indeed, when I ran a psychiatric ward and did "dream rounds" in the morning, depressed patients regularly reported dreaming of loved ones' faces.

Slowed data registration, processing, and analysis is more evident in major depression than in dysthymia. ERP (Event-Related Potential) studies show that dysthymics decrease early processing in the N1-P2 epoch (Yee, Delden, and Miller, 1992). In dysthymic college students, "the depressed group differed in arousal level or sensory sensitivity from the control group" (Burkhart and Thomas, 1993). As major depression deepens, neurophysiological defenses against rhinal cortical data registration and processing and prefrontal data assessment becomes bilateral.

In major depression, the discouraged person shuts down most prefrontal analysis. Beginning in the right hemisphere, all of the prefrontal zones enter into this slowing. Thus, the major depressive feels she does not belong in the world and stops observing what her experience really signifies. The dysthymic feels she *may* not belong in the world and *wonders* what her experience signifies.[1]

Biogenic amine hypotheses of depression cite reductions in available norepinephrine and serotonin, and sometimes dopamine, as causal factors in depression. If we accept the proposition that dopamine more heavily regulates the left hemisphere's metafunctions, then its causal role in depression applies only to atypical depression or to severe depression that secondarily involves the left hemisphere. The biogenic amines' immediate effects last long enough to maintain problem solving's efficacy for the second or two that it takes to analyze data. Thus, when prefrontal areas become depleted of biogenic amines, our emotional and cognitive capacity to appraise experience lapses.

Prolonged stress first increases then decreases the activity of both norepinephrine and serotonin. During the induction and maintenance of depression, the right hemisphere does not bind aggressive drive smoothly anymore. Perhaps an initial stress-related increase in serotonin contributes to hippocampal damping. As norepinephrine and serotonin resources diminish, the capacity to explore reality, deal with novelty, and regulate affects fails. Anger, denial, acceptance, and resignation are a well-known sequence of responses to unavoidable losses, as well as to prolonged stress.

Cognitive therapy aimed toward reestablishing response options and medication that increases the availability of biogenic amines allow the prefrontal cortex to reestablish a more normal pattern of responses to ongoing stress. In the case of the depressed day care center owner, tricyclic medication and consistent reassurance about the efficacy of her hard work slowly ameliorated the ordeal. Before she was placed on tricyclics, this patient overreacted to her stress and retraumatized herself further. She responded to the intimidation threats with avoidance and withdrawal. Among their effects, tricyclics inhibit presynaptic autofeedback receptors, which stabilizes the norepinephrine and serotonin systems so that a person feels as if stress has abated.

With pharmacological replacement and stabilization of biogenic amines, the prefrontal system increases its activity, perceptual defenses are allayed, and different somatic signals gradually bring cheerier feedback to the orbital cortex. Only after recovering from her major depression could the day care center owner safely become angry about the trauma she had been put through in the present and the abuse she had endured in the past.

THE THEORY OF BIPOLAR DISORDERS

There is no evidence of excitotoxicity in the formation of unipolar depression. Instead, there is a perceptual defense and a psychopathological lowering of stimulation and arousal levels. I posit, however, that bipolar disorder's severe depression is a reaction to the right hemisphere, limbic excitotoxicity.

I also posit that in bipolar disorder the left hemisphere compensates for both the overactive manic state, and the underactive depressed state. Studying bipolar disorder can therefore teach us more about the right hemisphere's role in affect regulation.

Recently, I saw a nineteen-year-old freshman student who had just arrived at the university. He complained of episodes of suddenly feeling as if the bottom were dropping out of his life. During these episodes, he becomes forgetful. This student disguises his lethargic episodes with a forced cheerfulness, so that no one knows what he endures. The initial diagnostic interview elicited similar, less frequent, episodes that began when the patient was twelve years old. In my office, the patient complained that although he has many friends—even in his new school—he tends to "carry" them emotionally. For this young man, carrying means more than support. For instance, he had a friend who committed suicide two years ago. The student still cannot let go of his friend's emotional problems.

During his teen years, this student had resorted to the use of "natural medicines" to try to restore his "energy balance." He believed that religious groups devoted to restoring energy balance could point him on his way to a reliable identity. In high school, he wrote a paper about bipolar disorder.

When I asked this young man about his family, he told me that his older brother had been diagnosed as having an attention deficit disorder. His brother has mood swings, however. Currently in a positive mood, the brother is making a lot of money. He also said that his father's mother had a nervous breakdown when she was fifty years old, after her husband died. She was given antidepressants, and "her brain turned to mush." The grandmother never recovered. She is currently languishing in a nursing home.

Mental status examination revealed that this patient feels his thoughts beginning to race our of control, particularly when he lies down to go to sleep. He feels an unpleasant excitement then and a kind of sexual tension as he tries to control his thoughts. Floods of sensory stimulation seem to flow from one thought to another. These episodes go on relentlessly, and because of them, the student had only slept for two hours on three consecutive nights during the week before our first visit. At other times, when lethargy overcomes him, this patient feels that he will actually lose himself at some point. He has considered suicide as a way of dealing with this contingency.

I propose that this young man suffers from a prodromal case of bipolar disorder, and that although he is still functioning normally, he is on the verge of developing a full-blown bipolar syndrome. As we will see, all of his symptoms are precursors of full-blown manic and depressive syndromes. What is more, although no one in his family has been given that diagnosis, his family history is consistent with a genetic predisposition to bipolar illness. I placed this patient on depakote, a mood stabilizer, as a prelude to giving him an antidepressant.

Let us assume that mania begins with a poorly modulated stress system that too easily induces LTP. Genetic predisposition causes the manic to register sensory and affect stimulation too easily in his right hemispheres. During high stress, floods of painful stimulation register. Instead of triggering the extensive episodic memory that gives rise to introjects in PTSD, in mania, the right hemisphere's amygdala reactively increases the left's dopaminergic pleasure processing (Flor-Henry, 1979). In this scenario, the manic person is deluged with facts, but forms a poverty of source memory.

In this view, the manic's left hemisphere increases its drive for consummation in response to increased pain assessment by the right hemisphere. Pleasure mitigates the manic's pain. In acute mania, waves of frustration are balanced by waves of expected consummation. Indiscriminately appraising floods of stimuli as both significant and salient, the manic does not know what is happening. Psychoanalytically conceived, the manic's drive pressures alternate rapidly, without sufficient binding or neutralization.

Here is my hypothesis about bipolar depression: *manic overstimulation causes excitotoxicity in the amygdala and in the hippocampus' explicit pathway. Then neurophysiological reactive damping blocks further explicit processing of data, which produces depression.* The retardation of data processing in bipolar depression is reactive, then, not primary as it is in unipolar depression. Post (1992) suggests that early bipolar manic episodes are induced by stressful experience, but later, rapid cycling induces endogenous episodes of excitotoxicity. Thus, excitotoxicity builds on itself as life proceeds.

In a manic or mixed bipolar episode, such as the one undergone by the sobbing, laughing patient discussed in Chapter 8, increased drive pressure depletes biogenic amines and depletes the capacity of neuromodulators to enhance neurotransmitter production and efficacy. Theoretically, the patient's quick changing sobbing and laughing accompanied the unbinding of her drives; the depletion of her drive resources enhanced her formation of hippocampal and amygdalar excitotoxicity.

A fifty-year-old bipolar type 2 woman in the midst of divorce proceedings was thrown into a manic episode after she took SSRI (selective serotonin reuptake inhibitor) medication. Before this, she had experienced episodes of depression, but only one prior hypomanic episode. She had a premorbid history of having an eidetic memory. She could explicitly process great volumes of visual information, which enabled her to run her "headhunter" agency in a superior manner without the aid of a computer.

Manic, her capacity to analyze information was so compromised that she did not know what day of the week it was. Her executive was so disconnected from her observer that she spoke about herself in the third person. She told me about a week's total insomnia as if she were speaking of a distant phenomenon. Her thoughts raced so fast that she could only tell one-tenth of them to me, but she assumed I knew all because we were both "smart." She could not stand the feeling that I, or anyone, would step into her articulatory breech and tell her what to do. She resisted all authority as a dangerous infringement on her holding forth in public. She emphatically did not want to be hospitalized. She was hospitalized, however, and her manic "delirium" responded favorably to a single ECT (electroconvulsive therapy) treatment.

When a hypomanic person is on his game, he has an increased capacity to process data explicitly. The hypomanic often shows the capacity to deal with a plethora of details. It is for this reason, I think, that hypomanics can learn languages so rapidly and enter into so many social arrangements. Unfortunately, the hypomanic's language skill is often an instrument of imitation, not meaning. The hypomanic's communication and socialization skills are only skin deep as we sense when listening to complaints and boasts that seem to lack substance and conviction.

The Chef Who Crashed

A thirty-one-year-old chef with bipolar disorder came crashing down into a suicide attempt. He had almost superhumanly run the kitchen of an upscale resort restaurant for fourteen hours a day, seven days a week, for seven weeks at the height of the Jersey Shore vacation season. His attention to detail was so fantastic that he almost singlehandedly shopped for, and prepared, 150 entrees nightly, and he dealt with all the disasters that befall a resort restaurant during a prolonged heat wave. For instance, with the refrigeration on the fritz, and the kitchen temperature at 140 degrees, he still had enough time and ingenuity to run out and get enough ice to save the vegetables.

He worked as if he were on stage, engaged in a public performance, or on a battlefield. He handled burning pots like hot potatoes in order to make his work go faster. Unfortunately, no one could help him because everyone else seemed to him bumbling or lazy. Moreover, his boss took terrible advantage paying him $600 in cash per week, without medical benefits, and wheedling for just one more bravura kitchen performance. After a shift, he would sleep for an hour or two, get up, and then go jogging. On his one day off from this work marathon, he went parachute jumping.

I prescribed depakote to try to tame his hypomania, and a nonbenzodiapine sleeping pill to promote sleep; but despite adequate levels of depakote, the chef's activity level was only mildly stilled. Now, he slept three or four hours nightly. Inevitably, as the final big weekend of the summer approached, a co-worker insisted on interrupting for some irrelevancy, and the chef hurled a cauldron of scalding water toward the fellow, who was not hurt. The chef ran out of the restaurant and proceeded to take all of his depakote and sleeping medication, which finally brought him to a hospital.

The chef felt that this was the only way to stop his work marathon, and indeed, he wanted to sleep forever, and to dampen his irritability permanently. Indeed, by the time he got to the hospital, this man could not say no to his boss, and he could not set limits on himself or make boundaries without becoming intensely irritable. The volume of sensory input he registered and processed so stressed him and so engaged his aggressive drive that he was absolutely vigilant. Under these circumstances, I posit, excitotoxicity, and then reactive damping must be biologically induced. This patient needed help; but as he said all along, to give in meant he was "just a baby."

The rationale for using depakote, and similar antikindling drugs in mania is that these medications inhibit excitatory transmission. We attempt to block the limbic system's data and affect overload. Lithium slows many levels of neural activity. Obviously, the chef's level of excitatory transmission was so high that it was relatively unaffected by depakote. We can presume that his manic episode had reached the excitotoxic stage.

In bipolar disorder, as well as in chronic major depression, the brain's temporal lobe volume declines bilaterally. This decline is due to shrinkage in the hippocampal formation. Magnetic resonance imaging (MRI) in both bipolar patients and major depressives shows bilaterally decreased temporal lobe volume (Hauser, Altschuler, and Berretini, 1989). I infer that in bipolar disorder, the hippocampus shrinks in the aftermath of excitotoxicity. Since there is no evidence for excitotoxicity in chronic major depression, but there is evidence for decreased early data processing, I assume that shrinkage in major depression is due to hippocampal dendritic atrophy secondary to hypercortisol effects on CA 3.

Since affect is dysregulated in bipolar disorder, let us consider evidence for how the brain processes affective stimuli. The right hemisphere affectively assesses both visual feedback from others and their aural prosody—speech melody. We read other's responses and hear their tone. One technique that has been used as a source of stimulation in ERP studies is the presentation of a chimeric face—one, for example, with an angry expression on the left side, and a happy expression on the right. Normally, the right parahippocampus reacts more highly to the angry side, while the left and right react equally to the happy side (Laurian et al., 1991). This reactivity is a signal system that assesses facial expressions in prelude to behavior.

A chimeric processing study showed that the known bias toward the right parahippocampal processing of the left, angry face decreases in bipolar depression, while the left processing of the happy right face increases in manics (David and Cutting, 1990). In bipolar depression, then, processing of facial signifiers decreases because the bipolar depressive has already shut down his affect options. The bipolar depressed patient just wants to stay in bed with his eyes shut. When he is still manic, however, he will look expectantly into your eyes, and quickly scrutinize your face because he is seeking a license for consummation. The reader may recall that face processing is our best way to assess the immediate impact of reality on our adaptive responses. Manics make overly quick, maladaptive, poorly processed face assessments.

Two neuropsychological techniques for presenting stimuli to the hemispheres separately are confining visual stimuli to one half of the visual field, and *dichotic listening*, which is a technique for feeding auditory stimuli to either ear separately. The left ear feeds auditory rhythm to the right hemisphere. When presented with a combination of half-field visual stimuli and dichotic listening during ERP testing, compensated manics showed a decreased p100 response to both auditory and visual stimuli presented to the right hemisphere, which shows the defense against stimulus arousal (Bruder et al., 1992). Thus, compensated manics use chronic damping—a perceptual defense—against any further outbreak of flooding stimuli and LTP.

In conclusion, the acutely manic or hypomanic person registers and processes a lot more stimulation than a normal person does. Hypomanic people may have the capacity to deal with a great deal of stimulation in creative ways. They can be wonderful at parties with strangers. They may seek stimulation because stimulation is followed by the induction of reactive pleasure. If we consider that a certain proportion of hypomanic individuals may increases social intercourse, we may conclude that this syndrome may represent one in a genetically determined stochastic array of possibilities for handling experience. Society can uses diverse problem solvers to ensure its survival.

In our fin de siècle, highly stressful world, there is an advantage in being able to process experience superficially. Managed care, for instance, requires a pragmatic, nonempathic approach to psychiatric care. In this world, it is a convenience to believe that mental illness is a "chemical imbalance." And, oddly enough, many psychopharmacologists I have known have hypomanic qualities. They can process patients quickly, know the details of drug interactions and side effects, do research, teach, administer, and provide convincing rationales for psychopharmacological interventions in patient management.

THE THEORY OF OBSESSIVE-COMPULSIVE DISORDER

The clinical, neural system's hypothesis about the formation of obsessive-compulsive disorder (OCD) must take into account that obsessions and compulsions impair behavioral regulation. A suitable hypothesis, then, will have to describe the neural transactions that interfere with the executive's translation of data assessments into behavioral decisions.

In OCD, anticipatory anxiety and novelty anxiety elicit defenses that inhibit decision making. Identity anxiety also introduces uncertainty into the executive's reliance on his own intrapsychic identity. Consequently, the person with OCD wants to believe in others' executive decisions. The obsessive-compulsive constantly substitutes the appraisals and the reflection of others for his own executive decision making process ("What should I do?").

There is evidence, I will cite presently, for the hypothesis that *OCD develops in response to bilaterally increased, orbital frontal, and insular cortex assessment of socially conditioned data, especially to the right hemisphere's episodic source memory.* Too many socially conditioned signals are received; and in response, the executive evokes too much explicit data and source memory. This results in a decreased capacity of the supplementary motor association cortex and its conjunctive caudate processing to help the executive interpret the overload of salience and significance.

We recall from Chapter 1 that articulatory rehearsal readies the supplementary motor cortex to elicit behavior derived from action and response programs. The patient with OCD cannot believe the salience and significance of signals processed by his caudate, and assessed in the orbital frontal cortex, because the signals are too many and too conflicting. With too much data, the executive's articulatory rehearsal is unreliable, and the typical obsessive lists reasons as intellectual rationales for decisions.

The Man with a Contaminated Brain

A twenty-year-old Asian college student had severe OCD. For the previous several years, he had increased difficulty in studying. When he tried to study, his mind was taken over by images of contamination. Too much input was too dirty and too dangerous. The question of how much contamination had spread to his various possessions required so much cognitive activity that he could not study. Because no one agreed with his contamination estimates, he wondered if something was wrong with his brain.

His father, who is an esteemed educator, had told the young man, "Your only legacy is your brain." His father insisted that the boy must be an outstanding scholar. The young man, however, never wanted to be a scholar. The secondary gain of his symptoms was an unconsciously defiant refusal to take responsibility for becoming a scholar. All of his cognitive activity was turned to examining and reexamining the likelihood of contamination. Because he is Asian, the patient rationalized that one should take off one's shoes before entering a living space. Otherwise, he believed, the living space was the same as the outdoors—contaminated by feces. The young man could not make his own decisions. He constantly polled others about what he should do. At his worst, he was afraid to leave his room or to touch anyone, lest he be contaminated, or contaminate others.

I treated the young man with an SSRI. After two months, his contamination symptoms became restricted to his stereo set, the source of respite from his symptoms. When he began behavioral therapy, his therapist asked him to stop cleaning. He was able to do this, but he felt he would have to throw away his stereo—his chief source of pleasure—if he could not clean it. He lamented his loss of contact with music, but the guilty side of his aggressive conflicts was allayed.

Sociocultural dislocation contributed to this young man's OCD. After moving to California from Asia when he was fifteen years old, the patient managed to adjust his identity feelings to being an American. Then, his father pulled the rug out from under him by deciding to return the family to Asia for two more years. When he went back, he felt that he no longer belonged in either culture, that he had no home, and that he could not express his feelings of anger to his father. When he returned to the United States, he went to college on the East Coast. He was now in a quandary about where he belonged, and he felt that he was losing his adolescence. In insight psychotherapy, after his obsessive-compulsive symptoms had cleared partially with the help of SSRIs and cognitive therapy, we uncovered his underlying depression and anger as well as his identity and social role confusion.

Like this young man, other patients with OCD are overly sensitive to the social manifestations of their aggressive drive. They cannot tolerate the sense that their own social self is as important as other's. They become morally sanctimonious; to preserve a sense that their social identity is acceptable.

The contamination symptom itself, harks back to the anal period of development when feces control develops in a context of abandonment anxiety. Doing one's "duty" binds the aggressive drive, which, if it were unleashed through contaminative defacation, would result in abandonment. The anal conditioning of social relationships that commences at age two continues to provide a right hemisphere foreground for many social functions.

The Man Who Sculpted His Body

A twenty-two-year-old sculptor with OCD presented himself to therapy in a "delirium" of anxious doubt about all his decisions. Should he marry his girlfriend? When? Should he live in the city or in the suburbs, where it would be easier to have a studio? Should he work full-time at his computer art job for television or should he become a bartender? When working on his computer art, he is terrified of not doing his duty of pleasing everyone. As a bartender, maybe he can make everyone happy. He constantly asks his mother, father, girlfriend, and male friends what to do.

The young man was placed on an SSRI, and his anxiety diminished considerably. However, his habit of indecision, his unreliable contact with his affect signals, and his ambiguous identity remained a problem to be worked through. The patient was unable to refuse any person's request for help. When he neglected what appeared to be a runaway dog, he went into paroxysms of obsessive ruminations about failing to do his duty. Twice, he made himself late for sessions while trying to save a dog.

His body image was very pliable. In college he "sculpted" his own body into a muscular state to be pleasing to his peers and his girlfriend. He complained that his sculptures always turned out to be the same: a headless torso, with hands and arms reaching out. He could not finish any sculpture because he was afraid it would not please people. When his girlfriend showed promise as an artist, he thought he would give up his art because she was the artist, not him. Thus, his whole sense of executive identity was compromised and distorted by his OCD.

We previously concluded that the right hemisphere's orbital frontal association cortex assesses socially conditioned somatic signals of affect. Dysfunction in this cortex trigger OCD. As serotonin's modulation of conditioned somatic signals in the right hemisphere's orbital frontal cortex decreases, its neutralizing—aggression binding—function declines. As levels of serotonin become functionally inadequate throughout the whole serotonin system, serotonin's capacity to damp data registration decreases. Data overload then evokes limbic anxiety and stress responses. The executive's articulatory rehearsal and reflective thought become overly intense and repetitive. Pressured to respond decisively, the OCD patients defends himself with *doing and undoing, isolating affect, and reaction formation—*screening an affect with an opposing affect ("that's disgusting").

From our present syndrome perspective, OCD defends against mania's excitotoxicity. The comparison between mania and OCD is highlighted by the hypomanic's capacity to process so much detail, while the obsessive-compulsive founders on detail. When affect data and signifiers stream into the prefrontal system unabated, a severe obsessive state—once called an *obsessive delirium*—may develop. This delirium may be mistaken for mania.

Various studies support the hypothesis that serotonin neutralizes affect signals in the right hemisphere's anterior cingulate and orbital frontal cortices. These studies are based on the well-known psychopharmacological fact that SSRIs, which enhance the availability of serotonin, are often effective agents in alleviating the symptoms of OCD. In a normal person's prefrontal cortex, serotonin levels are highest in the right orbital frontal cortex, more so in women (Arate et al., 1991).

It follows from what we have learned about laterality and the drives that serotonin's greater availability to the right hemisphere enhances that hemisphere's capacity to neutralize the aggressive drive. This may be one reason for women's greater capacity to modulate their expression of aggressive affects. During administration of a serotonin reuptake blocker (chlorimipramine), p300 shifted its peak amplitude to the right hemisphere (Arate et al., 1991). This shift corresponds to a shift to the right hemisphere's form of working memory. Thus, serotonin's increased availability enhances the right hemisphere's data processing.[2]

In the bouts of obsessive thoughts and compulsions that accompany indecision, regional cerebral blood flow (rCBF) is abnormally high in the orbital frontal association cortex (OFA), as well as in the head of the caudate. Since serotonin reuptake blockers normalized the high orbital frontal association cortex rCBF, serotonin inhibits the overactivity of this cortex (Insel and Winslow, 1992). Because indecision about acts with aggressive social consequences induces doubt in OCD decision making, I infer that the right hemisphere's orbital frontal hyperactivity induces social wariness in the OCD patient's observer. These patients complain that they have to "over-analyze everything."[3]

A person with lesions in the frontal lobe feels transient feelings of compulsion (Ward, 1988). Conceivably this is because the supplementary motor association cortex is disinhibited. As we have discussed, volition occurs late in the processing cycle, and it depends on the relationship between the supplementary association motor cortex, the orbital frontal association cortex, and the caudate. Thus, when supplementary motor association cortex receives signals to respond, and the orbital frontal association cortex fails to trigger a particular response program, doubt takes over the response. Feelings of doing and undoing, isolation, and reaction formation are all defenses that are activated in this interaction.

Lest we believe that people with OCD are innately deficient in affect, I would like to make the case that the reverse is often true. I have worked with several composers who show a modified OCD. When they are composing well, the music is a language that the composers process with exquisite sensitivity to both melody and affect. As Wallace Stevens said in his poem, *Peter Quince at the Clavier*, "Music is feeling then, not sound."

This line of poetry brings us back to the right hemisphere's function in obsessive-compulsive disorder. This hemisphere assesses affect reports and melody, as well as the visual world's context. The exquisite association between the details of affect and melody is the right hemisphere's language of music. When one of my composer patients worked well, he went to museums to stimulate his affect, and his composing capacity increased. When he became obsessively anxious, he developed hypochondriacal oversensitivity to his anxiety signals, and the obsessive concern that he could no longer compose—only imitate other composers. Imitation is the procedural self's mode when it lacks sufficient integration.

We have all had the experience of waking with a song in our heads that keeps coming back throughout the day. Maybe we whistle it or burst into song. Songs center our affect. They are an affect lesson that connects us with our episodic source memory. A song binds our frustration and our aggression.

THE THEORY OF DELUSIONAL DISORDERS

I diagnose two types of delusional disorders: left and right. *Type 1, delusional disorder per se* is a disorder of subjective identity, in which delusions of love, jealousy, grandiosity, persecution, and somatic disintegration are prominent and enduringly invested with intense emotional and cognitive energy. *Type 2 manifests quasi-delusions*—temporary, false social beliefs—which are caused by altered reality perceptions. Type 2 is due either to denial of reality because of overwhelming novelty and identity anxiety, or to organicity that alters perceptions. The executive provides the altered perceptions with quasi-delusional cognitive rationales.

Type 1: Delusional Disorder

The delusional man whose brother tortured him exemplifies Type 1. The patient would sink into such deep humiliation that he would feel shattered. He believed that people knew his intimate sexual secrets, and that they were playing tricks on him to get him to reveal even more. When he did admit how much he liked a particular homosexual man to another friend, he spent weeks of anguish about whether the friend had communicated this to the first man. The only way to end his anguish was to become delusionally certain that his communication had been betrayed. Feeling persecuted, he no longer had to feel humiliated.

Freud asserted that *delusional disorder per se* is always dynamically caused by *homosexual libidinal conflicts* (1922). When our homosexual love is rejected, our love turns to hate, our hate is projected, and the projected hate feels like persecution. Indeed, paranoia comes from the Greek for "knowledge away." In Freud's view, we are all endowed with bisexually directed libidinal energy. For most people, homosexual energy (narcissistic cathexis) is sublimated in the formation of ideals. In Type 1 delusional disorder, however, the cathexis is detached from socialized ideals, narcissistic object choice is repressed, and the cathexis is regressively diverted to infantile grandiosity. I have seen many patients who are fine when they have a homosexual relationship working for them, but they become paranoid and deny their homosexuality when their relationship goes bad. This is a common precipitant of inpatient admissions.

A variety of syndromes appear to me to depend on *distorted left hemisphere data analysis*. These syndromes all share a tendency toward egocentricity, oversubjectivity, aesthetic sensitivity, shame morality, and sensitivity to rejection. They include *narcissistic personality, avoidant personality, paranoid personality, schizotypal personality, sexual perversity,* and above all, *delusional disorder.* Paranoids and narcissists share the tendency to feel subjective identity shatter when they feel rebuffed. Humiliated, they experience rage and pursue revenge. Revenge is the left hemisphere's libidinal way of reliving, equivalent to the right's aggressive repetition-compulsion.

If bipolar disorder arises from the right hemisphere's overstimulation, then we may hypothesize that delusional disorder arises from the left's overstimulation. People with left hemisphere oversensitivity are "thin skinned." They quaver to the emotional meaning of responses to their communications. Consequently their communications are often veiled. Meaning and salience are overanalyzed. The person with a delusional disorder or with a paranoid personality characteristically says, "that is *not* what I mean!" Any variation in the listener's understanding of what is meant to be communicated is an affront.

Hypothetically then, *delusional disorder develops in response to the left hemisphere's increased hippocampal and amygdaloid processing.* In Chapter 7, we examined evidence for the left hemisphere's temporal lobe shrinkage in paranoid schizophrenia, and presumed that this is the result of excitotoxicity induced by overly intense emotional pressure for consummation. Clinically, we can see that the person with delusional disorder overcognizes salience. *Meaning* is too highly organized by working memory. Reading the newspapers, we realize that mass murderers' manifestos merge meaning overloads with the rage of revenge.

How do delusions form? The person with delusional disorder is intensely goal oriented and ready to act on the basis of intense libidinal pressure. But, his supervisor overloads. Error and identity anxiety disrupt salience processing. Action programs' failures produce intense humiliation. Losing face, the delusional paranoid experiences rage and intense autonomic reactions, which lead to subjective shattering.

Then, revived event-sourced memories of past humiliations inaugurate *delusions proper*—false cognitions based on fantasies that compensate for disillusionments. The supervisor's disintegration leads to failures in judgment and insight. When the patient no longer questions the delusions, the failure to resolve libidinal needs ends in reactive grandiosity, erotomania, and the surfacing of revenge motifs. These motifs are the left hemisphere's mechanism for reliving event-sourced memory. As we saw in the case of the man who disassociated during periods of intense humiliation, the delusion of persecution provides the executive with a humiliation-relieving cognitive rationale.

The executive accepts delusional identity because the supervisor cannot integrate the left hemisphere's false salience signals. Humiliated expectations can be relieved by false rationales—psychotic cognitions. *Significance experience* (salience experience) fixes false cognitions in delusions. In the typical salience experience, a delusional person acts on the basis of false evidence, because some event takes on private salience that he knows only he can understand. When his executive acts on the basis of his delusions, his intrapsychic identity changes. By the time our humiliated patient began to play tricks on others in order to catch them at their tricks, he was deeply ensconced in his delusional identity.

Type 2: Quasi-Delusional Disorder

Let us reserve *significance experience* as an explanatory concept for Type 2 paranoia. While forming delusional ideas, a person has an inexplicable experience that is so extraordinary that some quasi-delusional explanation becomes its rationale. It follows from what we know about prefrontal duality, that significance experience is a right hemisphere phenomenon. Reality is falsely signified.

In the *Capgras* and related organic syndromes, it is not possible for one's own social self or for others to be experienced as totally real. In Capgras, the social self cannot absorb an affect overload. Others seem robotic and phony and their faces are particularly strange. This *derealization* is the nidus of misidentification delusions. The Capgras symptoms of person misidentification and altered social self provoke false cognitive explanations—delusional ideas—as opposed to delusions proper.

Organicity can induce false perceptions of reality. Right hemisphere organicity often produces reality-denying delusional ideas (Cummings, 1988). Capgras-type syndromes correlate with both right hemisphere organicity and a high level of violence (Forstl, Almeida, and Owen, 1991). In Type 2 paranoids, "violent behavior may result from the unilateral (right hemisphere) destruction of amygdaloid nuclei . . . coupled with the paroxysmal stimulation of preserved limbic structures by the mechanism of kindling" (Tonkonogy, 1991). Carbamazapine, an antikindling drug, sometimes controls violence in this cohort. Thus, overvalued delusional ideas in organic paranoia can lead to violent acts.

I posit, then, that Type 2 paranoia occurs *when the right hemisphere's amygdala cannot condition painful experience and cannot regulate aggressive binding. The social self then cannot bind aggressive energy into self and object representations, and the executive fabricates compensatory delusional ideas.*

THE THEORY OF SOCIOPATHY

Just as we posited two types of paranoia that correspond to abnormal processing in the two hemispheres, we may also posit two types of sociopathy that correspond to abnormal processing in the two hemispheres. *The capacity of the left hemisphere's orbital frontal cortex to evaluate socially conditioned somatic signals of pleasure, and of the right's to evaluate socially conditioned somatic signals of pain is missing.*

Sociopathy is a syndrome in which either one or both of the orbital frontal association cortices cannot assess socially *unconditioned* somatic signals. Sociopaths cannot emotionally condition social experience. Because they have no capacity for emotional organization, sociopath's source memory has no relevance to behavior. In the Type 1 variant, the supervisor cannot mediate subjective identity development, and social consequences are excluded from behavioral decisions. I will discuss Type 1 in more detail because it is least examined.

Type 1 Sociopathy: Entitled

Cases of sociopathy have been traced to the left hemisphere's incapacity to effect orbital frontal association assessment. In contrast to obsessive-compulsive disorder, these cases show a *deficit* of orbital frontal association assessment. A. Damasio (1990) describes a man, E.V.R., who lost his capacity to evaluate the social consequences of his motivated behaviors after he developed a bilateral, orbital frontal tumor.

E.V.R. did not lose his cognitive power. Even though he lost his capacity for appropriate behavior, ran his business into the ground, divorced his wife, and married a prostitute after his tumor took hold, his I.Q. remained stable. Like Psyche's patient in her board exam, when he was asked to account for these actions, he was unable to rely on any overall capacity to evaluate their social effect, but when he was led through the sequence of events by the questioner, he could see they were inappropriate. He had lost his intuitive sense of what was involved in decision making.

Meyers and colleagues (1992) present a similar case in which the tumor was in the left hemisphere's orbital frontal association cortex. This man was also unable to evaluate the social effects of his actions. He became boastfully grandiose, but showed no cognitive defects. Left hemisphere sociopaths show persistent infantile grandiosity without overt delusions.

In this syndrome, wishes are horses. The Type 1 sociopath finds a horse, destroys its rider, and mounts the horse.

In Type 1 sociopathy, since social conditioning does not enter the assessment of event-sourced memory, a person with this syndrome cannot provide an emotion-based account of the sequence of decisions he has undertaken in formulating an action plan. Instead, events are cognitively sequenced as a series of contrived tricks that manipulate reality. Normally, narration uses event memory to explain what has happened within a social intersubjective context. Type 1 sociopaths are unable to switch the "principle (or basis) of action" to conform to social mores when they narrate their crimes (Pontius, 1980).

Type 1 sociopathy may be organic in origin, or it may be a product of emotional development. Type 1 sociopathy is a syndrome at the extreme end of the overentitlement continuum. Egocentric means justify any ends. There are no ideals, no intersubjectivity, and no shame in this sociopath's actions. Revenge is evanescent satisfaction. The impostor and the forger, both disguising their subjective identity, exemplify this type.

A young man was admitted to my ward after the police arrested him for stealing an airplane in Florida and flying it to New York. He had pretended to be a military pilot on assignment. After two days on the ward, he told me with devilish delight that he would escape that night. Sure enough, he managed to open the sixth floor hospital window, knot together enough sheets to make a rope, and let himself down to the ground. In his descent, he yelled up to the ward personnel, standing aghast at the window, "So long suckers!"

One week later, I received a call from a psychiatrist at an army boot camp in Georgia. He told me that an imposter dressed as a sergeant was drilling recruits. When the psychiatrist asked him who he was, he said that he was Dr. Harris's patient. For imposters, tricks of derring-do, lies, and social manipulations blend together to give thrills of the moment, which also make fun of authority.

Another Type 1 sociopath gave the following account of his childhood. He used to accompany his mother and his father's best friend to New York on "business trips," during the patient's latency years. He was the cover for the mother's sexual liaisons with this man. The lover lavished gifts on the patient and helped to protect the father's business interests. When the patient told his father about what was happening, the boy was accused of lying, and he became a pariah in the family. He was shut out of all family property after this. In adult life, the patient became a sociopath with no hesitancy about revenging himself against anyone. Eventually, he got into trouble when he double-crossed some drug dealers. His supposedly suicidal entrance into the mental hospital was a trick to evade these dealers. After his danger was over, he left the hospital in the usual way, conning various personnel into giving him some emergency "loans," and then eloping.

Type 2 Sociopathy: Amoral

In the childhood of persons with attention deficit disorders, who develop conduct disorders, and then sociopathy, there is a well-known deficient response to pain conditioning. Pleasure conditioning may be more normal. These are children who may take pleasure in torturing animals. They like to watch their pet snakes eat small rodents. Psychological testing often reveals that their sense of self is primitive and composed of part objects, never integrated as a whole person representation. Some Type 2 sociopaths may be on a continuum with Asperger's disorder, in which the self's and other's pain is unknowable.

Right hemisphere sociopathy corresponds to what has been termed "amoral" sociopathy. Here, the absence of morality leads to activities undertaken with no compunction, no guilt, and no awareness of moral strictures. Suffering has no significance. Affect is an imitation, not a part of an interobjective signal system. The amoral sociopath has no compunction or remorse about killing you. At a time when the death penalty was rarely allowed, a Type 2 sociopathic murderer was interviewed about his feelings about whether he should be the first person in his state to be put to death. Without hesitation, qualms, remorse, or feeling he answered simply that he should be put to death.

Sometimes, amoral sociopathy develops in orphans who have never had a sense of a compassionate adult. They learn to simulate affects, because that is what leads to their care and survival. In each new foster care situation, they begin by providing their parent figures with exactly what the parent figures seem to want. However, for them, affect, and responding to other's pain remains a trick.

In passing, I would like to discuss one predisposing neural tendency toward sociopathy. Sociopaths—as well as athletes—are quicker to process target stimuli. Perhaps this is because neither group has any recognition of emotional repercussions of stimuli. Decreased p300 latency in fifteen year olds is a predictor of sociopathy (Raines, Venables, and Williams, 1990). The capacity to quickly delineate *cognitive* target stimuli correlates with the capacity to be successfully sociopathic.

A thirty-four-year-old bond trader who works on the floor of the New York Stock Exchange must make lightning decisions about buying and selling bonds. He received his most relevant life training to be a trader when he was a professional athlete. Although he manifests the quick cognitions of the athlete, his sense of the animalistic trading floor was insufficiently sociopathic to allow him the same ease of decision making that allowed his more sociopathic peers to move up in the hierarchy to become specialists. His sense of failure led to a major depression. Our society rewards those with sociopathic traits in occupations such as the trading floor and professional athletics.

A HEMISPHERIC THEORY OF PERSONALITY DISORDERS

I posit that narcissistic and borderline disorders represent abnormal hemispheric processing tendencies. These abnormalities may be so pronounced as to constitute syndromes. The syndromatic processing tendencies are particularly evinced in the executive's incapacity to maintain a well-balanced sense of intrapsychic identity. Therefore, reflective synthesis is impaired in these syndromes. We can also take these syndromes as overarching examples of hemispheric personality distortions.

Type 1 Personality Disorders: Narcissism

Narcissism is a condition characterized by a depletion or overcompensating enhancement in the supervisor's assessment of the importance of the left hemisphere's experiential states:

- The lateral zone's agent fragments when inner speech is inhibited or overly facilitated in its access to motivated decision making.
- The intermediate zone's social subject manifests poorly bounded intersubjectivity, which impairs the supervisor's assessment of wishes as horses.
- The medial zone's subject manifests boastful or recessed capacity for love.

Goal formation, ideal formation, aesthetic sublimation and homosexual needs, all left hemisphere identity functions, are unbalanced, either increased or depleted in narcissism.

A thirty-five-year-old woman suffers from a syndrome of narcissistic depletion. Her mother had been psychotic, and unable to provide empathic reciprocity from infancy onward. Among her symptoms, the patient had a severe inhibition of confidence in her speech and planning. Like the case of Echo, she felt that she had to overmonitor her speech. She was constantly ashamed of either stumbling over her words, or lacking the spontaneity to say what she wanted without rehearsal.

Reticence, as we saw in the case of Echo in Chapter 4, is a sign of the narcissistic depletion syndrome in addition to verbal miscues. More often they are, as Freud said, part of the *Psychopathology of Everyday Life* (1902). Slips of the tongue often occur when we experience conscious identity conflicts. Fitting with the narcissistic phenomenology of everyday life, a person's identity is often overdetermined by his or her name. Lord Brain and Henry Head, both neurologists, lived their names. I invite the reader to find other examples.

Other Type 1 character disorders also find difficulty in translating meaning into expressive communication. Hysteria—in the sense of hysterical neurosis—is a good example of a condition in which libidinal wishes cannot find their way into direct articulatory rehearsal. Type 1, paranoid, schizoid, schizotypal, avoidant, and narcissistic characters are all overly concerned with expressing *and* disguising their meaning.

Type 2 Personality Disorders: Borderline

Because we discussed borderline disorder at some length in Chapter 8, I will simply summarize its hemispheric attributes. As a right hemisphere syndrome, borderline disorder manifests an inability to regulate affect. The borderline is characterized by a dysfunction in self-observation. This dysfunction impairs all of the right hemisphere's zones of identity integration:

- The self cannot regulate affect.
- The social self cannot integrate self and object images.
- The procedural self mixes with others' representation, in the expectation that others will mediate adaptation and responses to stressful situations.

There is no capacity to evaluate one's own social standing. Instead, blame and recriminations are used in the service of maintaining projective identifications. This mechanism is unavailable to introspection.

By definition, character disorder is *egosyntonic*—unavailable to self-observation. The egosyntonic aspects of Type 2 character pathology is particularly manifest. Perhaps this is because the right hemisphere's aggressive drive is tightly bound in its character formation. Aggression bound makes objective structure. Thus, Type 2 passive-aggressive, obsessive, dependent, masochistic, and sadistic characters share a tendency to develop affective disorder when their character structure loses integration. In all of these character types, the distinction between self and object is missing, and grieving therefore is either impossible or pathological.

CONCLUSION

Excitotoxicity and dendritic atrophy, as well as biogenic amine drive regulation have evolved as flexible mechanisms for adapting the mind/brain to the changing circumstances of human life. In other words, when the lessons of social conditioning and emotional source memory do not help us cope or adapt, we have to induce and integrate new long-term memory into the mind/brain system. When LTP gathers too much momentum, we form insufferable memories and glutamate populations are damaged. Damaged hippocampal formation glutamate populations lose their well-ordered capacity to register and select data for adult problem solving. The brain may then talk to itself in pathological ways. Even pathological discourse, however, is a syndromatic form of adaptation.

In the next chapter, we will follow the course of schizophrenia toward its ultimate burnout. In schizophrenic burn-out, there are progressively fewer acute psychotic episodes as glutamate facilitation dwindles (Ishimaru et al., 1992; Weller and Kornhuber, 1992). As we will see, left hippocampal excitotoxicity ultimately leads to less explicit processing of new experience.

Chapter 10

How the Schizophrenic Brain Talks to Itself

I have lived long enough, having seen one thing,
that love has an end;
Goddess and maiden and queen, be near me
now and befriend.
Thou art more than the day and the morrow,
the seasons that laugh or that weep;
For these give joy and sorrow; but thou,
Proserpina, sleep.

From *Hymn to Proserpine*,
Algernon Charles Swinburne

WHERE DOES THE MIND GO WHEN WE LOSE IT?

Schizophrenia is a journey to oblivion. The schizophrenic's subject loses "I am," his social subject loses "we are," and his agent loses "I will." Because his left hemisphere lacks a full measure of being, love, or volition, the schizophrenic backpedals in an autistic, symbiotic reverie.

In chronic schizophrenia, poorly stimulated prefrontal identity networks convey the executive a numbed life of the drives. The supervisor makes do with little salience, and in the right hemisphere, the observer has little significance to account. The result is a syndromatic identity based on both hemispheres' least neural metabolism. When, in extreme chronicity, the right hemisphere cannot observe any self, the patient starts to believe that God or the country's bureaucracy provides all necessary direction.

Chronic schizophrenics believe that their minds reside elsewhere—not in Penn Station, but in the historical remnant of a psychotic system. One learns to speak the psychotic language. Thus, I say to Steve, who is a chronic schizophrenic, "I understand your name is Steve." "That's what they say," he answers. "Good," I say, "they may want you to come to dinner now." *They is a linguistic construct, the extreme end of a collapsed delusional system once (and still, potentially) peopled by delusional others.*

"They" is an adaptive, psychotic construct that alleviates all anxiety when it works. The problem for the chronic schizophrenic is that his sense of exterior direction is extremely vulnerable to change. When the social worker in Steve's group residence changes jobs, his sense of "they" collapses, and he loses his sense of direction by others. This is when Steve reexperiences the panic and terror of acute psychosis—yet again.

God's long-muted voice, which speaks for they, reemerges when the social worker disappears. Steve was not symbiosed with this worker, only with the generalized other she represented. Adding the loss of "they" to the earlier loss of "I" and "we," which coincided with his chronicity, Steve's inner speech and social speech—his articulatory rehearsal—autistically fuse with his executive's identity, which manifests as divine hallucinations. Steve has to fuse in God's voice. God's autistic voice is all there is . . . until another social worker appears.

Persephone: The Woman Who Could Feel the Earth's Tremors

Proserpina is Latin for Persephone, and it is by this name that she is known in Swinburne's poem, quoted earlier. In that poem, Persephone is already queen of the underworld. Persephone, however, has a story of her own. In reviewing the case I am about to present, I realized that the patient's schizophrenic descent was much like mythical Persephone's experience of the underworld.

In myth, Hades, god of the underworld, steals Persephone, goddess of spring, from her mother, Demeter. Hades abducts Persephone in his chariot. As Hades whips his horses, a chasm opens into the bowels of the earth. Passing through it, they arrive in Hades' kingdom. Searching for her daughter, Demeter, goddess of fertility, wanders the earth, which she makes barren until, after a series of adventures, she reunites with Persephone. They reunite for half the year—spring and summer.

As queen of the underworld, Persephone inhabits a palace of gloom set in strange fields, haunted by bizarre apparitions. The lethal waters of the river Styx bound her abode. Now, we recall that, even in myth, the human spirit can not ordinarily withstand prolonged contact with the underworld. Descending into Persephone's underworld, for instance, was Psyche's hardest task. Psyche's goal was to bring out a box of the divine cosmetic that would restore Aphrodite's beauty. But, just as Persephone had to stay in Hades after eating its fruits, so Psyche succumbed to the eternal cosmetic's allure. Still human, Psyche wanted to be eternally beautiful for Eros's pleasure, even if she relinquished consciousness. Luckily for Psyche, Eros restored her.

We can take Persephone's tale as allegory for the fate of those who descend into the id, the underworld. Like Psyche, some of us can make successful regressions in the service of the ego. Artists are notable among the lot, but their regressions are in the service of the ego's goals, and they are partial. The artist makes a virtual visit: being, love and volition do not shut down. Therefore, the artist can return to his every day state. It is not so much that he does not regress, it is that he regresses in order bring about fruitful change—in his work in progress, and therefore in his own identity. The essential distinction is: artistic creation ends in construction; schizophrenic creation ends in destruction. Those who tarry in the underworld are likely to come back with the inspired change in identity we call psychosis (Harris, Jay, and Harris, 1984).

The patient I will call Persephone had primal delusions of having been a queen who was carried off to a sexual place beneath the earth. Let's take the underworld as an image of her id/unconscious, and let's take the bond between Persephone and her mother as an image of our Persephone's wish for symbiosis—life together. In each acute episode of schizophrenia, our patient Persephone descended to the underworld, and in each subacute phase she reemerged with her psychotic identity refurbished.

Some schizophrenics are doomed to remain forever in the underworld; some make a single trip, and others go repeatedly. They lose a portion of their human identity each time. Each trip is like a near-death experience. Each psychotic episode is a profound exogenous and endogenous trauma. As we saw in Chapter 7, the near-death experience produces a profound change, for good or for ill in a person's intrapsychic identity. As we will see, when our Persephone is giving birth the first time, she comes so far down the tunnel of death, that she sets up the prototype experience for her later psychotic regressions.

Persephone, a thirty-year-old Caribbean woman, felt that she had always been supersensitive. She believed that she could feel earth tremors when others could not. Schizotypal, she believed her spirit inhabited the depths of the earth. The only daughter of a possessive mother, she was the youngest of three children. Persephone's mother overprotected her because of her sensitivity.

In her childhood in Haiti, Persephone recalls wandering among the fields outside town and gathering flowers. She contrasts this with a memory of being forced to stay in bed, mute, all day every Sunday, while her relatives held secret political discussions, which must not be heard, or even mentioned to the neighbors. Neighbors were not to be trusted with any personal business. The family's survival depended on that.

Persephone learned to keep her feelings and needs to herself. When Persephone was nine, her family moved to New York, where she clung to them, having learned on her island that she must not talk to strangers. They might betray the family.

Persephone's fianceé courted her for years in her late teens and early twenties. A chaperone stayed with the couple at all times. Persephone succumbed to a strange, intense intimacy that overpowered her with the wish to let go of her mother and go into her future husband's world. Persephone was so sensitive that she always fainted when her fianceé left the house.

Persephone experienced the honeymoon as a nightmare of losing herself. The newly married couple went to a beach resort where Persephone's fear of submerging in lethal water overwhelmed new sexual pleasure. Later, in her treatment with me, she made learning to swim a goal. In spite of her avid wish, she never did accomplish this feat. When her son was three, Persephone took him for swimming lessons. He learned; she did not.

Persephone was terrified when she became pregnant with this son. She insisted on natural childbirth. During a prolonged delivery, however, she experienced pain so severe that she felt that her clenched teeth were imploding in her head. She did not tell the obstetrician, an attending physician, who supervised her husband in his ob-gyn residency. Nor did she tell her husband.

After thirty-six hours of labor and a Caesarian section, Persephone had to be separated from her son for a few days. When she returned home, she relied on her mother to care for her son. Although she had been dependent on her mother before, she now allowed her mother to choose her clothes (even though she did not like them), and to rearrange her kitchen (even though she did not like the new arrangement), and to shop for her (even though she did not approve the food). Her mother treated Persephone as if she did not know how to shop, cook, or dress and found someone to care for the baby. Persephone went back to her professional work as a nutritionist within a month of giving birth. At that point, she stopped breastfeeding, but her milk continued to flow for at least eight years.

Feeling that she was flowing like a fountain, and fearing that her brain was permanently injured by her imploding teeth, Persephone believed she had a tumor. Her husband and her endocrinologist became alarmed because Persephone's prolactin level remained extremely high. The high prolactin level predated her treatment with neuroleptics, which sometimes mildly raises prolactin levels. Later, when she was my patient, I had to sedate Persephone, and accompany her to have an MRI to make sure she had no pituitary tumor. She was as terrified of submerging her head in the machine's space, as she was of being in water or giving birth. Nevertheless, her MRI at that time was normal. As we will see later, schizophrenics' MRIs are often increasingly abnormal.

When she was moving beyond her prodromal phase, still before I treated her, Persephone decided to become an obstetrics and gynecology nurse. Her husband was graduating from his residency. Now, she planned to work with him in his office. She wanted to continue her full-time job, however. She had been raised to believe that she personally must work hard, become wealthy, and buy a mansion and restore it. At the same time, she felt that she must have more children, to prove that she was at least as fertile as her mother. She needed to have her mansion secured before her next child. Time, she felt, was short.

Because of these urgent, rigid goals, Persephone started nursing school while continuing her full-time job. Then, she added a lab technician stint early in the mornings. As she drove off to do her lab technician work at 5 a.m. one morning, Persephone began to hallucinate. Exhausted, she felt that everyone in the nursing school knew her business, had been talking about her, and insulting her. Overwhelmed, she heard a voice say, "turn right, turn left, turn right, turn left." Persephone kept driving, but the instructions misled her, and she became hopelessly lost. For the next few days, she could not work or go to school, and then she was hospitalized.

In the days of acute schizophrenia leading to her hospitalization, Persephone panicked continuously. Clenching her teeth, she believed she had shattered her face and brain by driving her lower jaw into her head—a sign that somatic delusions had shattered her image of mind and body. Her delusions, moreover, never connected with self-observed anxiety. Sleepless and pacing for several nights, Persephone suffered restless motoric agitation.

Persephone hated the Haldol that "they" gave her in the hospital. She felt it turned her into a zombie. She learned to stop revealing her voices to the staff so that they would let her out. Then, she could avoid the Haldol. When I first saw Persephone, soon after her discharge, she was still acutely schizophrenic and only partly in remission. Wondering if she might have a manic psychosis because of her increased activity before entering the hospital, I placed her on lithium. I also switched her from Haldol to Trilafon, hoping she would better tolerate this neuroleptic. Perhaps if she had made her feelings clear about the Haldol, and if she had continued with it, Persephone might have adjusted to it. Later, we stopped the lithium as it had no effect.

As Persephone stabilized, I gradually reduced the Trilafon, from eight milligrams (mgms) per day to two. At that point, despite adequate lithium levels, her acute symptoms returned. This time, however, her hallucinations began to make sense to her. She felt agitated, and voices commanded her to walk. As she paced, she felt relief, and she began to believe in her voices. In fact, when I tried to increase the Trilafon she balked. Persephone believed that the voices held an imminent solution to her problems, just beyond her grasp. She felt that if her psychosis went just a little farther, she could enter the light on the other end of the tunnel.

The integration of Persephone's psychotic identity began in this subacute stage. From a jumble of disconnected thoughts and fragmented hallucinations, the voices became compellingly cogent. Speaking her native Creole language, they told Persephone about her past. They told her that in a previous life she had been born a queen, but that she had been forced into prostitution. They told her she knew all there was to know about food, and that she could cook anything without recipes. And she did.

As she listened to the voices, the patient felt that she was special and chosen. Although neuroleptic medication relieved her symptoms and suppressed the voices, the patient wanted to stop the medication so that she could find the ultimate solution. She understood when I told her that if she stopped medication, she could lose her love for her husband and her son, but the imminent psychotic solution was so compelling that she did not care.

During the years I worked with Persephone, she had several acute psychotic episodes. Each occurred when I decreased her medication because she desperately wanted to have more children. She felt that her time was short, and feared the medication could harm the fetus. After recovering from each episode, she would undertake intense reading about the origins of her new identity. First, she studied the ancient history of her ancestors, then the more modern history of her birthplace. Later, she studied all the recipes she could find that were native to her region. She searched out herbs and plants that were included in ancient recipes. She studied art that was indigenous to her birthplace. She studied the brain and Jayne's *Bicameral Mind* (1976) to find the origin of her voices. Finally, she studied the effects of various drugs on fetuses.

After each episode, the patient's study became vaguer and more prosaic. Her subacute episodes began to last for longer periods. During the first four years of treatment, she became cognitively duller and her expressed feelings were less animated. She stopped longing for a solution through her voices, and she did not lament their disappearance.

However, she was as insistent as ever that she must have more children. I expressed reservations about her plan to have more, but she was not to be deterred. Finally, Persephone, her husband, her obstetrician, and I all agreed that she would continue on Trilafon, eight mgms, regardless of possible consequences to pregnancy. For three years, Persephone could not get pregnant.

Then, Persephone took fertility drugs and had triplets. All the babies were normal and showed normal development. In triumph, Persephone brought the babies to see me. Persephone took good care of her children, and remained symptom free, if dull and unanimated. From time to time, she had auditory hallucinations, but she said that she disregarded them.

What does this case show?

- Professionals are not gods. We cannot tell someone how to conduct his or her life, even if the person is schizophrenic.
- Mythology can help us understand our patients.
- The subacute stage fixes schizophrenia as a lifelong syndrome.
- Each syndrome is individualized.
- There need not be a known family history for schizophrenia.
- A genetic sensitivity to sensory and emotional experience, and rigid goals increases vulnerability to schizophrenia.
- Symbiosis with a strong mother predisposes to schizophrenia.
- Trauma before a first episode fixes the content of delusions.

Undoubtedly, Persephone experienced the birth of her son as a near-death trauma. Her prolonged, unbearable pain created the prototype for future acute, psychotic panics. Each acute episode included a repetition of teeth clenching so intense that Persephone felt her teeth driving into her head and her head collapsing—an image of her dread and desire for the dissolution of her identity. Her premorbid, rigid personality was no match for deep family romance fantasies. In Persephone's family, the mother, like the mythological Demeter, was the unopposable queen, and Persephone could only sometimes separate her own subjective identity from her symbiosis with her mother.

When the acute psychosis laid bare Persephone's past organizing fantasies, sexualized and grandiose materials from her childhood flowed, by way of her hallucinations, into her executive system for assessing her identity. For a while, Persephone was intensely creative, as she studied her origins and identified herself with her ancestors. She even told me on one occasion that she had seen a harvest picture in the Metropolitan Museum that had been ascribed to "unknown artist." Because of her studies of her native Creole art and culture, she knew, she told me, that the artist had been her ancestor. This discovery did not excite her, however. She was merely puzzled by the designation—*unknown*.

These excursions into her past identity soon lost their allure, and Persephone resigned herself to a limited role as an adjunct of her family's structure. Although in some cases it need not be, Persephone's willingness to take Trilafon was also a resignation of residual desire to become a unique person. Even though she understood, to some degree, that accepting her mother's direction robbed her of her own identity, and that her family's insistence on extreme secrecy prevented her from having friends, interpretation and reconstruction were of limited value in freeing her identity from its constrictions. The best that the transference could accomplish was compliance with medication and an acceptance of me as a parafamily member. Years later, I found to my surprise that the date of Persephone's first appointment with me was indelibly inscribed in her memory.

AN EXCITOTOXIC MODEL FOR SCHIZOPHRENIA

In the same way that Post (1992) argues that each manic episode is an endogenous neural event that leads to a kindled progression in bipolar disorder, I argue that each *acute* psychotic episode during the course of schizophrenia leads to endogenous excitotoxicity. I will present evidence that the schizophrenic syndrome progresses in stages from

1. prodromal amygdalar-induced, increased ventral tegmental system dopamine activity, to
2. acute hippocampal formation excitotoxicity, to
3. subacute compensatory amine system changes, to
4. chronic reduced glutamate conduction in all the limbic/prefrontal experiential loops.

In this model, each experiential loop undergoes *excitotoxic transfer potentiation,* which induces the executive to reorganize the prefrontal zones to form a psychotic identity. Each acute episode induces less flexibility in the parallel processing networks. When subacute stage, neurohormonal and biogenic amine compensations defend against excitotoxicity, the relieved executive believes she has resolved her identity problem.

Chronic schizophrenia, then, is demarcated by the amount of excitotoxic damage that occurs in the syndrome's progress. I have concluded that hippocampal formation destruction reduces hippocampal data registration and processing. Moreover, amygdalar emotional processing diminishes, and the prefrontal system increasingly hypofunctions in response to decreased input from the amygdala, the hippocampus, and the drives. Each person sustains different amounts of excitotoxic damage and prefrontal reorganization. The brain's decreased functioning provides a compensatory equilibrium that relieves chaotic, insufferable anxiety and emotional pain.

Obviously, research studies on schizophrenia mislead when they do not delineate the degree of acuteness, subacuteness or chronicity. As we will see, in acute states, brain activation is greater; in chronicity, it is greatly diminished. Chronic patients may nevertheless undergo an acute decompensation during a period when they are in a research protocol. Moreover, left hemisphere, prefrontal cognitive deficits occur throughout the course of schizophrenia. When attempting to delineate cognitive deficits, researchers must distinguish these assessment deficits from data-processing deficits in chronic schizophrenics (Hoff et al., 1992). With these caveats in mind, let us consider studies about the brain findings in schizophrenia as the syndrome progresses.

A UNIFIED THEORY OF SYNDROME PROGRESSION IN SCHIZOPHRENIA

Even though I am about to present a theory of syndrome progression in schizophrenia, I find I am also going to make remarks about how the left brain's prefrontal networks generate communication. The reason for this is that studying the schizophrenic's formal thought disorder leads to observations about how the normal brain talks to itself. That is why the following material has two goals. The primary aim is to see how the left dorsolateral cortex gradually loses both its integration of agency and its capacity to spontaneously generate verbally fluent language. The secondary aim is to recognize that a normally functioning left dorsolateral cortex generates agency as well as verbally fluent language.

How does the left hemisphere generate communication? As we saw in Chapter 1, the left prefrontal cortex evolved a capacity to generate verbal communication. In human beings,

1. the dorsolateral cortex generates fluently cognized salience;
2. the intermediate cortex generates motivated verbal fluency;
3. the medial cortex assesses the communication of need.

Supervision is the left prefrontal cortex's metafunction, and it regulates all three. Liddle says that schizophrenics cannot maintain *supervisory* processes. He defines these processes as "the initiation, organization and monitoring of self-generated mental activity" (1993, p. 5). What does this mean?

I have observed that a genetic predisposition to schizophrenia is a predisposition to supervisory impairment. Most studies of risk for schizophrenia have focused on oversensitivity to salience, inability to process pleasure, and prefrontal difficulties in assessing cognitive data. Persephone, for example, showed all three. Persephone was an oversensitive child. Afraid of her own pleasure, she felt no right to enjoyment, much less a right to express an opinion of her own. More than reticent, she grew up ashamed to have friends. In children who are predisposed to schizophrenia (as against children whose neurological destiny determines that they will be schizophrenic) a failure of pleasure, satisfaction, and communication increases the risk of supervisory disintegration.

A predisposition to schizophrenia occurs in those, like Persephone, who show premorbid functional deficits in identity regulation (Brown and White, 1992). This regulation, we know, depends on the left prefrontal cortex's integrative capacity. Event-related potential studies of data processing epochs find that children at high risk for schizophrenia show significant deficiencies. They show prefrontal incapacity to integrate data in the p400 to p600 epoch, e.g., an incapacity to distinguish mismatches from expected stimuli (Schreiber et al., 1992). Thus, children at risk for schizophrenia cannot assess unexpected data. What this means is, they cannot stand to know something that does not conform to their beliefs. Their identities are built on very restricted data sets. They become anxious when these expectations are violated. To see others giving in to a good time and a lack of control, leads children such as Persephone to recoil, and to appear to be overly good children.

A retrospective study of twins discordant for schizophrenia showed that in most cases the impaired twin's schizophrenia had significantly reduced the volume of the left hemisphere's hippocampal formation and that the illness had also decreased frontal, cognitive functioning. These findings pointed to prefrontal, limbic system dysfunction in schizophrenia (Weinberger et al., 1992). By controlling for genetic causes, these findings indicate that the schizophrenic process alters the brain's neural systems. Let us follow process neurally, phenomenologically, and linguistically.

Prodromal Stage

More frequently in males, but sometimes in females, the prodromal stage begins in adolescence. Why does adolescence increase vulnerability to schizophrenic induction? In Chapter 6, we said that the prelude to adult life, profoundly alters identity. Adolescent formal thinking emphasizes metareflection on identity. In late adolescence, as we think about who we are becoming, we develop a personal theory of mind in preparation for adult life. In schizophrenia's prodrome, however, metareflection on identity goes awry. Schizophrenics overgeneralize their reflection about identity. Typically, the schizophrenic makes statements about his identity that appear to us grandiose and overinclusive. In his prodrome, Steve declared, "I dedicate my life to the love of humanity." When a genetically vulnerable person is unable to establish a real sense of purpose for adult life because his pleasure and communication are blocked, identity, which is programmed to change, undergoes an increasing disequilibrium. To put the case neurally, dendritic lengthening in the hippocampus accompanies adolescent formal thinking and advances in metaidentity (Stevens, 1992). While the normal adolescent achieves a greater capacity for explicit processing and for prefrontal, hierarchical assessment, one who is genetically or organically inflexible in data analysis, is vulnerable to a failure of his developmental task of synthesizing metareflection and formal thought.

The adolescent onset of higher levels of sexual hormones increases limbic pressures for libidinal gratification. The prodromal adolescent undergoes desperate attempts to find love, intimacy, sexual gratification, and fulfillment of personal identity goals. In his prodrome, the adolescent schizophrenic appears to upregulate his ventral tegmental system's dopaminergic activity. But in his case, the upregulation only exacerbates a futile search for meaningful contact and pleasure. In my experience, such patients feel that their needs are inordinate.

In the long prodroma of her late adolescence and early adult years, Persephone could not tolerate the pleasure that would induce her to leave her mother and change her identity, as her fainting when parting from her fianceé dramatized. Perhaps Persephone's ventral tegmental dopamine system became dysregulated, and this putative dysregulation enhanced her prolactin levels. The dopamine system does participate in the regulation of prolactin levels. However this may be, another sign of Persephone's fear of pleasure was her fear of water, which exacerbated on her honeymoon. I thought this fear was symptomatic of her inability to relinquish her identity and to experience the pleasure of intercourse with her love.

For normal adolescents The Rolling Stones' "I can't get no satisfaction, but I try, and I try. . . . and ya get what ya need" is a theme for adjustment to the ventral tegmental dopamine system's upregulation. But the prodromal adolescent schizophrenic does *not* find that "he gets what he needs." We will see that some studies of schizophrenic's cognitive impairment focus on the abnormally increased numbers of dopamine receptors found in their caudate, prefrontal, and limbic assessment cortex, both premorbidly and morbidly. Despite *increased* dopamine receptors in the left hemisphere's nucleus accumbens, caudate, and amygdala, as schizophrenia progresses, PET scans show *decreased* activation of the left hemisphere's nucleus accumbens, and its anterior cingulate cortex (Reynolds, Czudek, and Andrews, 1990).

In Chapter 2, we saw that while solving problems of need, the left hemisphere's caudate assesses data's salience, after which its nucleus accumbens provides signals of imminent gratification, and finally its anterior cingulate cortex assesses signals of actual pleasure. I posit that in schizophrenia:

1. dopamine receptors' upregulation in the left hemisphere's caudate compensates for a low level of salience cues throughout syndrome progression, and therefore, that
2. dopamine receptors' upregulation in the nucleus accumbens compensate for an inability to achieve intimacy and pleasure.

The low activation of the anterior cingulate cortex shows that the compensations do not work. Why does not pressure for satisfaction generate productive behavior or communication?

In the prodrome, the supervisor loses its capacity to generate coherent volition. For volition to be organized subjective identity has to cohere. To achieve this the supervisor has to integrate satisfaction, reward, and verbal fluency. This integration forms the template for generating thoughts. The prodromal schizophrenic does not know how have the voluntary thoughts that generate reward. At a limbic level, consummation pressure is not supported by working memory's formation of meaningful structures of inner speech. This loss of logic's base produces a *formal thought disorder*. *We can define a formal thought disorder as an inability to smoothly integrate need, working memory, and identity in spontaneous communication.*

Unlike most of the Rolling Stones' audience, the prodromal schizophrenic finds need states unrewarding. We learned in our study of the amygdala's regulation of the dopamine system that unsustained satisfaction induces the amygdala to upregulate the left ventral tegmental dopamine system and caudate. When need assessment does not lead to satisfaction, the acute patient mobilizes intense error anxiety and identity anxiety. Then, regressive fantasies replace consummatory behaviors.

Acute Stage

A formal thought disorder becomes overt during the acute stage. Using PET scans to measure functional brain activity during "simple verbal fluency" (when the subject engages in spontaneous communication), and "motivated verbal fluency" (when the subject asks for something), Frith's group investigated how schizophrenics differed from normal controls. Normally, spontaneous communication activates the left hemisphere's dorsolateral association cortex, while asking for something activates that cortex *and* anterior cingulate cortex. Neither activation occurs in schizophrenics (1991).

Schizophrenics cannot reflectively evaluate the efficacy of their communications of need (Leudar et al., 1992). When they were asked about their communications, they did not know whether their intentions or needs had been communicated to others. When we interview a schizophrenic, we realize that something is missing in his empathic communication. He does not check back with himself about whether he is getting through.

My patient, Persephone, never spoke spontaneously in her sessions. She only responded to my questions. Then she would ask me a question about how my life was going. She did not feel she had any right to ask for anything she needed, and if I did not ask the right questions, she would leave a session without talking about her symptoms or her difficulty in functioning. Once, she did not ask me to fill out a form she needed for insurance, because I did not know to ask her about it.

In the acute stage then, all three of the left prefrontal system's zones disintegrate in a narcissistic collapse. The agent's sense of initiatory generation shatters. The social subject's esteem and confidence fails. The subject's signals of anticipated pleasure stop. Panic, humiliation, and rage interdict the executive's intrapsychic synthesis. Then the right hemisphere's identity integration also collapses.

Persephone had experienced panic that was so intense that for days on end, without sleeping, her clenched teeth seemed to smash her face and her identity completely. As she unsuccessfully tried to synthesize an identity as wife, daughter, mother, nutritionist, nurse, and lab technician, Persephone welcomed the voices that gave her direction and that told her she was a queen and a prostitute. When the voices told her to pace, or to drive left or right, the volition lent her seemed to relieve some of the panic. She felt that the voices gave her a special power. As we saw when we studied mammal's prefrontally mediated delayed responses, this cortex regulates decisions to stop or go, choose left or right, and it buffers salient data.

Lacking the intersubjective and interobjective foundations of mind, the acute schizophrenic produces primary delusions. These are cognized reflections on what it is like to lose one's sense of identity. The sense of collapsing mind comes and goes. When it goes, the acute schizophrenic person tells what it feels like as it is lost—someone or something is stealing thoughts, or putting thoughts into the mind. A patient feels he has telepathic powers. What else can he conclude? The *Schneiderian* phenomenology of thoughts inserted or taken away results from the executive's desynthesis of a reflective mind.

Prolonged panic accompanies the collapse of the executive's identity synthesis. I posit the following acute stage sequence:

- Unrelenting panic exhausts the capacity of GABA, adenosine, endogenous opioids, various peptides, and the ventral tegmental dopamine system to inhibit LTP in the amygdala and hippocampus.
- Prolonged sleeplessness exhausts the capacity of the serotonin system to modulate and neutralize the libidinal and aggressive drives,

and to inhibit LTP in the amygdala and orbital frontal and insular cortex, where serotonin modulation is high.
- Limbic overpotentiation forms ineradicable memories of the psychotic experience and destroys vulnerable glutamate neurons.

Anyone who has worked with acute schizophrenics is awed by their way of generating the most intense and prolonged panic as their identities unravel. Their mobilized drive systems arouse prolonged wakefulness. Luria (1980) shows an acute schizophrenic's computerized EEG, in which the frontal and prefrontal areas are lit up like a Christmas tree.

McCarley's group found that hippocampal pathophysiology correlated with increased latency in the early ERP epoch of acute schizophrenia. They hypothesize that:

> positive symptoms of schizophrenia are related to limbic system pathology and in particular to a dysregulation of the NMDA form of excitatory amino acid transmission, potentiated by stress, and leading to cell damage and death due to "excitotoxicity." (1992, p. 209)[1]

The unfolding phenomenology of acute schizophrenia is similar to that of the near-death experience. Like a person undergoing a near-death experience, the acute schizophrenic experiences a sense of timelessness and a detached self. Then he is flooded with reemerging identity states from the past. We've inferred that in the near-death experience these phenomena are due to stilled, then hyperactive LTP. Now, we can infer that frozen, then hyperactive LTP occurs in acute schizophrenia. Many schizophrenics conclude that their premorbid identity has died. In his acute phase Steve said, "That woman is not my mother; she's Steve's mother!" For him, the former Steve had died.

It seems to me that schizophrenic excitotoxicity disrupts source memory organization and produces floods of wishes and motivations from earlier stages. The intrusion of primitive derivatives corresponds to a *looseness of associations*, the preeminent sign of a formal thought disorder. For example, if I ask, "How did Steve die?" He answers, "The killing fields made his semen end." This phenomenology reveals the presence of a dynamic unconscious, consisting of wishes and motives present in earlier life stages. The perplexity in thought indicates a poor fit of these wishes and motives with stage-appropriate, executive organization, to say the least.

Auditory hallucinations are one gauge of the acuteness of limbic excitotoxicity. Schizophrenic patients with auditory hallucinations show increased regional cerebral blood flow (rCBF) in the hippocampus, amygdalae and cingulate cortex, with decreased rCBF in the prefrontal regions (Muselak et al., 1989). The combination of intense limbic activity and stilled prefrontal assessment leads me to this hypothesis: *auditory hallucinations flow from a disassociation between increased limbic processing and decreased prefrontal assessments* of the processed data. Thus, auditory hallucinations correspond to unassessed data's intrusion into inner speech and social speech.

Acute delusions form when the supervisor does not shepherd needful states into the proper channels. These primary delusions are called *thought insertion* and *thought broadcasting*. We all hold a dual theory of mind. An intersubjective one supports our belief that we all have our own needs, and an interobjective one supports our belief that we all have autonomous minds. Lacking an intersubjective context, the acute schizophrenic loses empathy—the sensed boundary between his needs and other's needs. Lacking an interobjective context, the acute schizophrenic loses the sense that others have autonomous minds. In their primary delusions, schizophrenics do not know any longer whose needs are failing and whose thoughts are losing their autonomy.

Selective attention wanes during the acute stage. Often, when we ask an acutely schizophrenic patient a question, we have to wait through a long pause while the patient assesses the query. Usually, the answer comes just as we pose the next. It is not only the premorbid deficiency in selective attention that is at fault here, but the morbid decrease in p300 processing that produces this blocking phenomenon. As the reader recalls, the p300 stage occurs when the initial confluence of data activates enough attention to mobilize working memory's structure of potential consciousness.

The schizophrenic with the longest latency p300 response to auditory stimuli, is the one whose magnetic resonance imaging scans (MRIs) shows the most shrinkage in his own left limbic cortex and amygdala relative to shrinkage in his own right hemisphere (Blackwood et al., 1990). Shrinkage in the left hippocampus and surrounding structures slows semantic processing. MRI scans show that the left hemisphere's lateral ventricular enlargement tends to correspond to the severity of schizophrenia over a two-year period (DeLisi et al., 1992). In schizophrenia research, this enlargement is thought to be caused by underlying shrinkage in the hippocampus. Conceivably, shrinkage gauges the amount of excitotoxicity that occurs over the syndrome's course.

Now let us consider how the right hemisphere responds to the left hemisphere's disintegration in acute schizophrenia. Because of its neural equilibrium, the right hemisphere also undergoes some limbic excitotoxicity that is transferred to the right hemisphere's prefrontal networks. *Depersonalization and derealization* are symptoms of the observer's inability to integrate familiar and significant products of limbic processing. Thus, the right hemisphere's experiential loops integrated by the self, social self, and procedural self all form symptomatic identity-centered phenomenology.

What happens to perceptual processing in schizophrenia? We saw in Chapters 1, 2, and 3 that the right hemisphere's parallel processing networks integrate perceptual representations based on visual analysis. To review the right hemisphere's visual analysis, in conjunction with its supplementary visual cortex, its caudate evaluates limbic signals of significance. The caudate reads significance when supplementary visual cortex fixates the eyes on signifiers. There is an extensive literature on skittish saccades in acute and chronic schizophrenia. The greater the chronicity, the greater the saccade abnormality.

Poor eye tracking is specific for schizophrenia (Muir et al., 1992). *Abnormal saccades* correlate with *bilateral shrinkage* in the lateral ventricles (Blackwood et al., 1992). Poor visual fixation erodes the capacity to evaluate reality. The right hemisphere's erratic motoric palpation of signifiers by the eyes is a symptom of apperceptive failure, comparable to the left's semantic processing failure. All this produces continuing disintegration of the right hemisphere's organization, and contributes to the derealization, depersonalization, and blunted or peculiar affect manifested in disorganized schizophrenia.

Subacute Stage

In Chapter 5, we said that in human neoteny, developmental stages cycle from one hemisphere to the other. This progressive spiral incrementally increases the capacity for organizing consciousness at higher levels. Similarly, the schizophrenic process ends its acute regressive phase in a progressive phase that reintegrates and resynthesizes identity. Make no mistake about it, the end of a phase of psychosis is the beginning of a profound change in reflective identity.

The formation of massive, new source memory that occurs in all excitotoxic syndromes is necessarily accompanied by changes in intrapsychic identity. Good clinical use can be made of this insight, because every person who undergoes a psychosis, even a schizophrenic one, can be commended on his need to reorganize need satisfaction as well as on the way he deals with the world.

Persephone found a new identity in her psychosis. She embarked on prolonged investigations of her past and the past of her Creole people. She created a pseudoscientific, often inspired portrait of her ancestors. She wanted to understand how her hallucinations were the voices of former, and now present lives. She wished to be permanently embraced by her ancestors. When she talked of these matters, she *was* spontaneous.

In one subacute stage of intrapsychic identity restitution, Persephone studied Jaynes' erudite *The Bicameral Mind* (1976). She desperately wanted to integrate her acute experiences of hallucinations and a loss of mental boundaries into a new theory of mind. She wanted Jaynes' book to help her understand how her hallucinations came from her ancestors, including her ancestors in the pre-Homeric Greek civilization. She was fascinated to find that her ancestors did not know the source of their own minds. As time went on, however, her own cognitive clarity and her study decayed into apathetic disinterest.

Schizophrenia's subacute phase inspires new reintegrations of reflective identity. Newly potentiated experience feeds the executive's secondary revision. Secondary revision is a mechanism for turning new experience into logical experience that is suitable for communication. Thus, in the subacute phase, the executive uses the psychotic experience to reorganize identity. Two major factors lend themselves to this resynthesis that creates an altered person. The first is the cognitive rationales that have been developed to explain primary delusions and hallucinations. The second is the *significance experience*. In their subacute phase, schizophrenics have significance experiences—coincidences between their perception and their secondary revision of their delusions. For example, when Steve, who was so alienated he had no one to confirm his thinking, heard two honks outside, it meant he was right in his delusional thinking. One honk meant that he could be wrong. During one subacute phase, Persephone was studying her native art in an attempt to systematize her family romance delusions. By coincidence, she found a Caribbean harvest picture in the Metropolitan Museum of Art. Suddenly, she was "sure" it was painted by a particular ancestor. This reconfirmed to her that she was descended from nobility. She scoffed that the curator attributed the picture to an unknown artist. What happened in these two cases? Welding perception with cognition, the schizophrenic's executive *systematizes* delusions.

I posit that significance and salience experiences arise from rapidly altering inputs into the prefrontal networks. These inputs come from the intensely potentiated amygdala and hippocampus. Limbic excitotoxicity inappropriately introduces source memories into prefrontal assessment. These memories and their attendant screen constructs and fantasies come unbidden into reflection. The executive seizes the moment to make new delusional source memory from old source memory.

Clinicians often see subacute and chronic schizophrenic patients whose intrapsychic identities clearly include transformed elements of their early childhood experience. Early childhood experience mixes into emotionally organizing structures from other developmental stages in a kind of identity *melange.* Typically, patients living in the resulting systematized delusional world say things such as, "My cousin is controlling my mind. He makes me pee when I do not want to, and he laughs at me." Having seen many patients go through this subacute phase, I conclude that once past source memories are incorporated into a systematized delusion, there is no turning back from psychosis.

It is often possible to see the moment when the patient incorporates new material into old identity structures. This moment of *significance experience* transforms acute to subacute schizophrenia. Significance experience latches onto an innocent detail that occurs during acute psychotic trauma, as a cognitive integer of newfound identity. It is the coincidence, the synchrony of the detail during significance seeking, that gives the experience its credibility.

From time to time, we all have the experience of thinking about a particular item at a moment when that item is said in a conversation, or is heard on the television. That synchronous moment feels odd. Many people find themselves thinking of a friend or relative at the very moment of that person's death, as they realize later. This causes even a normal person to believe that she has the powers of a witch, or that communication can occur telepathically. In schizophrenia, significance experience happens when the details and the context of data processing and working memory serendipitously coincide with articulatory rehearsal at a moment when identity is shattered.

It seems to me that significance experience explains psychotic inspiration—the "aha!" experience—and that the influx of old material into new source memory produces the nidus for a reassessment of new experience under the auspices of a secondary delusion. A secondary delusion, as I said before, enters intrapsychic identity as a new cornerstone of the social self. This is to say, a secondary delusion is a cognitive rationale for some previously unknown social force that organizes reality—"Now I know why the CIA has been bugging my phone."

As Freud noted in the "Schreber Case" (1911), these restitutive, schizophrenic delusions provide the basis for a psychotic rebirth of personal identity. Freud propounded his theory of paranoid schizophrenia in that case. He observed that Schreber's *restitution* of personal identity incorporated raw experience at a level close to that of cathexis. Schreber experienced intense sexual pleasure that was disconnected from any wishes that he knew. In a state of mind with no boundaries, disavowing love for his male therapist, Schreber ascribed the intense sexual feelings as "the rays of God." Freud deduced that Schreber's "rays of God" were sources of pure homosexual libido that were grandiosely brought into Schreber's psychotic rebirth.

It seems to me that as the subacute stage progresses, restitutive reorganization of neural networks occurs both limbically and prefrontally. Forced normalization brings excitotoxic reorganization to a standstill. When excitatory transmission damps, schizophrenic "depression" occurs. Evidence for increased norepinephrine activity and a lack of hypofrontality distinguish this from chronicity (van Kammen, 1990). This is the period after an acute psychosis, when a person realizes that life has gone on without furthering either ambition or needed intimacy. A tremendous narcissistic loss must be accepted. Just as after a stroke, a person has to process both the neurological deficits and the emotional deficits, so the schizophrenic has both kinds of deficits to account for.

Chronic Stage

We can gauge chronicity by the degree of hippocampal formation damage and shrinkage. Accumulating research confirms that each acute episode produces further movement toward deeper chronicity. The left hemisphere usually manifests the most severe hippocampal formation shrinkage, processing deficits, and impoverished arousal. As chronicity deepens, there is a tendency for increased bilaterality of the excitotoxic effects, and for an increased bilaterality of frontal and prefrontal hypometabolism.

Eventually, in chronic schizophrenia, a kind of *organic abulia,* or lack of volition, and an emptiness of the social subject's personal historical context occurs. *Crow's Type II schizophrenia,* which features negative symptoms and an enlarged left lateral ventricle, corresponds to this description (Crow, 1980). MRI and cerebral glucose utilization studies (PET scans) in schizophrenics show left hemisphere, hippocampal formation reduction in size and metabolism (Weinberger et al., 1992).

Let us continue reviewing evidence which suggests that burnout is literally excitatory burnout. In chronicity, researchers find bilateral shrinkage of the hippocampal formations, especially the left hemisphere's, and decreased bilateral, frontal rCBF (Cassanova, 1990). This corresponds to decreased neurons and NMDA receptors in the chronic schizophrenic's left amygdala, hippocampus and rhinal cortex (Reynolds et al., 1990). We must conclude that impaired limbic processing due to excitotoxicity results in decreased glutamate transmission of new experience, which correlates with the degree of chronicity.

A PET study of unmedicated schizophrenics showed bilaterally decreased hippocampal formation and anterior cingulate rCBF (Tamminga et al., 1992). Thus, data registration and processing as well as emotional assessment are compromised in chronic schizophrenia. The bilaterality of this hypometabolism, further confirms that as schizophrenia progresses both hemispheres are drawn into the process.

In 1974, Ingvar reported a thickened corpus callosum and metabolic hypofrontality in chronic schizophrenics. Goode and Manning (1988) found interhemispheric defects. These findings point to the chronic schizophrenic's progressive incapacity to systematically assess information. We may take this bilaterally decreased registration, processing, and assessment of cognitive and emotional data as the index of chronicity.

Frontal and prefrontal cognitive deficits increase in chronicity. Neuropsychological testing, such as the Wisconsin Card Sort Test, shows decreased bilateral frontal glucose utilization during testing. Schizophrenics manifest an impaired capacity to switch sets during the card sort test, which requires a person to switch organizational contexts while using shapes, sizes, and colors (Weinberger et al., 1992).

When schizophrenics move toward a negative state, all levels of data processing diminish. The schizophrenic's impoverished thinking slows and blocks. Regional cerebral blood flow is markedly decreased in the left hemisphere's prefrontal and parietal cortex (which provides semantic *context*), particularly in patients who show such negative signs as reduced spontaneous communication and psychomotor poverty (Friston et al., 1992; Ebert et al., 1991). Reduced working memory in schizophrenics shows up in reduced parietal lobe p300 amplitude in response to target tones, and in an almost absent, late frontal component (Michie et al., 1990; Muir et al., 1991).

To sum up, schizophrenia is the prime example of a syndrome that produces an equilibrium among genetic, biochemical, neural, familial, social, emotional, and experiential determinants. Genetically determined, frontal and prefrontal processing deficiencies lead to emotional difficulties in consummation, which ultimately leads to panic, and the endogenous onset of amygdaloid and hippocampal formation excitotoxicity. Since reactively increased dopamine processing tends to limit limbic excitotoxicity, the hyperarousal of need augments symptoms in the acute stage. This leads to regression and to all of the other phenomenology of the psychotic experience. The psychotic experience itself leads to further syndrome progression through subacute restitutive processes. Once a psychotic identity is formed, new acute episodes come about more easily. In this way, the syndrome progresses to chronicity.

TYPES OF SCHIZOPHRENIA

Many researchers have attempted to distinguish different types of schizophrenia on the basis of altered patterns of brain function correlated

with phenomenology and syndrome progression. PET scans have correlated three clinical types of schizophrenia with the amount of functional
brain metabolism in various areas of the brain (Friston et al., 1991; Brown
and White, 1992):

- *reality dissociation* with marked delusions and hallucinations
- *disorganized* thought, inappropriate motives, and affects
- *negative* symptoms—impoverished content, goals, and emotions

Although we could equate the first (Schneiderian) type with paranoid
schizophrenia, and the disorganized type with its own namesake, there is
little point in trying to hold on to past nosology. That nosology did not
sufficiently distinguish types from stages of schizophrenia. Moreover, the
not previously mentioned catatonic type may be a variant of psychotic
mood disorder. We can say, however, that some schizophrenics do not
progress to chronicity with negative symptoms and that others do. Given
the widespread use of neuroleptics, we rarely see cases that maintain a
natural progression as distinct syndromes.

I believe the three types are distinguished by the amount of acuteness or
chronicity they display. If that is so, then, these types are nothing more than
a way of classifying relative chronicity. Since some cases never do progress
to chronicity, I surmise that the Schneiderian type, with a greater degree of
acuteness, does not necessarily progress to chronicity. It follows that the
disorganized type progresses half way, and the negative type all the way.
The Schneiderian type also displays left hemisphere pathology, the disorganized type manifests both hemisphere's limbic and prefrontal pathology,
and the negative type reveals both hemisphere's prefrontal pathology.

All three types have some PET findings in common. Most notably, their
left hemisphere's parahippocampus is overactive, more so in acute Schneiderian patients. As we have seen, the parahippocampus is activated in long-
term memory formation and in recall. Since the left hemisphere's parahippocampus stores event-sourced memory, I posit that this memory source
mixes with onstream processing and helps to form the hallucinatory and
delusional contents that working memory so poorly processes. Thus, the
content of the acute schizophrenic's delusions and hallucinations mixes
with his archaic experience.

Friston's group found that the disorganization syndrome "was characterized by marked positive correlation in the anterior cingulate, and negative correlation in the right temporal-insular-prefrontal cortices" (1992,
p. 368). Thus, activating either medial cortex *increases* disorganization;
and activating the right hemisphere's intermediate cortex *decreases* disorganization.

Why is this? Since anterior cingulate cortex assesses need and affect signals, disorganized schizophrenics *cannot* deal with activation of this cortex. In my clinical experience, it is common for disorganized patients to experience affect, anxiety, and sexual and aggressive signals. They ascribe them to outside forces since they cannot locate their source in their own subject or self. This is the essence of the disorganization experience. The well-known maxim that schizophrenic patients should not be expected to deal with expressed emotion finds credence in this brain scenario. However, since the right intermediate prefrontal cortex assesses somatic indications of socially conditioned pain, when this cortex functions, disorganized schizophrenics can organize their past in a present context.

Friston's group found that negative patients' "psychomotor poverty correlated negatively with rCBF in the prefrontal and left parietal association cortices, with positive correlations in the caudate nuclei" (1992, p. 368). The less prefrontal and left parietal activation, the more negative systems. The more caudate activation, the more negative symptoms. Why is this?

Since the prefrontal system synthesizes reflective identity, its lack of activation results in little executive activity. As we saw in the ERP studies of Chapter 6, the left hemisphere's parietal association cortex integrates a context for working memory's semantic processing. Its deactivation accompanies semantic poverty. Presumably, in chronic schizophrenics the caudate nuclei increase their activation to compensate for decreased left hemisphere assessment of needs.

HOW SOME SCHIZOPHRENICS COPE

Through intense, continual effort, some schizophrenics can prevent their illness from progressing. These patients use their psychotherapy to develop a personalized theory of mind that fosters maturation. They massively identify with the therapist's theory of mind, which they use as an external template for generating thoughts about their illness and about their own identity.

I have know several patients who have developed a talent for following the course of their own semantic processing and who are aware of what they must do to develop an articulated communication that will mediate their social interactions. For instance, a patient who has sporadic auditory hallucinations and who believes that most people are out to get her, developed the capacity to communicate her sensitivity to people in her graduate school classes. She becomes symptomatic when she feels her boundaries infringed. In one instance, when another student began to flirt with her, the patient had to tell him, without seeming inappropriate, how dangerous this felt.

In discussing this incident, the patient had to find just the right way to communicate her experience to me. She said that she has learned the "linguistic code" for interpersonal communication. Slowly and hesitantly, she looked for the perfect way of telling me about this code. She wanted me to verify that it helped her test reality. For my patient, the problem was, would this man respect her dignity? She understood that he was violating her boundaries when he told her that he was a teacher *too,* although *she* is not. My patient told her classmate that she was not able to respond to him because that would interfere with her only purpose in the class, which was to learn. She told him that she was a student, not a teacher, and that only the teacher of the class was essential to her present situation.

My position in this session was similar to my position as the writer of this text. I try to understand what I learn from my patient, and to place that information in a context that can be communicated. I tried to participate with her in her formulation of the social problem, and how to generalize it, in order to enhance her sense of who she is, and how she can communicate that to herself and others. I commended her on her capacity to find just the correct way to tell me about the incident, and I agreed with her that her formulation of her inner semantic process was sound. Other than that, my position was simply to listen with all the understanding I could muster. We concluded that there might be some—just a few men out there—who would be able to listen to her, and who might become suitable as objects for intimacy in the future.

I realize that I am the student; my patients the teachers.

Chapter 11

How the Brain Reveals Its Mental Status

Because the wreckage has been under water for a month, some evidence has dissolved or washed away. If clear evidence is never found and a highly unusual mechanical malfunction is ruled out, Mr. Kahlstrom said, the FBI will face the challenge of pursuing a circumstantial case. That, he conceded, could be as unsatisfying to jurors as it is to the public.

—Don Van Natta,
The New York Times, August 16, 1996

We can take this statement about a public event, the crash of TWA Flight 800, as a metaphor for what happens after syndrome formation. The next two chapters pursue the evidence that a diagnostic interview and mental status examination (MSE) bring to the surface about changes in underlying brain function after syndromatic events. The goal of the interview is to use phenomenology to diagnosis the brain's mechanical function, even though we can only make a circumstantial case.

The MSE is a quick way to assess the range and degree of the brain's dysfunction. Each MSE category opens a window into one or more of the higher cortical functions or metafunctions. Taken together, all these views offer a *tableau vivant* of the patient's world. When used properly, the MSE is a wonderfully economical instrument for confirming hypotheses generated in the semistructured diagnostic interview.

In addition, the diagnostic interview and MSE open windows on phenomenology itself. Following the trail of evidence presented by the patient's account of his illness and the circumstances and background that led up to it, and using the assessment categories that have evolved through the years of using the MSE, one can comprehensively survey the working mind. If the assessor is cognizant of the neural system's approach to the mind, the assessment categories will provide as much information about the functional state of the brain as they do of the mind. This should be so. After all, the nature of psychological experience is inextricable from its neural foundations. What follows is a primer for generating credible hypotheses in diagnostic interviews, and an attempt to redefine the kinds of phenomenology that each category of the MSE addresses. (The figures The Origins of Syndromes supplement this primer.)

Why is it that the partly educated student interviewer comes up with a slim array of rote and standard hypotheses, whereas a naive *class* of beginning students can jointly observe a patient interview and collectively arrive at brilliant diagnostic inferences and dynamic understandings? Having taught uncounted psychiatric residents and medical students to perform the MSE, over the years I have learned that individual students are often too embarrassed to administer this test. The principal reason seems to be that the student does not know what kind of information each segment of the MSE exam highlights. Training the student's capacity for performing and methodically observing a patient makes most individuals as brilliant as the naive group.

The sophisticated interviewer interpolates MSE inquiries into the diagnostic interview by interweaving two cognitive frames. The first includes semistructured questions that tap into the phenomena of illness and past history. The second includes conventional categories of MSE observation and inquiry.

A student's capacity for diagnosis hinges on her synthesis of her own cognitive, social, and emotional zones of data analysis. By training each zone of a person's constituent identity metafunctions we train a person's professional identity, which helps the student overcome embarrassment.

- A student's cognitive evaluations are subject to *political bias.*
- Social evaluations arise from her own social conditioning, which causes *countertransference.*
- Affective evaluations derive from sensing her own *counteraffective response to the patient's emotional appeal.*

Let us expand on the interviewer's three mechanisms for assessing the interviewee. The interviewer's cognitive frame for assessing the patient is determined by what she values in the scientific literature, by her training, and by her understanding of diagnostic categories. The literature and training express politicized biases of which students are largely unaware.

Because all of us have conditioned social associations, during training, students develop or discover prototypical patients among friends or relatives who seem to incarnate each syndrome being discussed. As students learn about personality disorders, they usually come up with friends and relatives who fit the criteria. This is helpful, but tricky, because students' dynamics determine their *diagnostic countertransference.*

When we use countertransference to aid in diagnosis, we associate the somatic signals of our own emotional responses to the patient—our feelings—with our own explicit source memories of social experience. Supervision can correct the distortions that come from blind spots. For instance, one resident could not stand patients whom he thought were malingering. Their dishonesty made him feel personally angry and professionally frustrated. He blamed patients for rejecting his help.

Supervision revealed this resident to be his family's caretaker. As the doctor in the family, he had encouraged his mother to have a life-saving operation. Unfortunately, she became anoxic during the operation and consequently demented. The resident's hypocritical siblings blamed him from the sidelines. After the operation, they refused to help with the mother's care, as they had done before. Although the resident had two young children, he and his wife had to nurture the mother, who became a figurative albatross. What was most interesting was that the resident's siblings' hypocrisy formed the basis for the resident's angry countertransference to malingering patients. Once the resident connected his countertransference with his inability to empathize with patients who lied or refused to follow his advice, his diagnostic skills advanced rapidly.

If the student understands her own dynamics and biases, then the patient's affect will trigger counteraffective responses in the interviewer, and these will open a particular window into the patient's inner life. To give a quick example, if one feels sorry for a patient, this indicates that the patient experiences dependency and abandonment anxiety. At the end of a MSE, all interviewers should identify the moments in the interview when they have been emotionally touched, positively or negatively. If the interviewer understands how and why she was touched, a sense of the patient's dynamics will emerge. A good interviewer will learn the fit between dynamics and diagnosis because they fit like a hand in a glove.

DIAGNOSTIC INTERVIEWING: THE FIRST TWO MINUTES

After introducing yourself and explaining the purpose of the interview, you should begin with an open-ended question such as, "What led to your coming here?" Instead of interrupting the patient within a few seconds, as many physicians do, listen to and observe the patient. At the same time, observe yourself.

We learn half of what we need to know in the first two minutes. If the interviewee understands the reason for the interview, and shows a cooperative attitude, three-quarters of the work is completed. Now the interviewer knows that the patient is socially appropriate, and his judgment and insight are intact enough to form a capacity for reflection. A good working alliance indicates the interviewee can join the interviewer both intersubjectively (with mutual empathy) and interobjectively (with each in appropriate social roles). People are no longer strangers in this context of joined reflection. When the examiner and patient know they are working together, the examiner can be sure that the patient is not acutely psychotic and that organicity of recent origin is unlikely.

The game is afoot when something goes awry in forming the working *alliance*. It is up to the examiner to develop an array of hypotheses about *how* things have gone amiss. What is unusual or off-putting about the first interchange with the patient? This question should remain in the interviewer's mind as an essential one to be answered by the end of the interview.

Eye Contact

In those first two minutes, we can learn a lot from eye contact. A frank exchange of gaze acknowledges the mutuality of reflective consciousness. Gaze exchange tells us immediately that we have formed a working alliance. From infancy onward, interlocking gaze indicates that the parent's and the infant's attention systems are mutually engaged (Osofsky and Connors, 1979), even to the level of their amygdaloid processing. From infancy onward, gaze locking accompanies a state of full data processing. Throughout life, frank eye contact helps regulate decisions about how to behave.

In my experience, when a person turns his *eyes upward*, he is *reflectively self-observing*. When the *eyes turn down,* he is evaluating data that *working memory* is processing. Tai Chi begins with the following eye movements: one inhales, looks far, and sees nothing. Then the practitioner exhales and looks down. This relaxes reflection and open the gates for unselected data.

Ask someone what is going on in his or her mind when the person's eyes are looking upward, then downward. When the eyes are looking upward, the first response will be "nothing." "Nothing" means that the person you questioned is in a state of reflective analysis guarded by behavioral blockade. If you want to know what the person is really thinking, proceed delicately.

We can correlate upturned eyes with dissociation and hypnotizability. A hypnotized person is lost in a reflective state that does not feel as if it belongs to him. He grants the hypnotist the right to direct his executive identity functions. A hypnotized person assesses cognitive, social, and emotional data in a state of relinquished identity. Some traumatized people forego their own identity and enter dissociated states.

During mutual gaze locking, we do not engage both eyes at the same moment. We move back and forth between right-right, left-left, right-left and left-right engagement. Take a moment and check if this is not so. As you are checking, you will notice that you are interfering with a natural process. The other person may become uneasy. We learn a lot in those instants of eye contact. For instance, going down an urban street, we make eye contact with dozens of people and perhaps a dog in just a few seconds.

I observe that when a patient makes *right-right eye contact* with me (left hemisphere locking) in a therapeutic setting, he wants help with *need satisfaction*. A patient who makes *left-left contact* (right hemisphere locking) conveys frustration, anger, or difficulty in processing reality. His right to my left is an appeal. My right to his left shows my wish to help him. To an informed observer, eye contact shows which hemisphere and which data processing systems are engaged. Eye movements without eye contact are also significant. One patient reports that when he uses what is called *NMDR*, continuously moving his eyes back and forth while looking at nothing, *emotional source memories occur.*

Unlike the voluntary eye movements we have been talking about, in saccades, the eyes move involuntarily back and forth during feature detection. Saccade stops, i.e., fixation stops, supply working memory with salient and significant visual information. Functional brain imaging correlates erratic saccade fixation with abnormal brain activity. In schizophrenia, erratic saccades indicate that significant and salient stimuli are poorly scanned. Chronic schizophrenic's erratic, slowed saccadic movement indicates a poverty of right hemisphere feature detection during working memory (Luria, 1980).[1]

Evaluating Thought Process

Thought rides the ridge between data analysis and behavior. Social communication is our major problem solving behavior. By analyzing the social communication, we infer how a patient thinks. Consequently, as the interview goes on, we assess a patient's thought process by evaluating the nature of our cognitive interaction. In addition to the MSE inquiry of asking the patient about her thought processes, whether they race for example or proceed too slowly, we reflectively observe the impression the patient's speech pattern makes on us. A sense of oddity, of cognitive dissonance, should elicit a hypothesis of cognitive dysfunction. Psychopathological syndromes are more likely to elicit a sense of emotional dissonance.

Let us focus our discussion of thought disorder on two phenomena: *looseness of associations* and *flight of ideas*. In the MSE, "association" refers to the capacity to convey explicit semantic meaning, which is the basis of logic. Looseness of associations occurs when a patient cannot infuse articulatory rehearsal with the inner speech that mobilizes goal oriented needs. An "idea" conveys visual representation that is been transformed into social speech. *A flight of ideas is a difficulty in melding social speech into articulatory rehearsal.* For instance, a beginning social work student with incipient bipolar illness told me that when he looks at the black radiator in my office, he thinks of the color black, then black paving, then a street, then his racing thoughts are off and running.

Because the left hemisphere produces inner speech, and the right hemisphere social speech, I have concluded that looseness of associations is a left hemisphere phenomenon, and flight of ideas a phenomenon of the right. A patient can manifest both.

When we look at articulated communication, we particularly want to assess how well a patient can convey his needs and how he goes about satisfying them. The combination of delusions and loose associations can produce a very odd logic of purpose. For example, a schizophrenic man whose erotomania disguised his homosexual needs, said that he had *mailed his semen* to Jackie O. "Why?" I asked. The patient answered that by sending this "male" "see men" into Jackie's female "O," he conceived a beloved son. The patient lavished gifts on male friends who simply took advantage of him. He comforted himself with his belief that Jackie O. was in love with him. Using neologisms, incorporating them into his delusions, and acting on the basis of his loosely condensed associations, this patient delusionally provided himself with a loved son, which assuaged his homosexual needs.

In schizophrenia, looseness of associations results from an attention deficit in the left hemisphere's integration of working memory's semantic associations. Repression's verbally selective inhibition fails. The result, as we saw in the above example, is idiosyncratic and primitive associations that may condense into neologisms. This kind of interference with logic's base impairs the normal formation of articulatory rehearsal. Other phenomena of interference with articulatory rehearsal include impoverished content, blocked speech, tangentiality, and circumstantiality—all indications of a *formal thought disorder.*

Flights of ideas contain superficial ideas and words, incompletely processed by working memory and still laden with raw sensation and affect. Manic patients are hard to interview. They do not hold on to the meaning of questions. Therefore we have to take control of the interview and structure it highly. Rhyming, clanging, cadence, and images disorganize the manic's communication. If another patient in the hall says something barely audible, the phrase will enter right into the manic patient's response to the interviewer. For instance, once when I asked a patient what led him to come to the hospital, another patient was heard to say "cake" in the hall. My patient then said, "The cake made me take off cooking. My mother never makes cake. She called the police, so where's the beef?"

In this patient's flight of ideas, disinhibition of onstream processing and working memory allowed the abnormal entry of disorganized, unselected sensation, ideas, and imagery into his thought. As we know, the right hemisphere integrates affect with idiomatic social speech, and it also has a separate processing system for apperceiving visual stimuli. Normally, apperception of images precedes naming the image. In mania, imagery mingles with words, the manic is distracted, and words for the images disorganize speech production. We should therefore try to hold follow-up interviews of manic patients in low stimulus areas.

In both looseness of associations and flight of ideas, the patient's meta-functions cannot integrate working memory. The patient's executive function in turn cannot integrate a coherent sense of identity. In both acute mania and schizophrenia, poor frontal/prefrontal integration yields pressured, racing thoughts.

Mood

Mood, feeling, somatic states, and anxiety all have their experiential side, which constitutes their *phenomenology* and their objective manifestations, which constitute *signs*. When we observe trembling hands and wide eyes and hear a tremulous voice, we conclude these are signs of anxiety. When the patient knows these signs are evident, a vicious circle may begin. Now he has to deal with both his inner sensations of anxiety as well as a sense that he is humiliated socially, which triggers more anxiety. Let us study how people know what they are experiencing, which is the phenomenology they can share with us, if we know how to ask.

Moving, with *open-ended questions* to the patient's inner experience, we ask, "How is your mood," and we follow up with, "What does it feel like to you? Try to tell me more about it." In this way, we try to get to the feelings, i.e., to get to reports of somatic sensations that give rise to mood. The observer can also infer a person's mood by perceiving many signs. Affect is, after all, a social as well as an intrapsychic signal system.

For many years, I have evaluated what the two sides of the face tell about emotional states. Almost always, the *right side reveals the left hemisphere's libidinal tone of expressive emotion:* warmth, tenderness, and sensuality. Conversely, *the left face portrays* the right hemisphere's *aggressive, affect tone:* anger, death, sadness, seriousness, frustration, or relief. It is amazing how much character tone can be perceived if one simply images the two sides of the face separately, and then reconfigures the qualities portrayed in both sides.

Dissecting the bilaterality of emotional responses gives the examiner extra information. One sees conflict as well as senses emotion. Consider the *snarl* where the turned-down left cheek and lip portray deadly aggression. Also, consider the *wry* smile, where the right face tries to portray pleasure, only to be checked by the left face's failure to follow. You can observe resignation in a politician's face, for instance, by seeing the left face as expressionless and the right face as having warmth. Ask a patient to show a picture from his wallet. Analyze it this way.

Look at a picture of the *Mona Lisa*. Her left side conveys warmth, her right side, disinterest. This reverses the usual pattern. Leonardo DaVinci was left-handed, however, and I would guess that his dominance was completely reversed. Perhaps this is the secret of the Mona Lisa's enigmatic smile.

A person's feedback from his own facial expression reenforces his other somatic signals of emotional discharge. The right face conveys the expressive emotion that tracks the progress of action programs, while the left face portrays the affect that tracks ongoing response programs. Consider a depressed person's face. His right face conveys helplessness about achieving libidinal satisfaction, while his left conveys an affect of hopelessly dead aggression. The downcast eyes indicate a lack of reflection. Impoverished reflection correlates with decreased frontal and prefrontal processing.

Try this. Relax your facial muscles. Do you notice your mood change? Facial muscle feedback is habitual and constantly reverifies our mood. Consider the older dysthymic's furrowed brow, and the deeply etched worry lines that frame his nose's beginning near the forehead. Consider, on the other hand, the wise optimist's smile lines, deeply etched in his composure. Our most habitual expressions engrave our characters on our faces. We feel what we portray. We sense that our social self is false when our facial muscles tighten into a mask.

Our expressive muscles are only the most superficial, and most voluntary of our emotional feedback signals. Autonomic discharge into every organ produces feedbacks that we call *feelings*. We sample our amygdallar, hypothalamically channelled autonomic discharges in our anterior cingulate cortex. As Freud noted in his "Three Essays" (1901), we also receive feedbacks of pleasure or reactive displeasure from our *erogenous zones.*

Erogenous zones include the skin and mucous membranes. We receive feedback of socially conditioned erogenous signals in our insular prefrontal cortex. Eurynome, the patient whom we know from Chapter 7, was terribly ticklish. Her mother never held her, and as a young child, her skin's erotic needs were not stimulated, except by her seducer. Eurynome's boundary conflicts touched on her skin and mucous membranes. These conflicts balanced wishes to be held with the dread that touching brought more intensity than she could stand. Her fantasy of putting her head on her first therapist's lap was overcome by dreadful phallic mushroom images when her therapist became pregnant.

Feelings—somatic states—signal the executive to reregulate our behavior. When feeling signals are ambiguous, we invoke signals of socially conditioned somatic states associated with events and episodes. Visceral sensations, including taste and smell assessed in the insular cortex, are closely associated with source memories. Proust's famous madeleine reference exemplifies this visceral closeness to the roots of emotionally organizing source memory. Traumatized persons often reexperience somatic, visceral, and olfactory sensations associated with their trauma.

PSYCHOSOMATIC ILLNESS

Although we usually use somatic signals preconsciously, these signals can attract consciousness, particularly if we are trying to disregard them in order to proceed with behavior. *One theory of psychosomatic illness is that when we try to disregard somatic signals, and continue our problem solving behavior, these signals become stronger, and their autonomic discharge into our organs becomes syndromatic* (Hovanitz and Wander, 1990).

The particular psychosomatic syndrome depends on the genetic, developmental, autoimmune, or other vulnerability of the organ to autonomic overload. In psychosomatic syndromes, signals of organ dysfunction attract enough attention to get the executive to modify our social communication in a way that reduces stress. In other words, somatic illness produces a secondary gain that is socially conditioned to reduce stress.

I have known many couples who alternate in carrying the psychosomatic load. When interpersonal conflict is curtailed by one person's symptoms the other becomes symptomatic, and vice versa. Psychosomatic illnesses either trigger an interpersonal reestablishment of equilibrium, or they can lead toward death. By suppressing psychosomatic signals in order to satisfy a partner who cannot stand to deal with anxiety over the other's condition, the psychosomatic condition can become fatal.

In one couple, the man had Crohn's disease, with intestinal malabsorption, and the woman had somatization disorder with prominent, but undiagnosible arthritic symptoms. The man failed to attend to signs that his Crohn's disease was worsening. My patient, who was attuned to her own somatic signals as well as signs of her lover's condition, dreamt he was dying and told him about it. As soon he began to take care of his Crohn's disease, my patient's condition exacerbated. Then, when my patient resolved to take care of herself, her partner began taking cocaine to deny his illness. As my patient became more autonomous and the pendulum of their equilibrium swung toward my patient's health, her partner died from a combination of cocaine, alcohol, and his Crohn's disease.

How does the social regulation of autonomic discharge come about? In the first months of life, parents help regulate autonomic discharge. Infant colic, eczema, blushing, and asthma exemplify the fact that all the organ systems have a psychosomatic regulatory function that interacts with parental intervention. For instance, when an infant cries with colic, if the parents just let the infant cry because they are frustrated and do not understand lactose intolerance, the autonomic regulation of the digestive system loses its adaptive function.

Socially conditioned somatic signals convey intrapsychic social regulation that began early in life. Somatic signals convey conditioned implicit memory. We cannot completely articulate them. That is why they are a signal system. There is a tendency for infant autonomic dysregulation to develop into full blown psychosomatic illness in adult life.

Thus, the colicky infant may develop adult syndromes anywhere on the continuum from irritable bowel syndrome to colitis, to Crohn's disease of the middle bowel. The man who died from Crohn's disease was socially alienated, and felt that his parents had never understood him. As an adult, starving for companionship and relief from pain, he habitually detached himself with drugs and entered a vicious cycle of stress.

Women are particularly sensitive to their somatic signals and sensations. *The premenstrual syndrome manifests a change in somatic signalling when estrogen's neuromodulation is withdrawn.* In the prelude to their period, some women sense somatic signals of something missing. A premenstrual woman may feel less attractive, hungry, and hollow. When estrogen is physiologically withdrawn, there is decreased hippocampal stimulation, just as there is in corticoid withdrawal.

ANOREXIA AND BULIMIA

In anorexia and bulimia, patients ascribe their somatic signals to their food and their body sense is often expressed in their feelings about food. Looking at the face and body in the mirror, and being sensitive to somatic signals channels a patient's bulimic and anorexic behaviors. In anorexia and bulimia, patients feel a disturbance in their body images that relate to feelings about whether they deserve to be satisfied. In cases involving women, I have observed clinically that the intersubjective relationship with her mother feels disturbed all the way back to infancy. Most of her socially conditioned somatic signals are of displeasure. In anorexia, the woman attempts to perfect herself by believing she has no further needs.

In this way, she tries to constrain her somatic signals to the vanishing point.

Indeed, anorexia's physiological effect on the amygdala, hypothalamus, and the drive systems downregulates autonomic responses. With little feedback of need, anorexics begin to feel less pressure to satisfy themselves or others. They withdraw, and there is less executive pressure to synthesize a sense of human coherence. The pressure for being social recedes when a person relinquishes living for either his or her own needs or for other's. In this connection, it is notable that some ascetic sects collectively relinquish worldly concerns. Perhaps each member downregulates his/her drives and corticoids.

HYPOCHONDRIA

Hypochondria may be defined as an overconcern with somatic sensations. Thus, hypochondria has an opposite profile from psychosomatic illnesses. Psychosomatic illness occurs when a person attempts to deny the autonomic signals of distress. The hypochondriac attends to feeling states and amplifies the social repercussions of the assessed somatic signals. While the psychosomatic is reluctant to ask for help for somatic states, the hypochondriac clings and worries. Hypochondria triggers social dependency as somatic signals repetitiously instigate clinging. The hypochondriac cannot relinquish social contact.

Hypochondria is like an itch that never goes away. Do you remember a time when you were trying to go to sleep, and suddenly you became aware that your foot was itching? Perhaps it had been itching all day, but your attention was engaged elsewhere. No matter how hard you tried, you could not get your attention off that itch, not even when you tried to put all your attention on it, so that you knew you could endure the worst of it. In hypochondria, the sensations do go on all day, and the patient rarely directs attention away from them, except to worry about them and to tell others about them.

One patient feared she had cancer, because she had a vulvar itch for two years. Despite seeing many doctors, she could not be reassured. Her husband had just retired and the family had planned to move to Florida. She could not go because she needed to stay close to her doctors. Further investigation revealed that her favorite daughter was not going to move with the family. To move meant separation from this daughter and living with a husband she really did not love. This patient's hypochondria had the secondary gain of keeping the family intact in Long Island, and of keeping the husband at a distance from her sexual parts.

EVALUATING ANXIETY AND ANXIETY DISORDERS

Is anxiety an emotion? Freud tried to answer this question. In his *Inhibition, Symptoms and Anxiety* (1926), he could not decide if anxiety belonged to the anguish of depression or if it was an affect in its own right. He did conclude, however, that when anxiety regulates the mind, even faint signals of anxiety (small discharges of assessed anxiety) mobilize defenses. When defenses fail, many patients say they want to die and we conclude that they are depressed. It is often anxiety discharges they cannot stand for one more minute. They would welcome unending sleep.

How does the interviewer assess the patient's anxiety? One way is to ask about evidence for the autonomic discharges of anxiety: rapid pulse, dizziness, shortness of breath, etc. Still, that does not tell us whether it is vigilant, anticipatory, or identity anxiety. I posit that each hemisphere has a form of anxiety that regulates behavior:

- Left hemisphere *anticipatory anxiety signals* prevent erroneous and dangerous initiatives.
- Right hemisphere *vigilant anxiety signals* guard against threats from the outside by suspending ongoing responsive behaviors.
- Dual hemisphere *identity anxiety signals* combine anticipatory and vigilant anxiety to maintain a coherent sense of identity.

Thus, error, anxiety, and identity anxiety regulate action programs, response programs and identity synthesis, respectively.

Understanding and diagnosing these forms of anxiety gives us a leg up on formulating a dynamic diagnosis that is consonant with a syndromatic one. We will look at clinical syndromes that manifest hemispheric forms of symptomatic anxiety discharge. Hysteria, muscular tension states, claustrophobia, and learning inhibitions manifest left hemisphere anticipatory anxiety. Simple phobias, social phobia, obsessive-compulsive disorder, and agoraphobia manifest right hemisphere vigilant anxiety. Panic disorder, generalized anxiety disorder, and PTSD often manifest identity anxiety, although anticipatory or vigilant anxiety may be more pronounced.

Anticipatory anxiety signals regulate the behavioral discharge of action plans. The defenses anticipatory anxiety mobilizes can lead to strict inhibitions against proceeding with consummatory discharge behaviors. Moderate anticipatory anxiety often induces muscular tension. Thus, tension headaches manifest defenses against libidinized intentions. "I have a headache tonight dear," could mean "I'm having a tension headache because I imagine making love to someone else."

In generalized anxiety disorder, anticipatory signals proceed to anxiety discharges. The patient interprets his anxiety discharges as irretrievable errors in major areas of problem solving. For instance, one patient anticipated that no one would hire him as a salesman because he was too old. He experienced his anxiety as a choking sensation. That particular somatic discharge, one of many, was secondarily invested with the "proof" that he could no longer express confidence when he presented himself to potential employers or to potential customers. His supervisory identity inhibited his initiative, because he believed that he would always "choke."

A Rock Singer's Hysteria

Anticipatory anxiety regulates the interaction between fantasies and plans. One patient, a singer, describes his anticipatory anxiety—"What will happen if . . . ?"—as a line that must not be crossed. When he thinks of having an affair and is on the verge of doing something about it, he backs away and has fantasies instead. Then he feels somatic states of muscular inhibition that curtail his ability to dance on the stage as he performs at rock concerts.

We can understand the mechanism of *conversion disorder* by considering the libidinal drive's relationship to anticipatory anxiety in symptom formation. Fantasies are a compromise formation among shame, fixations, anxiety discharges and libidinal discharges. Fantasies carry the wishful libidinal energy to act. Both the singer and the salesman had exhibitionistic tendencies that underwent repression and produced conversion symptoms. In each case, anticipatory anxiety triggered muscular rigidity that interfered with voluntary action. The salesman's vocal cords became chronically stiff.

The *secondary gain* from muscular inhibition *maintains* symptom formation. The patient with choking sensations was unable to speak in a forthright voice and was unable to continue his sales. This constriction removed him from the anxiety situation, satisfied his need to be shamed because he expressed forbidden exhibitionistic impulses, and resulted in his increased dependency. Therapists, in such cases, must begin by working with the secondary gain. Insight oriented psychotherapists can interpret it, while cognitive and behavioral therapists can help the patient modify his pessimism and reenforce behaviors that promote better vocalization through the use of anxiety reduction techniques while vocalizing. In truth, many therapists do both, wittingly or unwittingly.

Some people feel trapped in enclosed spaces; others feel safe. *Claustrophobia* is the most profound state of anticipatory anxiety. The claustrophobic massively inhibits voluntary action. For him, being in an enclosed space represents more inhibition of initiation than he can withstand. One patient was so claustrophobic that he exercised until he was musclebound so that he could burst out of any room in which he might be closed.

Schizophrenics experience profound claustrophobia as they inhibit their wishes for mature gratification, shut down their intersubjective world, and curtail all motivated planning. Their libidinal energy for consummation attaches to primitive fantasies that arise in the place of shut down, mature problem solving. The derivatives of these primitive fantasies are regressive and dangerous. They can only be controlled by the supervisor's further disorganizing behavior.

In their acute stage, many schizophrenics enact both sides of regressive symbiotic fantasies. They rage against their parents whom they feel restrict their intentionality—control them—from the inside of their bodies and minds. This is precisely the moment when they become homeless, for the parent or parents bar the door after the episode of rage. On the streets, they delusionally dream that they are reunited with their parents.

The feeling of inhibited muscles that neuroleptics produce adds to the schizophrenic's claustrophobia. Muscular tension may be the major factor in schizophrenics' noncompliance with neuroleptics. Early in the taking of neuroleptics, blockaded dopamine in the basal ganglia produces a feeling of losing one's operative agency, of being unable to effectuate intentions. The feeling of Parkinsonian rigidity or restless akathesia adds to the sense of shattering subjective identity. A neuroleptic may induce a sense of inability to automatically do what one intends, causing a vicious circle of increasing anticipatory anxiety.

If claustrophobia is the prototype for left hemisphere anxiety syndromes, then agoraphobia is the prototype for right hemisphere anxiety syndromes. In my experience, all *agoraphobics are anxious about abandonment*. Agoraphobics resent the fact that they have to inhibit their social responses because they are anxious about abandonment. They feel that if this anger were known they would surely be abandoned. Consequently, they dutifully overcomply with other's directions, to the point of masochism, obsessive obedience, or overdependency. Depression occurs when character defenses fail to stave off abandonment.

To give an example, a fifty-four-year-old, usually bold, outspoken, and entrepreneurial hypomanic woman became absolutely agoraphobic about crossing the street. The agoraphobia began when she was having a thought that she might never again have a lover. This would prove to her that her mother had been right in seeing her as worthless all her life. In the moment that her agoraphobia began, she felt suicidal, as well as homicidal toward her mother. The patient was getting older. Her hypomanic tendencies had alienated her clients, friends, and lovers. As her agoraphobia deepened, the patient found herself unable to continue exploring the world. She felt that she would have to accept her mother's authority and even live with her mother, because she herself could no longer work as an entrepreneur.

Agoraphobia's usual secondary gain is to force someone else to be present when that other person does not want to be. The agoraphobic's resentment about shaping her activities to other's needs leads to unconscious power struggles that the agoraphobic rationalizes as a need to hold on to the other person. In this sense, the secondary gain of agoraphobia is part of an aggressive anxiety syndrome. The fear of open spaces is the fear of taking on the unknown, and of social abandonment. Agoraphobia impairs autonomy. The adaptive side of aggression—to explore—is replaced by an anxiety that everything is overwhelmingly novel.

The known correspondence between major depression and agoraphobia helps to locate the trigger for agoraphobic anxiety in the right hemisphere. Typically, when there is a threatened loss of an ambivalent relationship, the person who is developing a major depression retreats to her apartment. The ambivalence, as Freud pointed out in *Mourning and Melancholia* (1917), is based on unconsciously resenting dependency on an uncaring person. Whether this unconscious resentment has developed in the context of a masochistic relationship ("You'll eventually see how good I am and pay me back"), an obsessive relationship ("I have always done my duty by you"), or a dependent relationship ("I trusted you to take care of me and did whatever you asked"), the depression or the characterological bitterness is the same.

Agoraphobia develops when a person experiences a threatened outbreak of angry rebellion against the superficially accepted authority of the other. In these cases, the other person, who is supposed to handle what comes up in the social world, can be replaced by anyone who volunteers for this job. This superficial quality of relationships is due to the agoraphobic's unconscious resentment, which prevents an acknowledgement of mutual autonomy.

A beautiful, young, social work student presented with severe *panic disorder.* She had a month-long history of daily panic attacks characterized by rapid pulse, breathlessness, sweating, faintness, dizziness, and a sense that she was going crazy, losing control, and losing her mind. When not undergoing these attacks, she vigilantly dreaded their return. The panic attacks had immobilized her capacity to learn, undergo supervision, and initiate clinical placement. Her fiancée became sick of her drastic complaints. Although benzodiazepines stopped the anxiety discharges, they did nothing for her anticipatory dread of a recurrence. She felt she was no longer the same person she was before the attacks started. This case shows that panic attacks include anticipatory, vigilant, and identity-related anxiety.

It seems to me that panic attacks, which might better be called *terror attacks,* are triggered in the right hemisphere. People who undergo panic attacks often develop an agoraphobic aversion to public places, especially to places where they have had a panic attack. These people often feel that any novel situation might induce a recurrence. The lack of precipitating content in panic attacks may relate to the fact that the intensity of autonomic discharge overshadows any other concerns, but the lack of verbal content may also point to the right hemisphere's triggering the attack.

We may recall that the right parahippocampus is highly stimulated during panic attacks. Moreover, this cortex contains a vast associational matrix that processes facial disapproval. I infer that panic disorder plumbs the earliest era of social integration, when infants process faces and learn that their well-being depends on seeing the signifiers in these faces. The student social worker was exquisitely sensitive to my response to her, as if she could divine whether I would help her.

Perceptual Disorder

The phenomenology of hallucinations differs for each sensory modality. What does not differ is the possibility of aligning the trigger point of hallucinations hemispherically. Thus, the patient with a major depression, who continues to experience a dream image of a loved one after the morning REM period is over, is experiencing a right hemisphere visual hallucination, that corresponds to other right hemisphere dysfunctions. The major depressive's quasidelusional belief in ghosts, then, has a different origin from the schizophrenic's delusion that auditory hallucinations are explained by a conspiracy. Perceptual distortions, as opposed to hallucinations, are more likely to represent a brain's organically disrupted percept formations.

Every practitioner has had the experience of asking, "Do you hear voices?" and getting the response, "Yes doctor, I hear your voice." The patient is usually not joking. We would do better to ask an open-ended question such as, "Do you receive some special communications?" If the answer suggests possible auditory hallucinations we might follow up with, "What are they like?" Because some patients feel a very special relationship with their voices, we might further ask, "Do you mind my asking?"

Auditory hallucinations are mysterious. Nevertheless, in our MSE we place a high emphasis on exploring the nature of a patient's auditory hallucinations. The various kinds combine qualities of hearing, thought, and reflective self-observation. Belonging to "the ineluctable modality of the auditory," to quote James Joyce (1942), each hallucinatory syndrome has its own balance of qualities. If multiple auditory hallucinations seem to have a life of their own, especially if they talk to each other, we usually conclude that the patient is schizophrenic.

What do we know about auditory hallucinations so far? In Chapter 10, we concluded that *auditory hallucinations are the result of a dissociation between hippocampal explicit processing and prefrontal assessment of that data as thought.* Thus, functional brain imaging during auditory hallucinations shows increased hippocampal processing and decreased frontal and prefrontal processing. We concluded, that an attention deficit compromised working memory's thought foundations during the formation of auditory hallucinations.

Now, let us add to these conclusions. Thought is a prefrontal higher cortical function that mediates between data assessment and the preparation for social communication and behavior. The left hemisphere's agent induces voluntary action, converts goals into inner speech—into action verbs that predicate the immediate future action—while the right hemisphere's procedural self converts responses into *social speech*—socially introjected phrases that guide responsive behaviors. Synthesized as articulatory rehearsal, inner and social speech are the two constituents of thought. During the formation of auditory hallucinations, thought malfunctions.

Egosyntonic auditory hallucinations are more common in psychotic mood disorders, which are induced by the right hemisphere, than they are in schizophrenia, which is induced by the left. The term "egosyntonic," here, means that the auditory hallucinations are experienced as emanating from one's own mind and thought. Freud was extremely impressed by the quality of detached reflective morality that such egosyntonic auditory hallucinations can convey. For instance, when he talked about the "cap of hearing" that the ego wears as superego, he meant precisely the effect of an aural, organized agency set upon the ego, that comments on its functioning (Freud, 1923). Freud could never decide whether that agency was part of the ego or set apart. To this day, psychoanalytic thinkers are unsure whether to ascribe aural self-observation to the ego or to the superego. Freud was sure, however, that a critical observing structure evaluates our intentions and responses.

The major depressive condemns her own social identity. She is unwilling to explore the social world because her attempts will reenforce her degradation. The aggression that she would usually use to explore the social world and to introject it is left unbound, and it is directed against her social self. Her thought system loses the capacity to bind social speech in pragmatic ways. The withdrawal from others impoverishes ongoing introjections of social speech. Instead, the psychotically depressed person regressively liberates archaic fragments of social speech. This is why a psychotically depressed person experiences auditory hallucinations as socially critical, primitive judgements that emanate from her own mind. Having listened to patients describe this detached experience of social judgment, I infer that these auditory hallucinations escape the right hemisphere's integration.

In my clinical experience, condemning auditory hallucinations are most vociferous and irresistible in *alcoholic auditory hallucinosis*. I have seen patients so hounded by the derogatory chorus that they jump out of windows or have to be restrained from doing so. This is not because the voices tell them to jump—it is to get away from the voices' condemnation.

Many psychoanalysts have been struck by the phrases that contain powerful aggression directed against the social self during egosyntonic auditory hallucinations. These phrases are best characterized as preoedipal products of the anal period's conditioning that have been segregated from later periods of internalization of inner speech. The phrase *"Do* it this way" may have anally conditioned primitive power cadence, while "Do it *this* way" may be internalized at latency when instruction is welcomed. Superimposing the phrases during development, the more mature phrase develops an explicit function that subdues the earlier conditioned phrase.

The question here is how alcoholic hallucinosis marshalls the superego's preoedipal introjects in such a powerful vitiation of the adult social self. We may find the answer by listening to the alcoholic organics we see talking to themselves on the street. If we listen, we will observe that the alcoholic responds to a berating that obviously took place long ago. We may hear him muttering, "Go fuck yourself then," or "What is this fucking shit?" He is trying to defend himself against affectively trenchant, conditioned introjects by simultaneously using the same speech fragments that have been directed against him against the introjects. The conditioned demons lodged in the anal period and reenforced in latency, are released into the alcoholic's inner world where they torment the organically and affectively fragmented drop-out of countless rehab programs. As Freud said, abandonment by the superego represents the most profound anxiety an adult can undergo (1923).

Auditory hallucinations' effects in schizophrenia are just as catastrophic as abandonment by the superego. These hallucinations begin in a context of already shattered, left hemisphere supervisory metafunctions. When the social subject loses the capacity for empathy, the agent, who initiates, loses the capacity to communicate needs. Consequently, working memory's semantic processing for inner speech formation is badly compromised. Auditory hallucinations carry the function of inner speech into this void of perplexed planning.

If you were a schizophrenic, your auditory hallucinations would often begin with a sense of whispering, poorly heard semantic fragments, or the sound of someone laughing at you. A young female schizophrenic patient who experienced all three wrote the following "poem" to her unclear hallucinations.

> Speak up please,
> or leave me in peace.

She urgently wished the hallucinations would tell her what to do because she did not know what to do. At no time did the hallucinations seem to come from her own mind. They seemed to whisper to each other: sometimes they talked to each other, sometimes they gave commands.

One command came clearly. Feeling claustrophobic and panicky, the patient drove to her friend's house. She came to a red light. What should she do? The question didn't formulate itself in her mind. Instead, she heard a command: "Go through the light." She did. Cars swerved around her. Despite this, the patient still wanted the voices to clearly tell her what to do.

In schizophrenia, auditory hallucinations seem to consist of aural data that are incompletely integrated by working memory so that they are judged to be external. In my clinical experience, there is sometimes a stage in the formation of hallucinations when the patient feels that the radio or the television is commenting on his wishes, needs, and intentions. When this happens, the patient experiences deep shame and feels as if everyone knows his or her sexual wishes—often, wishes that are homosexual and denied. This appears to me to be a direct result of the loss of the sensed intersubjective boundaries. The schizophrenic no longer experiences his thoughts as verbally fluent (subjectively initiated). He attributes them to others instead. This way of forming primary delusions alters the executive function of reflection. Since inner speech is now heard in a state of failed, intersubjective boundaries, the schizophrenic can only reinstate boundaries through the delusional belief that the voices emanate from the outside world.

As we have seen, during the subacute stage of schizophrenia, the schizophrenic often invests his auditory hallucinations with other people's qualities—as autistically conceived. In that sense, they fill the intersubjective void and function as intrapsychic synthesizers—mental prostheses—which allow executive reflection and decision making to go on without forming articulatory rehearsal from working memory.

Schizophrenics with auditory hallucinations are less able than those without auditory hallucinations to "self-repair" errors in communicating their intentions (Leudar et al., 1992). In schizophrenia, command hallucinations compensate for a lack of intentionality. Restitutional auditory hallucinations in schizophrenia compensate for a lack of integration by the left hemisphere's prefrontal system. From this, I conclude that the phenomenological qualities of auditory hallucinations in schizophrenia can tell us much about the stage of the illness.

Auditory hallucinations in post-traumatic stress disorder are affect-laden, episodically sourced flashbacks, incompletely integrated by working memory, which intrude into articulatory rehearsal. A twenty-six-year-old patient came for a social security benefits examination soon after her release from prison. She claimed that she kept hearing a voice say, "Let me in! Let me in!" Her history revealed that in her late teens, her mother had remarried a man who beat the mother in front of the patient. One day, when the patient could not stand it any more, and when she was alone with this man, and her mother was out, the patient began to argue with this man about his beating her mother. They began to fight. The girl grabbed a kitchen knife, and as her mother came bursting into the house, hearing the commotion, the man released his hold on the patient's arm, and the patient accidentally plunged the knife into her mother's heart. As the reader has surmised, the hallucinated voice was the patient's mother yelling, "Let me in!" The poor patient heard it over and over during the four years she served in prison.

Another patient, who had been diagnosed as a schizophrenic because of her disorganization and the presence of auditory hallucinations, actually suffered from post-traumatic stress disorder. She had been savagely and repeatedly raped by her grandfather during her latency and early adolescence. He told her that he would cut her into pieces with his buzz saw if she told any one what he was doing to her. After an experience of date rape in college, which retraumatized her, and after she tried to tell her family of the early rapes by the grandfather, she became apparently psychotic. Her family members literally struck her as she tried to tell them what the grandfather had done. She began to hallucinate a voice telling her to be still, accompanied by the whining sound of her grandfather's buzz saw. She became catatonic, mute, and anorexic.

The traumatized patient presented earlier, who had to deal with her father's flashbacks of killing "Japs," was disturbed by hallucinations of voices arguing. She was afraid she was going crazy. However, she was able to identify the source of the voices. The voices she heard were those of her parents fighting, while her father was attacking her mother while reliving his wartime experiences. When they fought, she was a latency kid, listening upstairs with her ears glued to the floor. She was relieved when I told her that she was reexperiencing her parent's battles as a kind of memory that had evaded her in the past, because she needed to detach herself from her helpless terror. Clearly, plumbing the phenomenology of auditory hallucinations is critical to both diagnosis and treatment.

Thought Content

We often begin our inquiry into the presence of delusions with a question such as, "Do you feel that some people may want to harm you?" Phrasing the question in an open-ended way may elicit ordinary experiences of hurt. This is a more natural line of inquiry than the question, "Do you feel people are after you?" The less pejorative sounding first question is also more likely to trigger the descriptive outpouring of multiple episodes of strange pursuit than the second. In order to diagnostically explore the phenomenology of delusions, it helps to categorize syndromes that give rise to delusions.

Karl Jaspers (1923) distinguished between *delusional ideas—false ideas* that are held to be true despite evidence to the contrary—and *delusions proper—a system of false beliefs*. Jaspers did his pioneering work on phenomenology early in the twentieth century. His observations have proved as useful for understanding phenomenology as modern brain imaging techniques have been for localizing brain function.

I pose two hemispheric types of delusions:

- *delusional ideas*—right hemisphere false cognitions
- *delusions proper*—left hemisphere false cognitions (which we see in the delusional disorders)

In either type, the patient elaborates the false cognitions in order to maintain a sense of coherent intrapsychic identity:

- *Primary delusions* are his attempts to *synthesize identity.*
- *Secondary delusions* are his *cognitive elaborations.*

Jaspers noticed that *delusional ideas* emerge from: (1) preceding, untenable affects such as shattering, mortifying, guilt-producing experiences; or (2) false perceptions or derealization in organically altered states of consciousness. Thus, delusional ideas are due either to denying reality or to organic misidentification of person, place, or thing. In either case, when *untenable affects* or *false perceptions undermine the right hemisphere's capacity to integrate its identity, the observer constructs delusional ideas as identity prostheses.*

From a neural system's perspective, organic misidentification can be explained by the right hemisphere's working memory's organic failure to find significance in perceived self or object images during its integration of potential consciousness at p300. Both organic misidentification and dynamically determined denial of other's personal or emotional reality detract from the right prefrontal system's self-observing function. Benson and Stuss (1990) found such a correlation between prefrontal dysfunction and the presence of delusional ideas.

Unlike delusional ideas, *delusions proper are psychologically irreducible.* They are irreducible because no amount of evidence to the contrary, persuasion, psycho- or pharmacotherapy change them one whit. They are irreducible because the conflict that gives rise to them is overwhelmingly defended by massed defenses: regression, repression, denial, projection, rationalization, condensation, and displacement. People with delusional disorder experience homosexual needs that are so destabilizing to their subjective identity that they employ these drastic defenses against their wishes. The defenses against and the wish for intersubjective symbiosis condense as delusions proper.

A delusion proper encompasses so much of the patient's identity that his whole belief system alters. Delusions proper lead to secondary cognitive elaboration. In delusional disorder, any communication threatens the cognitive system that supports the delusion. The person with delusions proper fears that any communication can destabilize his sense of identity.

ALL THE DELUSIONAL DISORDERS THAT FREUD KNEW

Delusional disorder includes (1) grandiose, (2) persecutory, (3) jealous, (4) erotomanic, and (5) somatic types. Often mixed in the same individual, these delusions pervade identity. Psychoanalysts have long known that *all types of delusional disorder are grounded in homoerotic libidinal conflict.* Because they are libidinally driven, I conclude that delusions proper develop from left hemisphere dysfunction. Let us characterize each type of delusional disorder. I think the reader will be convinced that projected homoerotic conflicts are always the smoking gun that has given rise to delusional disorder.

Grandiose

Freud characterized paranoid *grandiosity* in his exploration of the Schreber case when he analyzed Schreber's belief that the homoerotic rays of God invested him with greatness (1911). Freud concluded that Schreber's rays of God were something like a pure culture of homoerotic libido. Freud posited that this equation between his drive theory and the deep phenomenology of delusions proper substantiated drive theory's clinical relevance.

Persecutory

In his analysis of the Schreber case and in *A Case of Paranoia Running Counter to the Psychoanalytic Theory of the Disease* (1915), Freud concluded that persecutory delusions always arise from an experience of unrequited homosexual love. In the 1915 paper, he described a woman who presented a delusion of male persecution. Looking deep, Freud found that unrequited love for a woman had launched the paranoia. Freud elaborated the general mechanism of persecution: love turns to hate, and hate is projected and experienced as coming from the persecuting love object. The origin of projection in paranoia, as the word implies, is *para away from* and *noia* (knowledge). Homoerotic projection turns into hate, "known" to come from the outside.

Sometimes a woman's *masochism converts to persecutory paranoia.* Typically, a woman sacrifices everything for a mother whom she feels will not otherwise survive emotionally. The mother demands the sacrifice of her daughter's life. The father is seen by mother and daughter as the enemy who must be placated. In the course of her life's emotional transference, the daughter's hatred for women is held at bay through a displacement of the hatred onto a close male figure.

Jealous

In *Some Neurotic Mechanisms in Jealousy, Paranoia and Homosexuality* (1922), Freud observed that in delusions of *jealousy* the paranoid person wants to have the experience that his love object is having. Thus, if he is insanely jealous of his wife who may or may not be having an affair with another man, unconsciously he wants to have that affair. One can be sure that if, in such a situation, the man kills the wife's "lover," that he is jealous of what he imagines his wife gets from the lover.

Erotomanic

A woman who worked as a model in her twenties developed a chronic *erotomania* in her thirties. She believed that a great twentieth century fashion mogul found her irresistible. She lapsed into a continuous autistic reverie of being irresistible. She spent years in a mental hospital bed, emerging only to admire herself in the mirror. When she was fourteen years old and a budding beauty, her mother had sent her away from her family in Algeria, to live with a much older brother in Paris, so that she could pursue a modeling career. She could not abide her mother's betrayal and abandonment.

Somatic

In his paper "On the Origin of the Influencing Machine" (1948), Victor Tausk showed that in *somatic* delusions, the patient feels unconsciously, that his sexual body parts have been invaded by his own homoerotic wishes, and projected into the outside world. An erection that is unconsciously animated by denied, projected homosexual wishes is experienced as if it were a visitation from an unknown influence. Many chronic delusional people feel as if some outside, demonic force is entering their genitals and causing unwanted sexual responses.

The Woman Whose Cousin Made Her Pee

A seventy-five-year-old black woman with a forty-year somatic delusional disorder came to therapy because she could no longer care for her physical needs, as she had congestive heart failure. She was unwilling to enter a nursing home because the delusional figure of her male cousin controlled every detail of her life. She felt that this male cousin forced her to have sexual feelings when she urinated, when she washed herself, and hundreds of times a day as she tried to take care of her physical needs.

When she was four years old, her mother had sent her away from the small southern rural community where they lived to be raised by her mother's affluent brother in Washington, DC. The delusional cousin figure was this uncle's son. Similar to the model with erotomania, this woman felt deeply betrayed by the loss of her maternal symbiosis, and all other families' members were poor substitutes for her mother.

The patient pursued a career in civil service during her twenties and thirties. When her uncle and her mother both died when she was in her mid-thirties, she moved to New York City to be closer to another branch of her mother's family. When the patient realized she could not turn to them, she developed the delusion that her cousin was running her life from the inside of her body and mind. For forty years, she felt his influence as unwanted sexual sensations. She was certain that he used these sensations to control her body and her mind. All day, every day, she blamed this cousin figure for making her unacceptable to her mother, because of the shameful sexual feelings he induced in her. Thus, her wish for a female symbiote was masked by the delusional presence of her cousin.

Clearly, a homoerotic, symbiotic wish is buried beneath the surface of every delusional disorder. Working with chronic paranoid patients, one learns that they form permanent, exclusive attachments. Beneath the barrier against closeness, this transference manifests the symbiotic wish. Paranoids are sticky.

Persons with paranoid personality have the same dynamics as those with delusional disorder, but their identities are less fragile. In paranoid schizophrenia, the homoerotic conflict leads to a desynthesis in intrapsychic identity and consequently to a schizophrenic illness. In delusional disorder the delusion proper is the glue that holds the crazed personality intact, while in paranoid schizophrenia, the glue fails to hold.

Since our minds, our knowledge of our minds, and our very belief in intrapsychic identity exist as the result of prefrontal system synthesis, the acute schizophrenic patient who suffers from *primary delusions* accurately reports that his mind has been taken from him. The only restitution for the subjective sense of losing one's mind is to substitute regressive versions of mind.

Primary delusions—delusions of influence, thought insertion, thought broadcasting, or thought theft—manifest a lost capacity to locate thoughts intersubjectively. In the attempt to maintain mental synthesis and to restore the sense of intrapsychic coherence, the schizophrenic often introduces homoerotically projected rationales for the primary delusional experience. When primary delusions become invested with homoerotic conflict, they can develop secondary elaboration.

A thirty-five-year-old schizoaffective woman, who had a history of a humiliating loss of her mother's love, became pregnant on a psychiatric ward. She was advised to have an abortion. Consciously, the pregnancy meant to her that her mother was right to see her as a "slut." Unconsciously the pregnancy meant getting close to her mother.

She experienced the ward's television as broadcasting her sexual secrets to her mother and to the whole world. Her loss of intrapsychic integrity came on so fast that she was unable to control her actions. A fury directed toward killing the progenitor of her pregnancy ended in a seclusion room suicide attempt as she tore the observation mirror from the corner of the ceiling. The patient used pieces of the mirror to slash her wrist, because she heard her shame broadcast from the mirror.

In this chapter, we have explored the phenomena that arises from experiential disturbances, which alter the brain's organic equilibrium. The next chapter explores organic damage, which alters the brain's experiential equilibrium. This distinction is fundamental for the mental-status examiner. Chapter 12 will also help the reader distinguish between organic and emotionally traumatic impairment of source memory.

Chapter 12

Mental Status:
Memory and Related Functions

We awake to a world—we want to explore—composed of qualities—we cannot ignore.

This chapter explores cognitive disorders as they reveal themselves in the mental status examination (MSE), and it explores ways that our brains deal with assaults to their integrity, while sustaining the life of the mind. Many conditions that are not syndromatic have organic effects, and we cannot ignore their cognitive and emotional ones either. Any organic or metabolic condition affects the way we organize our intrapsychic identity. The reader should keep this in mind as we look at such conventional cognitive disorders as the dementias.

Case in point: a fifty-year-old nurse who has suffered for many years with severe neurological impairment as a result of lyme disease has word-finding difficulty (anomia). On IV antibiotics, her confusion spreads to her sense of identity. Her husband, a physician, has wearied of his wife's condition, and is exploring other relationships. Recently, when I talked to this patient by phone because she was hooked up to her home IV, she noticed I had a mild cold. Her response was, "Who is going to take care of you up there?"

This response manifests anomia and anomie, as it refers to her lapsing sense of identity. If she is not at home in her own head up there, then who is going to take care of her identity? If her husband leaves her, who is going to take care of her in her home? In order to maintain her professional identity, she needs to take care of others. Her concern for me is confused with her concern with herself. Because she has mild dementia and delirium, her expression is confused. I think she senses she may be unable to solve her problems of daily living in a way that is compatible with her identity in the future.

Another patient, a seventy-five-year-old man with Alzheimer's disease, who had a previous history of a delusional disorder, is afraid to leave his house because he thinks the Mafia has sent an alligator to swallow him. This delusion explains to him how it is that he is losing his brain, his mind, and his identity. Without the delusion, there is only chaos.

Because our brains build our identities in stages, we have to have a way of building on our past sense of identity as well as holding on to information we need to go on solving problems. The integrity of the brain is assaulted by physiological processes, injury, psychological trauma, as well as its genetically programmed syndromes and obsolescence. I will present a case that illustrates a woman trying to deal with all these assaults. This woman lost the organic capacity to maintain her maturity.

A Modern Clytemnestra

A fifty-year-old Greek woman, a concerned mother and devoted wife, whom we will call Clytemnestra, had a heart valve repaired for the third time in her life. She developed a high fever after the operation. When she recovered, her personality had changed. She had an affair with her younger daughter's fianceé. We will call her younger daughter Electra.

In our consultation, Clytemnestra said that her husband, whom we will call Agamemnon, had deserted her emotionally every ten years when her heart valve had been repaired, at thirty, forty, and fifty years of age. He would turn his attention to their daughters and son. Clytemnestra wondered if Electra became too close to Agamemnon. Before her last operation, she did not think that. Clytemnestra wanted me to tell her if that is why she had the affair with Electra's fianceé. Without waiting for an answer, she said that she had stopped the affair, only to pursue a devious associate of her husband's, whom we will call Aegesthus. She stalked Aegesthus, and had sex with him whenever he would agree.

Clytamenstra told me that her husband was now having an affair with a younger woman whom we will call Cassandra. Clytemnestra confronted Cassandra, who told her that she no longer had a right to Agamemnon. Clytemnestra told me that she lurks outside Cassandra's house to catch Agamemnon and Cassandra together and that she will kill them. She feels a fury rise in her chest and knows there is no turning back. Despite her wish to repair her relationship with Agamemnon, she cannot stay away from Aegesthus. She told me, unabashedly, that in the middle of her menstrual month it is "as if I have a hard-on for Aegethus."

Since Clytemnestra's high fever, her source memory became pellucid. Seeing a soda bottle on my desk as I administered her MSE, she said that my questions made her feel exactly as she did when her father, whom we will call Zeus, used to question her about her school work. When he was drunk with wine, he would penetrate her with questions. The questions felt like lightning bolts in her heart, and to her it was as if the lightning signalled impending death. Even in childhood, when she was anxious, her loose heart valve fluttered like a cygnette in her chest. And that is why she told me: the soda bottle was her father's retsina bottle and my questions stirred the same dread—despite knowing the soda was not retsina, and I was not her father.

Through this transference, Clytemnestra drew me into her story. She believed that her next operation would kill her, and she wondered if the present heart valve was holding. She thought perhaps her near-death experience had precipitated her personality change. She knew that her liaison with Aegethus would destroy her family. She wanted me to tell her something, or give her some medication that would still her anguish, but follow-up has shown there is no medication. Antidepressants were irrelevant, and shreds of anxiolytics only put her to sleep.

Like Damasio's patient, E.V.R., whose personality changed after his orbital frontal cortex was damaged, this patient has brain damage resulting from her operation and infection. She is impulsive and disinhibited. In this case, however, the patient's source memory is so vivid that her transference to me and to every other person in her life issues directly from it. In a state of disarray, her own executive is tragically unable to mobilize a reflective identity that can withstand the onslaught of all her source memories and her drives. Despite dynamic insight that would do Freud proud, Clytemnestra helplessly watches her tragedy unfold with the inexorable pace of a Greek chorus.

Unlike Damasio's patient, Clytemnestra knows that she has lost the capacity to withstand her own dynamics. Her orbital frontal assessments fail when source memories arouse her drives. Since Clytemnestra has no insurance, it is not yet possible to do the functional brain imaging and neuropsychological testing that would help us say more exactly where her brain is injured. There are real questions about what and when to tell her family.

We can say with some certainty that the combination of her injury and the family's dynamics unleashes the same forces that Aeschylus and Euripedes dramatized. As Freud taught us, and as he used myths to demonstrate, our source memories have universal dynamic configurations and similar biological and developmental roots. The Greek myths and their dramatizations, and Freud's insight contribute to the evolution of our social controls.

When our mythical student, Psyche, took her board-style examination, and diagnosed her patient's orbital frontal meningioma, there was hope for cure. Psyche and Freud together could not reverse the course of Clytemnestra's brain's tragedy. That would take the mythical Zeus's turning the sun around in the sky to make time and space course backward.

Before we turn our attention to methodically surveying how to assess the tragic brain as it goes about forging human identity, under conditions of organic duress, let us make *subjective* time course backward for a while. Let us address the markers people use to keep track of their past identity organizations. This will be useful when we want to distinguish between organic, syndromatic, and emotionally traumatic effects on source memory.

A DIAGNOSTIC PSYCHOLOGY OF PERSONAL TIME

Stage changes universally trigger the formation of fantasies and constructs that contain *personal identity markers*. In the sophisticated diagnostic interview, we ask the patient to tell early memories, recurrent memories, present dreams, recurrent dreams, and the nature of adolescent masturbation fantasies. Recurrent dreams, fantasies, and screen memories carry stage-organizing, imbedded source memories.

Just as an exogenously traumatized person develops an endless flow of images, dreams, and memories that both screen the trauma and reveal it, so stage changes' endogenous traumata also give rise to compelling images, dreams, and screen memories. These images, dreams, and screen memories recur with variations. Each stage—infancy, young childhood, oedipal, latency, adolescence—has characteristic imagoes that occupy our unconscious life.

In the diagnostic interview, we want to understand how the brain talks to itself as it manifests its phenomenology of personal stage marker. The experience of timelessness is one of the markers. Consciousness emerges from infancy's timelessness. The realization that our consciousness has emerged from a timeless period leads to wishes for respite and nonbeing when We are beset by misfortune. For some, the quest for meaning in philosophy or religion is a quest for a more encompassing identity, that might provide comfort and reassurance.

PTSD, schizophrenic, and bipolar patients can all lose their sense of sourced time and experience timelessness. Patients with major depression often experience slowing in subjective time (Blewett, 1992). Freud equated timelessness with "the return of the repressed"—experience that had been buried in the dynamic unconscious. Our patient, Clytemnestra, dramatically demonstrated Freud's point when she lost the organic capacity to repress. Earlier, we hypothesized that in the near-death experiences, timelessness may correspond to extremely reduced glutamate transmission by the hippocampus and amygdala when neuromodulation blocks their NMDA receptors. When experience is under or overprocessed our time sense is impaired.

When a schizophrenic person regresses to reexperience an initial symbiosis, he loses his sense of subjective time. Every experience is as novel as it was in infancy, and he reexperiences the first kingdom. Thus, a schizophrenic patient may say he is ninety-nine-years-old, ageless, or newborn. *Psychosis is a new beginning in identity.* This is why the schizophrenic is often an existentialist or other type of philosopher. His sources of being are reflected upon within an impoverished state of adult identity.

Early childhood is filled with disconnected, *episodic memories* that link self and object with affect. The prototype of episodic, organizing memory is the *primal scene.* It gives birth to the new reality of an objectified self. The eighteen-month-old child immerses for the first time in a primal scene where her belief in transitional objects fails completely, and she clings to her newly detached observing consciousness as if she were a survivor of the *Titanic* clinging to a life raft.

This detached observation of one's own objectified self is what I call a *primal screen source memory.* If a person's first memory is being alone, screaming in the crib, but no one comes, we can infer that autonomy and abandonment issues will be paramount in diagnosis and treatment. One patient recalls escaping from a dream of falling into the burls of her cherry wood crib. She was enormously pleased to find herself sitting safely and alone on the mattress. Her life raft will carry her through.

"Abandon all hope, all ye who enter here." When the life raft does not hold, an adult with severe depression cannot shake his sense of falling into an *immersion state,* where personal identity is abandoned. Patients with major depression feel they are in a deep hole, from which there is no escape. All available source memories are the same, prototypically, crying alone in the crib and losing the self. The aggression and pain expressed in lamentations of abandonment reveal the patient's self-centeredness. Depressed patients immerse, licking their wounds. Emerging from depression, patients may enjoy regressive versions of a nursing experience, or begin to eat ravenously.

Event-sourced memory begins during the oedipal period when the *second signal system* provides higher level prefrontal assessment of motor representations that enables anticipation of the future. Oedipal fantasy play makes story narration a new way to keep track of subjective time. Although we create stories in retrospect to explain what happened to form our goals and beliefs and to stabilize our subjective sense of identity, the stories we narrate to ourselves and others feel like they predict the future. Fantasy becomes a second immersion state that can internalize elements of screen memories. The fantasy state is disconnected from the initiation of action and fantasy is distinguished from reality by reality testing—fantasy testing. An overabundant fantasy state is the hallmark of neurosis.

The sophisticated diagnostician will try to form an impression of the patient's prevailing fantasy life, and how important it is to him. The neurotic may, Walter Mitty–like, or *Dungeons and Dragons*–like, enter into fantasies of heroic performance, of rescuing, being rescued, etc. Nowadays many people enter into hours-long, hypnotic immersion in Internet or computer games, as their screen memories and fantasies of finding comprehensive solutions are entrained in their computer.

We are all aware of sometimes entering a *fantasy state* while studying. Examination anxiety suspends cognition and holds our identity in thrall. Time goes by as it does in sleep, and we suddenly realize we are staring at the same page, woolgathering about something else. Reality testing (fantasy testing) revives our cognitive processing when identity anxiety in our daydream suddenly relates to the cognitive problem solving. As we emerge from the fantasy state, the fantasy itself may be almost inaccessible. If we are astute, it occurs to us that examination or performance anxiety launched us into the fantasy state. We are then aware that the fantasy we just had was a way out.

Like dreams in sleep, fantasy states are disconnected from the action system, from inner speech, from articulatory rehearsal, from short-term memory, and from working memory. Registered, but incompletely processed data flows directly into fantasy as it does into hallucinations. A fantasy state is a regression to an oedipal way of experiencing subjective life as a story. Like a dreamer, a fantasizer is in touch with event-sourced memory, as that memory shapes the ongoing fantasy.

Fiction writers immerse in fantasy to find the avenues they wish to express in their fiction. Many fictional dramatizations use linguistic devices to show the creator's entrance into, and emergence from, fantasy mixed with event-sourced recollection. The *Custom House* essay that begins Hawthorne's *Scarlet Letter* is a notable example. It is about Hawthorne's attempt to find a source of material that will launch him into a productive literary fantasy (Harris and Harris, 1981).

To mine the treasure trove of subjective fantasy life in our diagnostic interview, we use the device of asking the patient to tell us about a book he has read, a play or movie he has seen, a television show he likes, or a favorite joke. We note the fantasy imbedded in the material and take the patient as the main character in his narration. The story will be a metaphor for the patient's own life, and his difficulty in resolving ongoing conflicts.

"It is only from the sixth or seventh year onward . . . that our lives can be reproduced in memory as a connected chain of events" (Freud, 1899, p. 303). The *latency child* never tires of hearing about her parents' childhoods. The comparison broadens the context of her own past. Drawing on the *capacity for continuous personal time,* the latency child thinks about historical time. Not only is she interested in her own past but in a mythology of her own past.

We expect a latency child to be cognitively focused. Intense immersion or fantasy states in latency that interfere with cognitive development often accompany physical trauma or sexual, fixating experiences. If a latency child seems to be in a world of her own, we may assume that her sense of experience is currently being overwhelmed. We may hypothesize that an adult who does not remember his latency has been abused or seduced in latency. *An inner silence, where there should be memories of latency, is a mark of abuse.* When an adult patient insists that he had "a happy childhood," I always wonder.

In latency, event and episode source memories intertwine with fantasies and screens. Children, especially abused children, often compensate themselves for feelings of degradation, or for feelings that their talents and capacities are overlooked, by creating a personal mythology that ties their origins to great figures. Artists and paranoids have a history of these very intense *family romance fantasies in their latency* (Freud, 1909). Family romance mythologies may reappear in paranoid delusions or in artistic works. Typically, a child who had been homosexually abused in childhood became a homeless schizophrenic adult who lived in a delusional family romance world, believing he was the son of a great American hero. Central Park belonged to him. *Family romance fantasies and screens characterize latency.*

Adolescence is characterized by an unsensed future. When an adolescent asks whether there is any noise if a tree falls in the forest, he is asking a highly egocentric question: "Do I have any impact on the world?" Adolescents tend to feel that their personal time does not coincide with actual time. This phenomenon is inherent in many adolescent suicide attempts. They do not understand that there will be survivors, possibly including their own adult selves, who will have to cope with their acts. When their peers commit suicide, they have difficulty separating their own sense of identity from their dead companion's.

During adolescence, *emotionally organizing masturbation fantasies shape emerging sexual identity.* If we are unsure about a person's sexual orientation, and often a person is himself unsure, the nature of his adolescent sexual fantasies is the most direct evidence we can find for the real nature of his sexual orientation. In order to be tactful, and not to arouse defenses concerning sexual issues, it is best to begin by asking some general questions such as, "How is your romantic life? What was it like as a teenager? What did you dream it would be like then?"

If an adolescent has tattoos or dresses oddly, or wears nose rings, tongue rings, or nipple rings, we can see these icons as an attempt to reinforce an emerging change in intrapsychic identity. We want to inquire gently into the meaning of the iconography and relate that to the adolescent's identity crisis or gender identity disorder. If a tattoo is a self-portrait, we may hypothesize narcissistic compensation; if it is "mother," and if the person is a machoman, we may hypothesize a denied dependency.

Attention

The *tragic brain* cannot reflect on its problems and how to solve them. We are about to embark on a technical journey of how to study organic disruptions in how the brain talks to itself while solving problems. The journey will provide a context for understanding the disruptions. It is up to the reader to grasp how to apply these understandings in the MSE portion of the diagnostic interview. I will, however, fully apprise the reader when I feel I have an original contribution to make to MSE phenomenology.

To keep body and soul together, our executive has to deal with many possible kinds of cognitive disruption. To be fully awake while doing so, the executive requires four consecutive *As:* (1) *alerting*, (2) *arousal*, (3) *awareness*, and (4) *attention* (Seib, 1990). We will take these up in turn . . . as the brain does.

1. *Any sensory signal alerts the reticular activating system* (RAS). The nonspecific nuclei of the thalamus convey RAS signals to the limbic cortex and the neocortex. Alerting facilitates the rhinal cortex's registration at p100, (Bruder et al., 1992). The ascending RAS also alerts the locus ceruleus. In the "what is it" vigilance response to novelty, the locus ceruleus feeds activation back and forth with the RAS and the nonspecific nuclei of the thalamus (Luria, 1980).
2. The alerted locus ceruleus' norepinephrine system activates the amygdala, which in turn recruits the ventral tegmental dopamine system. Together, *the two catecholamine drive systems arouse the prefrontal system to work.*
3. Conscious semantic and perceptual *awareness* begins at p300, up to a second before attention engages (Polich and Donchin, 1988). Awareness prepares the basal ganglia to mediate behavior (Sieb, 1990). Awareness also prepares the parietal cortex to provide context for actions yet to be taken.
4. Thalamic signals derived from the alerting, arousal, and awareness systems engage prefrontal *attention*. With help from the cerebellum, the prefrontal attention system selects lexical and perceptual items,

the contents of short-term-memory. To make the point psychoanalytically, attention hypercathects qualities of consciousness necessary for thought.

Thus, *functional consciousness* depends on:

- *Alertness*—simple readiness to register data of all kinds
- *Arousal*—drive activation for problem solving
- *Awareness*—working memory's data processing
- *Attention*—selective assessment of working memory

When we test attention in the MSE, we assess the patient's capacity to maintain a *focused, working alliance.* Attention requires RAS alerting, central acetylcholine facilitation, catecholamine arousal, serotonergic stabilization, neocerebellar selectivity, and prefrontally sustained effort and concentration. Functional consciousness is regulated by the prefrontal system's executive, supervisory and observant metafunctions. I find a sort of intellectual satisfaction in being able to relate neural system's higher cortical functions to metafunctions. Karl Jaspers, the father of phenomenology in psychiatry, did too.

The MSE questions, *Do you know who you are, where you are, and what day it is?* Address these metafunctions. Jaspers divided functional consciousness into three parts: (1) *awareness of experience,* (2) *self/object dichotomy,* and (3) *self-observant knowing* (1923). *Awareness of experience requires an intact left prefrontal system. Self/object dichotomy requires an intact bilateral prefrontal system. Self-observant knowing requires an intact right prefrontal system.*

DELIRIUM

To assess a patient's orientation to person, place, and time dimensions of functional consciousness (called the three spheres), the patient must be attentive, cooperative, and informed. A delirious patient shifts from oriented to subjectively impressionistic responses. If we ask the hospitalized patient, "Where are you now?" and he answers, "This is some kind of large building where people live, a hotel maybe," he's delirious.

Delirium is the inability to be awake enough to maintain focused communication. Inadequate *alerting* reduces the level of consciousness in a continuum stretching from delirium, to stupor, to coma. A delirious patient's wandering attention is caused by a definable metabolic pathology, often a medical illness, that interdicts medial or intermediate prefrontal system facilitation.

Moving to the pathology of arousal, *apathy* is left hemisphere inert *effort;* *indifference* is right hemisphere lackadaisical *concentration*. Left hemisphere strokes often cause apathy in their aftermath, while right hemisphere strokes cause indifference or disregard. Defects in awareness or attention cause *inattention*, the inability to selectively organize working memory's items. At a certain point in following the contribution of the four As to consciousness, we are hard pressed to distinguish delirium from dementia.

DEMENTIA

Technically, *dementia is cognitive dysfunction*. If the executive cannot organize data to solve problems because of organic inadequacy, semantic, perceptual or memorial defects occur. These cognitive functions are highly lateralized in the executive's prefrontal domain. As we have seen, each hemisphere provides either background or foreground to a particular cognitive function. For instance, the right hand gestures, while the left hand depicts the limits of that communication in the interpersonal air. Therefore, a knowledge of how the two hemispheres process information differently is necessary to a descriptive and pragmatic formulation of dementias. Subcortical dementias, such as those produced by many cases of vascular dementia (multi-infarct dementia), HIV dementia, or lime dementia have a spotty, collectively bilateral effect on cognition.

APHASIA

While dementia is a general term for cognitive dysfunction, distinct interference with inputs into left hemisphere higher cortical functions give rise to specific cognitive deficits:

- *apraxia:* inability to perform pragmatic acts such as tying one's shoes
- *agnosia:* inability to access what you know you know
- *aphasia:* inability to speak voluntarily

Interviewers may miss aphasia. An aphasic's disorganized speech may be mistaken for a psychotic's thought disorder. It is easy to make this mistake because aphasic patients may manifest apathy or euphoria, which mimic emotional dysfunction. One patient, for instance, had taken a designer drug which caused aphasia. She was diagnosed as psychotic until a functional brain imaging examination (SPECT) revealed an aphasia pattern. She had been unable to communicate that she had taken the street drug. As she recovered brain function over a period of months, her speech improved sufficiently that she could tell about taking the drug. The use of the SPECT exam spared her from being medicated with neuroleptics. Unfortunately, we often neglect to use this relatively inexpensive form of functional brain imaging.

The type of aphasia depends on which lateral systems are impaired. I will follow the definitions of aphasic language disturbance provided by Strub and Black in *The Mental Status Examination in Neurology* (1993). (The reader can find clinical examples of types of aphasia in that text.) Damage to the

- left, Broca's, prefrontal area disrupts spontaneous, fluent, *expressive speech.*
- left, Wernicke's superior temporal area impairs *comprehension* of aurally coded phonemes.
- left parietal cortex *disorganizes* complex grammar and syntax.
- right lateral prefrontal area impairs *imitative speech.*
- right superior temporal and parietal areas impairs the *reception of cadence and prosody.*
- right parietal area disrupts the *context for decoding metaphor.*

The difference between the left hemisphere's *operant* speech and the right's *procedural* speech can be dramatically seen in *global aphasics,* whose left hemispheres' expressive and receptive areas are both impaired. Global aphasics can produce a few stereotyped utterances. A global aphasic who cannot repeat, "I cannot," after the examiner, may say, "I cannot!" in exasperation. The exasperated utterance is the right hemisphere's affective ejaculation. Here, *the articulatory muscles are organized by a procedural, rather than by an operative function.*

Broca's aphasia manifests telegraphic, "nonfluent, dysarthric, effortful speech. The patient utters mostly nouns and verbs (high-content words) with a paucity of grammatical filters" (Strub and Black, 1993). Broca's area is therefore responsible for the smooth integration of inner speech's contribution to articulation. Broca's aphasics often show intense frustration and agitation, because, when the operative function is disrupted, communication cannot be consummated and their coherent identity is disturbed.

Wernicke's aphasia is "fluent, effortless, well-articulated speech. The output however, contains many paraphasias and is often devoid of substantive words. There is often a great press to speak" (Strub and Black, 1993). The uncomprehending Wernicke's aphasic communicates unaware of receptive deficit. Sensing that communication is going well, the person feels euphoric. Because they are unaware of the deficit, Wernicke's aphasics do not respond well to speech therapy. Perhaps in Wernicke's aphasia, consummatory signals are false positives, while in Broca's aphasia, they are blocked.

Simple anomia—forgetting words or names—from which I suffer, is a nonspecific indication of mild brain dysfunction that cannot be localized. Perhaps I should nevertheless undergo functional brain imaging while being asked to name the members of my department. That would be a large price for a small tragedy!

THE ORGANIC DISRUPTION OF METAFUNCTIONS

We can infer from our study of delirium and dementia as well as various neuro- and psychopathological syndromes that each can disorganize executive, supervisory, and observant metafunctions. Parkinson's disorder, for instance, can interfere with identity functions, as well as producing dysfunctional movement. The diagnostician has to distinguish among pathologies that can undermine the executive's reflective synthesis.

Subcortical dementias that interfere with immediate memory's registration or with working memory's precognition, also interfere with the prefrontal system's assessment. Discrete organic damage (e.g., stroke or tumor) that disturbs input into any of the prefrontal system's parallel processing networks reverberates in identity. This noticeably interferes with such metafunctions as knowing how memory is functioning (executive metamemory), apperception (observation of percepts), and anticipation of the future (supervision of plans).

CONCENTRATION AND EFFORT

The standard MSE assesses whether a fully conscious person can carry out a set task. We ask the patient to spell *world* backwards, or give the days of the week or months of the year in reverse order. Many students falsely test concentration with serial sevens (subtracting sevens consecutively from one hundred) by prompting the patient with "seven from that" and "seven from that." By prompting, the examiner may allay his own and the patient's anxiety, but he is not testing concentration. If we fail to pursue real phenomena, our MSE is unreliable.

We have to distinguish between the phenomena of effort and concentration when a person fails to carry through. As I said, *left hemisphere effort* and *right concentration* depend on available drive energy for their maintenance. I posit that effort and concentration measure libidinal and aggressive arousal, respectively. Effort maintains motivated behavior as a person initiates an action program. Effort requires sufficient dopamine and serotonin. Concentration maintains apperception as a person releases a response program. Concentration requires sufficient norepinephrine and scrotonin. Effort and concentration cannot be gauged unless the person's frontal lobes can monitor behavioral programs without retroactive (perseverative) interference from each last task segment.

MEMORY

Jaspers (1923) divided memory function into *registration, retention,* and *recall.* All three can be assessed in the MSE. Remember, though, that memory is an ambiguous term for a complex array of higher cortical functions. Let us review how different types of memory interact pragmatically.

Immediate Memory

Immediate memory (including after-images generated by sensory organs), multiply registers sense impressions. Within 200 msecs, sensory data is registered not only in the brain stem and in primary sensory cortices, but also in the thalamus, many secondary cortical association areas, in the rhinal cortex and the amygdala, in the basal ganglia, in the cerebellum, and multiply in the prefrontal and frontal cortex. Multiple data registration allows prefrontal distributed systems to work with corresponding data in their different networks.

Immediate memory forms contexts for intramodal and intermodal associations. For instance, in visual data gathering, color, shape, pattern, movement, and intensity are each intramodally configured in separate neural populations, and they are each intermodally associated with vestibular, aural, kinaesthetic, somesthetic and visceral sensations. As I understand it, during immediate memory, sense data are divided for refined analysis, while in later processing they are reconfigured, integrated, and synthesized to fit into potential structures of consciousness.

One aspect of immediate memory, *priming,* can extend all day. The rhinal cortex can hold primed, noncontextualized, nonattended data for potential entrance into associative context (see Chapter 2).

Working Memory

Once contextualized, data is processed in working memory's preassociated brain matrices, which are distributively linked to higher cortical functions. Working memory, the 300 to 600 msecs epoch creates items that can enter short-term memory. Our impression of how fast people process our communication, informs us about their working memory's function.

One adult patient had had a severe case of German measles, with high fever, at age six. He recalled that his father told him that after this fever, it would take him a long time to respond to verbal communications. Prior to this illness, he was a quick responder. As he grew up, people became impatient with him, and he was at a competitive disadvantage with his older brother, whom he had previously surpassed. The combination of slowed working memory and feelings of inadequacy caused the patient to become distractible and easily defeated. When I saw him at age thirty-nine, he had become a methodical person who was repairing his life by continuing his higher education.

Another patient was in an automobile accident at age sixteen, that left him in a coma for five days. The longer the coma, we know, the greater the likelihood of a general dementia, which manifests as slowed working memory. This patient developed auditory and visual hallucinations within a year of the accident. He was diagnosed as schizophrenic. Many years later, after he had been put on an antipsychotic medication, Clozaryl, his hallucinations stopped. He was able to return to school. On MSE, he had a slow, hesitant way of responding to questions. He had to check and recheck whether he had understood his instructions.

If one did not know the history of this patient's accident (and he had not been able to bring it up spontaneously before he had been put on Clozaryl) then, given his recurrent, troublesome hallucinations, his poverty of content, and slow, hesitant speech, one could easily diagnose him as having what DSM-IV calls *undifferentiated schizophrenia, episodic, with inter-episode residual symptoms and prominent negative symptoms.* Further examination, however, revealed that the patient had spunk and a sense of humor. These qualities and the fact that he had previously had visual as well as auditory hallucination tell us that the patient's closed head injury had caused both dementia and a propensity for psychotic disorganization. The fact is that such cases often have a better prognosis than cases of a slow endogenous slide into schizophrenia. This patient went on to complete college, where he mastered chemistry and calculus.

Short-Term Memory

Short-term memory (from 600 msecs to 30 seconds) coordinates the higher cortical functions that mediate between executive metafunctions and working memory. *Thought—articulatory rehearsal—resynthesizes the items in directed attention* during thirty-second episodes of short-term memory, beyond which we tend to forget what animated our thought in the first place, unless short-term memory is renewed.

Executive reflection renews attention, which leads to the reorganization of the contents of short-term memory, until a behavioral decision is reached. Luria (1972) describes a man who could go on reading and rereading a newspaper article that took thirty second to read, since he always forgot he had read it. This man's parahippocampus had been destroyed in World War II. He was unable to establish new memories.

When we give a standard short-term memory task such as remembering three objects, we are checking whether retention and recall are intact. Giving another three objects to remember before checking the first three examines whether the frontal lobes can renew the first set of data. The frontal lobes buffer items that must be kept available for problem solving during periods when attention is engaged elsewhere. *Tests of short-term memory access the reverberating circuits between short-term memory and frontal lobe action and response programs.* [1]

The research paradigm used to study short-term memory in its frontal renewal context is called *delayed response.* Delayed response occurs when the subject is in an expectant, consummatory state. When delayed response is measured by event-related potentials (ERP's), the subject is required to make a particular response when the target stimulus occurs. In delayed response tasks, the frontal lobes (including prefrontal areas) buffer— maintain activation of—short-term memory associations. ERP studies on working memory and short-term memory show that the frontal lobes augment predirected attention to *expected stimuli.*

A patient with left hemisphere, lateral-frontal damage cannot maintain sequenced programs. If we ask such a patient to remember three items and then ask her to remember three more, the first set proactively interferes with retention of the second. Thus, short-term memory is compromised by frontal lobe damage. When the left hemisphere's lateral-frontal lobe is damaged, even a slight increase in semantic complexity renders the patient unable to attend to stimuli necessary to discharge behavior.

Recent and Remote Memory

Tests of recent and remote memory are often used to gauge memory capacity. In this context, *recent memory refers to renewed short-term memory,* not to memory that has recently undergone consolidation and storage. *Consolidation and storage in intermediate memory occurs over a period of many hours. Remote memory usually refers to source memories*—events and episodes—that have been stored and consolidated weeks to years ago. Having recalled remote memories on many occasions, and having, therefore, generalized *semantic memory* to many different memory systems, it is hard for a person to know whether he is remembering his own verbal conclusions, false informations he has been told, or actual experience. *Flashbacks in trauma are episodes that have not been assimilated by semantic memory.*

When we check a person's capacity to store and retrieve recent memory, we need to ask questions that require the retrieval of newly learned, not habitual material. If we ask a patient what she ate for breakfast, her response may be to tell what she usually eats for breakfast. In one case, a woman with stroke damage to the rhinal cortex was unable to retrieve information about the new clothes she dressed her son in on the previous day. However, when her husband told what the clothes were, she could fill in details about what was worn, including colors and styles. Her incapacity for *retrieval* rendered her recent and remote memory anterograde to her stroke inaccessible.

When we ask a patient to renarrate a somewhat complex, emotional story we have just told him, we are checking to see if his retrieval, source memory, and semantic memory work properly together. Our tacit requirement is that he compare this story with all the other stories he has lived or heard. To renarrate a story, such as the one (which the reader may remember) of the crow who changed colors in a time of famine, the patient will have to use his habitual way of using source memories to come to conclusions about the meaning of new events. When repeating a sequenced narrative, patients with left rhinal cortex damage cannot order the events. When we ask a person with comparable right damage to tell the emotional lesson of a story, he cannot.

When a person brings new salient or significant items into articulatory rehearsal he begins the process of consolidating short-term memory. He is *learning* the new material. Studied repetition produces learning by inducing *intermediate-term memory*, which is data on its way to becoming source memory.

The phrase, "That did not register on me," indicates that a person is preoccupied, inattentive, or incapable of registering or processing new data. If my wife says something to me while I am writing this material, I am preoccupied and put her utterance on hold. Psychic trauma, drugs, or brain damage impede hippocampal registration or processing. For example, by its action on the NMDA glutamate receptor, phencyclidine (PCP) distorts registration and processing. In my clinical experience, patients who have taken phencyclidine, and who have had a bad trip merge present experience with past trauma.

Benzodiazepines and other sedatives can impair registration by facilitating GABA receptors, which inhibit excitation in the amygdala and hippocampus. They can block new learning, and even induce retrograde amnesia. Think of asking yourself one day after taking a sleeping pill on the plane, "How did I get to Europe?" One patient who has severe pain because of orthopedic injuries, and who is taking opiates for the pain, becomes amnesic and acts out aggressively at night when given benzodiazepine sleeping medication. Overactive GABA receptors block the CA 3 glutamate receptors that induce context in recent registrations.

Data can register without our noticing it. *Tachistoscopic data* (flashed faster than we can process), for instance, can be implicitly registered. Later, the data may enter dream formation. This is known as the *Poetzl phenomenon*. When frontal or prefrontal system damage renders the reflection on attended data impossible, executive functions such as metamemory are compromised. Unreflected information is irretrievable.

Metamemory

The question, "How is your memory?" gauges metamemory. Metamemory is an executive metafunction that is necessary for prolonged problem solving. *Metamemory, the reflective coordination of memory functions, renews short-term memory in the context of behavioral readiness.* This means that metamemory keeps track of the principle of proposed action. Patients with *Korsakoff's syndrome* (alcoholic organicity that impairs the limbic system's capacity to form new source memory) also lose their frontal capacity for metamemory. As contrasted with patients who have multi-infarct dementia, they do not realize their incapacity. You will find them at bars renarrating their old source memory, such as their war experiences, repetitiously.

Executive metamemory reflectively assesses the outcome of behaviors. The executive uses semantic memory, located in the lateral frontal and prefrontal cortex, to deduce plans and rules. *Plans are left hemisphere operative sequences and their verbal equivalents. Rules are the right hemisphere's procedural programs. They can be translated into verbal form.* Metamemory compares outcomes of action and response programs with the plans and rules for their conduct.

The executive uses frontal action and response programs to select and switch the *principle of action*. As we work on an extended task, we consciously divide these programs into practiced segments. Our executive checks these programs, as we reflectively interrupt our articulatory rehearsal to ask, "How am I doing?" The answer selectively modifies short-term memory items according to what is required for progress. Frontal deficits interfere with the capacity for renewal of short-term memory items that are needed for program completion.

If the writer of this text decides that he is not really communicating, he can reflect on how he is violating the rules he had set for himself. One of the rules was: if the material is too dense and abstract, use a metaphor to reenforce the point. Better yet, get someone to read the material and see if it comes across. The last time I did that, Dr. Balasz told me I needed to use more metaphor and to simplify the material even more. "If he cannot understand it, nobody can," I thought.

Executive reflection provides a semantic foreground for all of the pre-frontal zone's assessments. Thus, emotional, socially conditioned, verbal, and perceptual data are normally synthesized by executive reflection before the brain undertakes behavior. Even without functional brain imaging, we can make an educated guess about which prefrontal networks are compromised in particular neuropsychiatric syndromes.

We know clinically, for instance, that individuals become impulsive when the conditioned social networks assessed in the orbital frontal cortex are damaged. They can no longer use their past social lessons to regulate behavior. As we saw in our mythical board examination of diagnostic interviewing skills (see Chapter 3), when behavior is driven by needs alone, social lessons are disregarded. However, what kind of memory animates past social lessons that regulate behavior?

Source Memory (Emotionally Organized Long-Term Memory)

A consideration of source memory takes us into the heart of psychoana-lytic knowledge about human dynamic development. A brief developmental history helps the diagnostician sample the emotional forces that determined the patient's personality. We can count on the presence of a *central organizing conflict* that enters into (almost) every situation that leads a person to the psychiatric emergency room or to the therapist's door.

Conditioned experience leaves emotional tendencies in its wake. The examiner can sense an individual's *basic transference* by evaluating the patient's trust or distrust, optimism or pessimism, empathy or nonempathy, self-observation or self-disregard. A patient's transference often reenacts seminal source memories that make his emotionally conditioned experience directly available to his cognition. Pragmatically, *source memory is the capacity to recall the event or episode which gave rise to a particular emotionally organizing experience.*

The smell and taste of Proust's tea and madeleine (assessed no doubt in his insular cortex), brought him back into contact with source memories of his childhood experience of his mother. He needed that contact to initiate writing his *Remembrance of Things Past* (1924). When source memory aids problem solving, an individual can recollect his experience in tranquility. After he fully remembered what it was like in his childhood, there was no end to the memories that Proust resurrected and the lessons he learned from his reminiscences.

If we cannot remember the source, we have to rely too much on conditioned somatic signals of anxiety and emotion. We are also left with the *assumptive world's* cognitive organizers: semantic memory's generalized beliefs, values, standards, rules, goals, conclusions, judgments, and insights.

We cannot use old experience to form new lessons for the present. As we will see, sourcing memory is essential to diagnosing trauma and abuse.

If each new life stage begins with endogenous fixation or trauma, then, *each life stage leaves both conditioned tendencies and highly activated source memories in its wake.* These source memories contribute to our capacity to locate events and episodes in personal time, so that each individual has access to a sense of historical identity. As we age, intense experiences in our earlier life remain viable organizers of present experience, and indeed, as we age, we rely more on old source memory than we do on fresh emotional experience to solve our problems.

What Is Your Earliest Memory?

Patients who overcelebrate anniversaries of particular events are often depressed, or, the events are the screens for trauma. *Anniversary reactions and holidays are affect-laden reminders of painful social and interpersonal episodes.* Happy memories often screen unbearable disappointments or trauma. Consider a vignette of a patient who watched her younger sister being hit and killed by a truck just before Thanksgiving. As an adult, this patient dreamed of a happy turkey dinner when she was thinking about visiting her parent's house for Thanksgiving. Unfortunately, her sister was the turkey. In association to the dream, the patient expressed terror that if she were not eternally vigilant, her own daughter would be killed as her younger sister was.

Another patient said that her earliest memory was of when she was six years old, and seeing herself standing in her yard as her father backed his car out of the driveway. Her father hit her three-year-old sister, who was on her tricycle in the driveway. What she remembers after that is her sister being rushed to the hospital, and then the years of her parents' attention and concern for her sister, while she had to raise herself. Her lifetime dynamics were imbedded in this source memory.

In both of the above examples, a patient had developed difficulty in allowing herself to win a competition with other women. Both patients were inordinately guilty. Neither one felt entitled to enjoy her life. Learning to plumb the sources of present-day emotional experience to diagnose and treat neurotic conflicts, much less trauma, abuse, and seduction is not easy; it requires a familiarity with developmental dynamics.

SCREEN MEMORIES AND TRAUMA

In this era of social disorganization, social and family violence and abuse have increased exponentially. Therefore, we have to alertly diagnose PTSD and other syndromes that follow in the wake of trauma and abuse. To *reconstruct* abuse, we have to distinguish screen memories from source memories. As Freud originally defined them, screen memories are innocent memories that stand in the place of traumatic source memories (1899).

Freud noted that the hallmark of trauma is the presence of the self as an observer who is detached from experience in the screen memory or dream. *Detachment is the essence of the neurobiological and emotional defense against trauma.* Detachment is manifested in overgeneralization. A person who has no memories of a period of life, such as latency—only general impressions or unsourced memories—has probably been traumatized or abused during that period. A person, moreover, who speaks uncommonly much in metaphors, or in game parlance, is probably protecting himself from both the memories of and the sense of repetition of abuse. *Metaphors are the observer's refuge from trauma.*

A thirty-seven-year-old man presented to therapy because of fears of entering new business relationships. This interfered with his capacity to advance in the business world. His speech was full of metaphors, and he spoke about his plans in the language of game strategy. He dreaded interruption by the therapist because he could not stand to have something presented to him that he had not already thought of.

Analysis revealed that when he was growing up, his older brother, who was brain damaged and impulsive, would suddenly threaten to kill him or attack him. When he would complain to his mother, who worked until ten every night, she would side with her brain-damaged son. The patient feared the introduction of novelty, as anything could take him by surprise and threaten his existence. He also feared that if his own angry responses ever got unleashed, his retaliation would be complete. He walked on eggshells. His metaphorical speech and chesslike approach to life defended against retraumatization, contained his anger, and maintained his survival strategies. His memory of latency was almost void, just a few vague impressions of his brother's attempting to choke him to death.

When we perform a MSE, we ask the patient to narrate early memories. Often these memories are screens laden with dynamics, which composite intense memories with innocent impressions. The fit between innocent and intense memory betrays relevant dynamics.

Abused Ministers

As a consultant to pastoral counselors, I often saw ministers who chose their profession as a way of working out childhood sexual and physical abuse. By ministering to the wounded flock, they hoped to repair their own wounded inner child. These ministers often felt that God's perfect identity subsumed their fractured personal identity. In these cases, faith covered and fed on screen memories of abuse. God, the father or mother, glorified painful parental relationships. A faith that God will protect the victim from further abuse is extremely common among traumatized people. That we are all in God's hands is an article of faith for the abused members of AA and similar self-help, twelve-step programs.

As abused children, many ministers felt it their job to mediate for the whole family, which later became the whole congregation. Many of these ministers combined an emotional intensity, a high level of abstraction, a high capacity for metaphorical communication, and a pervasive desire to help others who are in the midst of trauma. Sensory permeability, emotional intensity, highly abstracted identity, a reliance on imagery in communication, and absent boundaries from others who are hurting typifies the adult life of abused children.

Therapy with abused persons shows that episodes of trauma give rise to an unending imagery stream. Recall the case of Eurydyce, the sexually abused woman who recurrently produced poetic, innocent images of bathing, that belied her swimming in the ocean during a hurricane and whitewater rafting in inadequate vessels. Symbolically, her transference response to her abuse transformed me as her therapist into a mermaid/merman, as I sat with my crossed legs resting on a hassock.

In their most condensed form, images and metaphors of abuse form symbols. *Symbols deal consciously with traumatic material that's otherwise too hot to handle.* The serpent-headed gorgon, Medusa, of Greek mythology shows how symbolism contains trauma. One look at Medusa turned men to stone. Athena turned Medusa's hair to snakes in order to embody her as a living horror, after Medusa had been raped by Neptune; Medusa's snaky hair conveys the image of a multiple female phallus, that hides the traumatic image of castration from the viewer. Compelled to use this kind of symbolism, many traumatized people become artists, writers, therapists, or fetishists so that they can vicariously deal with and be detached from the source memories of their own trauma.

Freud concluded that *repetition-compulsion is an attempt to master trauma* (1919). He reasoned that the ego needs to repair breeches in its integrity by repeating traumatic experiences until they can be mastered. Eurydyce, who was raped at age twelve by the man who bathed and seduced her in her latency, recurrently put herself in dangerous water. She dramatizes the force of the compulsion to reenact and master trauma.

Women who had abusive, alcoholic fathers and masochistic, fearful mothers often recreate these conditions in their own married life. "Codependent" women often identify with appeasing mothers and victimized children, and they tolerate and expect spousal abuse. Fearful mothers themselves, they allow their spouse or boyfriend to victimize their children. In this way, the vicious circle of childhood is recreated. The woman's overt identification with the victim, and covert identification with the aggressor takes the place of authentic identity.

In diagnosing traumatic abuse then, we look for signs of:

- detachment,
- cognitive overgeneralization,
- sensory and emotional oversensitivity and intensity,
- creative pressure,
- metaphorical speech,
- repetition-compulsion,
- repetitious dreams, and
- codependent, boundaryless relationships.

METAPHOR

A metaphor is an unstated comparison. The capacity for metaphor requires intact right hemisphere prefrontal networks. *Metaphor is a product of the observer's capacity to appropriately use socialized self-observation to generalize about a variety of episodic source memories.* From its three experiential networks, the observer generalizes: affect (self), rules (social self), and lessons (procedural self). When we interpret a phrase such as "Don't put all your eggs in one basket," we elicit several affect-laden images from episodic memory. These have to be unified into a socially relevant lesson and then translated into suitable verbal communication. If the patient just says the eggs will break, he cannot generalize rules from painful lessons.

The famous mental status proverb, "People who live in glass houses should not throw stones," is so compelling to paranoid patients that they cannot resist personalizing it. Typically, a paranoid person answers, "People cannot hurt me when they know I can get even." Paranoid vulnerability is often expressed in attacking speech. For patients with delusional disorder, paranoid personality, or paranoid schizophrenia, the image of breaking glass elicits a dreaded breaking of subjective boundaries. These patients feel that their identities are so fragile and their projections so vital, they cannot resist throwing the first stone that will reverberate to shatter their identities. The paranoid's answer is not a right hemisphere type of deficiency in metaphoric interpretation, rather it is an overly subjectified left hemisphere interpretation.

ABSTRACTION

The MSE tests a patient's right hemisphere's prefrontal lateral capacity for abstraction. Can the patient understand that two or more objects fit into the same general category? An orange and an apple, for instance, are both fruit. If we simply ask, "How are an orange and an apple alike?" what are we to make of the response "They are both round" or "They both have seeds?" We can prompt that "They are both fruit," and go on to ask how a telegram, a letter, and a telephone call are alike.

Categorical abstraction tests whether a patient has ever developed this capacity. Patients who are unable to let go of the evoked sensory image remain concretely fixed to it. A moderately retarded patient is likely to say concretely, "The orange is orange and the apple is red," and "The letter is something you write on, and a telephone is something you talk on." We can easily miss the fact that a patient is retarded if we gloss over testing abstraction.

SOCIAL JUDGMENT

An executive prelude to decisive action, social judgment is the capacity to behave appropriately. It requires understanding the social consequences of our decisions. We know that the *orbital frontal cortices inform social judgment by assessing socially conditioned somatic signals.*

The judgment question on the MSE is often "What would you do if you found a stamped, addressed envelope on the street?" In modern urban settings, the answer as often as not is something such as, "I would check to see if there was any money in it. If there was no money, I would probably mail it." This is not a sociopathic response. It shows adequate peer-related knowledge of what is socially appropriate. We should try to tailor judgment questions to the expected experience of the patient. If he is on welfare we might ask, "What would you do if your welfare check did not arrive?" If the patient is a doctor we might ask, "What would you do if your managed care claim was wrongfully denied?"

The impulsivity question on the MSE is often, "What would you do if you smelled smoke and saw evidence of a fire while you were in a movie theater?" An impulsive, frontally impaired patient who is unable to resist the image of fire would say, "I would run." The *frontal lobe syndrome* impairs impulse control when the left hemisphere's orbital cortex is damaged, and it impairs the capacity to regulate the appropriate communication of affects when the damage is in the right hemisphere's orbital cortex.

Patients who have undergone a prefrontal leucotomy (severing the thalamic connections to the orbital cortex) for intractable, serious psychopathology develop a frontal lobe syndrome. They cannot assess the consequences of past actions in their judgment about present ones. Clinically, I have noticed that patients with left hemisphere leucotomies lose subjective context for their source memory. Personal, historical time collapses. They do not know when events occurred in relation to other events.

People with orbital frontal damage develop impaired judgment

> due to an inability to activate somatic states linked to punishment and reward that were previously experienced in association with specific social situations, and that must be reactivated in connection with anticipated outcomes of response options. (Damasio, Tramel, and Damasio, 1990, p. 81)

The patients neither attended to, nor responded autonomically to socially significant, alarming stimuli.

ERP studies of sociopaths show their *diminished arousability*. Unlike normals, sociopaths respond the same to emotional words as they do to neutral ones (Williamson et al., 1991). Is this why some children with conduct disorders cannot be socially conditioned by reward and punishment? Many sociopaths are organically unable to develop the executive metafunctions that places decisions in an emotional, moral, and social context.

Like sociopaths, borderlines are unable to observantly integrate affect knowledge of social relationships. Judgment, executive reflection, and the observant capacity to modulate social responses through affect signals are notably diminished in borderline patients. There are some similarities between borderlines and sociopaths in terms of borderline's frequent antisocial or asocial behavior patterns. ERP studies show that borderlines are slower than normals in both registering and evaluating information (Kutcher et al., 1987; Drake, Phillips, and Pakalnis, 1991). Thus, borderline patients have less integrated signals upon which to base their decisions.

TWO KINDS OF INSIGHT

Insight includes a person's capacity

- to know he is ill, and
- to understand the cause and consequences of this illness.

Insight determines a person's right to enter into all social, economic, interpersonal, and legal contracts. If the patient understands the reason for the MSE, the chances are that she has insight. Insight is a product of all three metafunctions. It is the capacity to know that one is a socially functioning person.

Impaired self-observation is caused by *organic*—dramatically presented in anosagnosia (not to know that the left side is paralyzed)—or *dynamic* problems in any of the right hemisphere's experiential loops. Insight is absent when the observer cannot assess the significance of data. Since the patient cannot know this, the examiner must infer it.

In major depression, the right hemisphere's prefrontal assessment, rhinal cortical data registration, and working memory are all slowed. This impairs the observer's ability to know what is wrong. The depressed patient often loses track of his depression as it deepens. Depression seems forever. In schizophrenia, the attention system is deficient, and this impairs insight. Chronic alcoholics gradually lose the organic capacity to know that they are alcoholics. Insight can be impaired for organic or emotional reasons in many syndromes.

Chapter 13

A Manual of Structural Therapy

He that has and a little tiny wit,—
With hey, ho, the wind and the rain,—
Must make content with his fortunes fit,
Though the rain it raineth every day.

From *King Lear,*
William Shakespeare

When Lear relinquished dominion over his own mind, he relinquished sovereignty over his external kingdom. Lear had created a world that extended his healthy narcissism. His failing narcissism led him to relinquish the source of his love, as he renounced Cordelia, the one daughter who was ruled by love. In the interpersonal, social, political, and economic disintegration that followed, Lear's capacity to maintain his coherence was tested by a great symbolic storm. Like Lear, we are permeable to interpersonal, social, political, and economic feedback from a world we help to create. We lose our minds if we do not hold on to just one wit, one piece of our true identity.

As King Lear's fool (who spoke the above words), a therapist who treats people who have faulty egos helps to preserve one piece of identity to rebuild the whole. Patients who respond to adversity with illusions, false hopes, or hopelessness lose their integrity. A therapist who can share a little humor with the patient, however, can anticipate a favorable outcome. Chapter 13 asks how therapists can be one-tenth as smart as King Lear's fool. How can we offer a stable perspective to patients buffeted by relentless stress?

To do *structural therapy,* you have to know how to do therapy—and make some choices. Structural therapy unifies several therapies: *supportive, cognitive, family systems, dynamic reconstruction, and pharmacological interventions.* Structural therapy uses positive transference to reenforce the cognitive rationale for a patient's sense of human coherence. It uses negative transference to inform the therapist and patient how to target reconditioning.

Why should we formulate a new type of therapy when there is nothing wrong with the old ones? Living in an era of social disorganization, economic polarization, and endemic abuse and trauma, we have to tailor therapy to the types of patients who succumb to adversity. We also have to tailor it to managed care, which mandates periodic, brief interventions, that can help the individual remain functional.

Conventional diagnosis does not offer guidelines to the treatment of patients who suffer from the following disorders:

PTSD and Its Sequelae

We lack diagnostic categories for people who have been sexually or physically abused in childhood. As adults, they are frequently treated for depression, anxiety disorders, or even bipolar disorder because of the volatility in their emotional lives.

Cognitive Disorders Secondary to Various Organic Causes

People who grow up in violent surroundings, where the future may stop on a dime, frequently abuse opiates or alcohol, which impair brain function. Another cohort of narcissistically deprived individuals try to replace a lack of appropriate maturational stimulation with drug stimulation. They often take refuge in cocaine, marijuana, hallucinogens, "ecstasy," or "angel dust."

Psychotic Conditions That Are "Not Otherwise Specified"

Perhaps most of the patients admitted to acute inpatient services are psychotic, but they do not fit easily into a single conventional category of diagnosis. These patients often suffer from a perplexed and confused sense of identity. Their human coherence is not up to the task of dealing with the world.

Chronic, Stress-Related Depressions

Many dysthymic individuals develop a chronically pessimistic outlook that defends against interpersonal, family, social, and economic situations. Their dysthymia places them in a bind that resembles restraint stress. Their sense of identity is impaired, at the same time that they can latently cognize both their own situation and that of their surrounding in an accurate and perceptive manner.

Relatively Severe Mixed Personality Disorders

This diagnosis roughly corresponds to the designation "young adult chronics," which was popular in the 1980s. The patients have tended to give up leading conventional lives. Manifesting a mixture of dependent, borderline, narcissistic, sociopathic, impulsive, and masochistic traits, these individuals find that no social support system tolerates their behavior.

Many patients mix these "diagnostic" entities. Nevertheless, patients' impairments can be structurally formulated: i.e., which prefrontal identity zone contributes most to their impairment can be identified and studied

HOW TO MAKE A STRUCTURAL DIAGNOSIS

To proceed with structural therapy, the therapist begins by formulating a structural diagnosis. This formulation determines

- which hemisphere triggers syndrome formation, and which zones within each hemisphere are drawn into the formation of pathology.
- whether syndrome formation is due to excitotoxicity or defenses against excitotoxicity.
- whether the patient's problem arises from rigid conditioning, prolonged stress, or a current disequilibrium in interpersonal, family, social, or economic relationships.

We can assess characteristic phenomena that each hemisphere manifests. Here are a series of questions to ask.

The Agent in the Left Hemisphere Lateral Zone

- How strong and flexible are the individual's belief systems?
- How well can the individual formulate his goals and priorities?
- Is this person verbally inchoate?
- Can this person use computers and other tools pragmatically?
- Can he cogently and sequentially narrate his life events?

We can gauge the strength of a person's agency by answering such questions. *Poor agency suggests that the therapist use cognitive approaches to help the patient increase his pragmatic competence.*

The Social Subject in the Left Hemisphere Intermediate Zone

- Does this person heavily invest ideals in his belief systems?
- Does this person feel that he can be understood?
- Does this person expect pleasure in his relationships?

- Does this person try to exercise his talents?
- Does this individual resist a life of alienated futility?

The answers to questions such as these reveal one's conditioned, subjectively experienced personality tendencies. *Narcissistic pathology suggests that the therapist combine a self-psychology approach with reconditioning the patient's sense of confidence.*

The Subject in the Left Hemisphere Medial Zone

- Does this person respond to failure with resolve?
- Does error anxiety lead her to the need for perfection?
- Is this person inhibited, claustrophobic, or tense?
- Is separation anxiety tolerable?
- Does the patient experience humiliation, betrayal, and rages that can lead to explosive behavior?

The answers to questions such as these indicate how a person uses anticipatory anxiety and need as signal systems. *Impaired signals suggests using medication to treat these symptoms.*

The Procedural Self in the Right Hemisphere Lateral Zone

- Can a person follow a set of directions?
- Can a person understand and abide by rules?
- Can a person learn a procedure by imitation?
- Can a person usually find his things?
- Can a person understand a chain of command in a bureaucracy?

Answers to these questions gauge the procedural self's strength. *Weakness suggests that the therapist use cognitive and multimodal learning techniques.*

The Social Self in the Right Hemisphere Intermediate Zone

- Does this person value the law?
- Does this person feel guilty when he wrongs another person?
- Does this person feel another's physical or emotional pain?
- Does this person value his own self when making a decision?
- Can this person use humor and metaphor to alleviate stress?

Answers to such questions gauge the social self's conditioned, responses to the social world. *Low self-esteem suggests that the patient may be helped by supportive assertiveness training.*

The Self in the Right Hemisphere Medial Zone

- Can this person tolerate prolonged frustration?
- Does this person blame others who are faultless?
- Is this individual hypervigilant?
- Does this person quash his own social strivings?
- Does this person lose self-esteem in social binds?

Answers to these questions gauge the self's use of novelty anxiety and affect as signal systems. *Impaired use of novelty anxiety or affect signals suggests that the therapist use medications to enhance an individual's adaptation to stress.*[1]

Collectively, these assessments should guide the structural therapist's approach to the patient. With medial zone pathology, medication is indicated. Intermediate zone pathology will suggest the nature of reconditioning the patient requires. With lateral zone pathology, the therapist will determine which cognitive interventions the patient needs. Patients who suffer simple lapses in their sense of identity may be helped by reassurance that they are still the same person. More regressed patients may require years of intercurrent work.

HOW TO DO STRUCTURAL THERAPY

Explain exactly what you are doing and why you are doing it. There are no secrets in structural therapy. Because the patient tries to maintain coherence in the face of incoherence, he distorts his identity. The patient manifests contradictions, cognitive dissonance, and emotional dissonance. The therapist addresses contradictions by reframing them and pointing out their effect on a person's sense of integrity. In this way, cognitive therapy addresses the patient's distorted intrapsychic identity.

Address changes in a person's experience of his identity. The therapist explains that a person has to balance his cognitive, social, and emotional life. She explains that one's belief systems, social relationships, and emotional responses have to remain compatible during periods of stress. Unremitting, untenable experiences in the present or in the past induces changes in the established equilibrium and so induce changes in the sense of who one is. No one becomes syndromatic without experiencing a distortion in who he senses he is. No one benefits from therapy without changing his sense of who he is becoming. While reconstructing his life experience, the therapist accounts for how the patient's identity has altered.

Present a theory of mind that emphasizes identity formation. Symbiosis or poor boundaries block the formation of a cognitive framework for all the identity integers. The lack of a theory of mind is a benchmark for a patient's capacity to maintain identity coherence. Without a theory of mind, we cannot keep verbal order in our mental processing or understand how we relate to others. A cognitive theory of mind provides the frame for identity. A theory of mind provides reflective coherence.

Everyone develops a theory of mind. Usually it is hidden, like the weight bearing structures within the framework of a house. In structural therapy, the therapist educates the patient about how a theory of mind is an innate development that accounts for how a one relates to other people, family, and social structure. Nowadays, almost every one believes that the mind is a product of brain function. This enables the therapist to present a theory of mind and brain that accounts for the patient's distortion.

Explain how stress affects the brain to change one's mind. Since the brain and the mind are mutually regulatory, chronic or overwhelming stress alters the neurobiological foundations of a person's mental structure. Describe how stable identity regulates stress and relationships. Tell how this replicates a natural developmental process. The structural therapist can usually choose several of a patient's early memories and reveal how the patient's identity foundations are imbedded in them.

Explain how the social world impacts identity. In the course of therapy, the therapist will find herself explaining how the social world is organized, how it changes, and how it effects family equilibrium and personal identity. For instance, in her therapeutic neutrality, the therapist has to be prepared to empathize with a patient who is "pro-choice" or one who believes in the "right to life." The therapist can explain that either position is vested in a person's social identity.

We live in a changing social world. That world often presents us with ambiguous and dissonant rationales for its organization. A sociology lesson, tailored to the patient, may include the effects of ethnicity on subjective aspects of identity, or the effects of bureaucracy on one's objective identity. If the patient is a graduate student enslaved by a mentor's career in an institution, exploring that institution's organization is very relevant to the patient's experience. If the therapist practices for a long time in one community, her patient's will teach her all the local sociology she needs.

Learning some sociology is a therapeutic tool. For instance, ethnic groups tend to bias their members to see other members as human and outsiders as nonhuman. Members of a bureaucracy tend to identify themselves with the bureaucracy's social aggression, which maintains the members' social and economic advantages. Stress takes root in how a person fits into these social and economic institutions. Institutional structures can also pathologically distort their members' identities. The therapist needs sophistication and tact to clarify these social forces.

Foster transference that puts you in a position to provide a cognitive prosthesis for the patient's identity. Patients with poorly synthesized identity tend to form *transitional object transference.* This transference wields the brain's original, eighteen-month-old capacity to synthesize identity. It recapitulates the original synthesis of narcissism with object relationships. When the patient experiences the therapist as the source of mental integration, the patient internalizes the therapist's cognitive framework for emotional integration. This framework helps the patient relinquish the identity changes caused by trauma or unhealthy conditioning. As we go along, I will explain more about how the structural therapist can use transitional object transference.

STRUCTURAL THERAPY WITH PTSD PATIENTS

When a person undergoes acute, unremitting trauma, she feels her present identity is no longer effective—or even relevant to her situation. This is one of the factors that gives the abuser his power: identification with the aggressor (the Stockholm syndrome) facilitates failing personal identity. Many of us recall the televised image of Patty Hearst. In it, she holds a gun during a Symbionese Liberation Front bank robbery, that took place months after the radicals kidnapped her. Anyone familiar with the *Stockholm Syndrome* can guess what happened to the heiress who seemed to become a radical. She married her personal bodyguard, who watched over her as she waited for her trial.

Our patient Lida (see Chapter 2), who was molested by a youth gang, referred to herself in the third person. She felt that Lida had become a distant friend. At the same time, during an office visit, she saw a picture of an innocent girl holding flowers as a portrait of a girl wielding a knife.

Consider the case of a dentist falsely charged with sexual abuse. A phallic narcissist, my patient had always enjoyed being in control of helping others. Now, barred from practice, the dentist blamed himself for cavalierly treating a dental emergency during his dental assistant's lunch hour. Trauma produced fault lines along the coordinates of his personality. Instead of taking pride in his professional performance, he felt ashamed of his helplessness. Waiting months for a hearing, he felt he had no professional or personal identity. He languished, and in a certain way, he lost himself. Nothing, he felt, will come of nothing. Only his trauma had meaning.

Helping the patient rediscover his or her premorbid mainstays of identity is a critical intervention in treating PTSD. Unable to practice, the dentist ran out of money, his disability refused to pay, he had to sell his house, and his wife was angry because her husband did not even help with the children. Almost inevitably, the patient developed a major depression. In addition to pharmacological intervention with an MAO inhibitor, serzone, and trazodone, I explained to the dentist what trauma is and how it undermined his sense of self. I asked him to explain what he learned to his wife. I treated him as a professional person, but still a man. To help shore up his identity, I paraphrased the words of King Lear, who wrestled with his own coherence:

> Close pent up guilts
> Rive your concealing continents, and cry
> These dreadful summoners grace. I am a man
> More sinn'd against than sinning.

From *King Lear,*
William Shakespeare

Psychosis and suicide are common in people such as the dentist or Lida, because their identity disintegrates in their of trauma. They feel that *social authority deserts them.* Desertion by social authority is tantamount to desertion by one's own indwelling social world—by one's superego. Lacking a sense of a protective superego, *one becomes a narrowly focused, detached observer.* The traumatized feel that *there is no social authority except for those who cause the trauma.* The mind has to find someone or some social entity as responsible for the trauma. Otherwise there is chaos, anxiety, and stress so severe that *a person longs for the death of premorbid identity. Taking the blame oneself helps one to feel that there is still self and others in the world.* The world remains orderly if we can find reason or even fault.

Explaining these mechanisms, I tried to help the dentist:

- build a cognitive foundation for maintaining his identity,
- see how each of his children carried his identity strength,
- hold onto the sense of *when he resumes his practice,* and
- reconcile with his aged, once emotionally cold mother.

Many patients who suffer from PTSD or from depression and anxiety disorders, believe they have a "chemical imbalance." This presents a convenient, ambiguous rationale for therapists, patients, patients' families, and society at large. It is remediate for the structural therapist to clarify this ambiguous rationale, because patients feel that if the fault is in their genetics or chemistry, it is inexorably in their identity. The therapist can explain how remediating stress remediates brain effects, and restores a sense of coherent identity.

One can explain to the patient, as I did to the dentist, that chronic stress undermines premorbid adaptation. I explained to the dentist that his feelings of social failure and being backed into a corner, arose from finding himself in a position *equivalent to that of a person experiencing restraint stress*. When there are no correct options, a person feels his social being subordinate to arbitrary authority. In this case, the dentist felt he would be destroyed by the legal system and the media. Reframing this negativity as a temporary adaptation helped the dentist maintain the sense of continuity in his identity. However, when he developed severe diabetes, and realized that his health insurance had been cancelled, he gave up and committed suicide.

The structural therapist has to distinguish the effects of *mild, moderate, and severe* or *prolonged stress.* Mild to moderate stress can impair new learning, which is a familiar mystery to students. As we saw earlier in this book, prolonged moderate stress or brief severe stress can induce long-term potentiation in the limbic system. LTP causes the formation of new emotionally organized source memories. To the extent that we reference our identity with emotionally organizing source memories, severe trauma changes our sense of identity. The therapist has to know, and sometimes explain, that although identity changes are transferred from the limbic system to the prefrontal system, they are not necessarily permanent.

STRUCTURAL THERAPY WITH PSYCHOTIC PATIENTS

Psychosis directly disrupts one's sense of personal identity. Whether the patient feels that the world is coming to end, that we are entering an ice age, that people have become robots, that angels and devils are contending for his soul, that everyone judges and condemns him, that the CIA wants his secrets, that mankind needs saving, that aliens have invaded the earth, or even that he owns Central Park—the result is the same: a devastating change in the world and his own person. That is the onset of psychosis. The psychotic person's odd delusions and experiences are an attempt to explain otherwise inexplicable changes in his sense of identity. After a time, he internalizes a sense of psychotic identity, and becomes a person with a psychotic identity. *The therapist has to explain these identity changes to the psychotic person.*

The schizophrenic is sure that he is no longer the same person he was before the onset of his psychosis. That is why a schizophrenic may change his name or say that his mother is no longer his mother. Our patient,

Persephone (see Chapter 10) felt her clenched teeth imploding into her head, destroying her brain and her identity. She developed a delusional explanation for this experience to save herself from complete nonbeing. After several acute episodes, I could no longer visit Persephone's underworld to help her refind her premorbid identity.

For some patients, one episode is enough to form a delusional restitution of identity that is set in stone. Other patients can hold their premorbid identity through several acute episodes. As we will see, some highly motivated schizophrenic patients may even be able to resume their maturation after they have learned a theory of mind that is socially and personally relevant.

STRUCTURAL THERAPY
WITH CHRONICALLY DEPRESSED PATIENTS

Most practitioners treat chronically depressed, gloomy patients. These patients often suffer from double depressions. They are dysthymic most of the time, and intercurrently psychotically depressed. When psychotic depression lingers, they become reclusive and suicidal. These patients' ambivalence surfaces when their dependency needs are disappointed. This is when we hear that "people are no damn good."

A vignette shows how structural therapy helped this kind of patient maintain her coherent identity and her relationships. A seventy-five-year-old woman, whom I had seen off and on for over thirty years, suffered many major depressive episodes, some psychotic. She got a call one day from her eighty-year-old sister, who lives across the continent. During their conversation, the patient described her visit to the Holocaust Museum. The sister listened for a moment and said, "How lugubrious." At this point, the patient decided that although MCI was sponsoring a free day of calling anywhere in the United States, she would not call her sister back because she felt rejected as a Jew. Filled with ambivalent conflict, the patient thought to herself that she needed a rabbi. But she did not have a rabbi. Then she thought to herself, "What would Doctor Harris say?" She thought I would say, "Do not start a private holocaust with your sister. It is better to be disappointed than to have no sister." When the patient told me this I said, "I wish I'd said that."

This anecdote illustrates how *I represented the patient's theory of mind*—what one does with one's thoughts and feelings to resolve conflict and to have relationships. In the Shakespearian sense, I was her fool—the one who can overcome ambivalence to maintain relationships. By saying, "I wish I'd said that," I helped the patient further internalize her reparative identification. The patient felt that her decision not to start her own private holocaust belonged mentally to her, not to me.

Does it go without saying that when working with chronically depressed patients, we never side with pessimism? We have to show optimism about positive changes that life can always bring.

TECHNIQUES OF STRUCTURAL THERAPY

Reconstruction

Because reconstruction uncovers maladaptive responses to conditions beyond a person's control, *reconstruction is more essential than interpretation during socially disorganized eras.* For interpretation to transmute identity effectively, the person has to live in a world that lets him take responsibility for his actions and their consequences. The patients we are focusing on here are more in need of reconstruction.

Reconstruction is a technique for putting together the pieces of a person's life. Doing reconstruction is like working a puzzle that provides an up-to-date portrait. A chronically manic individual, for instance, whose disease medication has finally controlled, will have to deal with a long amnestic period, filled with partial and suggestive source memories. The gaps will need to be filled in, for without a sense of continuity of source memories, one cannot maintain a stable identity.

In one instance, a Southern woman who would become my patient lived with her husband in a trailer. The patient had gone through a long period of physical abuse by her husband. She called the sheriff, who raped her. Manic now, leaving her two young children behind, she fled to California. There, two men recruited her for a prostitution ring. She was transported to New York City, where used and abused, she found herself in a mental hospital. On admission, the patient could not recount anything that had happened to her. Her thoughts were scattered to the winds. After she stabilized on lithium, we had to reconstruct her story so that she would be able to narrate it to herself. She could go on to make viable life decisions, only after she owned her own story.

Two exercises provide a context for reconstruction. The first is the *standard family genogram.* Going back to his grandparents' generation, the patient diagrams three generations of his family history. The genogram includes the parents' and grandparents' siblings. The patient may include each relative's fate and psychiatric history. The second exercise involves asking the patient to *write his life history.* We can follow the brain's own way of tracking source memory by asking the patient write his history in two ways. In the first history, the patient *narrates events sequentially, from birth to the present.* In the second, he recounts *episodes. Here we ask the patient to rate episodes according to their affective pain.* These exercises can draw the patient into a working alliance that shortens therapy.

Reconstructing cases of childhood abuse can be difficult. To distinguish true memories from false, the patient and therapist need to reconstruct collaboratively (see Chapters 7 and 12). *The therapist's job is to believe the patient completely.* When elements of the patient's accounts conflict, as they did in the case of Echo (see Chapter 4), we wonder aloud how these conflicts may be resolved. Inevitably, the trail leads to *family distortions, and myths that have been planted in the patient's mind, usually to falsify accounts of true abuse.* Our reconstruction is often a corollary to the family's mythology that suggests reasons for it. A narcissistically shattered mother, who has been dominated by an abusing husband, for example, will sacrifice her daughter or son to the husband's abuse in order to engage in private self-soothing behavior. (See Titus's case in Chapter 2.)

Many abused people grow up in atmospheres permeated by family mythology and secrets. These people often develop acute observational skills, which, resentfully, they keep to themselves. *Abused people often develop strong family romance fantasies: they imagine having "real" parents more in keeping with their latent identity strivings.* Such abused people long for permission to tell the truth they know so well. The therapist must become an ally to their truth telling. I should say parenthetically here that both abused and nonabused persons who grow up in a mythologized atmospheres angrily reenact, as if to correct past distortions. Rather than focusing on the patient's anger, the therapist will do well to applaud the patient's need to set the record straight.

Primitive as he is, Titus insisted on making contact with a sexually abused sister who had been raised by a distant relative. Titus insisted on revealing the extent of his father's abuse, because, against all family opposition, he was determined to recover the whole truth of his early life. For this reason, Titus successfully reacquainted his siblings with their sister after his parent's death, which helped him find a viable identity.

Screen memories help us reconstruct. Early memories screen conflictual events and episodes that contribute to identity formation. We can take it as a general rule that *screen memories create metaphors—mental constructs— for aspects of developing identity that cannot be integrated into existing identity structures.* One patient's first memory involved walking down the street with his mother when he was three years old. The episode involved finding another street that he recognized from living there before. The memory concealed the trauma of his infancy, which was that his family had moved fifteen times to stay ahead of their creditors. The child became a counterphobic explorer, always on the lookout for new ways to get where he was going.

Using the Transference

To treat severe conditions, the structural therapist needs to focus on two types of maladaptive conditioning, each of which gives rise to a distinct form of transference:

- *Primary transference* (see Titus, Chapter 2) rigidly and inflexibly conditions the infant to pleasure/displeasure or pain/pain relief. Primary transference is implicit in the sense that a mass of nonverbal associations accounts for it.
- *Secondary transference* involves trauma or fixation which takes place after infancy, and which creates secondary conditioning and transference. Seemingly trivial source memories often symbolize traumatic conditioning. Secondary transference is the brain's way of remembering and externalizing emotionally organizing events or episodes.

Both primary and intense secondary conditioning give rise to hemispherically determined forms of transference:

1. The left hemisphere's libidinal transference gives rise to grandiose, idealizing/degrading narcissistic identifications, or else it yields narcissistic identifications that tend toward the emptily deprived/misunderstood.
2. The right hemisphere's aggressive transference results in identifications of an object-related type. These are either identifications with the aggressor or the victim (see Chapter 2).

Here, I posit a theory of personality formation that combines the cognitive, psychoanalytic, and neural systems approaches: *Identifications use unbound energy. They tie up catecholamine resources. In this sense, the drive energy attached to satisfaction/deprivation or pain/pain relief flows freely among the masses of implicit social associations that comprise the identifications. Grandiosity is thus fueled by unbound libidinal (dopaminergic) energy, while deprivation is underfueled. Identification with the aggressor is similarly fueled by unbound noradrenergic aggression, while identification with the victim is underfueled. A lack of catechomaline drive resources for behavior is experienced as unrelieved mental pain.*

The primitive quality of unbound drives gives rise to all or nothing expectations. Abused at twenty-two months of age, Sam (see Chapter 5) valued the primitive intensity that he felt both when sensing pervasive beauty and when expressing himself with excoriating sarcasm. Sam clung to his primitive identifications, because writing poetry came easily in energized states. I have seen many patients who cannot relate consistently to others because they cannot relinquish the intensity of primitively conditioned states. Romanticizing their unrequited yearnings for contact, these patients cling, marooned, to atypical depression.

Many of the patients we see these days who have severe mixed personality disorders also tend to experience unbound drives. Such patients feel fulfilled or empty, powerful or powerless. For mature people, anxiety and emotion function as signal systems that regulate the coherence of their identities. More primitive personalities covet the experience of the unbound drives and the resultant upsurge of ecstasy, revenge, joy, and reconciliation. They lack the knowledge that these states are wedded to panic, terror, ugliness, humiliation, suicidality, and aloneness.

The drugs these patients take provide the same "all-or-nothing" pleasure or pain. Pharmacologically induced states of unbound pleasure inevitably revert to unbound pain. In these patients' relationships, the other's identity, more than the patient's, determines the course of events. Among those mired in primitive transference, adolescents whose identity has yet to cohere, cannot resist the drug taking of their peers.

Grandiosity arises from unabated primitive transference in which the baby's sense of being special and entitled persists into adult life. The grandiose narcissist does not develop well-formulated goals. He feels instead, that by merely existing, he is entitled to instant gratification. In the idiom, such a patient is "spoiled rotten." Narcissistic deprivation arises as an extension of parental needs. The infant's needs are irrelevant. The infant strives to be perfect—a being without needs for gratification. In most cases, a grandiose, overly entitled mother produces a narcissistically deprived offspring who always feels imperfect.

Primitive identification with the aggressor arises from the experience of being allowed to feel more powerful than any young child could really be. The sadist takes pleasure in promising pain relief, and then rescinding his offers. Masochistic identification with the victim (by the sadist) sets up a mental stereotype of either holding onto or yielding all control and power to the other. The masochist yields to rigid superego precursors, so that when oppression is lifted, pain relief comes. The sadomasochist's social self immerses in identification.

Known to analytic practitioners as infantile imagoes and introjects, these identifications yield severe character pathology. In this pathology, sadism and masochism are not mutually exclusive. To be primitively socially conditioned is to be left with a doubly distorted personal identity. The sadomasochist is incomplete without his current object of identification. Without the organizing other, the sadomasochist is vulnerable to psychotic disorganization. These split off identifications form the basis of the borderline personality.

How do we use primary negative transference? The mother of the borderline patient discussed in Chapter 7 sadistically and openly reviled her daughter. Growing up, the patient's self-vilification was so severely stressful that it impaired her hormonal development. Obese, she developed hair on her face and chest, so dating was out of the question. The mother offered pain relief only when the daughter fell ill.

In her negative transference, the daughter, who later became my patient, felt that I was the sadistic object. In her negative transferential mode, the patient could not stand me, but she felt she would become a bag lady if she left me. I used the negative tranference to reconstruct her mother's unremitting aggression toward her. For months, she told stories of her mother's forcing her to undergo painful and unproductive electrolysis. This became a metaphor for her analytic sessions. Only after the patient understood this transference, could she experience a positive transference with me.

The patient let me know at this point that she kept a teddy bear in her closet. During her therapy, when she felt suicidal, she would bring her transitional object into bed with her. She had not been willing to share her transitional object with me as long as I was the bad mother. I showed deep respect for her transitional object, and I treated her references to it as reference to a treasured part of herself. We will soon see that *transitional objects often play a role in structural therapy.*

Short of the ten-year analysis this patient underwent, how can we help transform massively conditioned primary transference in order to give the patient the opportunity to mature? Another way of asking this question is: how do we, just as King Lear's fool, become mediators of personal restoration? The answer involves not only the use of the principles and techniques of structural therapy modified for brief use, but the use of adjunctive medications.

Let us look at the case of Salvatore, a fifty-six-year-old managed care patient with limited sessions, whom I saw because he wanted to take a buyout package and retire prematurely. The problem was that Salvatore's retirement income would depend on his average income for the last two years of his work, including overtime. Unfortunately, Sal could not ask for his share of overtime because when he thought about asking, he began reliving primary transference. Transferentially speaking, Sal's co-workers stood in for his family of origin.

Within a few sessions, we had reconstructed that this patient's mother had been sexually abused when she was growing up. Sal's mother had mentally divided her own kids into abusers and abused. As the youngest son, Sal was to be her confidant and hear how terrible his three brothers were. Sal was the good child. Being good meant that he could not go outside and play until he had done his chores. He did them the best he could. Then his mother would say he had to do them over again. When he whimpered, a strange calm would come over his mother. She would place him on the bed, take off his clothes and give him an enema. We reconstructed that in this way she played dolls with him. He was her little doll. As if in play, Sal's mother did to Sal what had been done to her.

A traumatized person manifests a never-ending stream of imagery that deals with his trauma and which contains attempts to structure an identity that can master his trauma. Traumatized imagery pervaded Sal's speech. To reconstruct, I simply had to follow the flow of his conversation, which was full of remarks such as, "What an asshole I am. I can't do anything right."

Narcissistic misunderstanding, one of the four basic types of primary conditioning, fitted Sal's development. Sal had been continually humiliated, and never expected satisfaction except for the satisfaction he could bring to being sodomized, or having a rage that would break the symbiosis once and for all.

Sal derived two organizing fantasies from his conditioning. First, he would save his siblings from his mother's humiliating degradation by absorbing it into himself. Second, he would choke his mother to death. These fantasies gave rise to obsessive defenses. Sal could not assert himself, except on behalf of the other workers, whom he experienced as his siblings.

The essence of the therapy was to work on reconditioning. I tirelessly reiterated, "Fair is fair; your share is your share." Sal's assignment was to ask his manager for his share of overtime. Because he could not tolerate an SSRI, I placed Sal on a high dose of BuSpar and a small dose of Wellbutrin. The BuSpar reduced his anxiety about reconditioning himself and the Wellbutrin energized him to counteract the energy loss that went into mulling over his past as he tried to change the present. I did not touch with a ten-foot pole the fact that he had married a bipolar woman, who reminded him of his mother.

TRANSITIONAL OBJECT TRANSFERENCE

In more complete structural therapy than Salvatore's, the therapist becomes the focus of the patient's primitive transference and an object of identification in short order. As I have been suggesting throughout, *the therapist uses the patient's positive transference and identification to help the patient absorb a more complete theory of mind* capable of structuring a new perspective. Providing support for mental structure is like placing an absorbable graft over a burn to provide structure for new skin growth. At the same time, *the therapist uses the patient's negative transference as a window that reveals what to reconstruct of the circumstances that led to the distortion of the patient's personality.* The therapist must be at odds with the lies and mythologies (both within the family and within the social structure) with which the patient has had to contend. This defuses the patient's anger.

Developmentally, formation of the transitional object is the first time an individual synthesizes identity. Bringing the subjective and objective integers of identity into a united frame is made possible by the maturation of the corpus callosum. Fortunately, *the capacity for transitional object synthesis continues throughout life. The therapist becomes the recipient of the patient's transitional object omnitranference as well as his omni-identification. The therapist becomes, in this way, an extension of the patient's subjective identity, at the same time that the therapist continues to be experienced as out there in reality.* Let us take a clinical look at the use of transitional object transference in structural therapy.

Sophia's Tower

Sophia is a thirty-three-year-old Italian-American who divorced a small-time Mafia worker whose activities horrified her when she discovered them. The marriage came to an end when Sophia tried to keep her husband from committing murder. Ethnic loyalty and fear kept Sophia from telling me about her former husband's connections for the first two years.

I happened to go on vacation soon after treatment began. While I was away, Sophia constructed a painted pasta tower, which she glued to an eight-by-eleven-inch cardboard. She mooned over this transitional object in my absence. It was the joy of her life to imagine throwing herself from the tower and falling to a shameful, disgraceful death. Sophia gave me the tower upon my return. During the next four years of psychotherapy, I placed the upright collage on my desk during each session. It became the centerpiece of the sessions. Sophia paid for psychotherapy with arbitrary support from her former husband, the proceeds of domestic work, and occasional prostitution. What emerged through discussion of the transitional object was Sophia's hallucination of its rhythmic beating. In one session, she finally remembered snuggling against her mother's chest as an infant. The rhythmic beating was her mother's heartbeat. The pasta tower was the mother's breast and Sophia's emotional nourishment. A worldly interpretation was not difficult to see. Sophia's divorce had separated her from her marriage and her family of origin. Sophia felt cast out.

After these revelations clarified her depression, Sophia began to date a charming Puerto Rican man, married him, and no longer needed her therapist or the transitional object. Finding a new family in her in-laws, Sophia happily dissolved her narcissistic depression and her ethnic loyalty.

Ruth's Puppet

Ruth was an oversensitive identical twin, talented and accomplished as a dancer, painter, poet, and actress. She and her identical twin both believed the world was literally coming to an end. They experienced this imminence repeatedly. As infants, she and her twin used an autistic language known only to them. As they grew, the family designated Ruth the bad twin because she had rages; her timid sister was the good one. The girl's parents were haughty, hard-to-please narcissists.

Ruth's father was a militant Zionist. While Ruth was growing up, he disappeared on secret missions. Ruth never knew if he would return. While he was away, Ruth would imagine her father's plane had crashed into the ocean. She believed these fantasies had caused her father's death up to the moment when he walked in the door. She felt guilty about wanting more of her father's attention. After all, who was she? Her father had told her about all the Jews who had died in the Holocaust. Basically, he would steal the stage with his thunderous "Never again!" What did it mean when he supported her art? When he came to see her perform, he was the expert who told her what she had done wrong.

Ruth's mother was a behaviorist child psychologist. When Ruth expressed anxiety about her absent father, her mother shut her down with remarks such as, "Don't be silly, girl." Ruth raged, and her mother shut her in a closet to get quiet.

In essence, Ruth was enormously talented, narcissistically deprived person with an unstable subjective sense of herself. Misunderstood and lacking mirroring, Ruth would blow up in paranoid rages so severe, she felt she was destroying the world. During these frequent episodes, she was psychotic and anorexic. She would fight with people on the street. Ruth was also endowed with an eidetic memory so strong, she recognized many people on the street. These were persons she had noticed before as strangers. At times in our sessions, she would absorb herself in the pattern of my office rug. Although unable to return to a sense of observing the whole world or her self, she had no auditory hallucinations. By the time she was twenty-seven years old, Ruth was snuffing out burning cigarettes on her skin, and engaging in other self-mutilative behavior.

When I first met her thirty years ago, Ruth was a twenty-eight-year-old, just discharged from a lengthy hospitalization, and was still psychotic. Her second psychotherapy began with a two-year inpatient stay. When we met, Ruth believed the world was coming to an end. She hallucinated drowning. I remember sitting with her in a therapy session, while she cowered in a chair trying to get away from the waves. Needless to say, my puerile attempt at testing reality by showing my dry legs had the brilliant effect of inducing terror. Ruth immediately saw me as the Grim Reaper, her image of death.

I became Ruth's long-term therapist in a curious way. When she was in the hospital, Ruth absorbed herself in a relationship with an art therapist. Ruth developed a twinship transference. At one point, she fainted after taking Thorazine, and she cut her lip in the fall. Blaming me, Ruth said I had taken away her physical perfection. Narcissistically deprived, her blame reproduced her transference to her mother. On the other hand, I had come late in the evening to check on her, and Ruth contrasted my concern for her with her father's lack of concern. From this positive transference, a therapeutic relationship was born.

I have treated Ruth for some thirty years. For the first ten years, she communicated with a puppet she made, a transitional object named "Jay." Between sessions, she talked constantly with the Jay puppet. Together, they discussed details of Ruth's daily life.

The first stage of therapy ended when Ruth decided to have a child whom she would raise with love. In a very real sense, that child became the transitional object who replaced Jay. Ruth relived each aspect of her development through her daughter's. I should add here that as Ruth's twin remained childless; Ruth differentiated from her sister by becoming a mother.

Ruth was able to empathize with her daughter in a mature way that far surpassed Ruth's mother's way of relating to her daughter. During each phase of this girl's development, Ruth went through a painful separation from her, but at the same time, Ruth went on adding to her own theory of mental development, and this burgeoning theory guided her self-observing maturation.

In her therapy, we constantly talked about the details of her life, and I had to repeat perspectives on what she could do to assert herself, over and over until she owned them, or until her puppet owned them. When Ruth's daughter went to college, Ruth was able to negotiate the major separation, although she marked the transition with a psychotic episode.

Ruth has taken a high dose of neuroleptics for thirty years. We cannot reduce the dose because Ruth becomes psychotic whenever we try. She also takes an MAO inhibitor, carbamazepine, and benzodiazepines. That said, it is a most remarkable feature of this story that Ruth resumed her artistic career after her daughter grew up. Not only did she resume her career, she gained public renown. Ruth's is a case of averted schizophrenia. Her sister succumbed to a life of chronic psychosis.

Richard's Magic Carpet

When I first met Richard, he was forty years old and schizophrenic. Ten years earlier, his illness forced him to leave his graduate English program: his voices would not let him concentrate. Since then, he had been on neuroleptics for several years, with only partial remission. Despite his schizophrenia, Richard was able to hold a simple civil service job. He lived in a single room with a fierce attack dog, which kept him isolated. At one time, Richard told me, he had been a homosexual prostitute. He had never slept with a woman.

When I saw Richard for the first time, I asked him to tell me what was on his mind. Richard agreed, but said he did not see the point because he "knew" I could read his mind. In the course of an early session, he told me his belly was soft and round like a woman's. I told him he was so mentally close to his mother that he could not tell the difference between his body and hers. This statement formed the basis for Richard's theory of mind.

One of the interesting things about Richard is that during the therapy, he became highly functional without the use of any further medication. Unlike many schizophrenics who lose their initiative, Richard was highly motivated to have a "normal" life. In fact, after a few sessions, Richard wanted to date.

He felt so humiliated, the first date he had with a woman, that he actually knocked the woman down. He wanted to kill her, even as he talked about it in his session. I understood this violence as a way of killing the symbiosis with his mother. The problem was that Richard had to distinguish between psychological and actual murder. To get Richard to see the difference, I said he had to decide if he would kill his date, his mother, or anyone else. I insisted that he had to make that decision. Happily for everyone, Richard decided that he would not kill anyone, ever. His decision controlled his primary depleted narcissistic transference, with the result that he then dated, and later married, a woman he had met in a therapy group. This woman had herself recovered from psychosis. These two people created a successful and prolific marriage, although it needs to be said that during intercourse with his wife, Richard had to imagine that a muscular man protected him against disappearing into his wife's vagina.

A transitional object mediated Richard's therapy. While Ruth lost herself in the oriental rug in my office, Richard became entranced by and enamored of it. The rug came to represent his interrupted aesthetic development and the progress in his therapy. A consequence of this interest was that Richard became an oriental rug expert. He bargained and built up a small fortune in carpets. He bought art objects for his wife on her birthdays, and these were always wise investments. Thus, Richard rebuilt his narcissism with the use of my rug as a transitional object that also represented his maturation and his therapy.

Dreams As Transitional Objects

Dreams can promote the development of personal identity. *Dreams from above* deal particularly with the maturation (see Descartes' dream in Chapter 6). The reason is not difficult to see. One's identity is always on one's mind; this is especially true during falling asleep or waking. For this reason, the therapist can take the part of each dream that records the entrance and exit to sleep as a dream about identity. Once the patient understands that these dreams promote identity maturation, it is likely that the therapy will promote many identity dreams. A common dream about identity involves building and rebuilding foundations for a dwelling.

As he was waking, one very paranoid patient recurrently dreamed about dwellings and construction. These dreams became keys to his structural therapy. In our discussions of these dreams, it was possible to use them in building up the patient's theory of mind. These dreams and his belief in psychoanalysis were, in essence, transitional objects. Our working alliance was built on using these dreams to build his sense of a theory of mind to guide his maturation.

The patient had been unable to complete his years away from home in a well-known academic college. He went to an analyst for help, but he was sorely disappointed because the analyst saw him as too psychotic to be able to undergo analysis. Nevertheless, he insisted, when he returned home in a very regressed state, that nothing but analysis could help him. After referral to me, he proceeded to lie on the couch where he would curl up in a fetal position and turn away from me. Then came the great revelation. If he told me his dreams, he could be in analysis.

The patient would have a dream of a building with no foundations, and we would spend a week or longer turning the dream every which way. The part of the structural therapy that dealt with his need for identity maturation took off from these dreams. He used psychoanalytic theory to attempt to create a theory of mind that would allow him to mature. Originally, he felt that I understood him no better than his father had. His father ordered him to leave home because his mother could not tolerate his regressed, symbiotic behavior.

The patient got a low-level administrative job, rented a cheap room, and spent most of his money on his therapy. Trying to build identity was life or death for him. After many years, and structurally analyzing literally hundreds of identity dreams, this patient completed college and became a lawyer.

Art Works As Transitional Objects

The utilization of art and poetry is often a good response to trauma. The therapist should encourage patients to bring in the art and poetry they create, and she should study patients' art as attempts to shore up their identity. Art objects, as we saw in Sophia's case, are transitional objects that can reform the structures of identity. Thus, if I see an artist, I will barter art for therapy, as long as we can use the art in therapy as an expression of the person's developing identity. A cardinal principle of such an arrangement is that the patient must never throw away a piece of art. That would be like throwing away the cornerstone of a building.

The collage artist whom I mentioned in Chapter 5 used the colors of my office repeatedly in his works. He was a wonderful colorist. The reader may recall that this man had come to America on a boat when he was eighteen months old. Thereafter, his life felt fragmented, like a collage. I used this analogy to present him with a theory of mind that accounted for his own development. I told him that he fragmented his thoughts, perceptions, and sense of himself as a feeling person in order to avoid being overwhelmed. He had been overwhelmed, both coming to the new world and witnessing his parents in a primal scene. For his part, he brought in artwork that represented the structural integration in his therapy. I hung two of his collages in my office, and they became transitional objects for the patient's mental integration. He began to render elements of real life episodes into his collages, which enhanced his art.

The structural therapist does well to frame reconditioning in metaphors. I gave the patient (mentioned in Chapter 1) who had to follow the edict, "father knows best," the assignment of changing the equilibrium in his marriage. He had learned in therapy what a relationship is, but his wife had not. Since he was both a professor and a cognitive therapist, I told him that he should imagine that he was giving a one-semester class in relationships. The students were his wife and a couple—he and his wife together. One content of the course was his narration of his life story as a vehicle that had conditioned him. The other part of the course involved getting his wife to do the same. Unfortunately, when his wife was given the opportunity to talk, she proved so vitriolic that my patient could say nothing. He absorbed the vitriol instead, and decided to limit the satisfaction he could expect in his marriage.

AN EXAMPLE OF STRUCTURAL THERAPY

We will use the case of Eurynome, presented in Chapter 8, to further exemplify the practice of structural therapy. When she first came to see me, Eurynome was taking perphenazine, a major tranquilizer. Her emotions and her sense of reality were both out of control. Eurynome did not know that she was suffering from PTSD. She thought the world was shimmering and ready to explode. As soon as I made a diagnosis, I told the patient that she was not psychotic. Her feeling that the world shimmered, ready to explode, was a symptom of her PTSD. I explained the disorder.

First, we reconstructed the way the patient's uncle had seduced her during childhood bathing, and raped her when she was twelve. I helped Eurynome reconstruct the scene of the rape. She remembered, "He told me to open up, and when I did, my whole body exploded in pain." After the rape, the reader recalls, intending to blow up the house, Eurynome turned on the gas stove. I interpreted that she wanted everyone to know what it felt like to explode from the inside. Later in her life, especially in her kamikaze woman alter ego, she undertook dangerous expeditions. Each element of this laborious and dramatic reconstruction was foreshadowed by Eurynome's becoming silent for much of a session. When I asked her about this, Eurynome expressed the wish—almost a belief—that I would know what she was going through, without her telling me. She could not tell me because she was convinced that I wanted to bathe and then seduce her. Like so many sexually abused people, she felt we should just get on with the seduction and abuse and get it over with.

At this point, Eurynome began to bring in poems and artistic renderings of a female in the bathtub. I reconstructed that her uncle had taken advantage of the maternally starved little girl by tenderly and seductively bathing her. I convinced Eurynome that I would not do that. At this point, Eurynome imagined that I was a mermaid/merman, a neutered water creature no different than she.

At this point, as reconstruction moved back into her early relationship with her mother, Eurynome brought Mumu to our sessions. Mumu was a life-sized doll that Eurynome had created, cathected as a transitional object. Mumu favored me, and I was able to talk to both Eurynome and Mumu about what had happened to Eurynome. I explained to them both how it was that Mumu was a transitional object. Eurynome and Mumu were both glad to learn this. I explained that one needs one's identity intact in order to move through life in a mature fashion. I explained that although Mumu had a life of her own, in many ways more mature that Eurynome's; Mumu was nevertheless an extension of Eurynome's need for her. One evidence was that Mumu's name was contracted out of *Mama, me,* and *you.* We all agreed that Mumu's judgment was always mature, accurate, and perceptive. Mumu became my therapeutic ally.

It was time to begin unraveling the family mythology that caught Eurynome in its web. Eurynome had been given the impression that she was the reason for her mother's marriage to an unfaithful husband. After she became pregnant with Eurynome, her mother felt trapped. Partly as an outlet for the mother, the family would leave the father at home while they summered at the ocean with the mother's sister, the wife of Eurynome's abuser. The father, in the meanwhile had two other children through an adulterous affair. Eurynome's mother needed to deny this other family. Eurynome and the other children had to pretend they did not know about it.

Eurynome became mute after her rape, but the muteness coincided with the covert revelation that the father had created another family. Believing it her job to keep the family together, Eurynome felt that if she said anything about the rape, her father would kill the perpetrator and her family would dissolve. Then, her father would move in with his other family. All of this had to be lifted into Eurynome's conscious memory in order to provide a rationale for the way Eurynome and her mother interacted. Eurynome loved her father.

The final phase of Eurynome's therapy dealt directly with her fear of abandonment. If she did not sacrifice herself, she felt that no one would want her. For Eurynome, reconditioning was a matter of using her identification with the therapist's attitude toward her. Eurynome had to learn to take herself into account and to value her life as much as she did other people's and Mumu's. Gradually, Eurynome mentioned Mumu less, the kamikaze woman became an assertive side of Eurynome's own nature; Eurynome allowed her sister to assume her mother's burden of preserving the family's mythology; and Eurynome developed a relationship with a woman who cared for her.

THE USE OF MEDICATION IN STRUCTURAL THERAPY

Let us see how medication fits into structural therapy. I offer here some principles that are useful in my practice. In cases of severe abuse, reconditioning cannot occur without the use of medication. This makes sense. Without medication, most people cannot stand the return of feelings during reconstruction.

Patients who are acutely psychotic need to be medicated so they do not develop long-term potentiation or excitotoxicity that permanently alters their stress systems and identities. Sometimes, in mania or in acute psychosis, the likelihood of excitotoxicity can make the use of glutamate synapse inhibitors such as valproate, carbamazepine, or the benzodiazepines critical interventions. We want to prevent the formation of limbic scars and identity-distorting source memories.

Patients with PTSD or severe personality distortion secondary to childhood abuse appear to do well with SSRIs. Increasing serotonin's availability in the orbital frontal and cingulate cortex appears to enhance the capacity to withstand the emotional intensity of flashbacks and reliving. SSRIs help the patient tolerate the inevitable sense of imminent retraumatization that accompanies the formation of a new, potentially transmuting, therapeutic relationship. In this connection, I note that many patients with PTSD appear to be bipolar. This is a result of these patients' alternating numbed and excited behaviors. If patients are bipolar, SSRIs can be psychopharmacologically destructive. Consequently, diagnosis is critical to the choice of medication.

Patients with primitive transference based on conditioning in early life or later trauma do better when their serotonin systems are stabilized with the use of agents such as BuSpar or serzone agonists to the presynaptic serotonin autoreceptors. As we learned in Chapter 3, serotonin stabilizes the catecholamine drive systems, and in this sense, serotonin stabilizers neutralize the primitive unbound drives in individuals whose drives are primitively unbound or destabilized by later trauma. Medications such as BuSpar or serzone can inhibit identity anxiety. In order to go through a maturational period of reconditioning, acting out has to give way to the use of signal anxiety and emotion.

Patients with PTSD are skittish about medication. Just as psychotic people and patients with panic disorder, traumatized individuals may feel their identities under attack when they feel side effects. Thus, complete explanation of the reason for the medication, careful explanation of what causes potential side effects, slow introduction of the medication, and praise for the patient's persistence with medication are all essential.

Diagnosis aimed at discerning which hemisphere is the triggering zone for psychopathology is paramount to psychopharmacological intervention. Thus, a patient with narcissistic, i.e., atypical depression, may do well with some stimulation of his dopamine system, which can be induced by medications such as bupropion (Wellbutrin) or an MAO inhibitor. Ambivalent patients with major depression secondary to right hemisphere triggering appear to do best with norepinephrine-serotonin-stabilizing medications such as the tricyclics. When chronic stress triggers major depression, then SSRIs appear just as useful as tricyclics; and they are also safer.

Freud's Last Recorded Words

> Space may be the projection of the extension of the psychical apparatus. No other derivation is possible . . . Psyche is extended; knows nothing about it. Mysticism is the obscure self-perception of the realm outside the ego, of the id. (Freud, 1938, p. 300)

In this quotation, Freud clings to the last shred of his identity as his ego and his brain succumb to the ultimate. Ultimately, our brains speak the language that has evolved to code the physical processes that account for the universe. Our brains give us an account of that universe, as they assess their neuronal systems' own processes. As social animals, our brains have created social structures that continue to evolve within the universe at large and within the universe as we have learned to experience it socially.

Throughout this text, we have considered the social world as a communal extension of the brain's processes. Collective entitlement, bureaucratic greed, social disorganization, political dehumanization, and transgenerational, drug-facilitated abuse cut us off from our social and historical sources. We live without them as poorly as a traumatized person lives without her personal source memories. When one's identity does not fit one's social world, the prefrontal cortex cannot regulate the drives, mediate stress, or maintain coherent identity.

The combined findings of cognitively and psychoanalytically informed neuroscience can be a force for human and moral good. If, however, we rationalize mental and emotional ills as the result of biological and genetic forces that create disease as mere "chemical imbalance," then our science betrays the reality of human experience. The brain talks to itself in the language of human experience, as well as in a genetic code.

If you, the reader, are still with me, your perspective must have changed. We have imaginatively ascended the Acropolis of Our Minds, intersubjectively with Psyche, and interobjectively with Freud. The journey has been like fresh data moving through the brain, finally helping to recast an intrapsychic identity that can reflect on its own progress. Some people never finish reading a book because they cannot let go of the characters. Some authors cannot relinquish the writing. In the end, for closure, the reader's feedback is as important to the author as the author's communications are to the reader.

Notes

Chapter 1

1. The research on which this chapter is based will be presented in subsequent chapters, where detailed analysis of converging evidence from multiple domains leads to the variety of conclusions that support this introductory synthesis.

2. The mobility of excitatory receptors on neocortical neurons contributes to neocortical plasticity (Huntley, Vickers, and Morrison, 1994). A protein called synapsin can enhance the mobility of these receptors over time (Sapolsky, 1992).

3. The prefrontal system includes the highly associative Brodman Areas (BAs) 9, 10, 11, 45 and 46 (Luria, 1980). Here, we need not concern ourselves with the microanatomical features that characterize these areas.

4. Embryologically, functional connections between excitatory neurons occur in response to the increase in growth regulating proteins (netrons) (Pfenninger et al., 1991). Growth-regulating proteins also increase in postnatal life when LTP forms the functional relationship between excitatory neurons.

5. We can specify many of the glutamate population's inhibitory and facilitatory processes. Sensitization downregulates (decreases) peptide, adenosine, and serotonin presynaptic inhibitory receptors (Lothman, 1991). Adenosine's presynaptic inhibition of excitatory transmission in the brain is well known. Since caffeine blocks the adenosine effect, caffeine increases the brain's excitation, which produces increased alertness and increased sensory processing. It also lowers the seizure threshold. Postsynaptic excitatory potentiation downregulates gabaminergic-A receptors' postsynaptic inhibition of glutamate transmission (Lothman, 1991). Therefore, postsynaptic potentiation lowers the threshold for LTP and kindling.

Full LTP increases (1) presynaptic capacity to depolarize, and (2) NMDA dendritic receptor density (Kuba and Kumamoto, 1990). Thus, full LTP produces permanent structural changes in excitatory synapses. Structural changes in the postsynaptic neuron make it more accessible to transmission, and produces exactly those biochemical conditions which feed back to permanently enhance presynaptic firing. There are three kinds of postsynaptic glutamate receptors: metabotropic (energy releasing) and NMDA and AMPA, which are ionic.

The AMPA glutamate receptors are responsible for the depolarization that is accompanied by Na^+ entrance into the postsynaptic cell. AMPA receptors must admit Na^+ to produce depolarization before NMDA receptors can enter a state of activation. It is only in the depolarized state that Mg^{++} blockade in the NMDA receptor is relieved so that both Na^+ and Ca^{++} can be admitted in its ionic channel. Thus, LTP can be induced only when ionic NMDA receptors colocalize with

AMPA receptors on postsynaptic dendritic spines (Izumi et al., 1990; Patel et al., 1990).

The colocalization of AMPA and NMDA receptors provides a mechanism for separating ordinary transmission from LTP. A large influx of Ca^{++} opens NMDA's ionic channel. Thus, LTP, which requires an intense Ca^{++} influx, and ordinary transmission diverge. LTP begins with waves of calcium that enter the NMDA channel and pervade the postsynaptic cytoplasm.

Full LTP requires (1) *induction* and (2) *maintenance*. Induction begins with bursting, high-frequency depolarizations that mobilizes *presynaptic* Ca^{++} to release enough glutamate and Ca^{++} to engage both NMDA and AMPA receptors. An NMDA channel binding site must allosterically orient (i.e., its configuration must be modified to open the channel) to induce *postsynaptic* Ca^{++} influx: (1) glycine must bind; (2) Mg^{++} must dislodge; (3) peptide and (4) opioid blockade must reduce (Kuba and Kumamoto, 1990). Glutamate binding to the metabotropic receptor enhances the NMDA cascade effect that occurs in LTP.

During LTP, the metabotropic receptor activates a G-protein second messenger (PIP), which enhances the activation of a cascade of protein kinases. This energy release mobilizes MAP 2 proteins of dendritic microtubules (Goedert, Crowther, and Garner, 1990) to release more energy-releasing bonds, which activates a protein kinase cascade (Halpain and Greengard, 1990). Thus, LTP induces an energy-releasing, structural reorganization within the postsynaptic neuron.

As the dendrites reorganize, their structural membranes release fatty acids (Shimiziu and Wolfe, 1990) and nitric oxide, which both diffuse (Bredt, Snyder, and Solomon, 1992) to the presynaptic membrane, where they upregulate glutamate autofeedback receptors (Herrero, Miras-Portugal, and Sanchez-Prieto, 1992; Nichols, 1992). The nitric oxide diffuses as an ionic gas within a few microseconds so that LTP maintenance is almost immediate. The upregulation *maintains* presynaptic glutamate production and Ca^{++} outflow beyond the LTP threshold (Fazelli, 1992).

Chapter 2

1. Understanding how the primate integrates prefrontal and hippocampal processing helps us imagine how the distributed visual system evaluates visual features during a task that requires delayed response. Inferotemporal neurons located next to the perirhinal cortex perform initial feature discrimination on visual data (Eichenbaum and Buckingham, 1995). During the delay period, the prefrontal system *buffers* (suspends deactivation of) neurons in the inferotemporal area. Responding to reward cues, inferotemporal neuron's processing determines whether features are salient (left hemisphere), significant (right hemisphere), or irrelevant to problem solving.

As the dorsolateral prefrontal system buffers inferotemporal neurons, other prefrontal distributed systems also assess visual data and contribute to its processing. Perirhinal cortex and amygdaloid populations—neural centers in which the cells constitute a group function—add significance and salience cues to the orbital, insular, and cingulate cortices' visual data. Prefrontal assessment of these cues adds emotional feedback about the social consequences of a visual, cue-dependent behavior. Thus, visual salience detection is a highly distributed function.

2. Startle responses are mediated by potentiated amygdaloid pathways at around seven milliseconds after an acoustic stimulus (Davis, 1992a). Startle responses can become conditioned to stimuli, which subsequently initiate a vigilance response. Then, the central nucleus of the amygdala recruits consciousness (an activation of fast waves) by arousing the *acetylcholinergic magnocellular basal nucleus:*

> the nucleus and its associated structures function . . . in the acquisition of . . . arousal manifested in a variety of conditioned responses which function to enhance sensory processing. This mechanism is rapidly acquired, perhaps via an inherent plasticity . . . in situations of uncertainty, but of potential import; for example when a neural stimulus (CS) precedes either a positive or negative reinforcing, unexpected event (US). (Kapp et al., 1992, p. 241)

3. Basolateral populations enhance rhinal cortical associations that are on their way to consolidation and storage as long-term memory (Izqiuerdo et al., 1992). When sensory stimulation is too novel, basolateral populations trigger the hypothalamus's aversive, instinctual responses. This response can be initiated by auditory signals conveyed to the lateral amygdala and visual signals conveyed to the medial amygdala (Ledoux et al., 1990).

A study of its lateral nucleus demonstrates how the amygdala participates in both conditioning and ordinary data processing (Ledoux, 1994). Auditory stimuli are transmitted from the thalamus to the lateral amygdala by two consecutive glutamate populations that have colocalized NMDA and AMPA receptors. This pathway becomes potentiated and produces quick processing. A second pathway from the rhinal cortex brings delayed and specific auditory input to the lateral amygdala for slow processing. A third pathway from hippocampal output brings contextualized data to the lateral and ventromedial amygdala.

Lateral and ventromedial populations respond to a noxious confluence of auditory, somesthetic, and visual inputs; they also respond to septal input. These populations, therefore, are intrinsic to aversive conditioning. These populations potentiate easily, they are accessed quickly, and their output via the basolateral nucleus of the amygdala to the hypothalamus leads to fear discharge. Thus, lateral amygdala populations participate in both onstream processing and conditioning.

4. The hypothalamus's lateral nucleus activates sympathetic discharges as central grey, trigeminal, and facial nuclei interrupt behavior and stimulate facial expression, and its paraventricular nucleus elicits lower centers' startle responses (Davis, 1992b).

5. Reports of hypothalamic autonomic discharges are processed by the *nucleus solitarus*, which distributes the somatic signals to the anterior and posterior cingulate association cortex (Friere-Maia and Azevedo, 1990). The anterior cingulate cortex assesses these signals in a sensory context, and the posterior cingulate cortex assesses them in a motor context. When in concert with the whole prefrontal

system, the cingulate cortex assesses mild fear signals, treating them as anxiety signals and inhibiting the amygdala's full-blown hypothalamic fear discharge.

6. • Amygdalar GABA damps fear response (Izquierdo and Median, 1991).
  • Amygdalar enkephalins damp fear response (Hanley, 1989).
  • Amygdalar vasopressin inhibits CA 1 (Smock, Albeck, and McMechen, 1991).
  • Outflow to the septum slows brain activation (Thomas, 1988).

7. When we are trying to solve problems, novelty can be handled in three different ways: (1) habituation to mildly charged data, (2) conditioning, and (3) long-term memory formation. Habituation configures novel data. The locus ceruleus induces a vigilance response mediated by norepinephrine that clears and readies the frontal and prefrontal systems to assess the novel data. At the same time, in the Ca 3 region, norepinephrine fibers enhance the mossy fiber transmission of data (Kandel, Schwartz and Jessel, 1991). It does not surprise us that hippocampal neurons show lower synaptic Ca^{++} currents during habituation, and higher ones during LTP (Disterhoft et al., 1991).

8. The potentiation of dentate cells is temporary. The synapses on the dentate cells become concave, and astrocytes invade the space of the synapse, which puts a stop to their LTP process (Desmond, 1994). In this case, potentiated dentate cells can transfer LTP to their output for a limited period of minutes. Afterward, they return to onstream processing.

The mossy fiber LTP that potentiates CA 3 neurons is a form of presynaptic LTP (Brown, 1994). Mossy fibers terminate on the *dendritic thorns* of CA 3 cells, which maintain their morphology. Thus, CA 3 cells undergo presynaptic sensitization, which does not change their morphology. CA 3's capacity to be sensitized by their mossy fibers for forty minutes is consistent with their role in habituation *and* in the production of polysensory context.

During intense Schaffer collateral stimulation of CA 1 cells, increased synaptogenesis occurs on CA 1's spiny dendritic processes (Desmond, 1994). Ca 1's postsynaptic receptivity to excitation increases. This indicates that CA 1 cells are capable of permanent facilitation by LTP.

Chapter 3

1. In a January 13, 1996, Grand Rounds at Stony Brook's Psychiatry Department, Peter Swales presented their view that the "analytic establishment" was "whitewashing Freud," and indulging in self-promotion by promulgating the retrospective as its own contribution to American culture. Swales said the *Times* misrepresented the signers' wish for fair representation. He decried the fact that after the signer's letter was received, the retrospective was cancelled without response or explanation.

2. *Presynaptic* excitatory dopamine-1 and alpha-1-norepinephrine, and *postsynaptic* inhibitory gabaminergic-A and serotonin-2 receptors modulate neocortical glutamate synapse's receptivity to LTP (Goldman-Rakic, 1990).

3. In primates, neocortical layers II, III, and V glutamate neurones manifest the colocalization of NMDA and AMPA receptors required for LTP (Jones and

Baughman, 1990). Billions of these layers' neurons form the neocortex's short-term and working-memory transcortical and transcallosal networks. Flexibility in these layers' modules may relate to the mobility and reserve capacity of excitatory receptors on these neurons (Huntley, Vickers and Morrison, 1994). Easily established LTP in the corticocortical, commissural, and local excitatory circuits of neocortex allows the brain to establish flexible communication pathways at the higher levels of its discourse with itself.

4. In the formation of a conditioned cerebellar motor schema, two consecutive glutamate inputs potentiate a Purkinje cell (Linden et al., 1991). Thereafter, this potentiated pathway is activated whenever the Purkinje cell's gabaminergic inhibition is lifted. Local gabaminergic inhibition by basket, stellate, and golgi cells pattern the Purkinje cells' cerebellar outflow. In turn, the output of the Purkinje cells induces selective gabaminergic inhibition in the striatum.

5. Morrison and Hof (1992) distinguished the effects of the aminergic systems in producing behavioral states:

- Dopamine and acetylcholine activate the prefrontal cortex during consummatory behaviors' *orienting* search for salience.
- Norepinephrine and acetycholine systems activate the prefrontal cortex during *vigilant* states' exploration of reality.
- Serotonin reenforces local prefrontal gabaminergic systems during *vitality* states' suspended activity. The serotonin system modulates every neocortical neuron.

6. The central and basal amygdaloid nuclei are profusely regulated by the aminergic systems (Fallon and Ciofi, 1992). The profusion and directness of these inputs suggest to me that the amygdala can be behavioral state driven as well as vice versa. Infusion of benzodiazepines into the central or basal regions of the amygdala show remarkable antianxiety effects (Ledoux, 1992; Davis, 1992b). Ledoux posits that sensory reports that reach the amygdala, already contextualized by the hippocampus and cognized by the neocortex are more likely to give rise to nonspecific anxiety than they are to fear discharge. As we saw in Chapter 2, during fear discharge, the central amygdala arouses the whole neocortex through its outflow to the central acetylcholine system. Arousal accompanies all types of anxiety discharges. During conditioned aversion the central nucleus of the amygdala conditions sensory signals from all modalities, while triggering fear discharge through the lateral hypothalamus (Kapp, 1992). Biogenic amines in the amygdala can modulate or even inhibit these responses (Davis, 1992b).

7. The serotonin modulation of the amygdala and the orbital frontal cortex are both extremely high (Amaral, 1992). Increased serotonin processing in the central amygdala is anxiolytic (Davis, 1992b). As we will document later, serotonin modulation of the orbital frontal cortex is also anxiolytic. For now, we can say that serotonin modulation is pivotal in allaying identity anxiety, and maintaining a sense of intrapsychic coherence.

8. Our neurobiological anxiety model provides the student of psychopharmacology with a means of understanding how anxiolytic drugs work. Drugs that augment the presynaptic autofeedback of dopamine, or that block postsynaptic

receptors (neuroleptics), reduce libidinal drive pressure, and therefore reduce *anticipatory anxiety.* Tricyclics quiet the locus ceruleus's aggressive drive through their presynaptic, (alpha-adrenergic) agonist action. A good example of vigilance anxiety occurs during opiate withdrawal. Because opioids inhibit the locus ceruleus, their withdrawal severely increases adrenergic pressure. (Consider the dilated pupils as signs of sympathetic stimulation.) Serotonin's evocation of identity anxiety is more complicated. It appears, however, that augmenting its presynaptic autofeedback effect with drugs such as buspirone produces an anxiolytic effect. Benzodiazepines, which enhance gabaminergic function, work directly on the amygdala to mitigate the intensity of all forms of anxiety *discharge.*

9. If feedback is on course, anterior cingulate association cortex dopamine-1 receptors damp gabaminergic inhibition of reward-conditioned operant behaviors (Strange, 1991).

10. The dorsolateral prefrontal cortex and the anterior cingulate prefrontal cortex are both heavily laced with ventral tegmental dopamine filaments. The auditory association cortex is also more heavily laced with dopamine regulation than is the visual association cortex (Morrison and Hof, 1992). These factors explain how dopamine regulates consummatory states, from salience, to reward, to planning, and to inner speech.

11. These studies presume that *alpha rhythm* (eight to twelve waves per second) indicates a cortex at rest, and suppressed alpha indicates a working cortex. The left hemisphere's frontal cortex suppresses alpha power, when we process salient stimuli (Sobotka, Davidson, and Senulis, 1992). The suppression disappears during actual pleasurable experience (Tomarken et al., 1992). Thus, suppressed alpha indicates libidinal *arousal*, while enhanced alpha indicates pleasurable libidinal *relief.*

12. The adaptive process begins in infancy, when the locus ceruleus's norepinephrine (LCN) system and thyroid hormone stimulate the hippocampus to develop type 2 glucocorticoid receptors. Later, these receptors respond to norepinephrine and endogenous cortisone by enhancing the stress response to novelty (Maccari et al., 1992). One of the ways we discover who we are is through self-observation of our ways of adapting to stress. Clearly some persons are mutable adapters.

13. Morrison and Hof (1992) reviewed the neocortical effects of norepinephrine. Norepinephrine fibers are particularly dense in neocortical visual processing zone's layers three and five. When we process unfamiliar stimuli's motion and position in space, norepinephrine increases our vigilant responsiveness to the visual input. Thus, norepinephrine determines the formation of our neocortical associations in response to spatial contexts.

Norepinephrine is notably lacking in the basal ganglia (Morrison and Hof, 1992). It is less dense in visual processing zones for assessing salience. From this we can conclude that it does not effect our action planning. However, norepinephrine fibers are very dense in motor areas that process our orienting response to novel stimuli. Thus, norepinephrine facilitates our response to novel reality and our exploration of it.

14. The locus ceruleus's norepinephrine system alerts: it promotes either vigilant interruption of problem solving, or enhanced reality exploration (Elbert et al., 1991). The central nucleus of the amygdala, which discharges fear or recruits arousal, has a strong input of norepinephrine neurons from the locus ceruleus (Amaral, 1992). The norepinephrine system interrupts executive processing when onstream processing registers novelty (Luria, 1980). Vacationing at the Mardi Gras, for instance, can completely reorganize our plans—for good or ill, and open our eyes to a thousand new details of life.

15. The right hemisphere suppresses frontal alpha when *potentially* painful stimuli are encountered (Sobotka, Davidson, and Senulis, 1992). Conversely, right hemisphere frontal alpha, but not left, increases when a person actually experiences painful stimuli (Tomarken et al., 1992). Dysphoria accompanies right hemisphere alerting to reality signals (Gur, 1984).

16. As we said before, serotonin fibers lace every neocortical neuron (Morrison and Hof, 1992). This means that serotonergic coverage of the neocortex is complete. It is most dense in layer four, the processing layer for specific thalamic inputs. These inputs bring processed sensory and emotional reports to the neocortex. In some species, serotonin has been shown to form a complete "basket" around layer four gabaminergic interneurons. This means that serotonin is capable of modulating and selectively inhibiting sensory and emotional input.

Chapter 4

1. In hippocampal tissue cultures, high glutamate and Ca^{++}, hence high LTP, destroys postsynaptic dendrites, while low glutamate and Ca^{++}, hence low LTP, destroys presynaptic connections (Mattson, Guthrie, and Kater, 1992). Ischemia-induced excitotoxic effects on CA 1 cells destroy postsynaptic dendritic microtubules, while presynaptic structures remain intact (Kitagawa et al., 1992).

2. On the basis of his work with gerbils, James Davis posited that the excitotoxicity that causes CA 1 cell death is mediated by intense glucocorticoid stimulation of their genome (personal communication). Reverberating increases in glucocorticoids mediate the DNA fragmenting cell death process—apoptosis. In severe stress, CA 1 cells evoke increased cortisone releasing factor (CRF), which elevates glucocorticoids to the point that their increasing CA 1 penetration produces apoptosis.

Corticoids determine cell growth, death, and networking in the neonatal rat dentate (Gould et al., 1991). Type 2 glucocorticoid, GABA A, and serotonin receptors are permanently enhanced in the handled neonatal rats' hippocampus, producing a lifelong, robust hippocampus that damps severe stress response (Meaney et al., 1991). Raised in a complex environment, rats permanently increase their functional hippocampal outflow (Green and Greenough, 1986). When young, these rats increase the synaptic density on their CA 3 cells (Greenough, 1994).

3. Amygdalar CRF directly enhances the hippocampus' memory formation (Chen, Chiu, and Lee, 1992). During habituation, data is processed faster because norepinephrine beta receptors in the hippocampus inhibit GABA A inhibition of

glutamate transmission (Izquierdo et al., 1992). Mild stress induces those transcription factors that accompany increased glutamate and peptide production in CA 1, hypothalamic and amygdala populations (Post, 1992). Rats' estrus increases their CA 1 dendritic spines, which contributes to their receptivity to new experience (McEwen et al., 1992). Can we conclude that female animals tend to be more receptive to fresh experience during their fertile period?

4. In acute stress, neuromodulation by cortisone, endogenous opioids, somatostatin, CCK, VIP, and other peptides inhibits glutamate synaptic transmission in the hippocampus. Indeed, in acute stress, glucocorticoids act directly on CA 1 cells to decrease glucose absorption, which prevents LTP maintenance (Maccari et al., 1992; McEwen et al., 1992). In many mammal species, acute stress, especially *restraint stress*, in which the animal is unable to take any action that will evade the noxious event, deregulates the postsynaptic CA 3 neurons. The adaptive deregulation is mediated by CA 3's type 1 (aldosterone) and type 2 (cortisol) receptors (McEwen et al., 1992). These effects all contribute to the major depressive's failure to suppress cortisone, and the accompanying decrease in new memory formation.

Chapter 5

1. As we will see in Chapter 6, semantic context is mediated by the left hemisphere's supramodal parietal cortex, while percept context is mediated by the right's "feature-detection" supramodal parietal neocortex (Geschwind, 1965). Quick-read feature detection provides the supplementary visual cortex integration of saccades with a new basis for integrating an observant sense of reality (Hikosaka et al., 1989).

Cognitive developments enable all this quick action and perception. Representational networks form throughout the oedipal stage and latency. Supramodal, parietal assessment cortex, an essential part of the second signal system, matures during the oedipal stage (Luria, 1980). This assessment cortex allows working memory to quickly scan sensory data and to form semantic and perceptual *contexts*. Supramodal cortex combines data from multiple modalities into a unified associational network. Geschwind surmised that the uniquely human capacity to approximate and generalize, despite discordant forms of data, relies on our evolutionarily enhanced supramodal parietal cortex (1965). This capacity helps the brain make quick cognitive judgments with minimal hippocampal data. The maturation of integrated frontal, prefrontal, and supramodal parietal networks during the oedipal stage paves the way for a new synthesis of latency identity.

Chapter 6

1. ERP is an extensive, still burgeoning field. To name some of its pioneers: Grey Walter contributed to its development; Charles Shagass applied it to psychopathology; Turan Itil used it pragmatically to profile types of psychoactive drugs; Baddeley related it to dichotomous working memory; Daniel Ruchkin extended

its reach to complex cognitive processing; Nancy Squires extended its methodology to noncomprehending subjects. Their work and others' underlies the following discussion.

2. Predirected attention augments the ERP response to expected stimuli, but does not effect the ERP response to indifferent stimuli (Paller, 1990). Thus, priming (rhinal cortex facilitation of indifferent stimuli) is neither enhanced nor inhibited in ERP, whereas cued or novel stimuli are augmented.

3. When, at the beginning of latency, a child can *anticipate* a particular stimulus, and use it a signal to react, p300 amplitude increases (Sommer, Matt, and Leuthold, 1990). Moreover, the latency child develops a capacity to categorize visual features that corresponds to increased and prolonged N2 waves (Robaey et al., 1989). As N2 prolongs, P3 develops. During P3, we *categorize* features and detect unusual ones. This gives rise to the abstract cognition that Piaget called operational thinking. In operational thinking a latency child learns to assess quantities and qualities. Early in latency, girls who can cognize the conservation of quality, show a maturation of P3 wave forms (Stauder, Molenaar, and van der Molen, 1993). Girls who perform this Piagetian milestone task lateralize their P3 waves anteriorly at 600 msecs. Girls who cannot do not lateralize their P3 waves.

4. Facilitated modules generate p300 in oddball, target stimulus paradigms (Polich and Donchin, 1988; Picton, 1992).

5. Because responding to unusual features or meanings requires a stronger inhibition of usual meanings or features, N2 is stronger in oddball paradigms (Jodo and Kayama, 1992).

6. In complex, visual-phonological, crossmodal tasks, visual processing resolves more quickly than semantic (Falkenstein et al., 1991). We see before we know we see. Comparing prolonged visual with prolonged verbal working memory, Ruchkin et al. (1992) evinced separate processing systems for each. During prolonged visual assessment, right hemisphere CNV waves shift to the central parietal region. During prolonged semantic assessment, left hemisphere's CNV waves shift to a slowly increasing, positive parietal wave for up to five seconds. Presumably, parietal areas provide a refined dual verbal and visual context for the assessed information.

7. During the spontaneous emotional imaging that accompanies prolonged executive reflection, the orbital frontal association cortex shows increased rCBF (regional cerebral blood flow). More data also registers during spontaneous imaging (Goldenberg et al., 1991).

Chapter 7

1. Excitotoxicity exemplifies the changes that occur rapidly, as opposed to slowly, in neural systems. On a massive scale, these changes can effect multisynaptic transmission permanently and induce syndromes. Various types of LTP that I have already cited cause incremental changes in neural function.

2. During LTP *induction,* acute hypoxia triggers a postsynaptic influx of Na+ and Ca++ through NMDA channels, as well as a strong activation of glutamate

AMPA and metabotropic receptors. This influx activates the energizing postsynaptic *second messengers*, PIP and diaglycerol. A high enough influx of Ca^{++} triggers an energizing biochemical process that lasts for about thirty minutes. Induction is attenuated by hypothermia, adenosine stimulation, and other measures that block the presynaptic release of glutamate. Since Mg^{++} and opioids block the NMDA channel, they might be useful. Caffeine, because of its adenosine blocking capacity, is contraindicated in acute hypoxia.

3. LTP moves toward permanency when the Ca^{++} influx triggers a more profound postsynaptic process. Amplification's postsynaptic cascade activates networks of Ca^{++} dependent kinases: "c-kinases, calmodulin-regulated enzymes, calpains and phospholipases . . . orchestrate the long-term enhancement of excitatory synaptic efficacy and circuit excitability" (Choi, p. 2485). After thirty minutes, exhausted pre- and postsynaptic GABA inhibition and increased glutamate transmission amplifies the excitement to other linked excitatory neurons. Since benzodiazepines increase GABA receptor efficacy, they tend to block amplification.

4. This stage of postsynaptic excitotoxic damage—genetically determined apoptosis—lasts for up to three days. When the protease calpain is activated, MAP 2 proteins of dendritic microtubules break down, phospholipases induce the breakdown of lipid cell membranes. This in turn generates arachadonic acid, free oxygen radicals, and nitric oxide. Ca^{++}-activated endonucleases induce DNA fragmentation in the postsynaptic cell. It is the DNA fragmentation that is irreversibly excitotoxic.

As we discussed in Chapter 2, during LTP, arachadonic acid and nitric oxide diffuse back to the presynaptic membrane, where they enhance further glutamate production and more Ca^{++} release. Presynaptic *overstimulation* induces axonal sprouting, which goes beyond LTP's presynaptic upregulation of glutamate production. The destructive waves of Ca^{++} produced presynaptically and postsynaptically, postsynaptic enzyme cascades, and structural damage to the presynaptic and postsynaptic cell turns LTP from a normal to an excitotoxic process.

NMDA antagonists effectively block the full expression of excitotoxicity in the *penumbra*, the area of incomplete ischemia, surrounding the completely hypoxic area. The penumbra is the area of excitotoxic cellular death for forty-eight to seventy-two hours after the stroke or head trauma. NMDA antagonists have been found to reduce morbidity in head trauma (Bullock, 1992). Clearly, if we can get drugs that block LTP through the blood/brain barrier, we will effectively reduce morbidity in strokes and head trauma.

5. Goldgaber (1994) found a genetic defect that decreases thyrotrophin releasing (*TTR*) production, a substance that keeps amyloid in solution. He found that soluble amyloid contributes to housekeeping after apoptosis, whereas precipitated amyloid physically increases local brain damage. Neurofibrillary tangles, the histological, pathognomonic sign of Alzheimer's dementia, are found primarily in the hippocampal formation and the middle neocortex, areas high in excitatory neurotransmission. They are composed, in part, of *tau proteins*, the microtubular structural protein elements in axons (Goedert, Crowther, and Garner, 1991). Pre-

synaptic axonal sprouting is one of the aftermaths of excitotoxicity. Conceivably, tau proteins are the remnants of this sprouting. Tau proteins and sprouting are highest in the subicular cortex. Since the subiculum contains the hippocampus's outflow, its damage interferes with onstream processing and the formation of new memory. Alzheimer's patients manifest severe deficits of new memory formation.

Chapter 8

1. Other investigators found low baseline cortisol and high MHPG—the breakdown product of norepinephrine—in veterans with PTSD (Mason et al., 1988; Yehuda et al., 1991). Since high norepinephrine usage occurs during increased onstream processing, Mason's and Yehuda's group studies demonstrated that the veterans showed a readiness for arousal and excitability. The low-resting cortisol indicated little capacity to modulate stress. Hoffman and colleagues (1991) found low plasma beta-endorphins in veterans with PTSD. Since these endorphins dampen the locus ceruleus's origin of the arousing norepinephrine system, this also indicates a diminished capacity to lessen arousal. These findings all indicate a tendency toward increased limbic excitability. I conclude that these physiological studies support the inference that veterans with PTSD are vulnerable to LTP-induced episodes of retraumatization.

Chapter 9

1. A position emission tomography (PET) study showed that (1) cognitive slowing, (2) decreased goal-oriented effort, and (3) reduced affect processing in *retarded major depression* corresponds to *bilaterally decreased* rCBF (regional cerebral blood flow) in (1) dorsolateral association cortex, (2) anterior cingulate cortex, and (3) insular cortex (Dolan et al., 1992). By definition, then, lateral, intermediate, and medial prefrontal cortical zones are all drawn into retarded major depression's hypofunction. A SPECT (single photon emission computerized tomography) study confirmed the hypofunction in dorsolateral association cortex and anterior cingulate association cortex in major depressed patients with psychosis, but not in dysthymics (Austin et al., 1992).

2. We may also infer from the finding of increased prefrontal serotonin binding capacity in brains of suicide victims that serotonin neutralizes the aggressive drive. Their postmortem brains showed an increased capacity to bind serotonin compared to controls (Arango, Underwood, and Mann, 1992). The finding indicates that these patients had a prefrontal serotonin deficit in life. Various studies have correlated raw aggressive behavior with decreased central serotonergic activity and upregulation of the serotonin postsynaptic receptors (Cocarro, 1989).

3. A high impetus to action and increased early data assessment in OCD patients may be inferred from an ERP study that showed significantly decreased latency in p300 processing and enhanced n200 in the left hemisphere of OCD patients compared to controls (Towey et al., 1990). I take the finding of quick processing of significance that this implies as an indication that OCD patients are pressured to respond.

Chapter 10

1. Further support for this view is the fact that schizophrenics have decreased binding sites for cholecystokinin (CCK), a neuromodulator that inhibits excitotoxicity in the hippocampus's Ca 1 region (Kerwin, Robinson, and Stevenson, 1992).

Chapter 11

1. In a combined magnetic resonance imaging (MRI) and event-related potential (ERP) study, schizophrenics' abnormal saccades correlated with decreased activation of the nondominant hemisphere's posterior cingulate association cortex (Blackwood et al., 1991). Because the cingulate cortex associates affect signals with social signals, I have concluded that schizophrenics' abnormal saccades are associated with a lack of response to social signals. The schizophrenic cannot determine what is socially and emotionally significant in what he sees.

Chapter 12

1. Both conscious attention and stimulus sequence expectancy enhance the p300 response to stimuli (Sommer, Matt, and Leuthold, 1990). Patients with prefrontal damage are less able to augment their p300 response (Nasman and Dorio, 1993). Selective attention during combined auditory and visual tasks (complex intramodal processing) frontally augments the p300 (Alho et al., 1993). Frontal lobe selective attention can even augment onstream registration of expected stimuli in the brainstem (Galbraith and Kane, 1993)! Thus, during short-term memory tasks, the frontal lobes facilitate processing of data that must be registered, retained, and attended in order to trigger discharge behavior.

Chapter 13

1. One could devise a questionnaire suitable to evaluating an individual's zonal functioning. Each question would become two questions emphasizing high or low function, and each would be scaled from one to five. Such a questionnaire would rate an individual both high and low for each zone's functioning. The total scores for each zone, would indicate the relative emphasis on each zone's identity integers. The present questions are meant to give the practitioner a sense of how to gauge each zone.

Bibliography

Abdullaev, Y.G. and Tsygankov, N.I. How to select epochs of cognitive event-related potentials for brain mapping, *International Journal of Psychophysiology* 1992:13 (2):181-184.

Adamac, R.E. Does kindling model anything clinically relevant? *Biological Psychiatry* 1990:27:249-279.

Aggleton, J.P. The functional effects of amygdala lesions in humans: A comparison with monkeys, in *The amygdala: Neurobiological aspects of emotion, memory, and mental dysfunction*, ed. by John Aggleton. New York: Wiley-Liss, 1992.

Alho, K., Kusular, T., Paavilainen, P., Summala, H., and Naatanen, R. Auditory processing in visual brain areas of the early blind: Evidence from event-related potentials, *Electroencephalography and Clinical Neurophysiology* 1993:86 (6):418-427.

Amaral, D.G. Is there channeling of information through the intrinsic circuit of the rat hippocampus? *Brain Research Review* 1991:16:200-201.

Amaral, D.G., Price, J.L., Pitkanen, A., and Carmichael, T.S. Anatomical organization of the primate amygdaloid complex, in *The amygdala: Neurobiological aspects of emotion, memory, and mental dysfunction*, ed. by J. Aggleton. New York: Wiley-Liss, 1992.

Arango, V., Underwood, M.D., and Mann, J.J. Alterations in monoamine receptors in the brain of suicide victims, *Journal of Clinical Psychopharmacology* 1992:12 (2 suppl):8s-12s.

Arato, M., Frecska, E., MacCrimmon, D.J., Guscott, R., Saxena, B., Tekes, K., and Tothfalusi, L. Serotonergic interhemispheric assymetry: Neurochemical and Pharmaco-EEG evidence, *Progress in Neuropsychopharmacology and Biological Psychiatry* 1991:15 (6):759-764.

Austin, M.P., Dougall, N., Ross, M., Murray, C., O'Carroll, R.E., Moffoot, A., Ebmeier, K.P., and Goodwin, G.M. Single photon emission tomography with Tc-exametazine in major depression and the pattern of brain activity underlying the psychotic/neurotic continuum, *Journal of Affective Disorders* 1992:26: 31-44.

Baddeley, A.D. *Working Memory*, Oxford Psychological Series II, Oxford, England, 1986: pp. 1-289.

Barnes, C.A. Presentation at *The Neurobiology of Learning and Memory*, conference at Stony Brook University, May 24, 1994.

Barnes, J.M. and Henley, J.M. Molecular characteristics of excitatory amino acid receptors, *Progress in Neurobiology* 1992:39:113-133.

Barrett, S.E. and Rugg, M.D. Event-related potentials and the semantic matching of faces, *Neuropsychologica* 1989:27:913-922.

Bauer, H., Rebert, C., Korunka, C., and Leodolter, M. Rare events and the CNV—the oddball CNV, *International Journal of Psychophysiology* 1992:13 (1):51-58.

Bear, D.M. Temporal Lobe epilepsy: A syndrome of senory-limbic hyperconnection, *Cortex* 1979:15:357-384.

Bechtereva, N.P. *The neuropsychological aspects of human mental activity.* New York: Oxford University Press, 1978.

Belleville, S., Peretz, I., and Arguin, M. Contribution of articulatory rehearsal to short-term-memory: Evidence from a case of selective disruption, *Brain and Language* 1992:43:713-746.

Benson, D.F. and Stuss, D.T. Frontal lobe influences on delusions: A clinical perspective, *Schizophrenia Bulletin* 1990:16 (3):403-411.

Berger, B., Gaspar, P., and Verney, C. Dopaminergic innervation of the cerebral cortex: Unexpected differences between rodents and primates, *Trends in Neuroscience* 1991:14:21-28.

Blackburn, J.R., Pfaust, J.G., and Phillips, A.G. Dopamine functions in appetitive and defensive behaviors, *Progress in Neurobiology* 1992:39:247-279.

Blackwood, D.H., Young, A.H., McQueen, J.K., Martin, M.J., Roxborough, H.M., Muir, M.J., St Clair, D.M., and Kean, D.M. Magnetic resonance imaging in schizophrenia: Altered brain morphology associated with P300 abnormalities and eye-tracking dysfunction, *Biological Psychiatry* 1991:30 (8):753-769.

Blanchard, E.B., Kolb, L., Prins, A., Gates, S., and McCoy, G.C. Changes in plasma norepinephrine to combat-related stimuli among Vietnam veterans with post-traumatic stress disorder, *The Journal of Nervous and Mental Disorders* 1991:179:371-373.

Blewett, A.E. Abnormal subjective time experience in depression, *British Journal of Psychiatry* 1992:161:195-200.

Brazelton, T.B. The origins of reciprocity, in *New Directions in Childhood Psychopathology*, ed. by S.I. Harrison and J.F. McDermott Jr. New York: International University Press, 1980.

Bredt, D.S., Snyder, S., and Solomon, H. Nitric oxide: A novel neuronal messenger, *Neuron* 1992:8:3-11.

Breier, A., Schreiber, J., Dyer, J., and Pickar, D. Course of illness and predictors of outcome in chronic schizophrenia: Implications for pathophysiology, *British Journal of Psychiatry* 1992:161 (suppl):38-43.

Bremner, J.D., Seibyl, J.P., and Scott, T.M. Depressed hippocampal formation volume in post-traumatic stress disorder, *Proceedings of the 145th Annual Meeting of the American Psychiatric Association*, Washington DC, 1992.

Brown, E.E., Robertson, G.S., and Fibiger, H.C. Evidence for conditional neuronal activation following exposure to a cocaine-paired environment: Role of forebrain limbic structures, *The Journal of Neuroscience* 1992:12 (10):4112-4121.

Brown, K.W. and White, T. Syndromes of chronic schizophenia and some clinical correlates, *British Journal of Psychiatry* 1992:161:317-322.

Brown, T.H. Calcium dynamics in hippocampal neurons, presentation at *The Neurobiology of Learning and Memory*, Stony Brook, New York, May 24, 1994.

Bruder, G.E., Stewart, J.W., Towey, J.P., Friedman, D., tenke, Craig, E., Voglmaier, M.M., Leite, P., Cohen, P., and Quitkin, F.M. Abnormal cerebral laterality in bipolar depression: Convergence of behavioral and brain event-related potential findings, *Biological Psychiatry* 1992:32:33-47.

Bullfinch, T. *Bullfinch's Mythology*, ed. by R. Martin, New York: HarperCollins, 1991.

Bullock, R. Introducing NMDA antagonists into clinical practice: Why head injury trials? *British Journal of Clinical Pharmacology* 1992:34:396-401.

Bunney, E., Jr., Goodwin, F.K., Murphy, D.L., House, K.M., and Gordon, E.K. The "switch process" in manic-depressive illness, *Archives of General Psychiatry* 1972:September:27

Burkhart, M.A. and Thomas, D.G. Event-elated potential measures of attention in moderately depressed subjects, *Electroencephalography and Clinical Neurophysiology* 1993:88 (1):42-50.

Caldecott-Hazard, S. and Engel, J., Jr. Limbic postictal events: Anatomical substrates and opioid receptor involvment, *Progress in Neuropsychopharmacological Biological Psychiatry* 1987:11:389-418.

Campbell, J. *Grammatical man*, New York: Simon and Schuster, 1982.

Caplan, L.R., Schahmann, J.D., Kase, C.S., Feldmann, E., Baquis, G., Greenberg, J.P., Gorelick, P.B., Helgason, C., and Hier, D. Caudate infarcts, *Archives of neurology* 1990:47:133-142.

Cassanova, M.F., Goldberg, T.E., Suddath, R., Daniel, D.G., Rawlings, R., Lloyd, D.G., Loats, H.L., Kleinman, J.E., and Weinberger, D.R. Quantitative shape analysis of the temporal and prefrontal lobes of schizophrenic patients: A magnetic resonance image study, *Journal of Neuropsychiatry and Clinical Neurosciences* 1990:2:363-372.

Cassell, M.D. and Gray, T.S. Morphology of peptide-immunoreactive neurons in the rat central nucleus of the amygdalla, *The Journal of Comparative Neurology* 1989:28:1320-1333.

Chen, M.F., Chiu, T.H., and Lee, E.H.Y. Noradrenergic mediation of the memory enhancing effect of cortocotrphin releasing factor in the locus coeruleus of rats, *Psychoneuroendocrinolgy* 1992:17 (2/3):113-124.

Choi, D.W. Cerebral Hypoxia: Some new approaches and unanswered questions, *The Journal of Neuroscience* 1990:10:2493-2501.

Chomsky, N. *Rules and representations*, New York: Columbia University Press, 1980.

Cleghorn, J., Garnett, E., Nahmias, C., Firnau, G., Brown, G., Kaplan, R., Szechtman, H., and Szechtma, B. Increased frontal and reduced parietal glucose metabolism in acute untreated schizophrenics, *Psychiatry Research* 1989:28:119-133.

Coccaro, E.F. Central Serotonin and impulsive aggression, *British Journal of Psychiatry* 1989:8 (suppl):52-62.

Cook, M.J., Fish, D.R., Shorvon, S.D., Staughan, K., and Stevens, J.M. Hippocampal volumetric and morphometric studies in frontal and temporal lobe epilepsy, *Brain* 1992:115:1001-1015.

Cooper, J.R., Bloom, F.E., and Roth, R.H. *The biochemical basis of neuropharmacology*, New York: Oxford University Press, 1991.

Corradetti, R., Ballerini, L., Pugliese, A.M., and Pepeu, G. Serotonin blocks the long-trem potentiation induced by primed burst stimulation in the CA1 region of rat hippocampal slices, *Neuroscience* 1992:46:511-518

Cortazer, J. *We love Glenda so much and a change of light*, New York: Vintage Books, 1984.

Courschesne, E., Townsend, J., Akshoomoff, N.A. Saitch, O., Yeung-Courschesne Leone, R., Lincoln, A.J., James, H.E., Haas, R.H., Schreibman, L., and Lau, L. Impairment in shifting attention in autistic and cerebellar patients, *Behavioral Neuroscience* 1994:108 (5):848-865.

Crick, F. The recent excitement about neural networks, *Nature*, 1989:337:12 January:129-133.

Crick, F. and Koch, C. The problem of consciousness, *Scientific American* 1992 (September):153-159.

Crow, T. Molecular pathology of schizophrenia: More than one disease process? *British Medical Journal* 1980:280:66-68.

Crowe, S.F. Dissociation of two frontal lobe syndromes by a test of verbal fluency, *Journal of Clinical and Experimental Neuropsychology* 1992:14 (2):327-339.

Cummings, J.L. Organic psychosis, *Psychosomatics* 1988:29:17-25.

Damasio, A.R., Tramel, D., and Damasio, H. Individuals with sociopathic behavior fail to respond to social stimuli, *Behavioral Brain Research* 1990:41:81-94.

Damasio, A.R. and Damasio, H. Brain and language, *Scientific American* 1992 (September):89-95.

David, A.S. and Cutting, J.C. Affect, affective disorder and schizophrneia, A neuropsychological investigation of right hemisphere function, *British Journal of Psychiatry* 1990:156:491-495.

Davis, M. The role of the amygdala in fear-potentiated startle: implications for animal models of anxiety, *Trends in Psychopharmacological Sciences* 1992a:13: 35-41.

Davis, M. The role of the amygdala in conditioned fear, in *The amygdala*, ed. by J.P. Aggleton, New York: Wiley-Liss, 1992.

DeGiorgio, C.M., Tomaiyasu, U., Gott, P.S., and Treiman D.M. Hippocampal pyramidal cell loss in human status epilepticus, *Epilepsia* 1992:33: (1):23-27.

DeLisi, L.E., Stritzke, P., Riordan, H., Holan, V., Boccio, A., Kushner, M., McClelland, J., Van Eyl, O., and Azad, A. The timing of brain morphological changes in schizophrenia and their relationship to clinical outcome, *Biological Psychiatry* 1992:31:241-254.

Demonet, J.F., Chollet, F., Ramsay, S., Cardebat, D., Nespoulous, J., Wise, R., Rascol, A., and Frackowiak, R. The anatomy of phonological and semantic processing in normal subjects, *Brain* 1992:115:1753-1768.

Dennet, J.D. and Kinsbourne, M. The color phi phenomenon, *Behavioral Brain Science* 1992:15:183-247.

Desmond, N.L. Presentation at *The Neurobiology of Learning and Memory*, Stony Brook, New York, May 24, 1994.

Disterhoff, J.F., Black, J., Moyer, J.R., and Thompson L.T. Calcium-mediated changes in hippocampal neurons and learning, *Brain Research Review* 1991:16: 196-197.

Dolan, R.J., Bench, C.J., Brown R.G., Scott, L.C., Friston, K. J., and Frackowiak, R.S.J. Regional cerebral blood flow abnormalities in depressed patients with cognitive impairment, *Journal of Neurology, Neurosurgery, and Psychiatry* 1992: 55:768-773.

Drake, M.E. Jr., Phillips, B.B., and Pakalnis, A. Auditory evoked potentials in borderline personality disorder, *Clinical Electoencephalography* 1991:22 (3): 188-192.

Dure, L.S., Young, A.B., and Penney, J.B. Excitatory amino acid binding sites in the caudate nucleus and frontal cortex of Huntington's Disease, *Annals of Neurology* 1991:30:271-283.

Ebert, D., Feistel, H., Burocka, A., and Kusckaw, M.T. A test-retest study of cerebral blood flow during somatosensory stimulation in depressed patients with schizophrenia and major depression, *European Archives of Psychiatry and Clinical Neuroscience* 1993:242:250-254.

Eccles, J.C. How the self acts on the brain, *Psychoneuroendocrinology* 1982:3: 271-283.

Eccles, J.C. Developing concepts of the synapses, *The Journal of Neuroscience* 1990:3769-3781.

Edelman, G. *Neural Darwinism*. Basic Books, New York, 1987.

Ehlers, C.L., Wall, T.L., and Chaplin, R.I. Long-latency event-related potentials in rats: Effects of doaminergic and serotonergic depletions, *Pharmacology, Biochemistry and Behavior* 1991:38 (4):789-793.

Eichenbaum, H. and Otto, T. The Hippocampus: What does it do? *Behavioral, and Neural Biology* 1992:57:2-36.

Eichenbaum, H. and Buckingham, J. Studies on hippocampal processing: Experiment, theory and model, in *Learning and Computational Neuroscience: Foundations of Adaptive Networks*, ed. by M. Gabriel and J. Moore, Cambridge, MA: The MIT Press, 1995.

Elbert, T., Ulrich, R., Rockstroh, B., and Lutdenberger, W. The processing of temporal intervals reflected by CNV-like brain potentials, *Psychophysiology* 1991:28 (6):648-655.

Eliot, T.S. *The Complete Poems and Plays,* New York: Harcourt, Brace and Co., 1952.

Everitt, B.J. and Robbins, T.W. Amygdala-ventral striatal interactions and reward-related processes in *The Amygdala: Neurobiological Aspects of Emotion, Memory, and Mental Dysfunction*, ed. by J. Aggleton. New York: Wiley-Liss, 1992.

Falkenstein, M., Hohnsbein, J., Hoorman, J., and Blanke, L. Effects of crossmodal divided attention on late ERP components II: Error Processing in choice reaction tasks, *Electroencephalography and Clinical Neurophysiology* 1991:78 (6):447-455.

Fallon, J. and Cioffo, P. Distibutions of monoamines within the amygdala, in *The Amygdala*, ed. by J.P. Aggleton, New York: Wiley-Liss, 1992.

Farwell, L.A. and Donchin, E. The truth will out: Interrogative polygraphy ("lie-detection") with event-related brain potentials, *Psychophysiology* 1991:28 (5): 531-547.

Fazelli, M.S. Synaptic plasticity: On the trail of the retrograde messenger, *Trends in Neuroscience* 1992:15:115-118.

Ferenczi, S. Thalassia. *Psychoanalytic Quarterly* 1938.

First, M.B. (ed.) DSM-IV, Washington, DC: American Psychiatric Association Press, 1994.

Fisher, C.M. Neurologic fragments II: Remarks on anosagnosia, confabulation, memory, and other topics; and an appendix on self-observation, *Neurology* 1989:39:127-132.

Flor-Henry, P. On certain aspects of the localization of the cerebral systems regulating and determining emotion, *Biological Psychiatry* 1979:4:677-694.

Fontana, D.J., Post, R.M., and Pert, A. Conditioned increase in mesolimbic dopamine overflow by stimuli associated with cocaine, in Abstacts of the 17th Meeting of the Society for Neuroscience, Society for Neuroscience, Washington, DC, 1991.

Foote, S.L., Berridge, C.W., Adams, L.M., and Pineda, J.A. Electrophysiological evidence for the involvment of the locus coeruleus in alerting, orienting and attending, *Progress in Brain Research* 1991:88:521-532.

Forstl, H., Almeida, O.P., and Owen, A.M. Psychiatric, neurological, and medicalaspects of misidentification syndromes: A review of 260 cases, *Psychological Medicine* 1991:21:905-910.

Frackowiak, R.S.J. The left medial temporal region and schizophrenia, *Brain* 1992:115:367-382.

Fraiberg, S. *Every child's birthright: In defense of mothering*, New York: Basic Books, 1977.

The following references are from *The Collected Words of Sigmund Freud, Volumes I-XXV*, London: Hogarth Press.

Freud, S. *Project for a scientific psychology*, ed. and trans. by J. Strachey. Standard Edition, Vol. I, (1950 [1895]).

Freud S. *Letter 125*, ed. and trans. by J. Strachey. Standard Edition, Vol I, (1950 [1899]).

Freud, S. *Screen memories*, ed. and trans. by J. Strachey. Standard Edition, Vol III, 1899.

Freud, S. *The interpretation of dreams*, ed. and trans. by J. Strachey. Standard Edition, Vols IV and V, 1900.

Freud, S. *Psychopathology of everyday life*, ed. and trans. by J. Strachey. Standard Edition, Vol VI, 1901.

Freud, S. *Jokes and their relation to the unconscious*, ed. and trans. by J. Strachey. Standard Edition, Vol VIII, 1905.

Freud, S. *Family romances*, ed. and trans. by J. Strachey. Standard Edition, Vol IX, 1909.

Freud, S. *Psycho-analytic notes on an autobiographical account of a case of paranoia (demential paranoides)*, ed. and trans. by J. Strachey. Standard Edition, Vol XII, 1911.

Freud, S. *On narcissism*, ed. and trans. by J. Strachey. Standard Edition, Vol XIV, 1914.

Freud, S. *Instincts and their vicissitudes*, ed. and trans. by J. Strachey. Standard Edition, Vol XIV, 1915.

Freud, S. *A case of paranoia running counter to the psychoanalytic theory of the disease*, ed. and trans. by J. Strachey. Standard Edition, Vol XIV, 1915.

Freud, S. *Mourning and melancholia*, ed. and trans. by J. Strachey. Standard Edition, Vol XIV, 1917.

Freud, S. *From the history of an infantile neurosis*, ed. and trans. by J. Strachey. Standard Edition, Vol XVII, 1918.

Freud, S. *The Uncanny*, ed. and trans. by J. Strachey. Standard Edition, Vol XVII, 1919.

Freud, S. *Beyond the pleasure principle*, ed. and trans. by J. Strachey. Standard Edition, Vol XVIII, 1920.

Freud, S. *Group psychology and the analysis of the ego*, ed. and trans. by J. Strachey. Standard Edition, Vol XVIII, 1921.

Freud, S. *Medusa's head,* ed. and trans. by J. Strachey. The Standard Edition, Vol. XVIII, 1922.

Freud, S. *Some neurotic mechanisms in jealousy, paranoia and homosexuality*, ed. and trans. by J. Strachey. Standard Edition, Vol XVIII, 1922.

Freud, S. *The ego and the id*, ed. and trans. by J. Strachey. Standard Edition, Vol XIX, 1923.

Freud, S. *Inhibition symptom and anxiety*, ed. and trans. by J. Strachey. Standard Edition, Vol XX, 1926.

Freud, S. *Fetishism*, ed. and trans. by J. Strachey. Standard Edition, Vol XXI, 1927.

Freud, S. *Some dreams of Descartes': A letter to Maxime Leroy*, ed. and trans. by J. Strachey. Standard Edition, Vol XXI, 1929.

Freud, S. *A disturbance of memory on the Acropolis*, ed. and trans. by J. Strachey. Standard Edition, Vol XXII, 1936.

Friere-Maia, L. and Azevedo, A.D. The autonomic nervous system is not a purely efferent system, *Medical Hypotheses* 1990:32:91-99.

Friston, K.J., Liddle, P. F., Frith, C.D., Hirsch, S.R., and Frackowiak, R.S.J. The left medial temporal region and schizophrenia, *Brain* 1992:115:367-382.

Frith, C.D., Friston, K.J., and Liddle, P.F. A PET study of word finding, *Neuropsychologica* 1991:29 (12):1137-1148.

Fuchigami, T., Okubo, O., Fujita, Y., Okuni, M., Noguchi, Y., and Yamada, T. Auditory event-related potenitals and reaction time in children: Evaluation of cognitive development, *Developmental Medicine and Child Neurology* 1993:35 (3):230-237.

Fuster, J.M. *Memory in the Cerebral Cortex*, Cambridge, MA: The MIT Press, 1995.

Galbraith, G.C. and Kane, J.M. Brainstem frequency-following responses and cortical event-related potentials during attention, *Perceptual and Motor Skills* 1993:76 (3):1231-1241.

Gangadher, B.N., Ancy, J., Janakiramaiah, N., and Umapthy, C. P300 amplitude in non-bipolar, melancholic depression, *Journal of Affective Disorders* 1993: 28 (1):57-60.

Gerfen, C.R. The neostriatal mosaic: comparmentalization of corticostriatal input and striatonigral output systems, *Nature* 1984:311:461-464.

Gerfen, C.R. The neostriatal mosaic: Multiple levels of compartmental organization, *Trends in Neuroscience* 1992:15:133-139.

Geschwind, N. Dysconnection Syndromes in animals and man, *Brain* 1965:88:1-3.

Ginzburg, I. Neuronal polarity: Targeting of microtubule components into axons and dendrites, *Trends in Biological Science* 1991:16:257-260.

Gloor, P. Inputs and outputs of the amygdala: What the amygdala is trying to tell the rest of the brain, in *Limbic mechanisms,* ed. by R.E. Livingston and O. Hornykiewicz. New York: Plenum Press, 1978.

Gloor, P. Epilepsy: Relationships between electrophysiology and intracellular mechanisms involving second messengers and gene expression, *The Canadian Journal of Neurological Sciences* 1989:16:8-21.

Gloor, P. Role of the amygdala in temporal lobe epilepsy, in *The amygdala: Neurobiological aspects of emotion, memory, and mental dysfunction*, ed. by J. Aggleton, New York: Wiley-Liss, 1992.

Gloor, P., Olivier, A., Quesney, L.F., Andermann, F., and Horowitz, S. The role of the limbic system in experiential phenomena of temporal lobe epilepsy, *Annals of Neurology* 1982:12:129-142.

Glowinski, J. Some properties of the ascending dopaminergic pathways: Interaction of the nigrostriatal dopaminergic system with other neuronal pathways, in *The Neurosciences*, ed. by F. Schmidt, Cambridge, MA: MIT Press, 1979.

Goddard, G.V., McIntyre, D.C., and Leech, C.K. A permanent change in brain function resulting from daily electrical stimulation, *Experimental Neurology* 1969:25:147-165.

Goedert, M., Crowther, R.A., and Garner, C.C. Molecular characterization of microtubule-associated proteins tau and MAP2, *Trends in Neuroscience* 1991: 14:193-198.

Goldenberg, G., Podreka, I., Uhl, F., Steiner, K., Willmes, K., and Deeke, L. Cerebral correlates of imagining colours, faces, and a map-1. SPECT of regional cerebral blood flow, *Neurobiology* 1991:27 (11):1315-1328.

Goldgaber, D. Presentation at *The Neurobiology of Learning and Memory*, Stony Brook, New York, May 24, 1994.

Goldman-Rakic, P.S. Working memory and the mind, *Scientific American* 1992 (September):111-117.

Goldman-Rakic, P.S., Lidow, M.S., and Gallager, D.W. Overlap of dopaminergic, adrenergic, and serotonergic receptors and complementarity of their subtypes in primate prefrontal cortex, *The Journal of Neuroscience* 1990:10:2125-2138.

Goode, D.J. and Manning, A.A. Specific imbalance of right and left sided motor neuron exciteability in schizophrenia, *Journal of Neurology, Neurosurgery, and Psychiatry* 1988:51:626-629.

Gould, E., Woolley, C.S., Cameron, H.A., Daniels, D.H., and McEwen, B.S. Adrenal steroids regulate postnatal development of the rat dentate gyrus: II. Effects of glucocorticoids and mineralcorticoids on cell birth, *The Journal of Comparative Neurology* 1991:313:486-493.

Green, E. and Greenough, W. Altered synaptic transmission in dentate gyrus of rats reared in complex environments: Evidence from hippocampal slices maintained in vitro, *Journal of Neurophysiology* 1986:55:739-750.

Greenacre, P. *Emotional Growth*, Vols. I and II, New York: International Universities Press, (1971 [1963]).

Greengard, P. The synapsins: Dual function neuronal phosphoproteins, Association for Research in Nervous and Mental Disease 75th Anniversary Program (Salmon lecture). New York, December 1, 1995.

Greenough, W.T. Presentation at *The Neurobiology of Learning and Memory*, Stony Brook University, May 24, 1994.

Grossman, A. Opioids and stress in man, *Journal of Endocrinology* 1988:119: 377-381.

Gruber, H.E. and Voneche, J. *The Essential Piaget*, New York: Basic Books, 1977.

Gur, E. Brain function in psychiatric disorders, *Archives of General Psychiatry* 1984:41:695-699.

Haley, J.E., Wilcox, G.L., and Chapman, P.F. The role of nitric oxide in hippocampal long-term potentiation, *Neuron* 1992:8:211-216.

Halgren, E. Emotional neurophysiology of the amygdala within the context of human cognition, in *The amygdala: Neurobiological aspects of emotion, memory, and mental dysfunction*, ed. by J. Aggleton, New York: Wiley-Liss, 1992.

Halpain, S. and Greengard, P. Activation of NMDA receptors induces rapid dephosphorilization of the cytoskeletal protein, *Neural Biology* 1992:57: 263-266.

Hanley, M.R. Peptide regulatory factors in the nervous system, *The Lancet* June 17, 1989:1375-1376.

Hargreaves, E.L., Cain, D.P., and Vanderwolf, C.H. Learning and behavioral long-term-potentiation: Importance of controlling for motor activity, *The Journal of Neuroscience* 1990:10 (5):1472-1478.

Harris, J.E. *Clinical neuroscience*, New York: Human Sciences Press, 1986.

Harris, J.E. and Harris, J.A. *The roots of artifice: On the origin and development of literary creativity*, New York: Human Sciences Press, 1981.

Harris, J.E. and Harris J.A. *Sigmund Freud, the one-eyed doctor*, New York: Jason Aronson, 1984.

Harris, J.E. and Newman, J. The emotional cost of war, *The Journal of Psychohistory,* 1986:14:2:153-164.

Harris, J.E. and Pontius, A. Dismemberment murder: In search of the object, *Law and Psychiatry,* 1975:3:1:7-24.

Hartmann, H. *Essays on ego psychology,* New York: International Universities Press, (1956, [1964]).

Hauser, P., Altshuler, L.L., and Berretini, W. Temporal lobe measurement in primary affective disorder, *Journal of Neuropsychiatry and Clinical Neuroscience* 1989:1 (2):128-134.

Havashida, S., Kameyama, T., Niwa, S., Itch, K., Hiramatsu, K., Fukuda, M., Saitch, C., Iwanami, A., Nakagome, K., and Sasaki, T. Distributions of the Nd and P300 in a normal sample, *International Journal of Psychophysiology* 1992:13 (3):233-239.

Heath, R.G. Pleasure and brain activity in man: Deep and surface encephalograms during orgasm, *The Journal of Nervous and Mental Disease* 1972:154:3-16.

Hendin, H. and Haas, A.P. *Wounds of war,* New York: Basic Books, 1984.

Henke, P.C. Stomach pathology and the amygdala, in *The Amygdala,* ed. by J.P. Aggleton, New York: Wiley-Liss, 1992.

Herrero, I.M., Miras-Portugal, T.M., and Sanchez-Prieto, J. Positive feedback of glutamate exocytosis by metabotropic presynaptic receptor stimulation, *Nature* 1992:360:163-165.

Hikosaka, O., Sakamoto, M., and Usui, S. Functional properties of monkey caudate neurons I. Activities related to saccadic eye movements, *Journal of Neuroscience* 1989:61:780-798.

Hoff, A.L., Riordan, H., O'Donnell, D.W., Morris, L., and DeLisi, L.E. Neuropsychological functioning of first-episode schizophreniform patients, *American Journal of Psychiatry* 1992:149:898-903.

Hoffman, L., Watson, P.B., Wilson, G., and Montgomery, J. Low plasma beta-endorphin in post-trumatic stress disorder, *Australian and New Zealand Journal of Psychiatry* 1989:23:269-273.

Hokfelt, T. Neuropeptides in perspective: The last ten years, *Neuron* 1991:7: 867-879.

Horowitz, M.J. (ed.). *Personal schemas and maladaptive interpersonal patterns,* Chicago: University of Chicago Press, 1992.

Hovanitz, C.A. and Wander, M.R. Tension headache: Disregulation at some levels of stress, *Journal of Behavioral Medicine* 1990:13:539-559.

Huntley, G.W., Vickers, J.C., and Morrison, J.H. Cellular and synaptic localization of NMDA and non-NMDA receptor subunits in neocortex: Organizational features related to cortical circuitry, function, and disease, *Trends in Neuroscience* 1994:17 (12):536-543.

Ingvar, D.H. Distribution of cerebral activity in chronic schizophrenia, *The Lancet* December, 21, 1974:1484-1486.

Insel, T.R. and Winslow, J.T. Neurobiology of obsessive-compulsive disorder, *Psychiatric Clinics of North America* 1992:15 (4):813-824.

Izquierdo, I. and Median, J.H. Memory: The role of endogenous benzodiazepines, *Trends in Pharmacological Science* 1991:12:260-264.

Izquierdo, I., Da Cunha, C., Rosat, R., Jerusalinsky, D., Ferreiara, M., Beatriz C., and Medina, J.H. Neurotransmitter receptors in volved in post-training memory processing by the amygdala, medial septum, and hippocampus of the rat, *Behavioral and Neural Biology* 1992:58:16-26.

Izumi, Y., Ito, K., Urono, K., and Kato, H. The role of quisqualate receptors in the induction of hippocampal long-term potentiation, *Medical Hypotheses* 1990: 33:89-93.

Jacobson, E. *The self and the object world*, New York: International Universities Press, 1954.

Jacobson, L. and Sapolsky, R. The role of the hippocampus in feedback regulation of the hypothalamic-pituitary-adrenocortical axis, *Endocrine Reviews* 1991: 12:118-134.

Jameson, F. *The Prison house of language*, Princeton: Princeton University Press, 1972.

Janowsky, J.S., Shimamura, A.P., and Squire, L.R. Memory and metamemory: Comparisons between patients with frontal lobe lesions and amnesic patients, *Psychobiology* 1989:17:3-11.

Jansen, K.L.R. Neuroscience and the near-death expereince: Roles for the NMDA-PCP receptor, the sigma receptor and the endopsychosins, *Medical Hypotheses* 1990:31:25-29.

Jaspers, K. *General Psychopathology*, Chicago: University of Chicago Press, 1963.

Javitt, D.C., Doeshka, P., Zylberman, I., Ritter, W., and Vaughan, H.G. Jr. Impairment of early cortical processing in schizophrenia: An event-related potential confirmation study, *Biological Psychiatry* 1993:33 (7):513-519.

Jaynes, J. *The origin of consciousness in the breakdown of the bicameral mind*, Boston: Houghton Mifflin, 1976.

Jodo, E. and Kayama, Y. Relation of a negative ERP component to response inhibition in a go/no-go task, *Electroencephalography and Clinical Neurophysiology* 1992:82 (6):477-482.

Johnson, R., Jr. Developmental evidence for modality-dependent P300 generators: A normative study, *Psychophysiology* 1989:26 (6):651-657.

Johnston, D. and Brown, T.H. The synaptic nature of the paroxysmal depolarizing shift in hippocampal neurons, *Annals of Neurology*, 1984:16 (suppl.):s65-s71.

Jones, K.A. and Baughman, R.W. Both NMDA and nonNMDA subtypes of glutamate receptors are concentrated at synapses on cerebral cortical neurons in culture, *Neuron* 1990:7:593-603.

Jones, R.S.G. Entorhinal-hippocampal connections: A speculative view of their function, *Trends in Neuroscience* 1993:16 (2):58-64.

Jonson, B. Hymn to Cynthia, in *Elizabethan and Jacobean Posts*, ed. by W.H. Auden and N.H. Pearson, New York: Viking Press, 1950.

Joyce, J. *A Portrait of the Artist as a Young Man*, New York: Random House (Modern Library), 1928.

Joyce, J. *Ulysses*, New York: Random House,1942.

Kaczmarek, P.L.J. Neurolinguistic analysis of verbal utterances in patients with focal lesions of the frontal lobes, *Brain and Language* 1984:21:52-58.

Kamphuis, G.W. and Lopes da Silva, F.H. A long-lasting decrease in the inhibitory effect of GABA on glutamate responses of hippocampal pyramidal neurons induced by kindling eleptogenesis, *Neuroscience* 1991b:41:425-431.

Kandel, E.R. From metapsychology to molecular biology: Explorations into the nature of anxiety, *The American Journal of Psychiatry* 1983:140:1277-1293.

Kandel, E.R. Presentation at *The Neurobiology of Learning and Memory*, Stony Brook University, May 23, 1994.

Kandel, E.R. and Hawkins, R.D. The biological basis of learning and individuality, *Scientific American* 1992 (September):79-86.

Kandel, E.R., Schwartz, J.H., and Jessell, T.M. (eds.). *Principles of neural science*, third edition, New York: Elsevier Scientific Publishing Co., 1991.

Kapp, B.S., Whalen, P.J., Supple, W.F., and Pascoe, J.P. Amygdaloid contributions to conditioned arousal and sensory infromation processing in *The amygdala: Neurobiological aspects of emotion, memory, and mental dysfunction*, ed. by J. Aggleton, New York: Wiley-Liss, 1992.

Keats, J. *Selected Poems and Letters,* Cambridge, MA: Houghton Mifflin, Riverside Edition, 1959.

Kernberg, O. *Borderline conditions and pathological narcissism*, New York: Jason Aronson, 1975.

Kerwin, R., Robinson, P., and Stephenson, J. Distribution of CCK binding sites in the human hippocampal formation and their alteration in schizophrenia: A post-mortem autoradiographic study, *Psychological Medicine* 1992:22 (1): 37-43.

Kestenbaum, R. and Nelson, C.A. Neural and behavioral correlates of emotion recognition in children and adults, *Journal of Experimental Child Psychology* 1992:54 (1):1-18.

Keyser, A. Basic aspects of development and maturation of the brain: Embryological contributions to neuroendocrinology, *Psychoneuroendocrinology* 1983:8: 157-181.

Kihlstrom, J.F. Hypnosis, memory, and amnesia, *Journal of the Neurological Sciences* 1995:134 (1):1-8.

Kitagawa, K., Matsumoto, M., Ohtsuki, T., Okabe, T., Hata, R., Ueda, H., Handa, N., Sobue, K., and Kamada, T. The characteristics of blood-brain barrier in three different conditions—infarction, selective neuronal death, and selective loss of presynatpic terminals-following cerebral ischemia, *Acta neuropathologica* 1992:84:378-386.

Klausner, J.D., Sweeney, J.A., Deck, M.D.F., Haas, G.L., and Kelly, A.B. Clinical correlates of cerebral ventricular enlargment in schizophrenia, *The Journal of Nervous and Mental Disease* 1992:180:407-412.

Kling, A.S. and Brothers, L.A. The amygdala and social behavior, in *The amygdala: Neurobiological aspects of emotion, memory, and mental dysfunction*, ed. by J. Aggleton, New York: Wiley-Liss, 1992.

Kohut, H. *The analysis of the self*, New York: International Universities Press, 1971.

Kounios, J. and Holcomb, P.J. Structure and process in semantic memory: Evidence from event-related brain potentials and reaction times, *Journal of Experimental Psychology* 1992:121 (4):459-479.

Kounios, J. and Holcomb, P.J. Structure and process in semantic memory: Evidence from event-related brain potentials and reaction time, *Journal of Experimental Psychology: General* 1992:121 (4):459-479.

Kriekhaus, E.E., Donahoe, J.W., and Morgan, M.A. Paranoid schizophrenia may be caused by dopamine hyperactivity of CA 1 hippocampus, *Biological Psychiatry* 1992:31:560-570.

Kritchevsky, M., Zouzounis, J., and Squire, L.L. Transient global amnesia and functional amnesia: contrasting examples of episodic memory loss, *The Journal of Neurological Science* 1995:134 (1):1-8.

Kroll, J. *PTSD/Borderlines in Therapy*, New York: Norton, 1993.

Kuba, K. and Kumamoto, E. Long-term-potentiation in vertebrate synapses: A variety of cascades with common subprocesses, *Progress in Neurobiology* 1990:34:197-269.

Kushwaha, R.K., Williams, W.J., and Shevrin, H. An information flow technique for category event-related-potentials, *IEEE Transactions on Biomedical Engineering* 1992:39 (2):165-175.

Kutcher, S.P., Blackwood, D.H., St Clair, D., Bakell, D.F., and Muir, W.J. Auditory p300 in borderline personality disorder and schizophrenia, *Archives of General Psychiatry*: 1989:44 (7):645-650.

Lalonde, R. and Botez, M.I. The cerebellum and learning processes in animals, *Brain Research Reviews* 1990:15:325-332.

Lauffer, M. The central masturbation fantasy, the final sexual organization and adolescence, *The Psychoanalytic Study of the Child* 1976:31.

Laurian, S., Bader, M., Lanares, J., and Oros, L. Topography of event-related potentials elicited by visual emotional stimuli, *International Journal of Psychophysiology* 1991:10 (3):231-238.

Laurien, S., Bader, M., Lanares, J., and Dros, L. Topography of event-related-potentials elicited by visual emotional stimuli, *International Journal of Psychophysiology* 1991:10 (3):231-238.

Ledoux, J.E., Cicchetti, P., Xagoris, A., and Romanski, L.M. The lateral amygdaloid nucleus: Sensory interface of the amygdala in fear conditioning, *The Journal of Neuroscience* 1990:10:1062-1069.

Ledoux, J.E. Presentation at *The Neurobiology of Learning and Memory*, Stony Brook University, May 23, 1994

Ledoux, J.E. Emotion and the amygdala in *The amygdala: Neurobiological aspects of emotion, memory, and mental dysfunction*, ed. by J. Aggleton, New York: Wiley-Liss, 1992.

Leiner, H.C., Leiner, A.L., and Dow, R.S. Reappraising the cerebellum: What does the hindbrain contribute to the forebrain? *Behavioral Neuroscience* 1989: 103 (5):998-1008.

Leudar, I., Thomas, P., and Johnston, M. Self-repair in dialogues of schizophrenics: Effects of hallucinations and negative sympoms, *Brain and Language* 1992:43:487-511.

Levinson, H.N. Learning disabilities in children, adolescents, and adults, *Perceptual and Motor Skills* 1988:67:983-1006.

Liddle, P.F. The psychomotor disorders: Disorders of the supervisory mental processes, *Behavioral Neurology* 1993:6:5-14.

Linden, D.J., Dickinson, M.H., Smeyne, M., and Connor, J.A. A long-term depression of AMPA currents in cultured cerebellar purkinje neurons, *Neuron* 1991:7:81-89.

Lisberger, S.G. Presentation at *The Neurobiology of Learning and memory*, Stony Brook University, May 23, 1994.

Lisman, J.E. and Harris, K.M. Quantal analysis and synaptic anatomy, *Trends in Neuroscience* 1993:16 (4):141-147.

Lothman, E.W. The biochemical basis and pathophysiology of status epilepticus, *Neurology* 1990:40: (suppl. 2):13-23.

Lothman, E.W. Functional anatomy: A challenge for the decade of the brain, *Epilepsia* 1991:32: (suppl. 5):s3-s13.

Luria, A.R. *The man with a shattered world*, New York: Basic Books, 1972.

Luria, A.R. *Higher cortical functions in man*, New York: Basic Books, 1980.

Lynch, G. and Baudry, M. The biochemistry of memory: A new and specific hypothesis, *Science* 1984:224: (June 8):1057-1063.

Maccari, S., Mormede, P., Piazza, P.V., Simon, H., Angelucci, L., and Le Moal, M. Hippocampal type I and type II corticosteroid receptors are modulated by central noradrenergic systems, *Psychoneuroendocrinology* 1992:17:103-112.

Mahler, M., Pine, F., and Bergman, A. *The psychological birth of the human infant*, New York: Basic Books, 1975.

Malcom, J. *In the Freud archives*, New York: Alfred Knopf, 1984.

Marangos, P.J. Adenosinergic approaches to stroke therapeutics, *Medical Hypotheses* 1990:32:45-49.

Mason, J.W., Giller, E.A., Kosten, T., and Harkness, L. Elevation of urinary norepinephrine/cortisol ratio in post-traumatic stress disorder, *The Journal of Nervous and Mental Disease* 1988:176:498-502.

Matsumoto, R.R. GABA receptors: are cellular differences reflected in function? *Brain Research Reviews* 1989:14:203-225.

Mattson, M.P., Guthrie, P.B., and Kater, S.B. Intracellular messengers in the generation and degeneration of hippocampal neuroarchitecture, *Journal of Neuroscience Research* 1988:21:447-464.

McCarley, R.W., Faux, S.F., Shenton, M.E., Nestor, P.G., and Adams, J. Event-related-potentials in schizophrenia: Their biological and clinical correlations and a new model of schizophrenic pathophysiology, *Schizophrenia Research* 1991:4 (2):209-231.

McDonald, J.W. and Johnston, M.V. Physiological and pathophysiological roles of excitatory amino acids during central nervous system development, *Brain Research Reviews* 1990:15:41-70.

McEwen, B.S., Angulo, J., Cameron, H., Chao, H.M., Daniels, D., Gannon, M.N., Gould, E., Mendelson, S., Sakai, R., Spencer, R., and Wooley, C. Paradoxical effects of adrenal steroids on the brain: Protection versus degeneration, *Biological Psychiatry*, 1992:31:177-199.

McGaugh, J.L., Introini-Collison, I.B., Cahill, L., Kim, M., and Liang, K.C. Involvement of the amygdala in neuromodulatory influences on memory storage in *The amygdala: Neurobiological aspects of emotion, memory, and mental dysfunction*, ed. by J. Aggleton, New York: Wiley-Liss, 1992.

Meador, K.J., Loring, D.W., Lee, G.P., Brroks, B.S., Nichols, F.T., Thompson, E.E., Thompson, W.O., and Heilman, K.M. Hemisphere assymetry for eye gaze mechanisms, *Brain* 1989:112:103-111.

Meaney, M.J., Mitchell, J.B., Aitken, D.H., Bhatnagar, S.R., Iny, L.J., and Saeeieau, A. The effects of neonatal handling on the development of the adrenocortical response to stress: Implications for neuropathology and cognitive defects in later life, *Psychoneuroendocrinology* 1991:16:83-103.

Merzenich, M.M. Presentation at *The Neurobiology of Learning and Memory*, Stony Brook University, May 24, 1994.

Meyers, C.A., Berman, S.A., and Scheibel, R.S. Case Report: Acquired antisocial personality disorder, *Journal of Psychiatry and Neuroscience* 1992:17 (3): 121-125.

Michie, P.T., Fox, A.M., Ward, P.B., Catts, S.V., and McConaght, N. Event-related-potential indices of selective attention and cortical lateralization in schizophrenia, *Psychophysiology* 1990:27 (2):209-227.

Miller, G., Pribram, K., and Galanter, E. *Plans and the Organization of behavior*, New York: Holt, 1960.

Miller, S.D. and Triggiano, P.J. The psychophysiological investigation of multiple personality disorder: Review and update, *American Journal of Clinical Hypnosis* 1992:35 (1):47-61.

Milner, B. and Teubar, H. Further analysis of the hippocampal amnestic syndrome: A 14-year followup study of H. M., *Neuropsychologia* 1968:6:215-234.

Minami, E., Tsuruu, N., and Okita, T. Effect of a subject's family name on visual event-related-potential in schizophrenia, *Biological Psychiatry* 1992:31 (7): 681-689.

Mishkin, M. Presentation at *The Neurobiology of Learning and Memory*, Stony Brook University, May, 23, 1994.

Morgan, J.M., Wenzel, M., Lang, W., Lindinger, S., and Deecke, L. Frontocentral DC—potential shifts predicting behavior with or without a motor task, *Electroencephalography and Clinical Neurophysiology* 1992:83 (6):378-388.

Mori, E. and Yamadori, A. Rejection behavior: A human homologue of the abnormal behavior of Denny Brown and Chambers' monkey with bilateral parietal ablation, *Journal of Neurology, Neurosurgery, and Psychiatry* 1989:52:1260-1266.

Morrison, J.H. and Hof, P.R. The organization of the cerebral cortex: From molecules to circuits, *Discussions in Neuroscience* 1992: IX:21:11-76.

Morrison-Stewart, S.L., Williamson, P.C., Corning, W.C., Kutcher, S.P., Snow, W.G., and Merskey, H. Frontal and non-frontal lobe neuropsychological test performance and clinical symptomatology in schizophrenia. *Psychological Medicine* 1992:22:353-359.

Muir, W.J., StClair, D.M., Douglas, H.R. Blackwood, A., Roxburgh, H.M., and Marshall, I. Eye-tracking dysfunction in the affective psychoses and schizophrenia, *Psychological Medicine* 1992:22:573-580.

Musalek, M., Podreka, I., and Walter, H. Regional brain function in hallucinations: A study of regional cerebral blood flow with 99m-Tc-HMPAO-SPECT in patients with auditory halluincations, tactile hallucinations and normal controls, *Comprehensive Psychiatry* 1989:30 (1):99-108.

Muselak, M., Podreka, H., Walter, S.E., Passway, W., Notzinger, D., Strobl, R., and Lesch, O.M. Regional brain function in hallucinations: A study of regional cerebral blood flow with 99m-TC-HMPAO-Spect in patients with auditory hallucinations, tactile hallucinations and normal controls, *Comprehensive Psychiatry* 1989:301:99-108.

Nasman, V.I. and Dorio, P.J. *International Journal of Psychophysiology*, 1993:41 (1):61-74.

Nelson, C.A. and Collins, P.F. Neural and behavioral correlates of visual recognition memory in 4- and 8-month-old infants, *Brain and Cognition* 1992:19 (1): 105-121.

Neshiga, R. and Luders, H. Recording of event-related-potentials (P300) from human cortex, *Journal of Clinical Neurophysiology* 1992:9 (2):294-298.

Nichols, D.G. A retrograde step forward, *Nature* 1992:360:106-107.

Nishijo, H., Ono, T., and Nishino, H. Topographic distribution of modality-specific amygdalar neurons in alert monkeys, *The Journal of Neuroscience* 1988: 8:3556-3569.

Olton, D.S., Golski, S., Mishkin, M., Gorman, L.K., Olds, J.L., and Alkon, D.L. Behaviorally induced changes in the hippocampus, in learning and memory, *Brain Research Reviews* 1991:16:206-215.

Osofsky, J.D. and Connors, K. Mother-infant interaction: An integrative view of a complex system, in *Handbook of Infant Development*, ed. by J.D. Osofsky. New York: Wiley, 1979.

Owen, J.E., Cook, E.W., and Stevenson, J. Features of "near-death experience" in relation to whether or not patients were near death, *The Lancet* 1990:336: 1175-1177.

Paige, S.R., Graham, R.M., Allen, M.G., and Newton, J.E.O. Psychophysiological correlates of posttraumatic stress disorder in Vietnam veterans, *Biological Psychiatry* 1990:27:419-430

Paller, K.A. Recall and stem-completion priming have different electrophysiological correlates and are modified differentially by directed forgetting, *Journal of Experimental Psychology* 1990:16 (6): 1021-1032.

Patel, J., Moore, C.W., Thompson, C., Keith, R.A., and Salama, A.I. Characterization of the quisqualate receptor linked to phosphoinositide hydrolysis in neocortical culture, *Journal of Neurochemistry* 1990:54:1461-1466.

Paulescu, E., Frith, C.D., and Frackowiak, R.S.J. The neural correlates of the verbal component of working memory, *Nature* 1993:362:342-345.

Pelosi, L., Holly, M., Slade, T., Hayward, M., Barrett, B., and Blumhard, L.D. Event-related potential (ERP) correlates of performance of intelligence tests, *Electroencephalography and Clinical Neurophysiology* 1992:84 (6):515-520.

Penfield, W. and Jasper, H. *Epilepsy and functional anatomy of the human brain,* Boston: Little Brown, 1954.

Pfenninger, K.H., dela Houssave, B.A., Helmke, S.M., and Quiroga, S. Growth-regulated proteins and neuronal plasticity, *Molecular Neurobiology* 1991:5 (2-4):143-151.

Pfurtscheller, G. and Berghold, A. Patterns of cortical activation during planning of voluntary movement, *EEG* 1989:12:250-258.

Piaget, J. *The construction of reality in the child,* New York: Basic Books, 1954.

Picton, T.W. The P300 wave of the human event-related potential, *Journal of Clinical Neurophysiology* 1992:9 (4):456-479.

Pinker, S. *The language instinct,* New York: Harper Perennial, 1995.

Polich, J. and Donchin, E. P300 and the word frequency effect, *Electroencephalography and Clinical Neurophysiology* 1988:70:33-45.

Pontius, A.A. Psychotic trigger reactions: Neuropsychiatric and neuro-biological (limbic) aspects of homicide. Reflecting on normal activities. *Integrative Psychiatry* 1987:5:116-139.

Pontius, A.A. and Yudowitz, B.S. Frontal lobe system dysfunction in some criminal actions as shown in the narrative test, *The Journal of Nervous and Mental Disease* 1980:168 (2):111-117.

Post, R.M. Transduction of psychosocial stress into the neurobiology of recurrent affective disorder, *The American Journal of Psychiatry* 1992:149:8:999-1010.

Post R.M., Uhde, T.W., and Ballenger, J.C. Prophylactic efficacy of carbamazepine in manic-depressive illness, *American Journal of Psychiatry* 1983:140:1602-1604.

Proust, M. *Remembrance of Things Past,* Vol. I, New York: Random House (Modern Library), 1934.

Purvis, D., Riddle, D.R., and Lamantia, A.S. Iterated patterns of brain circuitry. *Trends in Neuroscience* 1992:15:362-367.

Raine, A., Venables, P.H., and Williams, M. Relationships between N1, P300, and contingent negative variation recorded at age 15, and criminal behavior at age 24, *Psychophysiology* 1990:27 (5):567-574.

Rapoport, S.I. Integrated phylogeny of the primate brain, with special reference to humans and their diseases, *Brain Research Reviews* 1990:15:267-294.

Rehak, A., Kaplan, J., Weylman, S.T., Brendan, K., Brownell, H.H., and Gardnrer, H. Story processing in right-hemipshere brain-damaged patients, *Brain and Language*: 1992:42:320-336.

Reiman, E.M., Fusselman, M.J., Fox, P.T., and Raichle, M.E. Neuroanatomical correlates of anticipatory anxiety, *Science* 1989:243:1071-1074.

Remillard, G.M., Andermann, F., Franco, T., Aube, M., Martin, J.B., Feindel, W., Guberman, A., and Simpson, C. Sexual ictal manifestations predominate in women with temporal lobe epilepsy: A finding suggesting sexual dimorphism in the human brain, *Neurology* 1983:33:323-330.

Rescorla, R.A. Hierarchical associative relations in Pavlovian conditioning and instrumental training, *Current Directions in Psychological Science* 1992:1: 66-70.

Reynolds, G.P. The amygdala and the neurochemistry of schizophrenia, in *The amygdala: Neurobiological aspects of emotion, memory, and mental dysfunction*, ed. by J. P. Aggleton, New York: Wiley-Liss, 1992.

Reynolds, G.P., Czudek, C., and Andrews, H.B. Deficit and hemispheric assymetry of GABA uptake sites in the hippocampus in schizophrenia, *Biological Psychiatry* 1990:27:1038-1044.

Robaey, P., Laget, P., and Creff, J. ERP study of the development of the holistic and analytic modes of processing between 6 and 8 years, *International Journal of Psychophysiology* 1989:8 (2):145-153.

Roberts, G.W. Neuropeptides: Cellular morphology, major pathways, and functional considerations, in *The amygdala*, ed. by J. P. Aggleton, New York: Wiley-Liss, 1992.

Rolls, E.T. Neurophysiology and functions of the primate amygdala in *The amygdala: Neurobiological aspects of emotion, memory, and mental dysfunction*, ed. by J. Aggleton, New York: Wiley-Liss, 1992.

Ruchkin, D.S., Johnson, R. Jr., Grafman, J., Canoune, H., and Ritter, W. Distinctions and similarities among working memory processes: An event-related potential study, *Cognitive Brain Research* 1992:1:53-66.

Ruchkin, D.S., Johnson, R. Jr., Canoune, H., and Ritter, W. Short-term memory storage and retention, *Electroencephalography and Clinical Neurophysiology* 1990:76 (5):419-439.

Ryle, A. Object relations theory and activity theory: A proposed link by way of the procedural sequence model, *British Journal of Medical Psychology* 1991: 64:307-316.

Sacks, O. *The man who mistook his wife for a hat*, New York: Harper and Row, 1987.

Samson, Y., Justin, J.W., Friedman, A.H., and Davis, J.N. Catecholaminergic innervation of the hippocampus in the cynomogus monkey, *The Journal of Comparative Neurology* 1990:298:250-263.

Sapolsky, R.M. *Stress, the aging brain, and the mechanisms of neuron death*, The Cambridge, MA: MIT Press, 1992.

Schacter, D.L. Multiple forms of memory in humans and animals, in *Memory systems of the brain*, ed. by N.M. Weinberger, J.L. McGaugh, and G. Lynch. New York: Guilford Press, 1985.

Schreiber, H., Stolz-born, G., Kornhuber, H.H., and Born, J. Event-related potential correlates of impaired selective attention in children at high risk for schizophrenia, *Biological Psychiatry* 1992:32 (8):634-651.

Seib, R.A. A brain mechanism for attention, *Medical Hypotheses*, 1990:33: 145-153.

Sergent, J. Furtive incursions into bicameral minds: Integrative and coordinating role of subcortical structures, *Brain*: 1990:113:537-568.

Sergent, J., Shinsuke, O., and MacDonald, B. Functional neuroanatomy of face and object processing, *Brain*: 1992:115:15-36.

Shakespeare, W. King Lear (1605), *The Complete Works*, Baltimore: Penguin Books, 1969.

Shatz, C.J. Impulse activity and the patterning of connections during CNS development, *Neuron* 1991:7:745-754.

Shelley, P.B. Hymn to Apollo, in *An Oxford Anthology of English Poetry*, New York: Oxford University Press, 1956.

Shibisaki, H. and Miyazaki, M. Event-related potential studies in adults and children, *Journal of Clinical Neurophysiology* 1992:9 (3):408-418.

Shimiziu, T. and Wolfe, L.S. Arachadonic acid cascade and signal transduction, *Journal of Neurochemistry* 1990:55:1-11.

Slater, P., McConell, S., D'Souza, S.W., Barson, A.J., Simpson, M.D.C., and Gilchrist, A.C. Age-related changes in binding to excitatory amino acid uptake sites in temporal cortex of human brain, *Developmental Brain Research* 1992: 65:157-160.

Smock, T., Albeck, D., and McMechen, P. Peptidergic transmission in the brain III, hippocampal inhibition by the amygdala, *Peptides* 1991:12:47-51.

Sobotka, S.S., Davidson, R.J., and Senulis, J.A. Anterior brain electrical assymetries in response to reward and punishment, *Electoencephalography and Clinical Neurophysiology* 1992:83:236-247.

Sommer, W., Matt, J., and Leuthold, H. Consciousness of attention and expectancy as reflected in event-related potentials and reaction times, *Journal of Experimental Psychology* 1990:16 (5): 902-915.

Southwick, S.M., Krystal, J.H., Morgan, A., Johnson, D., Nagy, L., and Nicolaou, A. Abnormal noradrenergic funtion in post-traumatic stress disorder, *Archives of General Psychiatry* 1993:50:266-274.

Spenser, E. *The Poetical Works of Edmund Spenser*, ed. by J.C. Smith and E. De Selincourt, London: Oxford University Press, 1932.

Sperry, R.W. Hemisphere deconnection and unity in conscious awareness, *American Psychology* 1968:23:723-733.

Spiller, A. and Racine, R.J. Transfer kindling between sites in the entorrhinal cortex-perforant path-dentate gyrus system, *Brain Research* 1994:635: 130-158.

Spitz, R. *No and yes: On the genesis of human communications*, New York: International Universities Press, 1957.

Stauder, J.E., Molenaar, P.C., and van der Molen, M.W. Scalp topography of event-related brain potentials and cognitive transition during childhood, *Child Development* 1993:64 (3):769-788.

Stern, D. *The interpersonal world of the infant: A view from psychoanalysis and developmental psychology*, New York: Basic Books, 1985.

Stevens, J.R. Abnormal reinnervation as a basis for schizophrenia: A hypothesis, *Archives of General Psychiatry* 1992:49:238-243.

Stevens, W. *The Collected Poems of Wallace Stevens*, New York: Alfred A. Knopf, 1957.

Strange, P.G. Interesting times for dopamine receptors, *Trends in Neuroscience* 1991:14:43-45.

Strub, R.L. and Black, F.W. *Organic brain syndromes: An introduction to neurobehavioral disorders*, Philadelphia: F.A. Davis Co., 1993.

Stuss, D.T., Picton, T.W., Cerri, A.M., Leech, E.E., and Stethem, L.L. Perceptual closure and object identification: Electrophysiological responses to incomplete pictures, *Brain and Cognition* 1992:19 (2):253-266.

Sutherland, R.J. and Rudy, J.W. Configural association theory: The role of the hippocampal formation in learning, memory, and amnesia, *Psychobiology* 1989:17:129-144.

Swinburne, A.C. Hymn to Proserpine, in *An Oxford Anthology of English Poetry*, New York: Oxford University Press, 1956.

Tamminga, C.A., Thaker, G.K., Buchanan, R., Kirkpatrick, B., Alphs, L.D., Chase, T.N., and Carpenter, W.T. Limbic system abnormalities identified in schizophrenia using positron emmission tomography with fluorodeoxyglucose and neocortical alterations with deficit syndrome, *Archives of General Psychiatry* 1992:49:522-531.

Tausk, V. On the origin of the influencing machine in schizophrenia, *Psychoanalytic Quarterly* II, 1933.

Thatcher, R.W., Walker, R.A., and Giudice, S. Human cerebral hemispheres develop at different rates and ages, *Science* 1987:236:1110-1113.

Thomas, E. Forebrain mechanisms in the relief of fear: The role of the lateral septum, *Psychobiology* 1988:16:36-44.

Tomarken, A., Davidson, R.J., Wheeler, R.E., and Boss, R.C. Individual differences in anterior brain assymetry and fundamental dimensions of emotion, *Journal of Personality and Social Psychology* 1992:62: (4):676-687.

Tonkonogy, J.M. Violence and temporal lobe lesions: Head CT and MRI data, *Journal of Neuropsychiatry and Clinical Neurosciences* 1991:3 (2):189-196.

Towey, J., Bruder, G., Hollander, E., Friedman, D., Erhan, H., Liebowitz, M., and Sutton, S. Endogenous event-related potentials in obsessive-compulsive disorder, *Biological Psychiatry* 1990:28 (2):92-98.

Tulving, E. What is episodic memory? *Current Directions in Psychological Science* 1992:2:67-70.

van der Kolk, B.A. The body keeps the score: Memory and the evolving psychobiology of postraumatic stress, *Harvard Review of Psychiatry* 1994:1:253-265.

van Kammen, D.L. Norepinephrine in acute exacerbations of chrinic schizophernia: Negative symptoms revisited, *Archives of General Psychiatry* 1990:47: 161-167.

Van Natta Jr., D. FBI fear ocean won't yield bomb clue, *New York Times*, August 16, 1996.

Vygotsky, L.S. *Thought and language*, Cambridge, MA: MIT Press, 1962.

Waelder, R. The principle of multiple function: Observations on overdetermination, *Psychoanalytic Quarterly* 5:1936

Ward, C.D. Transient feelings of compulsion caused by henispheric lesions: Three cases, *Journal of Neurology, Neurosurgery, and Psychiatry* 1988:51:266-268.

Weiler, M.A., Buchsbaum, M.S., Gillin, J.C., Tafalla, R., and Bunney, W.E. Jr. Explorations in the relationship of dream sleep to schizophrenia using positron emission tomography, *Neuropsychobiology* 1990:23:109-118.

Weinberger, D.R., Berman, K.F., Suddath, R., and Torrey, F.E. Evidence of dysfunction of a prefrontal-limbic network in schizophrenia: A magnetic resonance imaging and regional cerebral blood flow study of discordant monozygotic twins, *American Journal of Psychiatry* 1992:149:890-897.

Weller, M. and Korhuber, J. A rationale for NMDA receptor antagonist therapy of the neuroleptic malignant syndrome, *Medical Hypotheses* 1992:38:320-333.

Welmoet B., Neylan, T., Shaw, D., and Linnoila, M. Norepinephrine in acute exacerbations of chronic schizophrenia: Negative symptoms revisited, *Archives of General Psychiatry* 1990:47:161-167.

Werner, H. *Comparative psychology of mental development*, New York: Harper and Row, 1940.

Williams, J.M.G. and Scott, J. Autobiographical memory in depression, *Psychological Medicine* 1988:18:689-695.

Williamson, S., Harper, T.J., and Hare, R.D. Abnormal processing of affective words by schizophrenics, *Psychophysiology* 1991:28 (3):26-73.

Winnicott, D.W. *The maturational process and the facilitating environment*, New York: International Universities Press, 1965.

Winocur, G. Functional dissociation of the hippocampus and prefrontal cortex in learning and memory, *Psychobiology* 1991:19:11-20.

Wu, J.C., Testing the Swerdlow/Koob model of schizophrenia pathophysiology using positron emission tomography, *Behavioral and Brain Sciences* 1990:13: 168-175.

Yeats, W.B. *The Collected Poems of W.B. Yeats*, New York: Macmillan, 1957.

Yee, C.M., Deldin, P.J., and Miller, G.A. Early stimulus processing in dysthymia and anhedonia, *Journal of Abnormal Psychology* 1992:101 (2):230-233.

Yehuda, R., Giller, E.L., Southwick, S.M., and Mason, J.W. Hypothalamic-pituitary-adrenal dysfunction in posttraumatic stress disorder, *Biological Psychiatry* 1991:30:1031-1048.

Index

Page numbers followed by the letter "i" indicate illustrations.

Order Your Own Copy of
This Important Book for Your Personal Library!

HOW THE BRAIN TALKS TO ITSELF
A Clinical Primer of Psychotherapeutic Neuroscience

_____ in hardbound at $69.95 (ISBN: 0-7890-0408-9)

_____ in softbound at $39.95 (ISBN: 0-7890-0409-7)

COST OF BOOKS_____

OUTSIDE USA/CANADA/
MEXICO: ADD 20%_____

POSTAGE & HANDLING_____
(US: $3.00 for first book & $1.25
for each additional book)
Outside US: $4.75 for first book
& $1.75 for each additional book)

SUBTOTAL_____

IN CANADA: ADD 7% GST_____

STATE TAX_____
(NY, OH & MN residents, please
add appropriate local sales tax)

FINAL TOTAL_____
(If paying in Canadian funds,
convert using the current
exchange rate. UNESCO
coupons welcome.)

☐ **BILL ME LATER:** ($5 service charge will be added)
(Bill-me option is good on US/Canada/Mexico orders only;
not good to jobbers, wholesalers, or subscription agencies.)

☐ Check here if billing address is different from
shipping address and attach purchase order and
billing address information.

Signature_____

☐ **PAYMENT ENCLOSED: $**_____

☐ **PLEASE CHARGE TO MY CREDIT CARD.**

☐ Visa ☐ MasterCard ☐ AmEx ☐ Discover
☐ Diner's Club

Account # _____

Exp. Date _____

Signature _____

Prices in US dollars and subject to change without notice.

NAME _____

INSTITUTION _____

ADDRESS _____

CITY _____

STATE/ZIP _____

COUNTRY _____ COUNTY (NY residents only) _____

TEL _____ FAX _____

E-MAIL_____
May we use your e-mail address for confirmations and other types of information? ☐ Yes ☐ No

Order From Your Local Bookstore or Directly From
The Haworth Press, Inc.
10 Alice Street, Binghamton, New York 13904-1580 • USA
TELEPHONE: 1-800-HAWORTH (1-800-429-6784) / Outside US/Canada: (607) 722-5857
FAX: 1-800-895-0582 / Outside US/Canada: (607) 772-6362
E-mail: getinfo@haworth.com
PLEASE PHOTOCOPY THIS FORM FOR YOUR PERSONAL USE.

BOF96